Selling in 6™

PLATINUM EDITION

Mark Jewell

@SellingEnergy
info@sellingenergy.com
415-814-3744

sellingenergy

Turbocharging Success

www.SellingEnergy.com

This workbook belongs to:

Name: _____

Phone Number: _____

Table of Contents

www.SellingEnergy.com

Lesson 1
Why Selling in 6™?

Presented by
Mark Jewell
@SellingEnergy
info@sellingenergy.com

"The best way to prosper yourself is to prosper others."

-Walter Jewell*

*Mark's wise and loving father

"Successful people do what unsuccessful people are unwilling to do."

-Jeff Olsen

Q:

So **why** should you invest your time viewing this Selling in 6™ program?

You are about to begin a journey that has brought **sales success** and **personal fulfillment** to many fellow professionals.

Thousands have taken Selling Energy's award-winning sales training in-person. **Their accomplishments** prove its value.

Higher closing %, shorter sales cycles...

Higher revenues and income...

Plenty of specific success stories...

Plenty of business and personal a

Mark Jewell
• Sales Trainer / Education Leader of the Year (2x Stevie® Awards)
• Wall Street Journal and Amazon bestselling book

IDEAS & ACTIONS

Award-winning sales training firm...

- *Selling Power* magazine:
  - Top 20 Sales Training Companies in 2017
- *Training Industry* magazine
  - Companies to Watch List 2018
- *Inc.* magazine
  - 16th fastest-growing education company in the US

For every person I've taught in-person over the last several years, there are at least a hundred others who could have benefited from the same training had it been more convenient to experience.

Q:

So **why** did we create Selling in 6™?

1. To give more energy professionals **cost-effective, time-efficient** access to our award-winning training

- The energy field is full of "accidental salespeople*"
- Large and/or geographically dispersed teams need training
- Our graduates wanted a path to training their colleagues
- The energy space needs more skilled sales professionals

2. To change a "fire hydrant flow" into **"drip irrigation"**

- Drip-irrigation enhances comprehension and application
- Learners progress at their own pace
- Playlists can be assigned, with post-viewing discussion
- Lessons can be searched by topic or keyword
- Lessons can be revisited throughout the subscription
- Questions reinforce the learning and encourage commitments

3. To make our training **easier to approve** and **implement**

- No calendar coordination
- No minimum or maximum audience size
- No travel time or expense
- No training venue/catering/AV coordination or cost
- No lost selling time

- *Less cost means higher return on the training investment*
- *Tracked viewing makes it easy to confirm engagement*
- *Ease of deployment and use removes all excuses*

4. To make our training **easier to share**

- Best way to prosper yourself is to prosper others
- Brand the training to give a gift that keeps on giving
- Insert custom lessons to advance the sale of your offerings
- Share lessons with internal champions at your prospects' orgs

5. To make it practical to **expand the target audience**

- Make it part of your onboarding process
- Use it for professional development and performance reviews
- Use custom playlists to ensure relevant and engaging content
  - Lead generators
  - Customer service staff
  - Field technical staff
  - Marketing staff
- Past grads get a refresher and a clear path forward
- Sales meeting attendees leave with lesson playlists

IDEAS & ACTIONS

6. To leverage **learner preferences** and the **latest tech**

- People prefer m-learning over in-person or long online courses
- Blended learning = ^comprehension and persistent application
  - Selling in 6™ mobile-learning 6-minute lessons
  - Selling in 6™ Playbook w/slides, exercises, templates and more
  - Monthly Mastermind Group coaching conference calls
  - Autographed copy of our Wall Street Journal bestselling book
  - Audio-only version, for listening on the go

Q:

So how can you maximize the effectiveness of Selling in 6™?

Commit to embracing your inner sales professional

- Find the best time to do your lesson(s) every day, if possible
- Pause, reflect, and address each question or exercise
- Listen to each lesson more than once, if possible

Use *all* the dimensions of this Selling in 6™ program

- Selling in 6™ mobile-learning 6-minute lessons
- Selling in 6™ Playbook w/slides, exercises, templates and more
- Monthly Mastermind Group coaching conference calls
- Autographed copy of our Wall Street Journal bestselling book
- Audio-only version (great for windshield time!)

Discuss these lessons with your peers

- Make this content a regular agenda item at sales meetings
- Form a Selling Energy Club to review lessons with colleagues
- Share your successes with management
- Stay connected to the Selling Energy community

Commit to creating and using the Success Tools™

- Elevator pitch
- Three-sentence solicitation
- One-page proposal
- One-page financial analysis (featuring the proper metrics)
- Success Story Archive™
- Objections Archive™
- Digits-to-Widgets™
- C-Suite Talking Points™
- Segment Guides™

Continue your Selling in 6™ journey

- Silver, Gold and Platinum Editions build on each other
- Selling Energy exists to make you successful, so stay in touch!

selling in 6™

Lesson **2**
The importance of sales professionalism

Presented by
Mark Jewell
@SellingEnergy
info@sellingenergy.com

sellingenergy
Turbocharging Success

IDEAS & ACTIONS

Q:

How important is professional selling in our industry?

39%

The percentage of B2B buyers who select a vendor according to the skills of the salesperson rather than price, quality or service.

Universities offering psychology degrees outnumber those offering sales degrees by a factor of 6 to 1.

In the US, sales-related jobs outnumber psychology-related jobs 93 to 1.

Most MBA programs offer no sales-related courses at all, and those that do offer a single course in sales management.

350,000
170,000

The number of students each year who earn bachelor's degrees in business and MBAs, respectively, from American universities.

Only a tiny fraction have been taught anything about sales.

---

3 days

The average salesperson has received 3 days of sales training in their career...

...and most of that was likely product-knowledge training

Never planned on a *sales* career?

The Accidental Salesperson

How to Take Control of Your Sales Career and Earn the Respect and Income You Deserve

Chris Lytle

Copyright 2000 Chris Lytle

Guiding Principles

Energy-related products, services and programs all require effective selling.

IDEAS & ACTIONS

_____

_____

_____

_____

Guiding Principles

Professional sales skills make you more successful at advancing any energy-related initiative, regardless of your role in the process.

Guiding Principles

You need to think of yourself as a sales professional even if your job title does not include the word "sales."

Lesson 3
"Selling" vs. "customer engagement"

Presented by
Mark Jewell
@SellingEnergy
info@sellingenergy.com

Turbocharging Success

Q:

What is "customer engagement"?

Customer engagement is the **emotional connection** your customer has with your brand.

Q:

Why is "customer engagement" so important?

Customers who are "more highly engaged" **buy more...** **promote more...** and are **more loyal.**

Customers who are "more highly engaged" **also deliver higher customer satisfaction scores.**

IDEAS & ACTIONS

www.SellingEnergy.com

Q:

So what can *you* do to drive "customer engagement"?

You can strive to meet and **exceed** each customer's expectations.

Q:

What is cross-selling?

Selling an additional product or service to an existing customer

Increases the income derived from the customer and/or protects the relationship with the customer

Q:

Is cross-selling different from upselling or "up-serving"?

Upselling is selling more expensive items, upgrades, or other add-ons

Objective is to increase the income earned from a transaction

IDEAS & ACTIONS

Benefits for the customer

Benefits for the customer

It's easier to increase revenues through cross-selling and up-selling than through approaching additional prospects.

How do "customer engagement," "cross-selling" and "upselling" apply to what you do every day?

They give you the opportunity to earn your customer's respect and praise.

Plan your service offerings logically so that they enhance the probability that cross-selling can occur

Q:

How do you set the stage for effective cross-selling and upselling?

Which add-on services make the most sense to offer?

IDEAS & ACTIONS

Train yourself to confidently cross-sell and upsell... for the customer's benefit

Understand what your customers are trying to achieve...

...and create offerings that really complement each other

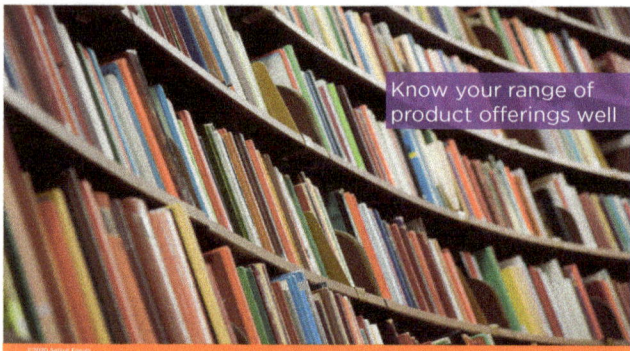

Know your range of product offerings well

Timing is important

Utilize expert recommendations... including your own

Capitalize on cross-selling & upselling potential during the initial interaction

Keep your eyes and ears open for additional needs while you're with the customer

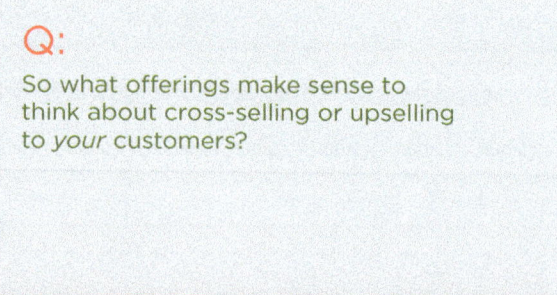

Q:

So what offerings make sense to think about cross-selling or upselling to *your* customers?

IDEAS & ACTIONS

_____

_____

_____

_____

Q:

And by the way, are there other ways to "extend the sale" even beyond this customer's property?

Yes!

Do they have a **relative, friend or neighbor** who uses energy?

Do they **own a business** that uses energy?

Do they **work for a business** that uses energy?

Referrals!

selling in 6™

Lesson **4**
Is what you're doing now working?

Presented by
Mark Jewell
@SellingEnergy
info@sellingenergy.com

sellingenergy
Turbocharging Success

"The quality of your life is directly related to the quality of the questions you ask."
- Anthony Robbins

Q:

Is what you're doing now working?

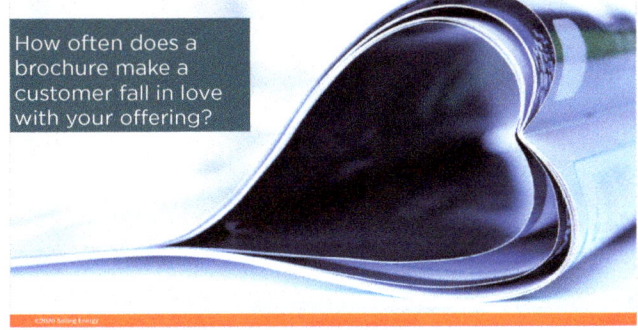

How often does a brochure make a customer fall in love with your offering?

IDEAS & ACTIONS

www.SellingEnergy.com

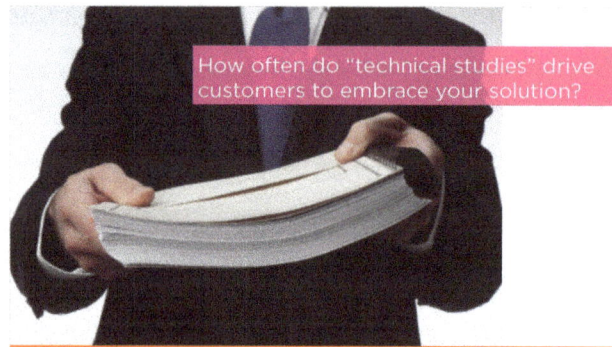

How often do "technical studies" drive customers to embrace your solution?

How many customers base decisions on "saving the environment"?

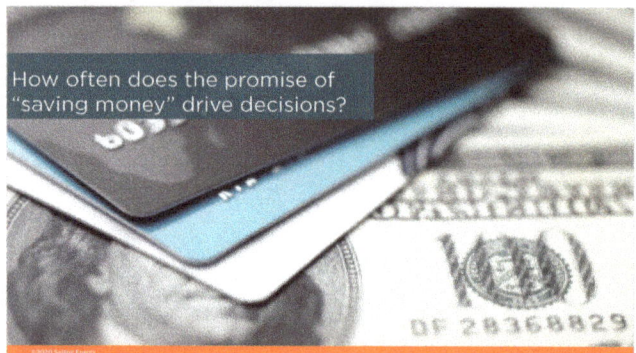

How often does the promise of "saving money" drive decisions?

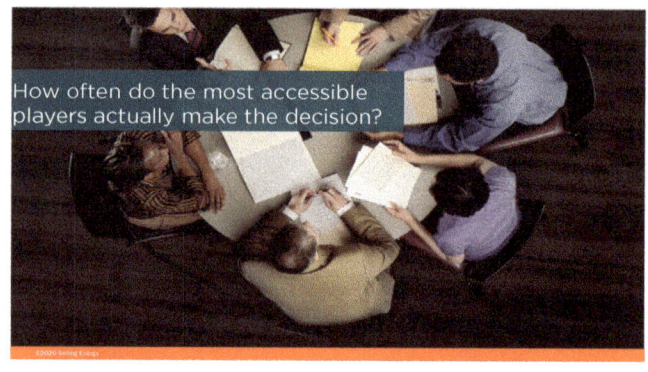

How often do the most accessible players actually make the decision?

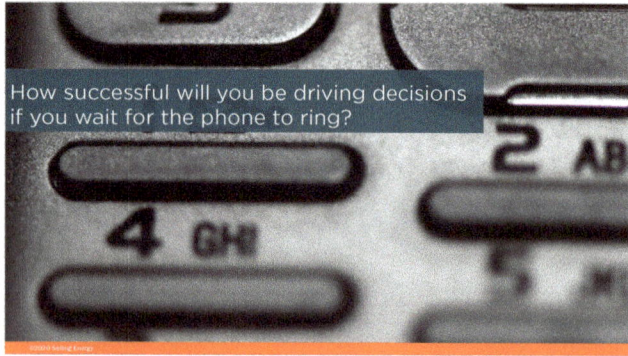

How successful will you be driving decisions if you wait for the phone to ring?

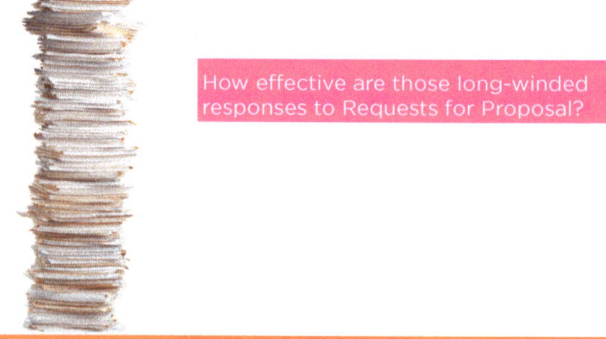

How effective are those long-winded responses to Requests for Proposal?

IDEAS & ACTIONS

How often does a single-page "quote" or "bill of materials" drive the decision?

Lesson 5
What prospects actually care about

Presented by
Mark Jewell
@SellingEnergy
info@sellingenergy.com

Q:

What do your prospects really care about?

Q:

Do they care about kWh, kW, therms?

Q:

Do they care about your "bits, bytes and blinking lights"?

"Market Segmentation"

The practice of aggregating your prospects into **"segments"** (and then **"sub-segments"**) that have common needs and would **likely respond similarly to your messaging.**

The more specific, the better...

Segments
Real estate
Retail
Healthcare
Manufacturing

Sub-segments
Shopping centers, multifamily housing...
Grocery, department stores...
Hospitals, medical office...
Chemicals, food processing...

Various dimensions of segmentation

Your messaging needs to be sensitive to each segment's uniqueness...

- Interest in energy as a controllable expense
- Non-utility-cost financial benefits
- Non-financial benefits
- Jargon, yardsticks
- Decision-making processes
- Sound bites that will capture attention
- And much more...

IDEAS & ACTIONS

Q:

So what do grocery stores care about?

- Sales per square foot
- Dwell time
- Shelf life of perishable items
- Security
- Other...

Q:

What do RE investors care about?

- Rent per square foot
- Occupancy percentage
- Landlord's share of operating expenses
- Percentage rents
- Capitalization rate
- Asset value
- Other...

Q:

What do manufacturers care about?

- 28 Manufacturing metrics that matter, such as...
  - Total manufacturing cost per unit excluding materials
  - Downtime in proportion to operating time
  - Reportable health and safety incidents
  - Energy cost per unit
  - Other

Q:

What do hotel operators care about?

- Average Daily Room Rate (ADR)
- Revenue Per Available Room (RevPAR)
- Press releases and accolades that boost bookings
- Sustainability badges that support event revenue
- Other...

Q:

What do K-12 schools care about?

- Student attendance
- Teacher attraction, retention, and attendance
- Standardized test scores
- Security
- Other...

Q:

What do fitness centers care about?

- New members signed on the spot
- New members signed within 30 days
- Membership renewals
- Pro shop and juice bar revenue
- Security
- Other...

Q:

How about small business owners?

- Surviving wage and other cost pressures
- Health and safety requirements
- Regulatory compliance
- Corporate improvement initiatives
- Maintenance
- Productivity
- Other...

Q:

What does the CEO care about the most?

- Will what you are proposing make my organization **easier to manage?**
- Will what you are proposing make my organization **more valuable?**

IDEAS & ACTIONS

www.SellingEnergy.com

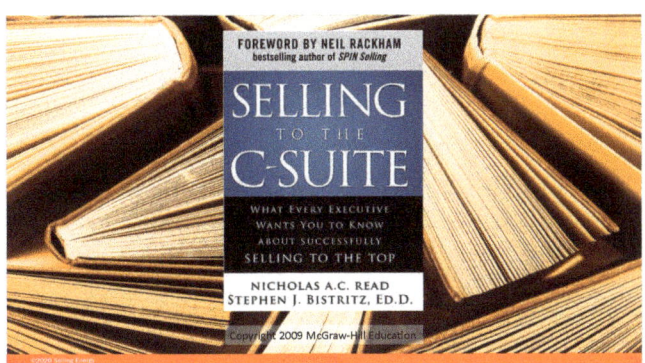

Q:
How about a non-business-owner in a B2B sales setting?

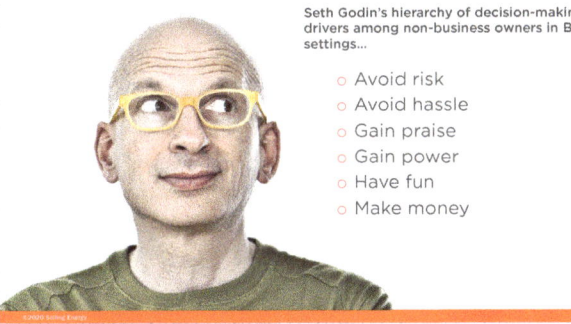

Seth Godin's hierarchy of decision-making drivers among non-business owners in B2B settings...

- Avoid risk
- Avoid hassle
- Gain praise
- Gain power
- Have fun
- Make money

Sales professionals migrate the discussion away from features and beyond benefits, putting all the focus on the customer's values.

They also reframe benefits so they can be measured with the customer's yardstick.

Most people don't make decisions...

...they make comparisons.

And even when they do make decisions...

...they make emotional decisions first, and then they justify them financially.

There will be no forward motion without motivation...

and there will be no motivation without emotion.

IDEAS & ACTIONS

selling in

Lesson 6
Leading with the "Why"

Presented by
Mark Jewell
@SellingEnergy
info@sellingenergy.com

sellingenergy
Turbocharging Success

Focus on the *why* before the *how* or the *what*

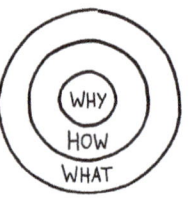

Simon Sinek's Golden Circle
As cited in his 2009 TED Talk

"People don't buy WHAT you do, they buy WHY you do it."
-Simon Sinek

What can this industry learn from TIVO?

How much of your conversation with your customer should be focused on the engineering?

How many of your conversations are with the right execs, rather than with their technical lieutenants?

Who is your best customer, and what is that customer really buying?

What would happen if you stopped "talking shop" with the technical professionals and started talking "business outcomes" with the actual decision-makers with the budget dollars to spend?

IDEAS & ACTIONS

_____

_____

_____

_____

www.SellingEnergy.com

Lesson 7
Connecting the dots for your prospects

Presented by
Mark Jewell
@SellingEnergy
info@sellingenergy.com

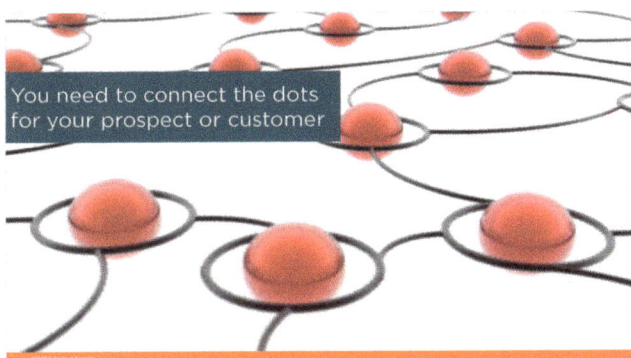

You need to connect the dots for your prospect or customer

Remember to address all four levels of the decision

- Segment-specific
- Organizational
- Professional
- Personal

Where do you find all the data and insights needed to make a compelling pitch?

It isn't enough to be an expert in whatever you are selling

You need to be an expert in your prospect's realm!

Do your research

Where do they get their industry news?

IDEAS & ACTIONS

_____

_____

_____

_____

Read *their* industry publications

Attend *their* conferences – and not just to network

Understand metrics that matter to them

HINT: It's not kWh or BTUs

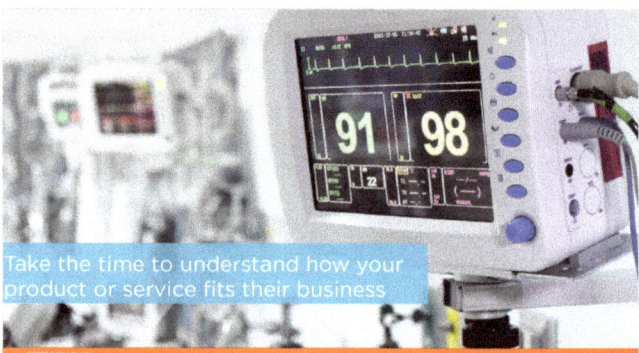

Take the time to understand how your product or service fits their business

Think systems, not pieces

Find out what matters most

Ask customers if you can do a "ride along"

1. Immerse yourself in the segment
   Conversations with your customers
   Trade orgs and journals
   Reviews of 10Ks and earnings calls
   Conferences, white papers, articles
   Success Story Archive™ entries
   Segment Guides™

IDEAS & ACTIONS

_____

_____

_____

_____

2. Know the org's values & goals

Chat with your internal champion
Review their website & press releases
Find their execs on LinkedIn, etc.
Examine their 10Ks, brochures, etc.
Talk to their customers
Ask their other vendors
Know their competitors

3. Understand your prospect's role

Ask how the decision will be made
Find the decision-makers & influencers
Inquire about previous experiences

4. Know what moves the individual

Look at LinkedIn, other social media
Look for articles or presentations
Talk to others who may know them
Build rapport in every interaction
Identify the personality style
Locate the emotional triggers
Empower them as internal champion

Lesson 8
Addressing all 3 benefit categories

Presented by
Mark Jewell
@SellingEnergy
Info@sellingenergy.com

Q:

What value do you provide your customers?

Do you focus on the money?

Moving beyond utility-cost savings...

1. Utility-cost financial benefits
2. Non-utility-cost financial benefits
3. Non-financial benefits

   What are some examples of each?

Non-utility-cost financial & non-financial benefits...

1. Better employee attraction/retention
2. Higher employee productivity & morale
3. Improved health and safety
4. Increased throughput or less downtime
5. Improved process control
6. Reduced scrap rate
7. Greater process visibility
8. Reduced emissions
9. Increased retail sales
10. And, of course, many more...

IDEAS & ACTIONS

Q:

How many of those benefits can be quantified and monetized?

Q:

And how many decisions are driven by qualitative factors?

selling in 6™

Lesson 9
The real meaning of "efficiency"

Presented by
Mark Jewell
@SellingEnergy
info@sellingenergy.com

sellingenergy
Turbocharging Success

Q:

What is "efficiency"?

"Efficiency is the (often measurable) ability to avoid wasting materials, energy, efforts, money, and time in doing something or in producing a desired result."

SOURCE: https://en.wikipedia.org/wiki/Efficiency

"In a more general sense, efficiency is the ability to do things well, successfully, and without waste."

SOURCE: https://en.wikipedia.org/wiki/Efficiency

Q:

What are "smart energy technologies"?

Smart energy technologies involve either adding an electricity-powered process or fuel-switching to electricity.

IDEAS & ACTIONS

_____

_____

_____

_____

www.SellingEnergy.com

Smart energy technologies hold the potential to use less BTUs overall, drive productivity, improve product quality, improve safety, and/or reduce greenhouse gas emissions.

Q:
What is "efficiency"?

Lesson **10**
Connecting dots with business acumen

Presented by
Mark Jewell
@SellingEnergy
info@sellingenergy.com

Turbocharging Success

Q:
Why might your prospect be interested in your solutions?

Saving energy

Saving money

CB 214

What's the secret to making compelling value propositions to your commercial customers?

What's the secret to making compelling value propositions to your commercial customers?

Business acumen.

IDEAS & ACTIONS

Business acumen.

"Intuitive and applicable understanding of how a company makes money."

---

3 Levels of Business Acumen

Level **1**
Fundamental

Being able to connect the dots, extending the benefits of energy projects to consider non-utility-cost and non-financial benefits in addition to lower utility bills and rebates.

Q:

What are some examples of energy efficiency measures that would yield benefits far greater than the energy savings?

---

1. More efficient lighting, HVAC, and/or controls to improve **office worker** comfort and convenience

Energy savings
Maintenance savings
Better control of building systems
Better lighting, thermal comfort, IAQ
Fewer occupant complaints
Higher worker productivity

Impact of energy efficiency on productivity

- Assume $40,000 average salary and benefits per person
- Assume 200 square feet per person
- $200/SF in payroll vs. $2/SF in utilities
- **What if your efficiency campaign boosted productivity by just 1%?**

- Lockheed
  - 15% rise in production
  - 15% drop in absenteeism
- West Bend Mutual Insurance
  - 16% increase in claims processed
- ING Bank
  - 15% drop in absenteeism
- Verifone
  - 5% increase in productivity
  - 40% drop in absenteeism

Productivity benefits of EE

GREENING THE BUILDING AND THE BOTTOM LINE

---

2. More efficient lighting, HVAC, and/or controls to improve **school** comfort and convenience

Energy savings
Maintenance savings
Better control of building systems
Better lighting, thermal comfort, IAQ
Higher student and teacher attendance
Better learning and higher test scores
Perhaps larger state school subsidies

What's the value of a "butt in a seat"?

Could an increase in **Average Daily Attendance subsidies** exceed the energy savings?

IDEAS & ACTIONS
_____
_____
_____
_____

3. Fan arrays in the air-handling systems of **critical environments**

Save energy and maintenance cost
Lower life-cycle cost
Easier to install and repair
Less noise and vibration
More reliable critical space conditioning

What's the value of uninterrupted data center operation?

Cost of data center downtime averages **$7,900 per minute** with an average incident length of **86 minutes** for a total cost of **$690,200.**

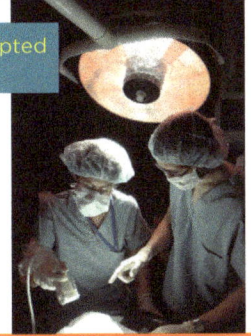

What's the value of uninterrupted surgical operations?

How much revenue would you **lose per day** if you could no longer properly pressurize the surgical suite?

4. More efficient lighting in **retail** settings.

Energy savings
Maintenance savings
Better control of lighting
Less load on AC and refrigeration
Less heat on merchandise
Higher retail sales
Potential higher percentage rent

Could higher ice cream sales trump lighting energy savings?

19% higher sales after upgrading to LED lighting?

5. More efficient lighting or ventilation in **agricultural** settings

Energy savings
Maintenance savings
Better control of building systems
Better lighting, thermal comfort, IAQ
Increased milk production
Higher-quality produce
Improved crop yields

"Got Simple Payback Period?"

Could you reduce the payback from 4 years to only 3 months by including the 6% increase in milk production?

Use strong, persuasive language

IDEAS & ACTIONS

www.SellingEnergy.com

Larger, more colorful, less bitter and more marketable lettuce?

What's the project's real "yield"?

Could you increase greenhouse yield by 15% with efficiency measures that also optimize CO_2 levels?

Bonus Lesson 10A
Connecting *all* the dots, not just energy

Presented by
Mark Jewell
@SellingEnergy
info@sellingenergy.com

selling energy
Turbocharging Success

Q:

Assume you are purchasing a fryer for your new restaurant. Should you choose an electric fryer or a gas fryer?

Q:

Does energy represent the largest portion of a fryer's operating cost?

What **other factors** might come into play when comparing **electric vs. gas fryers**?

Which fryer uses less energy during standby?

Which fryer reaches temperature sooner?

Which fryer has a faster recovery time?

Which fryer produces the most consistent product?

Which fryer requires less labor to maintain?

Which fryer makes the oil last the longest?

Which fryer puts less waste heat into the kitchen?

Which fryer has lower maintenance and longer life?

What **other factors** might come into play when comparing **electric vs. gas fryers**?

Electric fryers have quicker preheating and recovery times than their gas counterparts because they directly heat the oil, not the kettle.

What **other factors** might come into play when comparing **electric vs. gas fryers**?

Faster recovery means higher production while optimizing the flavor and appearance, even during peak serving times.

IDEAS & ACTIONS

_____

_____

_____

_____

What **other factors** might come into play when comparing **electric vs. gas fryers**?

Under idle conditions, electric fryers can use 2/3rds less energy than gas fryers.

What **other factors** might come into play when comparing **electric vs. gas fryers**?

Electric fryers reduce oil replacement and disposal costs. Their deep "cold zone" in the kettle reduces oil scorch from heavy breading.

What **other factors** might come into play when comparing **electric vs. gas fryers**?

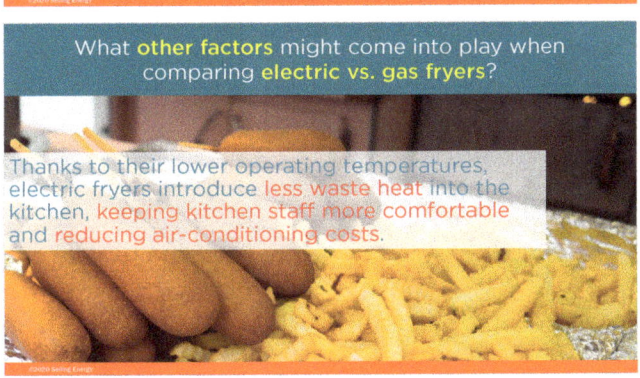

Electric fryers also reduce fat breakdown and boil-off because they operate at lower temperatures than gas fryers.

What **other factors** might come into play when comparing **electric vs. gas fryers**?

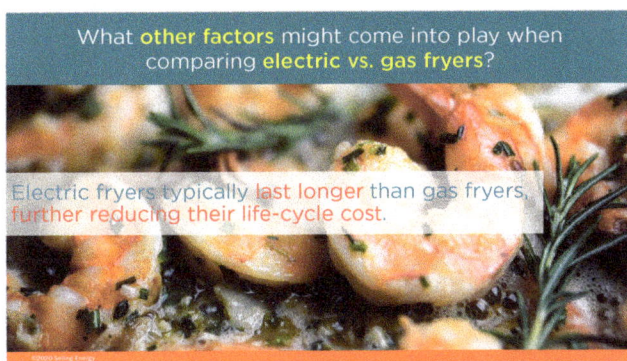

Electric fryers do not require heat shields, which allows for additional flexibility in kitchen layout.

What **other factors** might come into play when comparing **electric vs. gas fryers**?

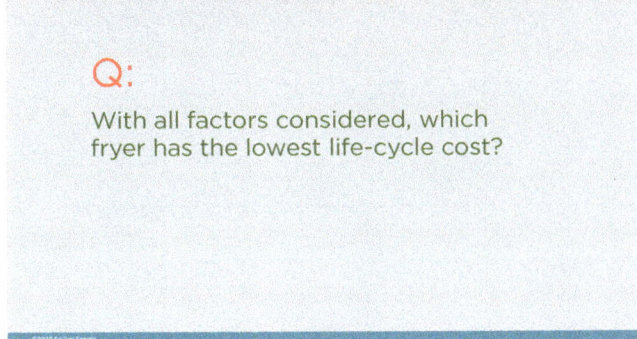

Thanks to their lower operating temperatures, electric fryers introduce less waste heat into the kitchen, keeping kitchen staff more comfortable and reducing air-conditioning costs.

What **other factors** might come into play when comparing **electric vs. gas fryers**?

Electric fryers typically last longer than gas fryers, further reducing their life-cycle cost.

Q:

With all factors considered, which fryer has the lowest life-cycle cost?

selling in 6™

Lesson 11
The value of smart energy technologies

Presented by
Mark Jewell
@SellingEnergy
info@sellingenergy.com

selling energy
Turbocharging Success

IDEAS & ACTIONS

www.SellingEnergy.com

Q:

What are some examples of smart energy technologies (electrification, for example) that can be linked to huge benefits provided you properly connect the dots?

---

1. Comfort cooling for workers in unconditioned workspaces

Additional electricity expense
Additional maintenance expense
Improved thermal comfort
Increased worker productivity
Reduced worker turnover

*Incentives or rebates may be available to help offset first cost

---

2. Low-velocity ceiling fans in a high-bay pharma warehouse

Additional electricity expense
Additional maintenance expense
Effective destratification of thermal gradients
3rd tier of racking passed FDA inspection
Prevented 33% loss of storage capacity

*Incentives or rebates may be available to help offset first cost

---

3. Reverse osmosis equipment in a metal cutting shop to address the disposal of oil/water mix

Additional electricity expense
Additional maintenance expense
Allows for on-site separation of cutting oil/water
Reduces disposal costs significantly
Makes high-quality RO water available for reintroduction into manufacturing process

*Incentives or rebates may be available to help offset first cost

---

4. WiFi-enabled electric fryers, combi ovens & induction cooktops

Potentially higher first cost than gas models
Likely savings in fuel, fat, maintenance, longevity
Remote monitoring of quality, portions & food safety
Higher-quality product via programming ease
Less waste due to tight tolerances and programming
Less-skilled workers can still produce quality product
Less potential for theft of prepared food

*Incentives or rebates may be available to help offset first cost

---

5. Electric non-road vehicles

Higher first cost than propane, gas or diesel models
Lower operating costs of fuel and maintenance
Cleaner operation
Safer to operate
Lower life-cycle cost
Lower emissions profile

*Incentives or rebates may be available to help offset first cost

---

6. Adding lighting to outdoor space that is presently not lighted

Additional electricity use
Additional maintenance
Pride of ownership and better curb appeal
Increased light level allows the property to be used safely and effectively after dark

*Incentives or rebates may be available to help offset first cost

---

7. Fuel-switching to electric to reduce embedded energy per widget, improve product quality, and/or increase plant throughput

Makes the plant more profitable
Better positions the plant to attract new contracts
Could decrease emissions inventory
Preserves jobs and sets the stage for expansion

*Incentives or rebates may be available to help offset first cost

---

IDEAS & ACTIONS

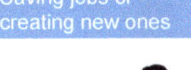

Saving jobs or creating new ones

Lesson 12
Business acumen in income property

Presented by
Mark Jewell
@SellingEnergy
info@sellingenergy.com

Turbocharging Success

More efficient equipment in **income-producing** property

Energy savings
Maintenance savings
Improved equipment longevity and control
Better look and feel of the space
Better tenant attraction and retention
Higher net operating income
Higher asset value

Efficiency is vital to income property

- "The building is the business"
- Energy is a very large portion of operating expenses
- You need to know how costs/benefits would be shared, AND...
- You need to know how owner's share would affect value

Sources and benefits of higher Net Operating Income (NOI)

$$\frac{\text{Net operating income}}{\text{Capitalization rate}} = \text{Asset value}$$

- Higher rent
- Lower vacancy
- Lower landlord share of operating expenses

Income properties

More Competitive	More Profitable	More Valuable
Lower occupancy cost	Better tenant retention & attraction	Higher rent revenue increases cash flow
Enhanced comfort & productivity	Lower vacancy rates result in higher rent revenue	Lower operating costs increase cash flow
Sustainability that gives marketing advantage	Lower tenant utility bills support higher base rents	Higher net operating income (NOI) supports higher appraisal

---

Market Premiums of ENERGY STAR-labeled U.S. Commercial Buildings

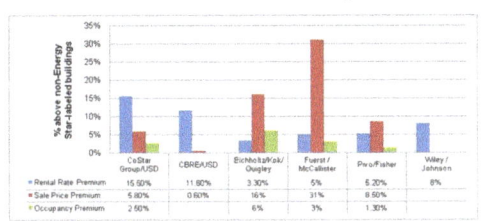

	CoStar Group/USD	CBRE/USD	Eichholtz/Kok/Quigley	Fuerst / McCallister	Pivo/Fisher	Wiley / Johnson
■ Rental Rate Premium	15.50%	11.80%	3.30%	5%	6.20%	8%
■ Sale Price Premium	5.80%	0.60%	16%	31%	8.50%	
▢ Occupancy Premium	2.50%		6%	3%	1.30%	

See www.imt.org/rating-value for more information

How costly is tenant turnover?

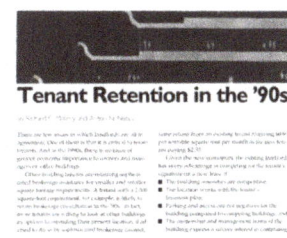

Tenant Retention in the '90s

IDEAS & ACTIONS

_____

_____

_____

_____

Lesson 13
Equating projected savings to revenue

Presented by
Mark Jewell
@SellingEnergy
info@sellingenergy.com

Turbocharging Success

---

3 Levels of Business Acumen

Level **2**
Intermediate

Being able to translate projected savings to
equivalent revenue using the prospect's net margin
percentage…

…and then converting that incrementally higher
revenue to "widget equivalents"

The "Profit" on the "P&L"

Bottom line is "net profit."

Dividing the projected savings by net margin will yield
the equivalent dollars of revenue needed to deliver a
similar impact in a prior fiscal period.

At a Net Margin of 4%…

$$\frac{\$1 \text{ savings}}{4\% \text{ net margin}}$$ $25 revenue

Net margin, net profit margin, profit margin, and net
profit ratio all refer to a measure of profitability that is
calculated by finding the net profit as a percentage of
revenue.

NOTE: A more conservative analysis might use Contribution Margin,
EBIT/Sales, or EBITDA/Sales rather than Net Margin in this context.

---

as of Jan 2019 Industry Name	Net Income Based Net Margin
Advertising	3.10%
Aerospace/Defense	7.92%
Air Transport	7.86%
Apparel	4.52%
Auto & Truck	1.82%
Auto Parts	4.92%
Bank (Money Center)	23.46%
Banks (Regional)	28.99%
Beverage (Alcoholic)	24.35%
Beverage (Soft)	8.76%
Broadcasting	9.59%
Brokerage & Investment Banking	14.23%
Building Materials	5.29%
Business & Consumer Services	6.47%
Cable TV	25.44%
Chemical (Basic)	9.90%
Chemical (Diversified)	4.87%
Chemical (Specialty)	8.29%
Coal & Related Energy	7.50%
Computer Services	4.03%
Computers/Peripherals	12.74%
Construction Supplies	7.47%
Diversified	8.70%
Drugs (Biotechnology)	-1.61%

Finding Margins by Industry

SOURCE: Stern School of
Business at NYU, using data from
S&P Capital IQ, Bloomberg and
the Federal Reserve.

---

as of Jan 2019 Industry Name	Net Income Based Net Margin
Drugs (Pharmaceutical)	10.94%
Education	6.81%
Electrical Equipment	6.31%
Electronics (Consumer & Office)	-4.07%
Electronics (General)	2.30%
Engineering/Construction	2.18%
Entertainment	13.43%
Environmental & Waste Services	9.19%
Farming/Agriculture	3.44%
Financial Svcs. (Non-bank & Insurance)	20.06%
Food Processing	11.98%
Food Wholesalers	2.05%
Furn/Home Furnishings	2.20%
Green & Renewable Energy	10.02%
Healthcare Products	5.80%
Healthcare Support Services	2.46%
Healthcare Information and Technology	9.55%
Homebuilding	7.19%
Hospitals/Healthcare Facilities	0.78%
Hotel/Gaming	17.62%
Household Products	6.79%
Information Services	18.41%
Insurance (General)	-1.61%
Insurance (Life)	11.24%

Finding Margins by Industry

SOURCE: Stern School of
Business at NYU, using data from
S&P Capital IQ, Bloomberg and
the Federal Reserve.

---

as of Jan 2019 Industry Name	Net Income Based Net Margin
Insurance (Prop/Cas.)	9.51%
Investments & Asset Management	24.52%
Machinery	7.74%
Metals & Mining	8.33%
Office Equipment & Services	3.84%
Oil/Gas (Integrated)	9.23%
Oil/Gas (Production and Exploration)	9.94%
Oil/Gas Distribution	5.98%
Oilfield Svcs/Equip.	3.25%
Packaging & Container	7.30%
Paper/Forest Products	3.07%
Power	9.57%
Precious Metals	-5.90%
Publishing & Newspapers	-1.00%
R.E.I.T.	24.44%
Real Estate (Development)	18.42%
Real Estate (General/Diversified)	41.23%
Real Estate (Operations & Services)	5.87%
Recreation	3.25%
Reinsurance	13.53%
Restaurant/Dining	12.11%
Retail (Automotive)	3.90%
Retail (Building Supply)	7.29%
Retail (Distributors)	5.63%

Finding Margins by Industry

SOURCE: Stern School of
Business at NYU, using data from
S&P Capital IQ, Bloomberg and
the Federal Reserve.

---

as of Jan 2019 Industry Name	Net Income Based Net Margin
Retail (General)	1.90%
Retail (Grocery and Food)	2.85%
Retail (Online)	11.34%
Retail (Special Lines)	4.00%
Rubber& Tires	2.72%
Semiconductor	21.47%
Semiconductor Equip	15.61%
Shipbuilding & Marine	8.69%
Shoe	5.59%
Software (Entertainment)	18.91%
Software (Internet)	1.88%
Software (System & Application)	10.45%
Steel	7.32%
Telecom (Wireless)	14.88%
Telecom. Equipment	2.11%
Telecom. Services	18.76%
Tobacco	31.42%
Transportation	6.74%
Transportation (Railroads)	50.93%
Trucking	7.82%
Utility (General)	11.49%
Utility (Water)	15.06%
Total Market	**8.89%**
Total Market (without financials)	**8.01%**

Finding Margins by Industry

SOURCE: Stern School of
Business at NYU, using data from
S&P Capital IQ, Bloomberg and
the Federal Reserve.

IDEAS & ACTIONS

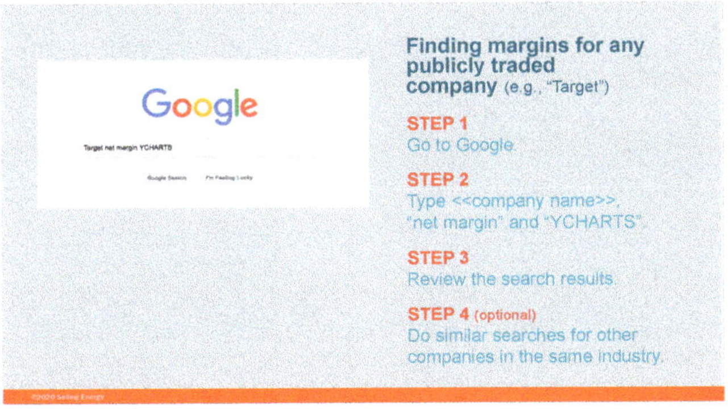

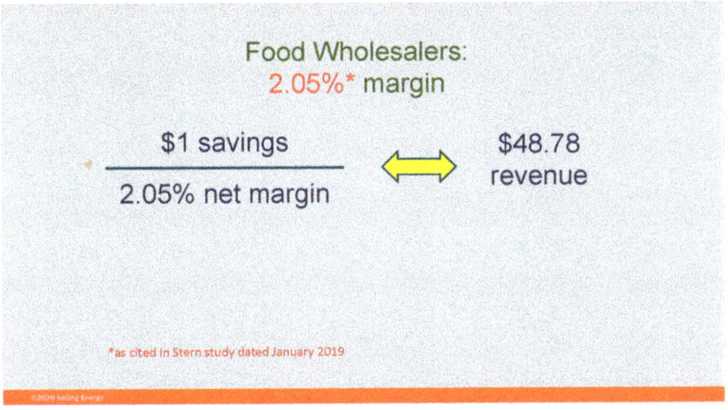

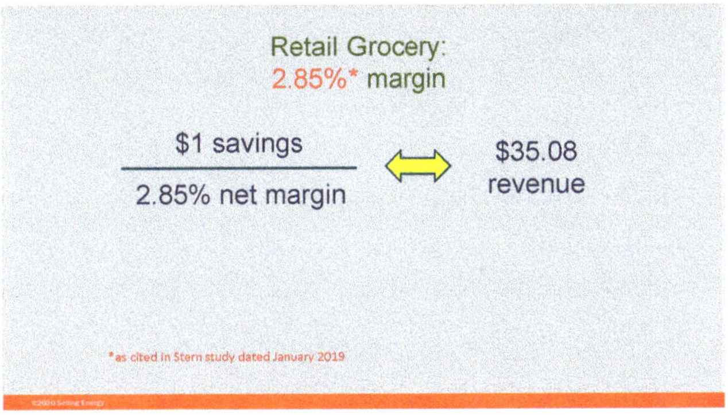

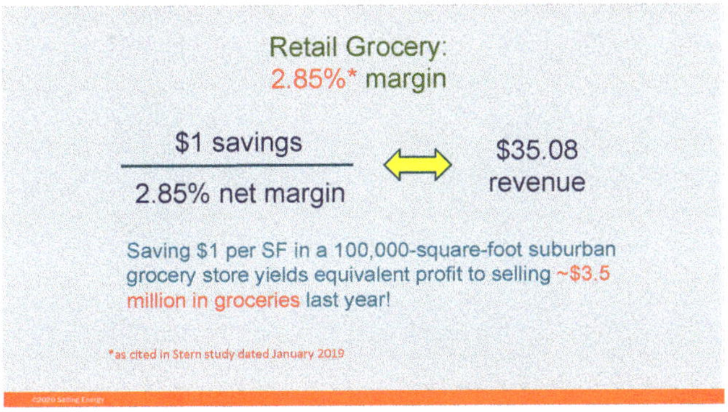

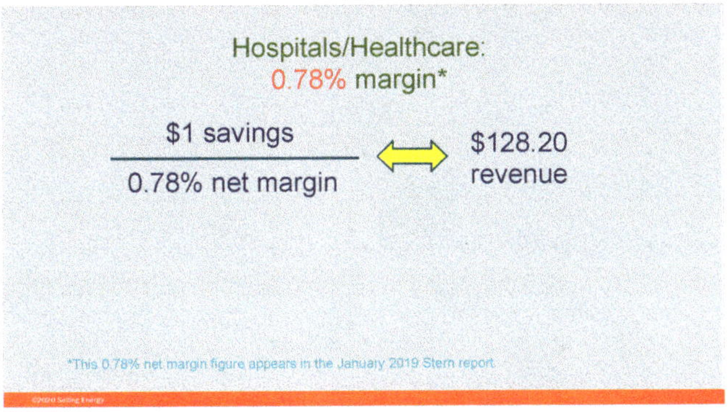

Finding margins for any publicly traded company (e.g., "Target")

Google

Target net margin YCHARTS

Google Search   I'm Feeling Lucky

STEP 1
Go to Google.

STEP 2
Type <<company name>>, "net margin" and "YCHARTS".

STEP 3
Review the search results.

STEP 4 (optional)
Do similar searches for other companies in the same industry.

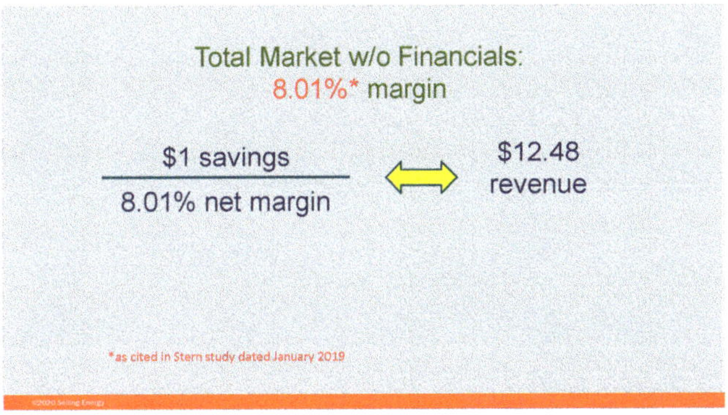

Total Market w/o Financials:
8.01%* margin

$$\frac{\$1 \text{ savings}}{8.01\% \text{ net margin}} \iff \$12.48 \text{ revenue}$$

*as cited in Stern study dated January 2019

Food Wholesalers:
2.05%* margin

$$\frac{\$1 \text{ savings}}{2.05\% \text{ net margin}} \iff \$48.78 \text{ revenue}$$

*as cited in Stern study dated January 2019

Retail Grocery:
2.85%* margin

$$\frac{\$1 \text{ savings}}{2.85\% \text{ net margin}} \iff \$35.08 \text{ revenue}$$

*as cited in Stern study dated January 2019

Retail Grocery:
2.85%* margin

$$\frac{\$1 \text{ savings}}{2.85\% \text{ net margin}} \iff \$35.08 \text{ revenue}$$

Saving $1 per SF in a 100,000-square-foot suburban grocery store yields equivalent profit to selling ~$3.5 million in groceries last year!

*as cited in Stern study dated January 2019

Sell 15,000 bushels of peaches.
Or switch to LED lighting.
Same results, your choice.

DUKE ENERGY.

Hospitals/Healthcare:
0.78% margin*

$$\frac{\$1 \text{ savings}}{0.78\% \text{ net margin}} \iff \$128.20 \text{ revenue}$$

*This 0.78% net margin figure appears in the January 2019 Stern report.

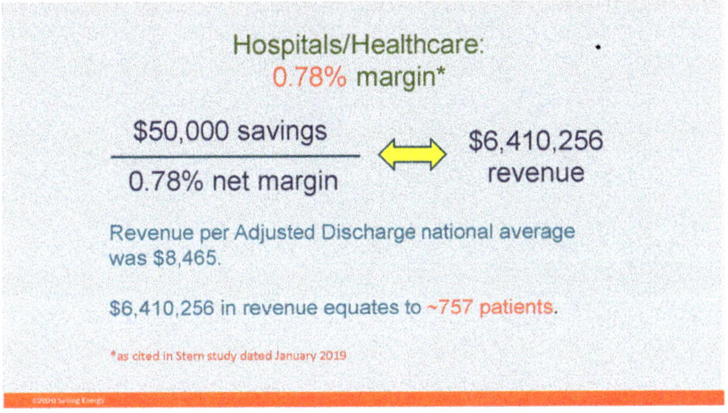

Hospitals/Healthcare:
0.78% margin*

$$\frac{\$50,000 \text{ savings}}{0.78\% \text{ net margin}} \iff \$6,410,256 \text{ revenue}$$

Revenue per Adjusted Discharge national average was $8,465.

$6,410,256 in revenue equates to ~757 patients.

*as cited in Stern study dated January 2019

IDEAS & ACTIONS

What's a "widget"?

An abstract "unit of production" that represents what a business makes and sells to generate its revenues.

Used to express the quantity of goods or services that need to be produced to generate a given amount of revenue.

EXAMPLES: Meals served, patients treated, gallons of milk produced, or bushels of peaches sold...

Sales professionals migrate the discussion away from features and beyond benefits, putting all the focus on the customer's values.

They also reframe benefits so they can be measured with the customer's yardstick.

Lesson 14
Equating savings to revenue for SMB

Presented by
Mark Jewell
@SellingEnergy
info@sellingenergy.com

Q:

Does this segment-specific sales concept apply to small and medium-sized businesses (SMB)?

Q:

How many "widgets*" did your prospect have to sell last year to match each $1,000 in savings your project could deliver?

*For the following examples, we employ a simplifying assumption that the margin of the typical widget is the same as the margin for a typical enterprise in that segment.

Q:

What's the net margin of a coffee shop?

10%

IDEAS & ACTIONS

2,500 cups of coffee

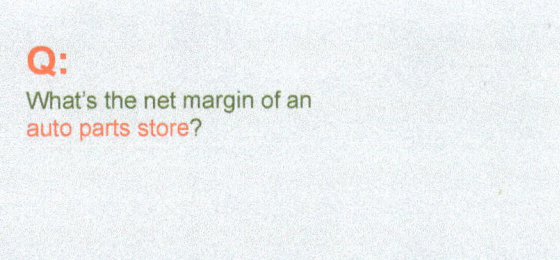

Q:
What's the net margin of an auto parts store?

3.4%

7,267 quarts of oil

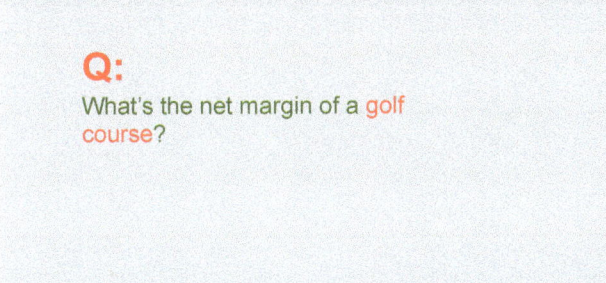

Q:
What's the net margin of a golf course?

2.7%

740 rounds of golf

Q:
What's the net margin of the typical farm?

IDEAS & ACTIONS

www.SellingEnergy.com

3.1%

7,298 bales of hay

Q:

What's the net margin of a casual dining establishment?

5%

1,455 meals

Q:

What's the net margin of a fine dining establishment?

6%

584 meals

IDEAS & ACTIONS _____

_____

_____

_____

Q:

What's the net margin of a
fitness center?

8.6%

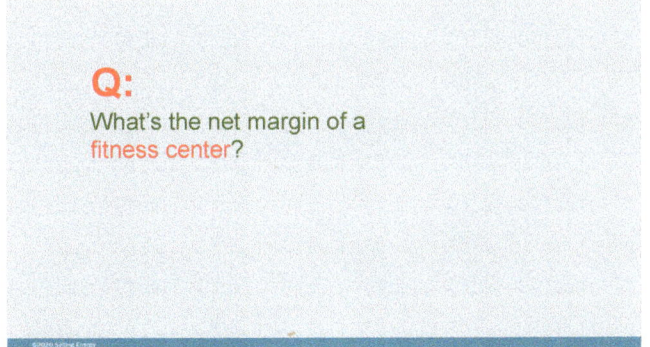

48 members @ $240/yr.

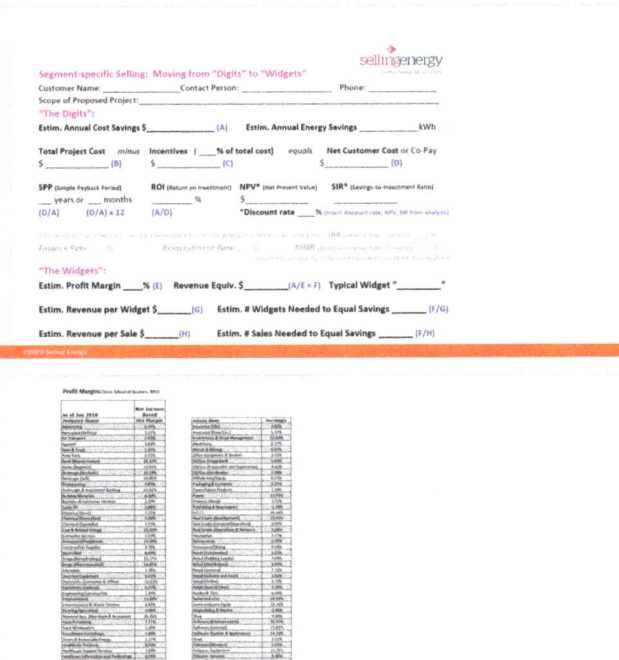

Q:

Could an LED lighting retrofit equate to
having 3,700 customers patronize a small
plumbing supply store?

IDEAS & ACTIONS

Q:

Are you committed to test-driving this Digits-to-Widgets approach to see how well it works for you?

selling in 6™

Lesson 15
Using the proper margin in Digits-to-Widgets™

Presented by
Mark Jewell
@SellingEnergy
info@sellingenergy.com

sellingenergy
Turbocharging Success

At a Net Margin of 4%...

$$\frac{\$1\ savings}{4\%\ net\ margin} \longleftrightarrow \$25\ revenue$$

Net margin, net profit margin, profit margin, and net profit ratio all refer to a measure of profitability that is calculated by finding the net profit as a percentage of revenue.

NOTE: A more conservative analysis might use Contribution Margin, EBIT/Sales, or EBITDA/Sales rather than Net Margin in this context.

Q:

So what does using "net margin" mean when using a Digits-to-Widgets™ analogy?

Q:

What is net margin*?

*Net margin, net profit margin, profit margin, and net profit ratio all refer to a measure of profitability that is calculated by finding the net profit as a percentage of revenue.

Calculating Net Profit and Net Margin

Revenue − Operating Expenses − Interest − Taxes − Preferred Stock Dividends = Net Profit ($)

$$\frac{Net\ Profit}{Revenue} = Net\ Margin\ (\%)$$

Q:

What is contribution margin?

Contribution Margin and Contribution Margin Ratio

Net Sales − Variable Product Costs − Variable Period Expenses = Contribution Margin ($)

$$\frac{Contribution\ Margin}{Net\ Sales} = Contribution\ Margin\ Ratio\ (\%)$$

IDEAS & ACTIONS

Q:

So, is your proposed project generating the same bottom-line impact witnessed in the prior fiscal period from producing "x" number of widgets?

Q:

Or is it generating the same bottom-line impact that would have been witnessed if they had produced "x" more widgets?

HINT:

If your prospect produced "x" more widgets without adding any fixed costs, would the incremental bottom line impact be a function of the "net margin" or the "contribution margin"?

The smaller the denominator, the larger the impact...

$$\frac{\$1\ savings}{4\%\ net\ margin} \longleftrightarrow \$25\ revenue$$

$$\frac{\$1\ savings}{25\%\ contribution\ margin} \longleftrightarrow \$4\ revenue$$

Respecting the difference between net margin and contribution margin

$$\frac{\$10,000\ savings}{4\%\ net\ margin} \longleftrightarrow \$250K\ revenue\ equivalent$$

"Given your net margin of 4% last year, your team had to make and sell $250,000 worth of widgets – that's a half-million widgets at 50 cents each – to see $10K hit your bottom line. This upgrade is projected to drop $10K to your bottom line every year – plus inflation – for the next 10 years."

If they could produce 500K more widgets with no additional fixed cost, it would **not** be accurate to say...

"This project is the equivalent of selling another half-million widgets this year..."

Bonus Lesson 15A
Understanding measures of profitability

Presented by
Mark Jewell
@SellingEnergy
info@sellingenergy.com

At a Net Margin of 4%...

$$\frac{\$1\ savings}{4\%\ net\ margin} \longleftrightarrow \$25\ revenue$$

Net margin, net profit margin, profit margin, and net profit ratio all refer to a measure of profitability that is calculated by finding the net profit as a percentage of revenue.

NOTE: A more conservative analysis might use Contribution Margin, EBIT/Sales, or EBITDA/Sales rather than Net Margin in this context.

3 key GAAP*-approved measures of profitability

1. Gross profit margin
2. Operating profit margin
3. Net profit margin

* GAAP refers to "Generally Accepted Accounting Principles"

IDEAS & ACTIONS

www.SellingEnergy.com

Q:

What is cost of goods sold*?

*also known as COGS

Calculating Cost of Goods Sold

$$\text{Fixed Product Costs} + \text{Variable Product Costs} = \text{Cost of Goods Sold}$$

Cost of Goods Sold *excludes* Selling and Administrative Expenses

Cost of Goods Sold *includes* Direct Material, Direct Labor and Factory Overhead

---

Bonus Lesson 15B
Understanding gross margin

Presented by
Mark Jewell
@SellingEnergy
info@sellingenergy.com

sellingenergy
Turbocharging Success.

---

3 key GAAP*-approved measures of profitability

1. Gross profit margin
2. Operating profit margin
3. Net profit margin

* GAAP refers to "Generally Accepted Accounting Principles"

Q:

What is gross margin*?

*also known as gross profit margin

Calculating Net Sales, Gross Profit, and Gross Margin

$$\text{Gross Sales} - \text{Sales Discounts, Returns, and Allowances} = \text{Net Sales (\$)}$$

$$\text{Net Sales} - \text{Cost of Goods Sold} = \text{Gross Profit (\$)}$$

$$\frac{\text{Gross Profit}}{\text{Net Sales}} = \text{Gross Margin (\%)}$$

Bonus Lesson 15C
Understanding operating margin

Presented by
Mark Jewell
@SellingEnergy
info@sellingenergy.com

sellingenergy
Turbocharging Success.

---

3 key GAAP*-approved measures of profitability

1. Gross profit margin
2. Operating profit margin
3. Net profit margin

* GAAP refers to "Generally Accepted Accounting Principles"

IDEAS & ACTIONS

Q:

What is operating income*?

*also known as income from operations, operating earnings, or operating profit

---

Calculating Operating Income and Operating Margin

$$\text{Operating Revenue} - \text{Operating Expenses} = \text{Operating Income (\$)}$$

$$\text{Net Sales} - \text{COGS}^1 - \text{SG\&A}^2 - \text{Impairment Charges}^3 = \text{Operating Income}^4 \text{ (\$)}$$

$$\frac{\text{Operating Income}}{\text{Revenue}} = \text{Operating Margin (\%)}$$

[1] COGS is Cost of Goods Sold, which is the component of operating expenses that is deducted from Net Sales to calculate Gross Profit, and in turn Gross Margin (see previous slides)
[2] Sales, General and Administrative may include depreciation/amortization and/or research and development
[3] Examples include long-lived assets whose market values have declined significantly
[4] Operating income is shown before provision for income tax and before investment income, interest expense, or other non-operating income or expense items

---

Operating margin, also referred to as operating profit margin, is one measure of the company's profit level. It is shown as a percentage of total sales revenue with all costs of doing business factored into the equation except for taxes, interest, profit or loss from investments, and any extraordinary gains or losses from events outside of the company's regular business dealings, such as selling real estate or buildings.

SOURCE: https://www.investopedia.com/ask/answers/010915/what-difference-between-operating-margin-and-ebitda.asp

---

"Costs included in figuring the operating margin include wages and benefits for employees and independent contractors, administrative costs, the cost of parts or materials required to produce items the company sells, advertising costs, and depreciation and amortization. Examining the operating margin helps companies analyze, and hopefully reduce, variable costs involved in conducting their business."

SOURCE: https://www.investopedia.com/ask/answers/010915/what-difference-between-operating-margin-and-ebitda.asp

---

Bonus Lesson 15D
Understanding contribution margin

Presented by
Mark Jewell
@SellingEnergy
info@sellingenergy.com

Turbocharging Success

Q:

What is contribution margin?

Contribution Margin and Contribution Margin Ratio

$$\text{Net Sales} - \text{Variable Product Costs} - \text{Variable Period Expenses} = \text{Contribution Margin (\$)}$$

$$\frac{\text{Contribution Margin}}{\text{Net Sales}} = \text{Contribution Margin Ratio (\%)}$$

SAMPLE COMPANY	Net Sales	Variable	Fixed
Net Sales	$600,000		
Cost of Goods Sold		$120,000	$200,000
Selling & Admin Expenses		$40,000	$150,000

$$\text{Net Sales} - \text{Cost of Goods Sold} = \text{Gross Profit (\$)}$$

$$\$600K - (\$120K + \$200K) = \$280,000$$

$$\frac{\text{Gross Profit}}{\text{Net Sales}} = \text{Gross Margin (\%)} \quad \frac{\$280K}{\$600K} = 46.7\%$$

IDEAS & ACTIONS

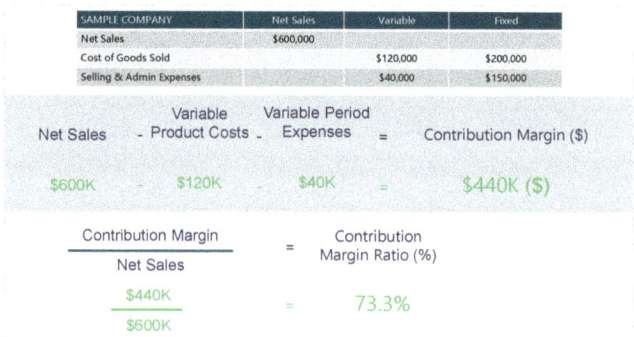

SAMPLE COMPANY	Net Sales	Variable	Fixed
Net Sales	$600,000		
Cost of Goods Sold		$120,000	$200,000
Selling & Admin Expenses		$40,000	$150,000

Net Sales − Variable Product Costs − Variable Period Expenses = Contribution Margin ($)

$600K − $120K − $40K = $440K ($)

$$\frac{\text{Contribution Margin}}{\text{Net Sales}} = \text{Contribution Margin Ratio (\%)}$$

$$\frac{\$440K}{\$600K} = 73.3\%$$

---

3 key GAAP*-approved measures of profitability

1. Gross profit margin
2. Operating profit margin
3. Net profit margin

* GAAP refers to "Generally Accepted Accounting Principles"

Q:

What is net margin*?

*Net margin, net profit margin, profit margin, and net profit ratio all refer to a measure of profitability that is calculated by finding the net profit as a percentage of revenue.

Calculating Net Profit and Net Margin

Revenue − Operating Expenses − Interest − Taxes − Preferred Stock Dividends = Net Profit ($)

$$\frac{\text{Net Profit}}{\text{Revenue}} = \text{Net Margin (\%)}$$

---

2 non-GAAP*-approved measures of profitability

1. **EBIT**
   Earnings Before Interest and Taxes

2. **EBITDA**
   Earnings Before Interest, Taxes, Depreciation and Amortization

* GAAP refers to "Generally Accepted Accounting Principles"

"Two of the most common non-GAAP profitability metrics are earnings before interest and taxes (EBIT) and earnings before interest, taxes, depreciation and amortization (EBITDA). While they bear close resemblance to their GAAP counterparts in some ways, there are crucial differences. For example, gross profit reflects revenue minus only those costs directly associated with production of goods for sale. Operating profit is equal to gross profit minus any other overhead, operational or sales expenses necessary to run the business, including depreciation and amortization of assets."

SOURCE: https://www.investopedia.com/ask/answers/032715/what-difference-between-ebitda-margin-and-profit-margin.asp

---

IDEAS & ACTIONS

_____

_____

_____

_____

"EBITDA essentially splits the difference between these two metrics by accounting for all expenses generated by production and day-to-day operations, but adding back in the cost of depreciation and amortization. Like its GAAP counterparts, the EBITDA profit margin is equal to the EBITDA divided by revenue."

SOURCE: https://www.investopedia.com/ask/answers/032715/what-difference-between-ebitda-margin-and-profit-margin.asp

©2020 Selling Energy

"The difference between the EBITDA profit margin and standard profit margins is simply a matter of its exclusion from the GAAP principles. The EBITDA is still a profit margin, but prudent corporate and stock valuation includes analysis of this metric in addition to the GAAP margins rather than instead of them."

SOURCE: https://www.investopedia.com/ask/answers/032715/what-difference-between-ebitda-margin-and-profit-margin.asp

©2020 Selling Energy

Q:

What is EBITDA*?

*Earnings Before Interest, Taxes, Depreciation, and Amortization.

©2020 Selling Energy

Calculating EBITDA and EBITDA Profit Margin

Net Profit + Interest + Taxes + Depreciation + Amortization = EBITDA ($)

$$\frac{EBITDA}{Revenue} = EBIDTA\ Profit\ Margin\ (\%)$$

©2020 Selling Energy

"Although the figures used for calculating operating margin and EBITDA somewhat overlap, EBITDA is commonly considered more closely related to net profit margin, because the net profit provides the base number from which EBITDA is calculated."

SOURCE: https://www.investopedia.com/ask/answers/010915/what-difference-between-operating-margin-and-ebitda.asp

©2020 Selling Energy

"Net profit is the bottom-line calculation for a company's profitability, as it includes all of the company's costs and expenses, including taxes, interest, and one-time or extraordinary expenses, figures that are not included in the calculation of operating profit."

SOURCE: https://www.investopedia.com/ask/answers/010915/what-difference-between-operating-margin-and-ebitda.asp

©2020 Selling Energy

"EBITDA represents the net profit amount with taxes, interest, depreciation and amortization added back to that amount. Thus, EBITDA includes both **items usually categorized under net profit** (taxes and interest) and **items usually categorized under operating profit** (depreciation and amortization). The EBITDA figure is helpful in comparing the net profitability of different companies by factoring out of the comparison decisions related to financing and accounting."

SOURCE: https://www.investopedia.com/ask/answers/010915/what-difference-between-operating-margin-and-ebitda.asp

©2020 Selling Energy

Lesson 16
Driving enterprise value via energy projects

Presented by
Mark Jewell
@SellingEnergy
info@sellingenergy.com

©2020 Selling Energy

IDEAS & ACTIONS

3 Levels of Business Acumen

Level **3**
Advanced

Being able to connect proposed energy improvements to non-utility-cost and non-financial benefits…

…and highlight potential positive impacts on the prospect's profit and loss statement and/or balance sheet.

Q:

How else might enhanced energy use benefit a fitness center?

Put on Your Business Broker's Hat

1. How quickly do prospects sign-up?
   "First visit sales" average 30%
   "Additional sales within 30 days" average another 35%
2. Membership retention averages 65%

Could the "look and feel" (lighting, thermal comfort, indoor air quality, etc.) influence these stats?

Q:

How is a fitness center valued upon sale?

5x EBIT

Put on Your Business Broker's Hat

Let's assume the sales price is set at 5x EBIT*

Fitness Center Owners should focus on the
$5 in higher enterprise value
they get for every
$1 of higher earnings**

* "EBIT" stands for "Earnings Before Interest and Taxes"
** Lower utilities and maintenance; better member recruitment/retention; etc.

Lesson **17**
Driving benefits far beyond savings

Presented by
Mark Jewell
@SellingEnergy
info@sellingenergy.com

IDEAS & ACTIONS

Moving beyond utility-cost savings…

1. Utility-cost financial benefits
2. Non-utility-cost financial benefits
3. Non-financial benefits

What are some examples of each?

Non-utility-cost financial & non-financial benefits…

1. Better employee attraction/retention
2. Higher employee productivity & morale
3. Improved health and safety
4. Increased throughput or less downtime
5. Improved process control
6. Reduced scrap rate
7. Greater process visibility
8. Reduced emissions
9. Increased retail sales
10. And, of course, many more…

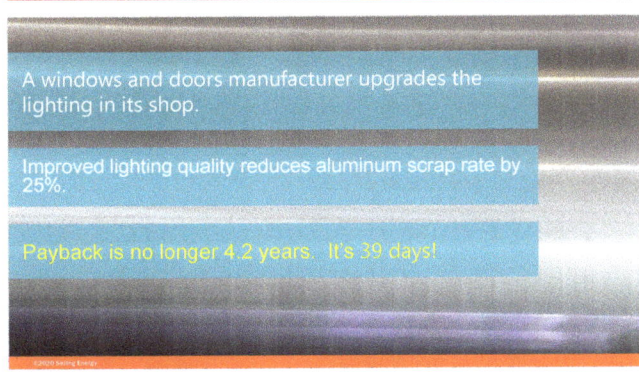

A windows and doors manufacturer upgrades the lighting in its shop.

Improved lighting quality reduces aluminum scrap rate by 25%.

Payback is no longer 4.2 years. It's 39 days!

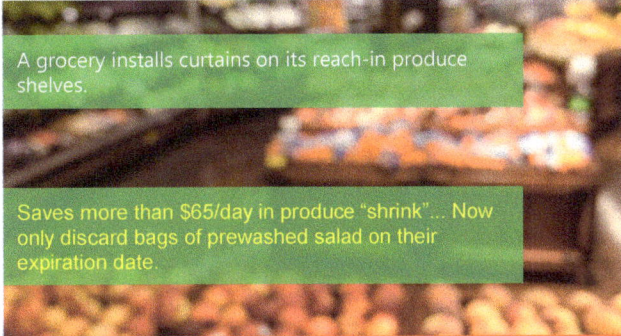

A grocery installs curtains on its reach-in produce shelves.

Saves more than $65/day in produce "shrink"… Now only discard bags of prewashed salad on their expiration date.

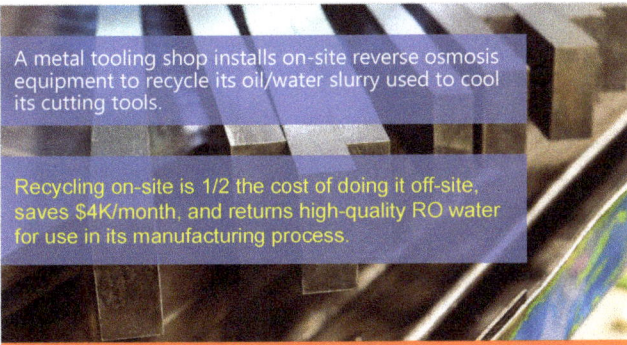

A metal tooling shop installs on-site reverse osmosis equipment to recycle its oil/water slurry used to cool its cutting tools.

Recycling on-site is 1/2 the cost of doing it off-site, saves $4K/month, and returns high-quality RO water for use in its manufacturing process.

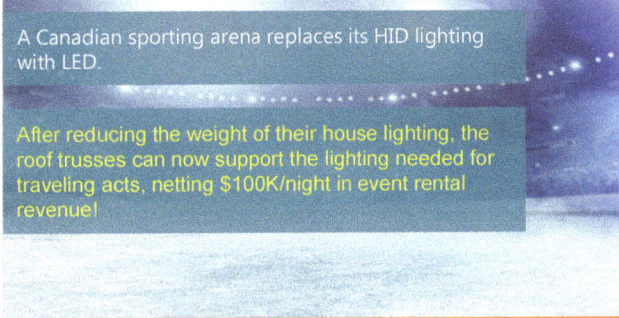

A Canadian sporting arena replaces its HID lighting with LED.

After reducing the weight of their house lighting, the roof trusses can now support the lighting needed for traveling acts, netting $100K/night in event rental revenue!

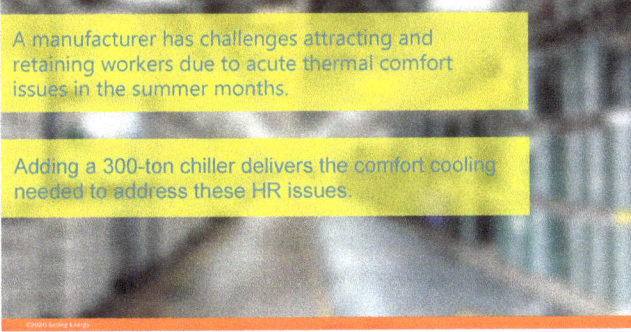

A manufacturer has challenges attracting and retaining workers due to acute thermal comfort issues in the summer months.

Adding a 300-ton chiller delivers the comfort cooling needed to address these HR issues.

A hospital installs VFDs on selected motors.

When surveyed 6 months later, plant engineers noted that their chronic need to replace pump seals has vanished.

IDEAS & ACTIONS

www.SellingEnergy.com

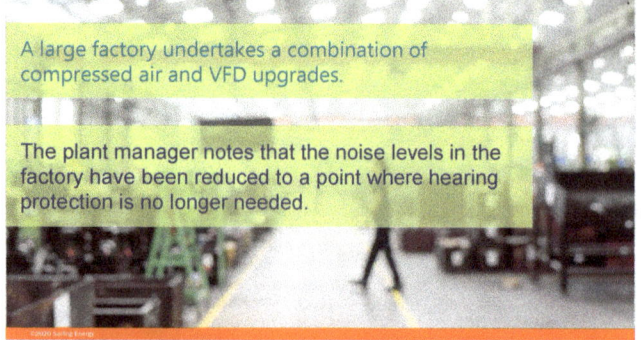

A large factory undertakes a combination of compressed air and VFD upgrades.

The plant manager notes that the noise levels in the factory have been reduced to a point where hearing protection is no longer needed.

Electric forklifts yield a multitude of benefits.

More maneuverable, permitting narrower aisles.
Quieter: drivers more aware of surroundings.
No emissions means less need for outside air.
No need to store flammable fuel.
Less maintenance overall.

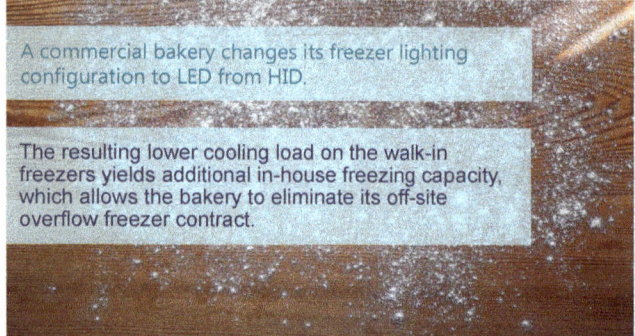

A commercial bakery changes its freezer lighting configuration to LED from HID.

The resulting lower cooling load on the walk-in freezers yields additional in-house freezing capacity, which allows the bakery to eliminate its off-site overflow freezer contract.

Lesson 18
Reframing savings to be more compelling

Presented by
Mark Jewell
@SellingEnergy
info@sellingenergy.com

Q:

Could financial savings be reframed to be even more compelling?

Funding more research with the savings

Lesson 19
Leveraging non-financial motivators

Presented by
Mark Jewell
@SellingEnergy
info@sellingenergy.com

Q:

What could be even more important than saving energy or even money?

IDEAS & ACTIONS

Reducing carbon emissions

Addressing tenant comfort complaints

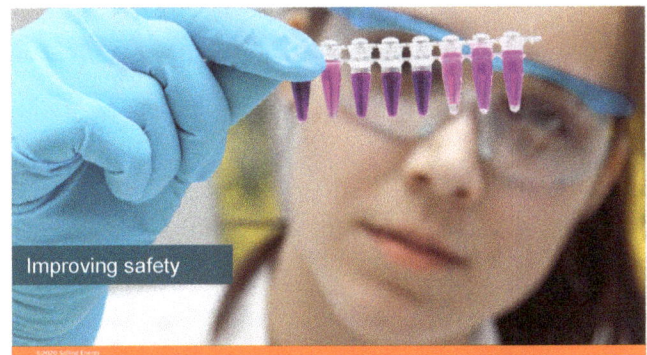
Improving safety

Ensuring regulatory compliance

Emulating best practice facilities

Avoiding obsolescence

Upgrading the user interface

Earning the ENERGY STAR® or LEED® certification

IDEAS & ACTIONS

www.SellingEnergy.com

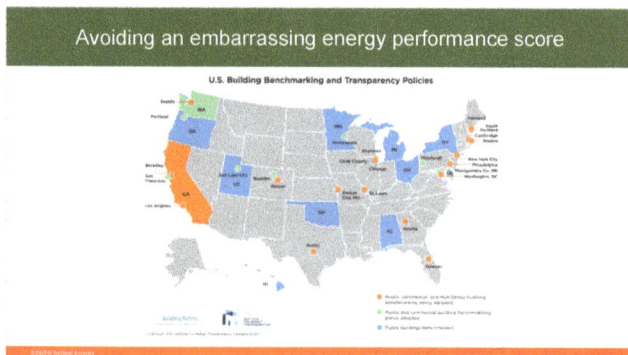

Avoiding an embarrassing energy performance score

U.S. Building Benchmarking and Transparency Policies

Avoiding budget cuts

Saving jobs or creating new ones

Lesson 20
Winning with market segmentation

Presented by
Mark Jewell
@SellingEnergy
info@sellingenergy.com

"Market Segmentation"

The practice of aggregating your prospects into "segments" (and then "sub-segments") that have common needs and would likely respond similarly to your messaging.

The more specific, the better…

Segments
Real estate
Retail
Healthcare
Manufacturing

Sub-segments
Shopping centers, multifamily housing…
Grocery, department stores…
Hospitals, medical office…
Food processing, chemicals…

Segment Guides™

- Commercial RE
- Dairy
- Data Centers
- Education
- Electrification
- Government
- Greenhouses
- Grocery
- Healthcare
- Hospitality
- K-12
- Large Assembly
- Manufacturing
- Parking Garages & Lots
- Residential
- Restaurants
- Retail
- Senior Living
- Warehouses & Cold Storage
- Water & Wastewater

…with frequent updates and additions to the database!

And many more…

- Advanced Manufacturing
- Agriculture
- Biotech / Laboratories
- Colleges / Universities
- Food Processing
- Livestock
- Service Retail
- Small / Medium-sized Businesses
- Other

IDEAS & ACTIONS

Your messaging should resonate with each segment's uniqueness

- Interest in energy as a controllable expense
- Non-utility-cost financial benefits
- Non-financial benefits
- Jargon, yardsticks
- Decision-making processes
- Sound bites that will capture attention
- And much more...

What's a "widget"?

An abstract "unit of production" that represents what a business makes and sells to generate its revenues.

Used to express the quantity of goods or services that need to be produced to generate a given amount of revenue.

EXAMPLES: Meals served, patients treated, cars sold, or gallons of milk produced

1. Identifying and expressing segment-specific, non-utility-cost financial benefits and non-financial benefits.

Why?

Because they tend to be far more compelling than the more obvious utility-cost financial benefits.

2. Understanding each segment's business dynamics (e.g., profit margin).

Why?

So that the savings that an energy project would deliver to the bottom line can be translated into the amount of revenue typically needed to create a similar bottom-line impact for that given segment.

3. Understanding what a typical "widget" might be in that segment.

Why?

Translating the revenue required to deliver a similar bottom-line impact into "widget equivalents" typically makes the comparison even more visual and more compelling.

IDEAS & ACTIONS

Fine-tune your pitch and *prove* that the non-utility-cost financial and non-financial benefits are way more compelling than the energy savings.

The anatomy of Segment Guides™

- Overview of the segment
- Role of energy in that segment's decision-making
- Yardsticks used to gauge success
- Sound bites, particularly on non-utility-cost financial and non-financial benefits
- Trade organizations
- Trade publications

Segment Guides™ tell you the role of energy in each segment.

Total Energy Use in Office Buildings by End Use

Energy consumption in greenhouses varies greatly depending on size, construction, controls, lighting and crop being grown.[20] However, the average cost of energy has been estimated at 8.5% of sales, including fuel, gas/diesel, electricity, and trucking costs,[25] and energy is the third largest cost in greenhouses (15%);[30] heating (75%) and electricity (15%) comprise most of the industry's energy needs.[31] In terms of desire to implement energy efficient measures, a 2008 survey of New Jersey greenhouse growers found that 45% of the respondents had implemented energy saving technologies since 2003 and that 39% were considering implementing energy efficient measures. Nine percent were not sure what energy efficient measures to adopt, but were considering all options.[32]

Segment Guides™ tell you the yardsticks and margins you need to be seen as a peer rather than a vendor.

- **On-Time Delivery to Commit** – This metric is the percentage of time that manufacturer completed product on the schedule that was committed to customers.
- **Manufacturing Cycle Time** – This metric measures the speed or time it takes for man produce a given product from the time the order is released, to production, to finished
- **Time to Make Changeovers** – This metric measures the speed or time it takes to switc manufacturing line or plant from making one product over to making a different prod
- **Yield** – This metric is an indication of the percentage of products that are manufactur to specifications the first time through the manufacturing process without scrap or re
- **Customer ...**

- **Sample Net Margins**
  - Auto Dealers (New Cars) - 0.5%
  - Bicycle Shops - 4.2%
  - Book Stores - 2.3%
  - Convenience Stores - 1.3%
  - Clothing Stores - 5%
  - Florists - 3.2%
  - Furniture Stores - 4.5%
  - Garden Centers - 3.3%
  - Gas Station - 1.5%
  - Gas Station with Convenience Store - 2.8%
  - Grocery Stores - 1.62%
  - Music Stores - 2%
  - Office Supply and Stationery Stores - 1.9%

- **Prime Cost** – This is a benchmark that takes into account the related paper products) and labor costs (including taxes, wor good Prime Cost benchmark is 60% or less of total revenue.
- **Cover** – The term "cover" refers to a meal served to a single di beverages, appetizers, entree, desserts, etc. A table with four regardless of the number of available seats at that table. If the four, the restaurant would record a total of 8 covers for the ni
- **Guest check size** – In 2014, full-service restaurant visit check checks averaged $7.40, and quick-service restaurant checks a
- **Average yearly sales** – In 2013, full-service restaurants saw y while quick-service restaurants had average yearly sales of $8

Sell 15,000 bushels of peaches.
Or switch to LED lighting.
Same results, your choice.

Segment Guides™ give you the figures you need to equate your projected savings to what your customer had to do last year to see that same bottom-line benefit.

Segment Guides™ give you the sound bites you need to capture attention and then close the sale.

RETAIL: "…sales increase by 10% after improving the store's lighting quality by replacing downlights with LED PAR38 lamps"[14]

GAS STATION/CONVENIENCE STORE: "…in the first three months after the retrofit, complaints were down 47% and theft went from 8 incidences to zero "[13]

GROCERY: "…a high-quality lighting design increased sales at a grocery store by 1.93%… representing over $518,000 in additional annual revenue"[20]

DAIRY: "…8% higher milk production, more docile cows, no need for supplemental fixtures for lower light levels, no interference with electronic identification systems for cows…"[51, 54, 57]

Segment Guides™ footnote each statistic and sound bite, complete with hyperlinks for easy retrieval

SOURCES

[1] Walker, J.N. and Duncan, G.A. (n.d.) Greenhouse structures. Retrieved from https://www.uky.edu/bae/sites/www.uky.edu.bae/files/AEN-12.pdf

[2] 2012 Census of Agriculture United States Summary and States Data, Volume 1. Retrieved from (2014), United States Department of Agriculture. Retrieved from https://www.agcensus.usda.gov/Publications/2012/Full_Report/Volume_1,_Chapter_1_US/usv1.pdf

[3] 2012 Census of Agriculture United States Summary and States Data, Volume 1. Retrieved from (2014), United States Department of Agriculture. Retrieved from https://www.agcensus.usda.gov/Publications/2012/Full_Report/Volume_1,_Chapter_1_US/usv1.pdf

---

Segment Guides™ tell you where to get the inside scoop, with hyperlinks to take you there.

TRADE ORGANIZATIONS AND PUBLICATIONS

Organizations
- American Horticultural Organization: http://ahsgardening.org/
- The Hobby Greenhouse Association: https://www.hobbygreenhouse.org/
- The National Greenhouse Manufacturers Association: https://www.ngma.com/

Publications
- Greenhouse Management Magazine: http://www.greenhousemag.com
- Garden and Greenhouse: http://www.gardenandgreenhouse.net
- Greenhouse Product News: http://www.gpnmag.com

IDEAS & ACTIONS

Using the proper jargon and yardsticks

Presented by
Mark Jewell
@SellingEnergy
info@sellingenergy.com

Turbocharging Success

Sales professionals migrate the discussion *away from features* and *beyond benefits*, putting all the focus on the **customer's values**.

They also *reframe benefits* so they can be measured with the **customer's yardstick**.

Segment Guides

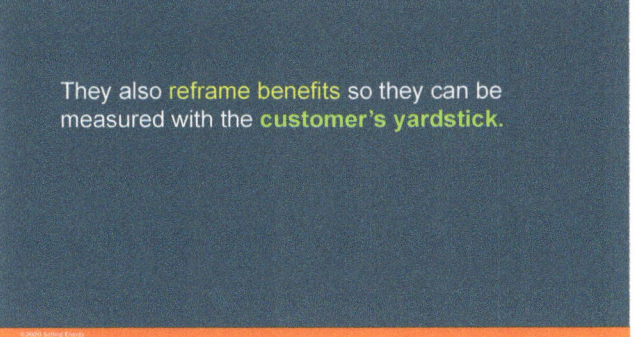

Data Centers

Manufacturing

ROLE OF ENERGY

28 Manufacturing Metrics That Matter

12. Reportable Health and Safety Incidents
15. Percentage Planned vs. Emergency Maintenance Work Orders
16. Downtime in Proportion to Operating Time
19. Total Manufacturing Cost per Unit Excluding Materials
21. Net Operating Profit
25. Energy Cost per Unit

Most people don't make decisions...

...they make comparisons.

IDEAS & ACTIONS

And even when they do make decisions…

…they make emotional decisions first, and then they justify them financially."

Most people are visual, so the more vivid the comparison, the more compelling it is.

Sell 15,000 bushels of peaches.
Or switch to LED lighting.
Same results, your choice.

If a picture is worth a thousand words…
…a story is worth a thousand pictures.

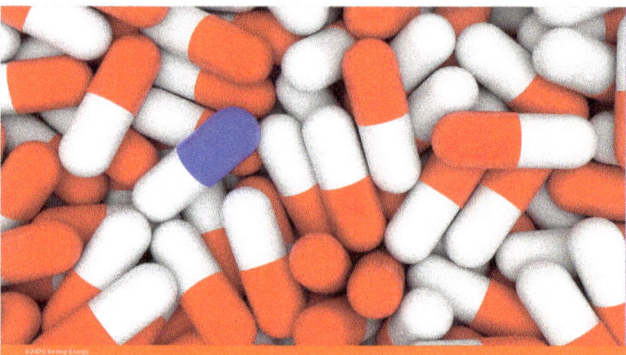

30% fewer dispensing errors

For a busy pharmacy averaging 250 prescriptions filled per day, that could mean more than 400 fewer dispensing errors per year.

SOURCE: As cited in Selling Energy's Segment Guides™

Police calls down 47%;
thefts went from eight to zero

A gas station in a high-crime area replaced its antiquated lighting system with LEDs, vastly increasing lighting levels. Before the retrofit, over 2,000 calls were made to the police in the prior two years. In the first three months after the retrofit, complaints were down 47 percent and theft went from eight incidences in the prior three months to zero.

SOURCE: As cited in Selling Energy's Segment Guides™

IDEAS & ACTIONS

Lesson 22
Quantifying and monetizing benefits

Presented by
Mark Jewell
@SellingEnergy
info@sellingenergy.com

Q:
What value do you provide your customers?

Do you focus on the money?

Moving beyond utility-cost savings...

1. Utility-cost financial benefits
2. Non-utility-cost financial benefits
3. Non-financial benefits

What are some examples of each?

Non-utility-cost financial & non-financial benefits...

1. Better employee attraction/retention
2. Higher employee productivity & morale
3. Improved health and safety
4. Increased throughput or less downtime
5. Improved process control
6. Reduced scrap rate
7. Greater process visibility
8. Reduced emissions
9. Increased retail sales
10. And, of course, many more...

Q:
How many of those benefits can be quantified and monetized?

Q:
And how many decisions are driven by qualitative factors?

Lesson 23
"Popular" vs. "proper" financial metrics

Presented by
Mark Jewell
@SellingEnergy
info@sellingenergy.com

IDEAS & ACTIONS

Which financial metrics should you avoid?

"Popular" metrics
- Simple Payback Period (SPP)
- Return on Investment (ROI)
- Internal Rate of Return (IRR)

Migrate the discussion away from these metrics as quickly as possible.

Which financial metrics should you emphasize?

"Proper" metrics
- Present Value (PV)
- Net Present Value (NPV)
- Modified Internal Rate of Return (MIRR)
- Savings-to-Investment Ratio (SIR)

Q:

What's the best way to migrate the conversation to focus on a more useful financial metric?

Your prospect asks...

"What's the payback?"

You confidently reply...

"It's 3.7 years. And I think what you'll find to be more interesting is that the project has a Savings-to-Investment Ratio of 2.9... which means that over the next 10 years it should return $2.90 – in today's dollars – for every dollar you invest.

Lesson 24
Using the right metrics for each scenario

Presented by
Mark Jewell
@SellingEnergy
info@sellingenergy.com

Turbocharging Success

Which financial metrics should you avoid?

"Popular" metrics
- Simple Payback Period (SPP)
- Return on Investment (ROI)
- Internal Rate of Return (IRR)

Migrate the discussion away from these metrics as quickly as possible.

Which financial metrics should you emphasize?

"Proper" metrics
- Present Value (PV)
- Net Present Value (NPV)
- Modified Internal Rate of Return (MIRR)
- Savings-to-Investment Ratio (SIR)

Principal Investment Scenario #1

"Mutually Exclusive"

- Selecting from two or more choices when only one will be implemented

IDEAS & ACTIONS

_____

_____

_____

_____

Principal Investment Scenario #2

"Non-mutually Exclusive"
(also called "Independent")

- Selecting one or more measures from a list of two or more possible expense-reducing opportunities

Selecting the Best Project to Fund

"Mutually Exclusive"

1. Calculate the **life-cycle cost** of each alternative
2. Select the alternative with the **lowest life-cycle cost**

.

Selecting the Best Project to Fund

"Non-mutually Exclusive"

1. Consider only **lowest-life-cycle-cost** alternatives
2. Eliminate alternatives with negative **NPV**
3. Calculate the **MIRR** or **SIR** of each
4. Fund them in order of descending **MIRR** or **SIR**

Two Special Circumstances

"Non-mutually Exclusive"

1. If you have a system in danger of failing, **prioritize its replacement**
2. If two or more selections make sense to do simultaneously, **group them** before ranking projects for funding

.

But what about SPP, ROI and IRR?

But what about SPP, ROI and IRR?

They may be popular metrics...
However, they are not proper metrics.

Should you still calculate the "popular" metrics?

Should you still calculate the "popular" metrics?

Yes...

Just make sure you migrate the conversation away from the "popular" metrics and toward the "proper" metrics to support smarter decision-making.

IDEAS & ACTIONS

Q:
Assume you're investing for your retirement. Should you be more interested in how fast you'll get your initial investment back...

...or *how many times* you'll get your investment back before you retire?

Q:
Do your prospects usually focus more attention on Simple Payback Period or Savings-to-Investment Ratio?

selling in 6™

Lesson 25
Emotional vs. financial decision-making

Presented by
Mark Jewell
@SellingEnergy
info@sellingenergy.com

selling energy
Turbocharging Success

Most people don't make decisions...

...they make comparisons.

And even when they do make decisions...

...they make emotional decisions first, and then they justify them financially."

There will be no forward motion without motivation...

and there will be no motivation without emotion.

Q:
What are some examples of people making emotional decisions and then justifying them financially?

ENERGY STAR® Label for Buildings and the US Green Building Council's LEED® both rely on emotional drivers to attract/retain buildings.

Many buildings became interested in getting one or both of those awards once they realized that they would lose competitive footing in the marketplace without them.

IDEAS & ACTIONS _____

_____

_____

_____

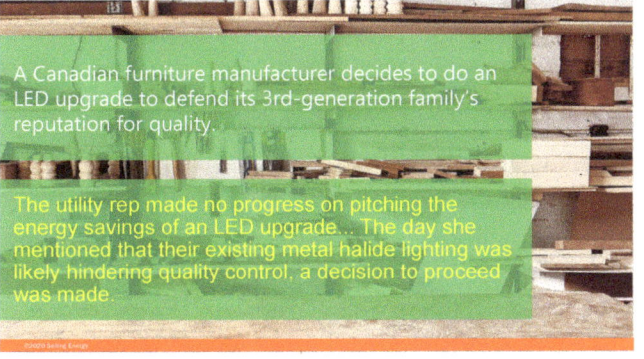

A Canadian furniture manufacturer decides to do an LED upgrade to defend its 3rd-generation family's reputation for quality.

The utility rep made no progress on pitching the energy savings of an LED upgrade... The day she mentioned that their existing metal halide lighting was likely hindering quality control, a decision to proceed was made.

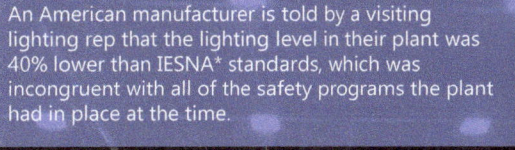

An American manufacturer is told by a visiting lighting rep that the lighting level in their plant was 40% lower than IESNA* standards, which was incongruent with all of the safety programs the plant had in place at the time.

The VP Operations immediately decides to authorize the upgrade, telling the plant manager to use the safety budget to fund it.

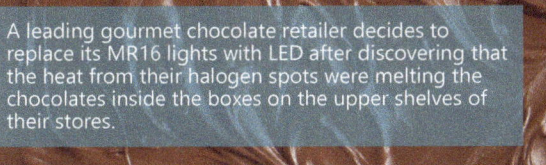

A leading gourmet chocolate retailer decides to replace its MR16 lights with LED after discovering that the heat from their halogen spots were melting the chocolates inside the boxes on the upper shelves of their stores.

The need to protect their reputation for quality drove an immediate project approval.

A European manufacturer of precision car parts wants to showcase its state-of-the-art factory to all potential customers.

Shortly after the LED upgrade, a major car manufacturer's parts buyer visits, looks up at the ceiling, and declares aloud that the factory looked "clinical – almost laboratory-like," and shortly thereafter proceeds to award a large and high-profile contract to the parts vendor.

Parking garage operators know that there is a direct relationship between adequate lighting, perceived safety, and the frequency of both crime and accidents in their facilities.

The fact that LED lighting enhances the views afforded by security cameras seals the deal.

A large restaurant chain is motivated to begin tracking product quality and installing controls to limit employee theft throughout its stores.

With the installation of efficient, WiFi-enabled fryers and ovens, headquarters begins to track portion quantities, cooking times and temperatures, and even programs the cooking sequences so that less-skilled employees can consistently produce a quality product.

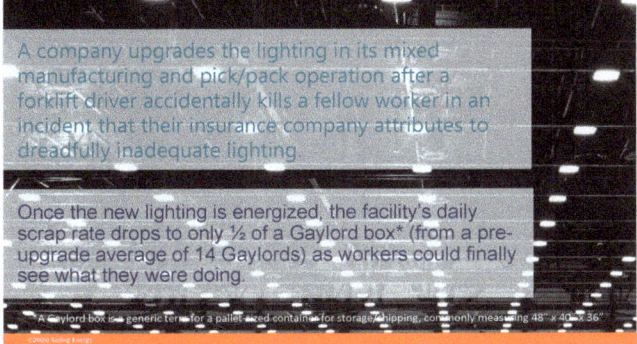

A company upgrades the lighting in its mixed manufacturing and pick/pack operation after a forklift driver accidentally kills a fellow worker in an incident that their insurance company attributes to dreadfully inadequate lighting.

Once the new lighting is energized, the facility's daily scrap rate drops to only ½ of a Gaylord box* (from a pre-upgrade average of 14 Gaylords) as workers could finally see what they were doing.

*A Gaylord box is a generic term for a pallet-sized container for storage/shipping, commonly measuring 48" x 40" x 36".

selling in 6™

Lesson 26
The contrarian view to creating value

Presented by
Mark Jewell
@SellingEnergy
info@sellingenergy.com

sellingenergy
Turbocharging Success

IDEAS & ACTIONS

www.SellingEnergy.com

Q:

How do we ensure that decision-makers appreciate the significant non-utility-cost and non-financial benefits of energy projects?

21%

27%

21%   Hurdle rate for "core" projects

27%   Hurdle rate for "non-core" projects

Q:

Do "core" or "non-core" projects actually hold the greater potential to deliver surprising benefits for your prospect?

Which bucket is likely larger, #1 or #2?

1. Utility-cost financial benefits
2. Non-utility-cost financial benefits
3. Non-financial benefits

And could bucket **#3** produce additional "core-business benefits"... perhaps even support additional benefits in bucket **#2**?

Lesson 27
Helping prospects visualize the savings

Presented by
Mark Jewell
@SellingEnergy
info@sellingenergy.com

Q:

How do we ensure that decision-makers and influencers actually grasp the magnitude of potential benefits and are emotionally motivated to take action?

IDEAS & ACTIONS

Visualize these facts involving a major university:

Feasibility study has identified $52M in energy projects with a projected average return of 30%/year

University has $450M in deferred maintenance

State is unwilling to fund more capital spending

The endowment has $226M and has earned an average return of 5.9% over the last 10 years

---

$0.27
of every tuition dollar was spent on energy

And what would the prize look like?

Fund the $52M in projects using a revolving loan from the endowment and earn 5x the historical return... Perhaps 6-10x once rebates/incentives are factored in

Preemptively address deferred maintenance by replacing the oldest, most inefficient equipment first

Get the teachers/students involved with a STEM focus

And what would the prize look like?

Impress touring parents/students with proactive approach to sustainability on campus

Improve the learning environment

Impress alumni donors who are now seeing the endowment yield higher returns while advancing a variety of important objectives on campus

---

Q:

What does a million pounds of paper look like?

Lesson 28
Circling back for unanticipated benefits

 Presented by
Mark Jewell
@SellingEnergy
info@sellingenergy.com

Q:

Do you typically make the effort to circle back with your customers after the sale?

Q:

Have you thought about all the potential upsides of circling back... and the risks of not doing so?

IDEAS & ACTIONS

www.SellingEnergy.com

The upsides of circling back...

1. Suggests a long-term client relationship rather than a transactional one
2. Provides honest feedback on why they bought
3. Ensures they had a positive experience, and allows you to correct any issues
4. Gives insight into unanticipated non-utility-cost and non-financial benefits they now enjoy
5. Provides opportunity to cross-sell, up-sell, and/or ask for referrals
6. And more...

The downsides of not circling back...

1. What if they had a bad experience and never took the time to tell you?
2. And you lost the opportunity to differentiate yourself from the typical salesperson who just makes a sale and moves on...
3. And you lost the opportunity to gain the insights mentioned on the previous slide...
4. And more...

Imagine these conversations...

"Oh, I've been meaning to call you..." <<good>>
"Wow, glad I called... When did your manager say he wanted your other 12 facilities upgraded?"

"Oh, I've been meaning to call you..." <<not good>>
"Wow, that's not in keeping with our service commitment. Are you there today? I'll come right over to fix it myself..."

Imagine these conversations...

"I really like the fact that we can now..."
"Glad to hear that... Do you know anyone else in your circle of friends or sphere of influence who would appreciate that benefit as well?"

"Funny you should ask... Our pick-and-pack accuracy is way up ever since we did that upgrade!"
"Congratulations... From the sound of it, it seems as if you're getting 10x the energy savings we used to get the project approved thanks to less frequent shipping errors... Has anyone told the CFO yet?"

Lesson 29
Selling "values" vs. "features and benefits"

Presented by
Mark Jewell
@SellingEnergy
info@sellingenergy.com

The Psychology of Selling and Advertising
Edward Kellogg Strong

1925

Copyright 1925, McGraw-Hill Book Company

What do today's prospects want?

Features and benefits?
They can find that on the internet with a few clicks and swipes...

How your offerings compare to others?
See above.

What others think of your product?
See above.

People don't buy features, they buy benefits that are **linked to their values**

IDEAS & ACTIONS

Sales professionals migrate the discussion **away from features** and **beyond benefits**, putting all the focus on the **customer's values.**

They also **reframe benefits** so they can be measured with the **customer's yardstick.**

Lesson 30
Escaping the price-driven sale

Presented by
Mark Jewell
@SellingEnergy
info@sellingenergy.com

Turbocharging Success

"Value" does not equal "price"

Adapted from *The Little Red Book of Selling* by Jeffrey Gitomer

---

"The unassailable value equation"

"VALUE = BENEFITS MINUS COSTS"

Adapted from *Escaping the Price-Driven Sale* by Tom Snyder and Kevin Kearns

---

"The unassailable value equation"
"VALUE = BENEFITS - COSTS"

BENEFITS

"**INSIGHT** and **DISCOVERY** that the customer receives from the buying experience"

Adapted from *Escaping the Price-Driven Sale* by Tom Snyder and Kevin Kearns

---

"The unassailable value equation"
"VALUE = BENEFITS - COSTS"

COSTS

"Not just price – from the standpoint of the buying experience itself, it is the **TIME and EFFORT** that the customer is devoting to being SOLD TO"

Adapted from *Escaping the Price-Driven Sale* by Tom Snyder and Kevin Kearns

---

"The *actual* unassailable value equation"

VALUE   equals   BENEFITS   minus   COSTS
                   INSIGHT   TIME
                   DISCOVERY   EFFORT

Adapted from *Escaping the Price-Driven Sale* by Tom Snyder and Kevin Kearns

---

IDEAS & ACTIONS

Take price off the table by...

revealing an unrecognized problem...
finding an unanticipated solution...
creating/revealing an unseen opportunity...

If your prospect wants a better deal, add more value rather than lower your price.

You may think you lost a deal based on "price."

In reality, you probably lost on "value."

"The quality of your outcome is directly related to the quality of the evaluations you're prepared to make."

- Anthony Robbins

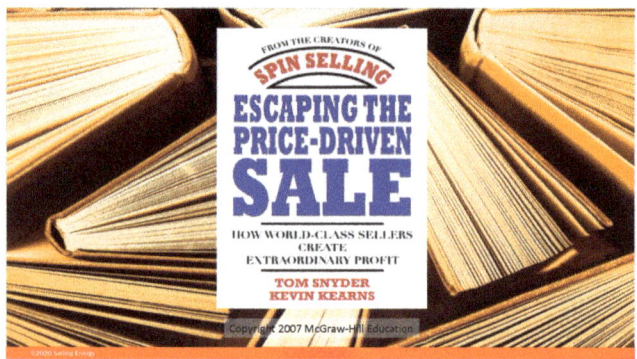

FROM THE CREATORS OF
SPIN SELLING
ESCAPING THE PRICE-DRIVEN SALE
HOW WORLD-CLASS SELLERS CREATE EXTRAORDINARY PROFIT
TOM SNYDER
KEVIN KEARNS
Copyright 2007 McGraw-Hill Education

Beyond PRICE
Differentiate Your Company in Ways that Really Matter
MARY KAY PLANTES
ROBERT D. FINFROCK
Copyright 2008 Greenfield Book Group LLC

selling in 6™

Lesson 31
Escaping "three-bids" syndrome

Presented by
Mark Jewell
@SellingEnergy
info@sellingenergy.com

sellingenergy
Turbocharging Success

Q:
So what happens when your prospect is convinced to buy, and then announces an intent to solicit three bids?

IDEAS & ACTIONS

Question #1
"Have you ever done a project like this sole-source, without using a bidding process?"

If the answer is YES, find out how similar your offering is…

Question #2A
"Is it safe to assume you could use that same process to approve this project?"

If the answer is NO, you need to understand what criteria will be used to select the winning bidder.

Question #2B
"If you do a bidding process, will price be the only deciding factor?"

If the answer is YES and lowest price always wins, you can take the high road and ask…

Question #3A
"Do you evaluate bids based on lowest first cost or lowest life-cycle cost?"

If the answer is YES and lowest first cost always wins, you might be tempted to ask…

Question #3B
"How is that working out for you?" ☺

Statement #3C
"We do subcontracting from time to time, and we've found that unless our prospective subcontractor can answer the following questions to our satisfaction, it doesn't matter what price they offer."

Statement #3D
"In fact, on the reverse side of that vendor screening questionnaire, you'll find our answers to our own questions."

Statement #3E
"By the way, here's another sheet that you can share with your colleagues in Procurement. It lists several of our clients, many of them household names, who use us not *despite* the fact that we're not the lowest price, but *because* we're not the lowest price."

"They understand the *risks* that come with basing a decision on lowest first cost alone."

IDEAS & ACTIONS

www.SellingEnergy.com

You may think you lost a deal because the prospect found a lower price elsewhere.

In reality, you probably lost the deal because the prospect perceived greater value elsewhere.

Now it is possible that the prospect just selected the option with the lowest price...

Did you make an effort to help the prospect gain the understanding he/she needed to make an informed evaluation and ultimate decision...

Or did you let the prospect think that your offering is a commodity and price would drive the decision?

"The quality of your **outcome** is directly related to the quality of the **evaluations** you're prepared to make."

- Anthony Robbins

Lesson 32
Selling to small business owners

Presented by
Mark Jewell
@SellingEnergy
info@sellingenergy.com

Q:

Should you modify your sales approach when dealing with small businesses?

Tips for dealing with small businesses...

1. They are (at least) as busy as C-level execs
2. They appreciate concise communication
3. They are not necessarily less sophisticated
4. They can still make better decisions using Savings-to-Investment Ratio and life-cycle cost; however, you may need to tone down the "finance speak"
5. They are often on the front lines and should identify well with a Digits-to-Widgets exercise

---

Lesson 33
The problem with "relationship selling"

Presented by
Mark Jewell
@SellingEnergy
info@sellingenergy.com

IDEAS & ACTIONS

Q:
How often do you think relationships are the reason you win business?

Q:
And are those relationships the *cause of* or the *result of* successful selling?

Q:
In fact, in the typical sales situation where there are multiple players involved in the decision, with whom do you actually have a relationship?

Q:
And does that person have the ability to decide unilaterally, or is consensus more the norm in your typical prospect's organization?

Q:
How often do you think you get to know, much less communicate with, all of the people who are either decision-makers or influencers in the decision?

Q:
Do you know who is meeting to evaluate your proposal? When they meet? Where they meet?

Q:
Do you need a relationship, or do you need rapport?

Q:
And in fact, if you have a relationship, but you don't have genuine trust and rapport, how likely is it that your internal champion would risk their career to back your proposal when they're not certain of the outcome?

IDEAS & ACTIONS

Your best approach with "internal champions"...

1. Understand what your champion is excited about and emotionally committed to achieving
2. Make the project "their" project as quickly and powerfully as possible
3. Give them the tools to prevail without relying upon their oratorical or debating skills
   - An elevator pitch that is worth repeating
   - Success stories from your archive
   - A one-page proposal centered on the "why"
   - A one-page financial analysis with the proper metrics

Lesson 34
Winning strategies require winning mechanisms

Presented by
Mark Jewell
@SellingEnergy
info@sellingenergy.com

Turbocharging Success

Q:

What strategies and tactics do winning sales professionals have in common?

Winning strategies

1. Industry foreknowledge about the target's segment and precisely how your solution creates value
2. The ability to capture the attention of a busy and distracted decision-maker or influencer
3. The ability to maintain the decision-maker's focus long enough to generate emotion that motivates action
4. The ability to prove the project's financial merits using the proper metrics
5. The ability to preemptively and/or reactively address any objections that may arise

---

Copyright 2001 Harper Business

"Every winning strategy requires a winning mechanism."

- Jim Collins, author, *Good to Great*

Winning mechanisms

1. Segment Guides™ or similar sources that will provide industry foreknowledge of exactly how your offering will create value for your prospect
2. An 15-second elevator pitch to capture attention
3. A one-page narrative proposal focused on "why"
4. A one-page financial analysis focused on the right metrics
5. A Success Story Archive™ and an Objections Archive™ that will build confidence and address any resistance

---

Lesson 35
The importance of making better evaluations

Presented by
Mark Jewell
@SellingEnergy
info@sellingenergy.com

Turbocharging Success

"The quality of your outcome will be directly related to the quality of the evaluations you are prepared to make."
-Anthony Robbins

IDEAS & ACTIONS

Q:

In what circumstances could your ability to make higher-quality evaluations help close more business?

The quality of your evaluations really matters

1. Who are your best customers and why?
2. Who are your worst customers and why?
3. Which market *sub-segments* contain prospects who could benefit the most from your offering?
4. What exactly is your competitive advantage?
5. How would you precisely connect the dots between your offering and your prospects' yardsticks for success?
6. And more...

"Arsenal of Competitive Advantage"

Sales team	Trust, differentiation, strategy, linkage, expert product/industry knowledge, exec presence, strategic literacy
Industry focus	Industry expertise & network, market share, tailored solutions
Product/solution	Functionality, features, technology, quality, value, ease of use, availability, brand loyalty, advertising, price, speed
Service	Service, responsiveness, people, customer satisfaction, results, performance
Company	Brand loyalty, financial stability, reputation, quality, other products, experience

Adapted from "Hope is Not a Strategy" by Rick Page, ©2003 McGraw-Hill Education; based on Michael Porter's work at Harvard

---

Q:

And by the way, how much more business could you generate by helping your prospects make higher-quality evaluations?

Lesson 36
SUCCESS TOOL #1
The Elevator Pitch

**Presented by
Mark Jewell**
@SellingEnergy
info@sellingenergy.com

Turbocharging Success

Elevator Pitches

Q:

Can you tell me in 15 seconds or less how you will create value for me?

Q:

And can you make it memorable enough to be worth repeating to others?

IDEAS & ACTIONS

_____

_____

_____

_____

www.SellingEnergy.com

Don't confuse your customer

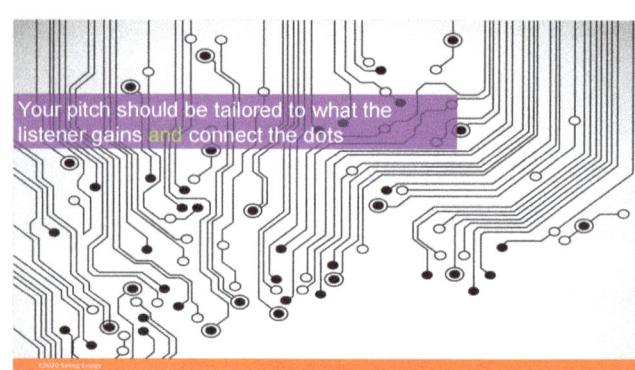

Your pitch should be tailored to what the listener gains and connect the dots

People don't buy features, they buy benefits that are **linked to their values**

Make your pitch easy to understand and repeat

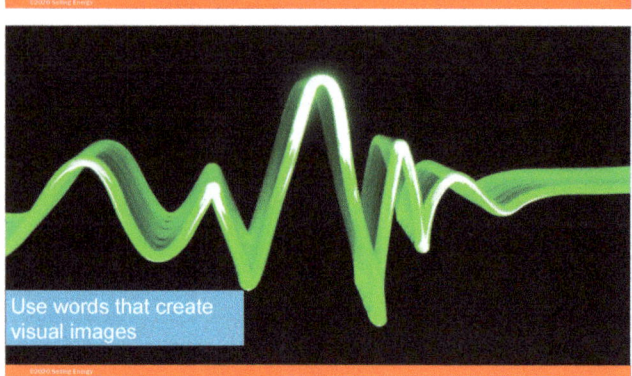

Use words that create visual images

Avoid acronyms and jargon

Make it compelling

Use strong, persuasive language

IDEAS & ACTIONS

Reduce, Reuse, Recycle
Veni, Vidi, Vici   Ready, aim, fire
Life, liberty, and the pursuit of happiness
Lights, camera, action
Blood, sweat, and tears
Location, location, location
People are comfortable with the rule of threes
Three blind mice
Knife, fork, spoon
Appetizer, entrée, dessert

Suggestions for delivering your perfect "elevator pitch"...

Practice, practice, practice

Make sure you find out about the other person first

Visualize the outcome of the conversation

and where you want it to end up.

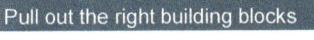

Pull out the right building blocks

Stay calm and pace yourself

Sound excited and be excited

IDEAS & ACTIONS

_____

_____

_____

_____

People value what they ask for more than what they are offered unsolicited.

Utilize your hook

Have people introduce you to others

Think of the world as one big elevator

EXERCISE
The Elevator Pitch

selling in 6™

Lesson 37
Fine-tuning your elevator pitch

Presented by
Mark Jewell
@SellingEnergy
info@sellingenergy.com

sellingenergy
Turbocharging Success

Tips for delivering a truly compelling elevator pitch

1. Be conversational – use questions, pauses and humor to bring the prospect into the conversation
2. Keep it accessible – avoid jargon and acronyms
3. Use words that create visual images – it will be more memorable

Tips for delivering a truly compelling elevator pitch

4. Slow and steady wins the race – or in this case, the pitch
5. Focus on having an impact
6. Make sure it has a "hook" and have a follow-up plan in mind

IDEAS & ACTIONS _____

_____

_____

_____

Tips for delivering a truly compelling elevator pitch

7. Have a whole quiver of elevator pitches
8. Practice, practice, practice... and look for shining eyes
9. Focus on giving, not taking
10. Remember that the whole world is an elevator

Lesson 38
SUCCESS TOOL #2
The 3-Sentence Solicitation™

Presented by
Mark Jewell
@SellingEnergy
info@sellingenergy.com

A **3-sentence solicitation** that gets the conversation started...

"Over the last **3 years** we've helped **8 hospitals within 10 miles** of yours reduce their utility bills for an **average savings of more than 15%**.

"It occurred to me as I was driving by your facility last night that your patient room lighting is **the same system we removed from 5 of those hospitals**, at an **average savings of 25% in lighting energy**.

"If you'd be interested in **exploring** how we might **extend the success** we've had with those other hospitals to your facility, I'd be **open to a discussion**."

A **3-sentence solicitation** that gets a smart energy technology conversation started...

"Over the last **3 years** we've seen **8 plants within 100 miles** of yours **improve worker productivity and morale** and **cut employee turnover by at least 75%** simply by adding comfort cooling.

IDEAS & ACTIONS

"I learned from your plant manager that several of your departments are also **finding it difficult to retain workers** due to excessive temperatures in those locations

"If you'd be interested in **exploring** how we might **extend the success** we've seen in those other plants to your facility, I'd be **open to a discussion**."

EXERCISE
The 3-Sentence Solicitation

Lesson 39
SUCCESS TOOL #3
The One-Page Proposal™

Presented by
Mark Jewell
@SellingEnergy
info@sellingenergy.com

What's the ideal length for a proposal?

This industry could learn a lot from...

What is it?

- "Succinctly expresses all the facts, reasoning, and conditions surrounding an undertaking or project.
- "Uses persuasive language to build a case for approval.
- "Proposes a specific course of action.
- "Fulfills all these qualifications within a single printed page"

Adapted from *The One-Page Proposal*, Patrick G. Riley

Why only one page?

"Identify a clear objective, focus on it, ferret out the pitfalls, sharpen your thinking, and pitch an idea perfectly."

Adapted from *The One-Page Proposal*, Patrick G. Riley

IDEAS & ACTIONS

_____

_____

_____

_____

Why only one page?

"400 words will take an average reader 3 to 4 minutes to review – the attention span of many high-level decision-makers."

Adapted from The One-Page Proposal, Patrick G. Riley

- Title and Subtitle
  - Label and define the entire proposal
- Target (and Secondary Targets)
  - Identify the goals of the proposal
- Rationale
  - Delineates why the proposed action is necessary

Adapted from The One-Page Proposal, Patrick G. Riley

- Financials
  - Quantifies the costs and benefits
- Status
  - States where things stand at the moment
- Action
  - Clarifies exactly what the recipient should do

Adapted from The One-Page Proposal, Patrick G. Riley

Lesson 40
Keys to writing One-Page Proposals

Presented by
Mark Jewell
@SellingEnergy
info@sellingenergy.com

Turbocharging Success

Tips for writing a truly compelling one-page proposal

1. All the key points fit on one page without tiny font, small margins or other tricks.
2. Title and subtitle capture and retain interest, encouraging the senior exec to read further.
3. Each target or sub-target is quantitative rather than generic or fluffy.

Tips for writing a truly compelling one-page proposal

4. Phrasing is authoritative, no-nonsense, and written in third-person.
5. Layman's language is easily understood by a non-technical decision-maker.
6. Sentences tend to be short and to the point; all excess words are eliminated.

Tips for writing a truly compelling one-page proposal

7. With few exceptions, every point is made once – repetition squanders word count.
8. Financials appear in tabular form, making them easier to scan.
9. While all financial metrics are listed, the important ones are referenced in the narrative that introduces that section.

Tips for writing a truly compelling one-page proposal

10. Benefits are prioritized according to their relative importance to the anticipated reader.
11. Non-utility-cost financial and non-financial benefits are featured prominently.
12. Think like a senior manager – what needs to be asked and answered in the affirmative to give you comfort to take the requested action

---

IDEAS & ACTIONS

Tips for writing a truly compelling one-page proposal

13. The action statement is specific, and ends with "Notice to Proceed" or similar language, which emphasizes the goal and time-sensitivity.
14. If at all possible, include an emotional trigger to catalyze action.
15. Use a style guide to avoid grammatical errors, wordiness, etc. and create templates to quickly customize future one-pagers.

Tips for writing a truly compelling one-page proposal

16. Before beginning, assemble all salient facts into folders.
17. List "big ideas" from each folder.
18. Select and prioritize the "big ideas" that actually qualify as being one-pager-worthy.

Tips for writing a truly compelling one-page proposal

19. If it genuinely helps build the case, consider including it; if not, save for the Appendix.
20. Assume the persona of the non-technical decision-maker.
21. Make sure the questions you would want to have answered are preemptively addressed in the one-pager.

Lesson 41
Ideal uses for One-Page Proposals

Presented by
Mark Jewell
@SellingEnergy
info@sellingenergy.com

Several ideal uses for a one-page proposal

1. Initially proposing a project
2. Revitalizing a project that has stalled or been rejected
3. Soft-circling approval in advance of sending a "global" one-page proposal
4. Submitting a "weighted-average" one-page proposal to pique interest and set the stage for a specific one-pager for their facility

20% More Light with 40% Lower Energy Cost for the Parking Garage at 123 Market Street
Improving security, saving energy, lowering operating costs, and boosting the ENERGY STAR score

TARGET: TO IMPROVE PARKING-AREA LIGHTING WITH ENERGY-EFFICIENT, LONG-LASTING LED TECHNOLOGY

- To address tenant safety concerns by increasing average lighting levels by 20% and moving to "whiter" light, enhancing visibility for both occupants and security cameras
- To reduce operating and maintenance costs for parking-area lighting by $15,000 the first year (10-year NPV of over $53,000[1])
- To capture $15,400 in Energy Trust incentives, covering 24% of project cost
- To avoid a quarter-million pounds of CO_2 emissions annually, boosting the ENERGY STAR score to 70 from 68

Over the last 12 months, 4 of 10 tenants have raised concerns about the lighting in and around the 5-level garage at 123 Market. A qualified lighting contractor has studied the situation and confirmed that the existing inefficient, 14-year-old fixtures deliver inadequate lighting levels. Changing to LED fixtures would increase lighting levels by approximately 20% while reducing annual operating expenses by about 40%. Moreover, LED technology produces "whiter" light, which improves "visibility" for both occupants and security cameras, even at low light levels.

Initially proposing a project...

Could Better Lighting, Pumps and Fans Mean 95,630 Gallons of Milk?
Lower energy and maintenance costs yield higher net profit; better lighting improves milk production as well

TARGET: IMPLEMENT LIGHTING, PUMP AND FAN EFFICIENCY IMPROVEMENTS TO BOOST YOUR PROFITABILITY

- The money you are now wasting in utilities could be better used to feed three more milk-producing cows.
- Studies suggest that you could also see 6% to 8% higher milk production overall by switching to LED lighting.
- At your net profit margin of 5%, saving $1 in energy is equivalent to driving $20 in revenue.
  - $108 per year saved on *each* 400W metal halide to LED upgrade equates to $2,160 in revenue.
  - $1,680 per year saved on free stall fans equates to $33,600 in revenue.
  - Adding variable frequency drives to cooling fans and irrigation pumps further increases your savings.
- Your business pays into the Public Benefits Fund, which entitles you to rebates to help fund your project.
- Since your project also qualifies for On-Bill Financing, any first cost not covered by rebates could be financed by <<Your Utility>> with $0 out of pocket and 0% interest. Your loan would be repaid on your monthly utility bill using a formula that limits the monthly debt service amount to the utility savings generated by the project.
- *This project's payback is less than one year, so you will pay for the project this year whether you do it or not.*

Revitalizing a project...

Soft-circling approval after mapping relationships

IDEAS & ACTIONS

Presented by
Mark Jewell
@SellingEnergy
info@sellingenergy.com

Turbocharging Success

Using a "weighted-average" one-page proposal

One-page proposal contributions from engineers

1. What are the most compelling reasons to pursue your recommendations?
2. Any past successes that could build confidence to invest further?
3. Do your recommendations build on well-recognized successes elsewhere?

One-page proposal contributions from engineers

4. Have submetering, pilots or other approaches already been undertaken to reduce project risk?
5. How would you prioritize your recommendations if you were the host facility?
   ➤ Addressing complaints
   ➤ Equipment nearing/beyond end-of-life
   ➤ Best savings per dollar invested
   ➤ Impending regulations or expiring incentives
   ➤ Other

One-page proposal contributions from engineers

6. Are there benefits to packaging measures
   ➤ Shared labor
   ➤ Beneficial interactivity
   ➤ Bonus incentives
   ➤ Volume discounts
   ➤ Reduces access equipment rentals
7. Who worked with you on-site?
   ➤ What did each say about energy initiatives (past, present or future)?
   ➤ What did each share about the decision-making environment?

One-page proposal contributions from engineers

8. Any mention of selling or refinancing the property?
9. Any history with (or aspirations toward) EPA ENERGY STAR® and/or LEED®?
10. How are energy decisions made?

One-page proposal contributions from engineers

11. When are capital budgets prepared and approved?
12. What guidance has been given to field staff re: required yields, preferred financial metrics, etc. when requesting capital?

One-page proposal contributions from engineers

13. Any sub-goals or "hot buttons" to mention in the title, targets, or rationale section of the one-pager?
14. Which projects have been proposed, rejected, or approved in the recent past... And why?
15. What is the best (worst) thing that will happen if this energy project is (not) approved?

IDEAS & ACTIONS

_____

_____

_____

_____

Lesson **43**
The anatomy of a One-Page Proposal

Presented by
Mark Jewell
@SellingEnergy
info@sellingenergy.com

This industry could learn a lot from…

THE ONE-PAGE PROPOSAL

HOW TO GET YOUR BUSINESS PITCH ONTO ONE PERSUASIVE PAGE

PATRICK G. RILEY

- Title and Subtitle
  - Label and define the entire proposal
- Target (and Secondary Targets)
  - Identify the goals of the proposal
- Rationale
  - Delineates why the proposed action is necessary

Adapted from The One-Page Proposal, Patrick G. Riley

- Financials
  - Quantifies the costs and benefits
- Status
  - States where things stand at the moment
- Action
  - Clarifies exactly what the recipient should do

Adapted from The One-Page Proposal, Patrick G. Riley

Page "0":
Cover Page
(with contact info on the reverse)

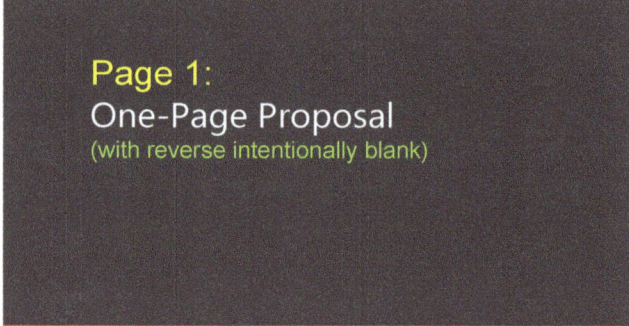

Page 1:
One-Page Proposal
(with reverse intentionally blank)

Page 2:
One-page financials
(with reverse intentionally blank)

Page 3:
Cost of delay
(with reverse intentionally blank)

IDEAS & ACTIONS

_____

_____

_____

_____

Page 4:
Sheet of colored paper
("Technical Appendix")

Pages 5+:
Everything else...

EXERCISE
The One-Page Proposal

Lesson 44
Using multiple One-Page Proposals

Presented by
Mark Jewell
@SellingEnergy
info@sellingenergy.com

Q:

Would there ever be a situation where you would want to draft and submit multiple one-page proposals?

Map the relationships between players

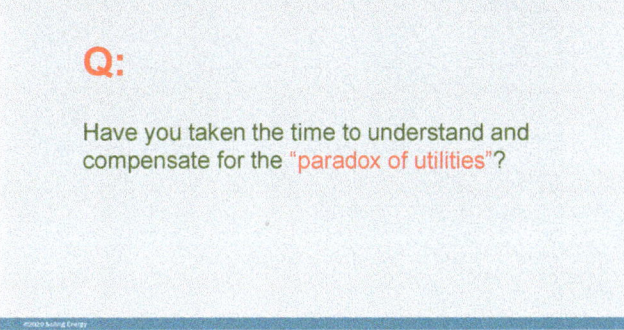

Q:

Have you taken the time to understand and compensate for the "paradox of utilities"?

IDEAS & ACTIONS

_____

_____

_____

_____

How important is the "utilities" line item?

- Little time looking at the utilities line item
- Small % of revenues for most customers
- Too many CFOs: "Utilities are a fixed cost"
- Many weary of energy-related sales pitches

How important *should* this topic be?

- Utility cost financial benefits
- Non-utility-cost financial benefits
- Non-financial benefits
- Revenue or "widget" equivalents
- Other ways to reposition the value

Fine-tune your message to resonate with each influencer

- The operation becomes easier to manage or more valuable
- Improved visibility into their operations
- Better employee hiring/retention/morale/productivity
- Lower cost of goods sold and/or factory overhead
- Greater sustainability (and associated accolades)
- Bragging rights on earnings calls and in press releases
- Higher product quality or throughput
- Improved safety/regulatory compliance
- Lower cost per unit produced
- And so many more…

Q:

As an example, why would each of the following stakeholders within an organization be motivated to support an energy management system?

Chief Executive Officer

"Would this installation make my organization easier to manage?"

"Would this make my enterprise more valuable?"

"Would my people perform better with this technology"

Chief Sustainability Officer

"Would installing this technology entitle us to additional LEED® points?"

Chief Engineer

"How much more visibility would I have into the operation of our chillers/pumps/etc.?"

Chief Financial Officer

"Would installing an energy management system be a viable alternative to purchasing additional equipment to address occupant comfort concerns?"

IDEAS & ACTIONS

_____

_____

_____

_____

www.SellingEnergy.com

Mechanical Engineering Firm

"Is this a profitable extension of work I already do for my customer?"

"Will it give us greater visibility to help diagnose problems, improve comfort, and enhance customer loyalty?"

"Could we leverage it to recapture scope normally given to the controls contractor?"

"Provide a lower-cost solution to the problems we've been asked to solve?"

Controls Contractor

"Could this give us additional visibility to inform and/or validate our controls strategy?"

"Could this help us commission or retro-commission the building over time?"

Consulting Engineer

"Could this provide a lower-cost solution to the problems we've been asked to solve?"

"Could this provide our client with flexibility as building loads change and/or plant performance degrades over time?"

Q:

How else could we express the "Why" when it comes to supporting an energy management system?

- Capital cost avoidance
- Control
- Credentials
- Confidence
- Other...

Capital cost avoidance

Potentially less expensive approach to improve comfort or satisfy new load without adding capacity

Control

Knowing that finite Operations and Maintenance (O&M) efforts are allocated optimally

Credentials

Earning LEED® points or boosting the ENERGY STAR® score

IDEAS & ACTIONS

www.SellingEnergy.com

Confidence
Visible evidence that savings is occurring

Lesson 45
The weighted-average One-Page Proposal

Presented by
Mark Jewell
@SellingEnergy
info@sellingenergy.com

Q:

What successes have you had with customers who are similar to the targets you have decided to focus on?

Q:

Is there an opportunity to "clone" those successes by assembling every target that looks a lot like your past projects?

Q:

Could you produce a "weighted-average" one-page proposal describing the success you've had with other similarly configured customers?

EXAMPLE: A weighted-average condo board proposal

EXERCISE
The "Weighted-Average" One-Page Proposal

Lesson 46
Using One-Page Proposal templates

Presented by
Mark Jewell
@SellingEnergy
info@sellingenergy.com

IDEAS & ACTIONS

This industry could learn a lot from...

THE ONE-PAGE PROPOSAL

HOW TO GET YOUR BUSINESS PITCH ONTO ONE PERSUASIVE PAGE

PATRICK G. RILEY

Copyright © 2002 Patrick G. Riley

How many variations would be in your pick list?

- Title and Subtitle
  - Label and define the entire proposal
- Target (and Secondary Targets)
  - Identify the goals of the proposal
- Rationale
  - Delineates why the proposed action is necessary

Adapted from The One-Page Proposal, Patrick G. Riley

How many variations would be in your pick list?

- Financials
  - Quantifies the costs and benefits
- Status
  - States where things stand at the moment
- Action
  - Clarifies exactly what the recipient should do

Adapted from The One-Page Proposal, Patrick G. Riley

selling in 6™

Lesson 47
Sending even less than a single page

Presented by
Mark Jewell
@SellingEnergy
info@sellingenergy.com

sellingenergy
Turbocharging Success

Q:

Could you motivate a prospect to pursue an energy project with something even shorter than one page?

YES!

Subject: Compressed air opportunity financial estimation

John,
Based on electricity at $0.14/kWh, your compressed air system costs over $50,000 a year to run, excluding the dryer.

A couple of new air compressors with additional storage and a pressure controller would reduce energy expenditures by $18,000 a year, increase reliability, and be eligible for a $14,000 incentive from <<Your Utility>>. Budget $60K to $70K for these benefits.

Example adapted with permission from a submission by Selling Energy graduate David Elfstrom, Toronto Hydro

The next steps are to size the equipment properly; develop a spec for quotation; prove the baseline energy consumption; and, qualify for an incentive. To do that we need to have some power, flow and pressure measurements done, costing about $1,800.

David

Example adapted with permission from a submission by Selling Energy graduate David Elfstrom, Toronto Hydro

IDEAS & ACTIONS

Q:

So, do you think it worked?

Example adapted with permission from a submission by Selling Energy graduate David Elfstrom, Toronto Hydro

©2020 Selling Energy

1. The email was forwarded to the owner, who responded within 3 hours, instructing the sender to proceed to the next step.

Example adapted with permission from a submission by Selling Energy graduate David Elfstrom, Toronto Hydro

©2020 Selling Energy

2. The measurements were useful and the project was approved and successfully implemented.

Example adapted with permission from a submission by Selling Energy graduate David Elfstrom, Toronto Hydro

©2020 Selling Energy

3. After the project was completed, the first thing the Operations Manager noted was how much quieter the new air compressor was and how efficiently and smoothly it was all operating.

Example adapted with permission from a submission by Selling Energy graduate David Elfstrom, Toronto Hydro

©2020 Selling Energy

4. He was greatly relieved that he no longer had to worry about the compressors. Plant pressure is superbly stable now. He didn't say anything about how much money he was saving.

Example adapted with permission from a submission by Selling Energy graduate David Elfstrom, Toronto Hydro

©2020 Selling Energy

Elements to notice in this email...

1. Use a short, accurate subject line.
2. Was easy to forward to the owner of the company.
3. Contained no attachments and was brief enough to read on a phone.
4. All figures were listed in dollars, rather than energy units.

Example adapted with permission from a submission by Selling Energy graduate David Elfstrom, Toronto Hydro

©2020 Selling Energy

More elements to notice...

5. Used highly defensible $0.14/kWh when it was more like $0.16/kWh.
6. Focused on how much the current system costs annually to operate. This is a large figure, approximately equal to the entire plant's monthly electric bill.
7. Visually minimized the capital cost by using "K" for thousands of dollars, while using all digits for savings.
8. Used the phrase "reduce energy expenditures" instead of "savings."

Example adapted with permission from a submission by Selling Energy graduate David Elfstrom, Toronto Hydro

©2020 Selling Energy

More elements to notice...

9. Used the word "benefits" to imply both cost savings and non-financial benefits (e.g., improved reliability).
10. Did not calculate a simple payback period; however, provided enough info to let the reader calculate it if desired.
11. Clearly stated what the next steps would be and what the entire initiative would likely cost.

Example adapted with permission from a submission by Selling Energy graduate David Elfstrom, Toronto Hydro

©2020 Selling Energy

IDEAS & ACTIONS

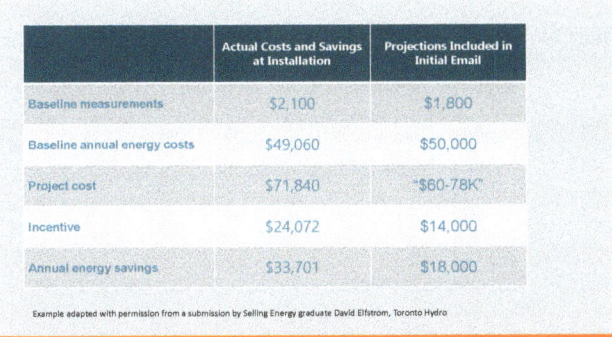

	Actual Costs and Savings at Installation	Projections Included in Initial Email
Baseline measurements	$2,100	$1,800
Baseline annual energy costs	$49,060	$50,000
Project cost	$71,840	"$60-78K"
Incentive	$24,072	$14,000
Annual energy savings	$33,701	$18,000

Example adapted with permission from a submission by Selling Energy graduate David Elfstrom, Toronto Hydro

Lesson 48
SUCCESS TOOL #4
The One-Page Financial Analysis™

Presented by
Mark Jewell
@SellingEnergy
info@sellingenergy.com

Decisions are often driven by emotion...

...and then justified with the financials.

The right metrics and presentation format facilitate confident decision-making.

What is "financial analysis"?

And is it different for energy efficiency vs. smart energy technology projects?

Accurate cost/benefit analysis

How did you calculate your costs?

- Local labor and material figures?
- Prevailing wage considerations?
- Demolition, recycling, disposal?
- Soft costs?
- Contingency added?
- Rebates, incentives, tax benefits deducted from the first cost?
- Who is actually paying?

How did you calculate your savings?

- Which utility tariff?
- Savings start?
- Measure interactions?
- Who gets the savings?
- Quantified and monetized non-utility-cost financial savings?

IDEAS & ACTIONS

www.SellingEnergy.com

Moving beyond utility-cost savings…

1. Utility-cost financial benefits
2. Non-utility-cost financial benefits
3. Non-financial benefits

Remember to consider, quantify and monetize as many non-utility-cost financial benefits as possible

Non-utility-cost financial & non-financial benefits…

1. Better employee attraction/retention
2. Higher employee productivity & morale
3. Improved health and safety
4. Increased throughput or less downtime
5. Improved process control
6. Reduced scrap rate
7. Greater process visibility
8. Reduced emissions
9. Increased retail sales
10. And, of course, many more…

Most
decisions
are made
emotionally
and then
justified
financially

The ideal financial summary?

The ideal financial summary?

A single page.

Is it transparent and compelling?

- Shows all inflows and outflows?
- All benefits quantified/monetized?
- Reasonable discount rate?
- Credible inflation rate?
- Uses proper financial metrics?
- One-page financial summary?

ENTERING THE CORRECT INPUTS

INPUTS FOR FINANCIAL ANALYSIS	
Discount Rate:	10.0%
Finance Rate:	10.0%
Reinvestment Rate:	10.0%
Utility Inflation Rate:	3.0%
Non-utility Inflation Rate:	3.0%

YR1 SAVINGS ASSUMING 100% INSTALLATION OF MEASURE(S)	
Energy	$10,000
Maintenance	$5,000
Other Benefits	

MID-YEAR CONVENTION	
"Y" or "N"	Y

PROJECT START (optional)	
Enter "Date 0"	

REBATE AMOUNT AND TIMING	
Avail. Rebate	$15,400
Rebate Timing	SEE OUTFLOWS

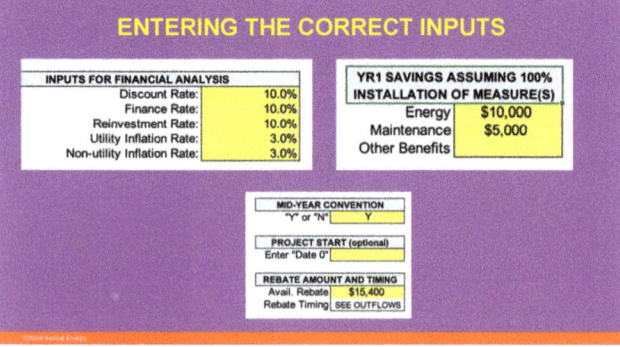

IDEAS & ACTIONS

_____

_____

_____

_____

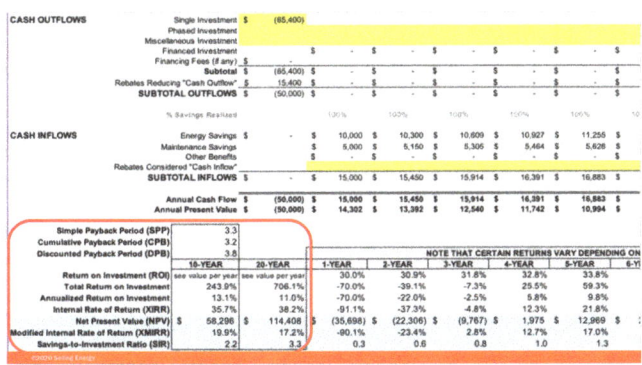

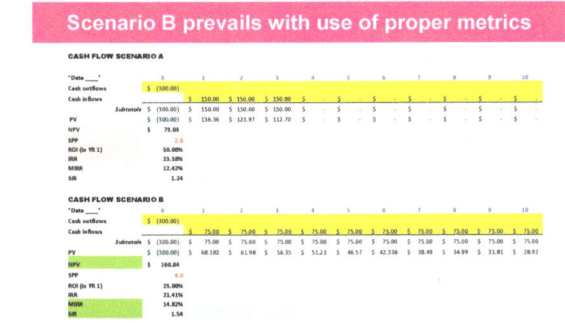

Scenario B prevails with use of proper metrics

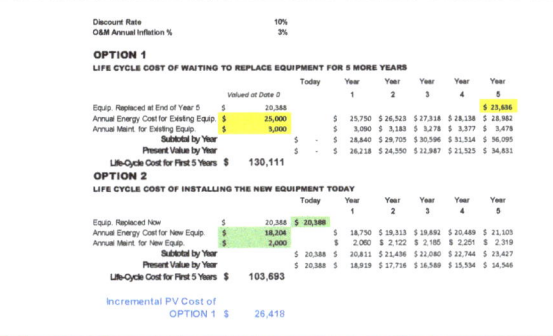

"Value is created by the compression of time."
— Peter Drucker

Finally, you need compelling evidence that *motivates action rather than delay*.

"Value is created by the compression of time"
– Peter Drucker

Assume 10 upgrade projects
(five 4-year SPP & five 2.5-year SPP)

	Scenario A 10 projects this year	Scenario B 2 projects per year
Total Cap Ex	$1,681,000	$1,764,503
PV of Investment	$1,681,000	$1,241,656
NPV	$1,016,071*	$578,366
NPV of "avoided cost of delay"		$437,705

*75% higher NPV helps build shareholder value faster

Lesson 49
Monetizing *non-utility-cost* financial benefits

Presented by
Mark Jewell
@SellingEnergy
info@sellingenergy.com

IDEAS & ACTIONS

www.SellingEnergy.com

Q:

Are there other studies cited in Segment Guides™ or other authoritative sources that you could use to quantify the non-utility-cost financial benefits?

Q:

Would it be useful to assume a small percentage of the quantified savings to enhance credibility even further?

Q:

Could you share a story of producing similar benefits for another customer, with contact info for that customer so they could compare notes?

Q:

Have you done enough sensitivity analysis to feel confident changing the non-utility-cost financial estimates in real time as you field questions?

Lesson 50
Including *all* financial benefits in the analysis

Presented by
Mark Jewell
@SellingEnergy
info@sellingenergy.com

Turbocharging Success

Q:

What happens if your project has an Simple Payback Period of 2 years, but your prospect needs it to pay back within a single year?

- Assume the savings is $10K per year for a 2-year SPP
- You need $10K more in savings to make it a 1-year SPP
- What is the average salary and benefits per worker?
- How many workers are there?
- What is the total payroll each year?
- What percentage of that payroll is $10K?
- How many more minutes of productivity per worker is that?
- Is it obvious that your upgrade will sufficiently improve comfort and convenience to support that many minutes of additional productivity per worker per day?

IDEAS & ACTIONS

- **Assume the savings is $10K per year for a 2-year SPP**
- **You need $10K more in savings to make it a 1-year SPP**
- What is the average salary and benefits per worker? **$50K**
- How many workers are there? **50**
- What is the total payroll each year? **$2.5M**
- What percentage of that payroll is $10K? **0.4%**
- How many more minutes of productivity per worker is that? **(0.4% x 8 hours x 50 minutes per hour = 1.6 minutes)**
- Is it obvious that your upgrade will sufficiently improve comfort and convenience to support **1.6 minutes of additional productivity per worker per day**?

Lesson **51**
SUCCESS TOOL #5
The Success Story Archive™

Presented by
Mark Jewell
@SellingEnergy
info@sellingenergy.com

Sales Success Tools™
How many potential energy solutions could be reduced to elevator pitches, 3-sentence solicitations, one-page proposals, financial analysis templates, etc. to benefit the entire "sales tribe"?

The Success Story Archive™
How many of the "wins" that your sales team has catalyzed (or even witnessed) have been catalogued so that everyone can benefit from the collective wisdom of the entire "sales tribe"?

Are you willing to create and maintain a Story Archive?

A **6-column worksheet** that allows anyone in your organization to leverage any of your best stories helping customers

---

1. Customer segment
2. Technology or approach
3. "The win" in 75 words or less
4. Location of the win
5. Where to get the whole story
6. Date added to the Archive

EXERCISE
Success Story Archive™

IDEAS & ACTIONS

www.SellingEnergy.com

Lesson 52
SUCCESS TOOL #6
The Objections Archive™

Presented by
Mark Jewell
@SellingEnergy
info@sellingenergy.com

Turbocharging Success

The Objections Archive™
How many of the myths and objections that your sales team has heard have been answered and catalogued so that everyone can benefit from the collective wisdom of the entire "sales tribe"?

Are you willing to create and maintain an Objections Archive™?

---

8 steps to a winning Objections Archive™

1. Have everyone list 10+ most commonly heard objections
2. Collect, review and de-duplicate to create a master list
3. Ask whole team to prioritize, adding new ones as needed
4. Everyone preps answers for a subset for each sales meeting
5. Brainstorm, archive and distribute the best responses
6. Test for "muscle memory" in meetings, ride-alongs, etc.
7. Add all new objections (and their responses) to the Archive
8. Include the Objections Archive™ as part of onboarding as well

---

EXERCISE
Objections Archive™

Lesson 53
SUCCESS TOOL #7
Digits-to-Widgets™

Presented by
Mark Jewell
@SellingEnergy
info@sellingenergy.com

Turbocharging Success

The "Profit" on the "P&L"

Bottom line is "net profit."

Dividing the projected savings by net margin will yield the equivalent dollars of revenue needed to deliver a similar impact in a prior fiscal period.

At a Net Margin of 4%...

$$\frac{\$1 \text{ savings}}{4\% \text{ net margin}} \quad \longleftrightarrow \quad \$25 \text{ revenue}$$

Net margin, net profit margin, profit margin, and net profit ratio all refer to a measure of profitability that is calculated by finding the net profit as a percentage of revenue.

NOTE: A more conservative analysis might use Contribution Margin, EBIT/Sales, or EBITDA/Sales rather than Net Margin in this context.

IDEAS & ACTIONS

_____

_____

_____

_____

Sell 15,000 bushels of peaches.
Or switch to LED lighting.
Same results, your choice.

Q:
How many "widgets" did your prospect have to sell last year to match the $1,000 in benefits your project could drop to the bottom line?

Segment-specific Selling: Moving from "Digits" to "Widgets"

Customer Name: _____ Contact Person: _____ Phone: _____
Scope of Proposed Project: _____

"The Digits":
Estim. Annual Cost Savings $_____ (A)   Estim. Annual Energy Savings _____ kWh

Total Project Cost   minus   Incentives (___% of total cost)   equals   Net Customer Cost or Co-Pay
$ _____ (B) $ _____ (C) $ _____ (D)

SPP (Simple Payback Period)   ROI (Return on Investment)   NPV* (Net Present Value)   SIR* (Savings-to-Investment Ratio)
___ years or ___ months   _____ % $ _____   _____
(D/A)   (D/A) x 12   (A/D)   *Discount rate ___% (insert discount rate, NPV, SIR from analysis)

"The Widgets":
Estim. Profit Margin ___% (E)   Revenue Equiv. $_____ (A/E = F)   Typical Widget "_____"

Estim. Revenue per Widget $_____ (G)   Estim. # Widgets Needed to Equal Savings _____ (F/G)

Estim. Revenue per Sale $_____ (H)   Estim. # Sales Needed to Equal Savings _____ (F/H)

"The Widgets":
Estim. Profit Margin ___% (E)   Revenue Equiv. $_____ (A/E = F)   Typical Widget "_____"

Estim. Revenue per Widget $_____ (G)   Estim. # Widgets Needed to Equal Savings _____ (F/G)

Estim. Revenue per Sale $_____ (H)   Estim. # Sales Needed to Equal Savings _____ (F/H)

- Looking over this proposal, I see it features an Estimated Annual Cost Savings of $_____ (A).
- That's a lot of money that could drop right to your bottom line once you implement this project. <<pause>>
- Personally, I think comparisons are often more compelling than calculations, so I did a little homework and found that businesses in the _____ industry have an average Profit Margin of _____ % (E).
- Would you say that your profit margin is close to that industry average? <<pause>>
- At a profit margin of _____ % (E), every $100 in revenue earns you $_____ (100 x E) in profit.
- Does that make sense? <<pause>> OK, so let's do the math.
- You have to generate $_____ (F) in sales to make the same $_____ (A) that should drop to your bottom line in the form of cost savings once you do this project. That's a lot of sales you have to make to see the same impact on your bottom line that this project could deliver for you.
- Taking it a step further, let's say your average sale is $_____ (H). You have to make _____ # (F/H) sales each year to see the same benefit. That's a lot of customers to bring in to earn that same profit.
- Looked at another way, I know you sell a lot of _____s. If you charge $_____ (G) each, you have to sell _____ # (F/G) _____s each year to generate enough profit to match the cost savings that would drop right to your bottom line once you do this project. That's a lot of _____s!
- So, you can either sell _____ # (F/G) _____s a year and make $_____ (A) earning your profit the "old-fashioned way"... or you could do this upgrade and see a similar amount of profit go right to your bottom line thanks to what you'll save each year by doing so. Same results. Your choice!

Selling Energy © 2016 | info@sellingenergy.com | Adapted from a draft submitted by a Selling Energy graduate, Eric Desmatis, with his permission.

EXERCISE
Digits-to-Widgets™

Lesson 54
SUCCESS TOOL #8
C-Suite Talking Points™

Presented by
Mark Jewell
@SellingEnergy
info@sellingenergy.com

Turbocharging Success

C-Suite Talking Points™
How do you make the most of a 30-minute meeting with the C-Suite when you need to discuss and secure agreement on multiple measures?

An 8-column worksheet that highlights the talking points, with one row for each initiative to be discussed.

IDEAS & ACTIONS _____

_____

_____

_____

1. What the initiative is (in plain English)
2. Why the initiative is necessary
3. Cost of the initiative
4. Any amount paid by another party
5. Simple Payback Period (SPP)
6. Net Present Value (NPV)
7. Savings-to-Investment Ratio (SIR)
8. Next step(s) to make it happen

Lesson 55
SUCCESS TOOL #9
Segment Guides™

Presented by
Mark Jewell
@SellingEnergy
info@sellingenergy.com

Why was Segment Guides™ created?

• Learn who the players are
• Learn what they really care about
• Reframe energy projects with the prospect's yardsticks
• Cite benefits beyond obvious utility savings
• Escape the "bits, bytes and blinking lights" thinking
• Learn "sound bites" that grab attention
• Translate savings into compelling metrics
• *It is not a guide to energy conservation measures by segment*

Cite non-utility-cost financial and non-financial benefits that are more compelling than energy outcomes.

The anatomy of Segment Guides™

• Overview of the segment
• Role of energy in that segment's decision-making
• Yardsticks used to gauge success
• Sound bites, particularly on non-utility-cost financial and non-financial benefits
• Trade organizations
• Trade publications

Segment Guides

Data Centers

Segment Guides™ tell you the role of energy in each segment.

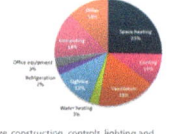

Total Energy Use in Office Buildings by End Use

Energy consumption in greenhouses varies greatly depending on size, construction, controls, lighting and crop being grown. However, the average cost of energy has been estimated at 8.5% of sales, including fuel, gas/diesel, electricity, and trucking costs, and energy is the third largest cost in greenhouses(15%). Heating (75%) and electricity (15%) comprise most of the industry's energy needs. In terms of desire to implement energy efficient measures, a 2008 survey of New Jersey greenhouse growers found that 45% of the respondents had implemented energy saving technologies since 2003 and that 39% were considering implementing energy saving technologies. Nine percent were not sure what energy efficient measures to adopt, but were considering all options.

Segment Guides™ tell you the yardsticks and margins you need to be seen as a peer rather than a vendor.

• **On-Time Delivery to Commit** – This metric is the percentage of time that manufacturer completed product on the schedule that was committed to customers.
• **Manufacturing Cycle Time** – This metric measures the speed or time it takes for manufacturer produce a given product from the time the order is released, to production, to finished...
• **Time to Make Changeovers** – This metric measures the speed or time it takes to switch manufacturing line or plant from making one product over to making a different product...
• **Yield** – This metric is an indication of the percentage of products that are manufactured to specifications the first time through the manufacturing process without scrap or re...
• **Customer**...

• **Sample Net Margins**
  • Auto Dealers (New Cars) - 0.5%
  • Bicycle Shops - 4.2%
  • Book Stores - 2.3%
  • Convenience Stores - 1.3%
  • Clothing Stores - 5%
  • Florists - 3.2%
  • Furniture Stores - 4.5%
  • Garden Centers - 3.3%
  • Gas Station - 1.5%
  • Gas Station with Convenience Store - 2.8%
  • Grocery Stores - 1.62%
  • Music Stores - 2%
  • Office Supply and Stationery Stores - 1.9%

• **Prime Cost** – This is a benchmark that takes into account the related paper products) and labor costs (including taxes, wor good Prime Cost benchmark is 60% or less of total revenue.
• **Cover** - The term "cover" refers to a meal served to a single di beverages, appetizers, entrée, desserts, etc. A table with four regardless of the number of available seats at that table. If th four, the restaurant would record a total of 8 covers for the ni
• **Guest check size** - In 2014, full-service restaurant visit check checks averaged $7.40, and quick-service restaurant checks a
• **Average yearly sales** - In 2013, full-service restaurants saw y while quick-service restaurants had average yearly sales of $1

IDEAS & ACTIONS

Sell 15,000 bushels of peaches.
Or switch to LED lighting.
Same results, your choice.

Segment Guides™ give you the figures you need to equate your projected savings to...

...how hard your customer had to work *last year* to see that same bottom-line benefit.

Segment Guides™ give you the sound bites you need to **capture attention** and then **close the sale**.

RETAIL: "...sales increase by 10% after improving the store's lighting quality by replacing downlights with LED PAR38 lamps" [14]

GAS STATION/CONVENIENCE STORE: "...in the first three months after the retrofit, complaints were down 47% and theft went from 8 incidences to zero." [13]

GROCERY: "...a high-quality lighting design increased sales at a grocery store by 1.93%... representing over $518,000 in additional annual revenue" [20]

DAIRY: "...8% higher milk production, more docile cows, no need for supplemental fixtures for lower light levels, no interference with electronic identification systems for cows..." [51, 54, 57]

Segment Guides™ footnote each statistic and sound bite, complete with hyperlinks for easy retrieval

SOURCES

[1] Walker, J.N. and Duncan, G.A. (n.d.) Greenhouse structures. Retrieved from https://www.uky.edu/bae-sites/www.uky.edu-bae/files/AEN-12.pdf

[2] 2012 Census of Agriculture United States Summary and States Data, Volume 1. Retrieved from (2014). United States Department of Agriculture. Retrieved from https://www.agcensus.usda.gov/Publications/2012/Full_Report/Volume_1,_Chapter_1_US/usv1.pdf

[3] 2012 Census of Agriculture United States Summary and States Data, Volume 1. Retrieved from (2014). United States Department of Agriculture. Retrieved from https://www.agcensus.usda.gov/Publications/2012/Full_Report/Volume_1,_Chapter_1_US/usv1.pdf

---

Segment Guides™ tell you where to get the inside scoop, with hyperlinks to take you there.

TRADE ORGANIZATIONS AND PUBLICATIONS

Organizations
- American Horticultural Organization: http://ahsgardening.org/
- The Hobby Greenhouse Association: https://www.hobbygreenhouse.org/
- The National Greenhouse Manufacturers Association: https://www.ngma.com/

Publications
- Greenhouse Management Magazine: http://www.greenhousemag.com
- Garden and Greenhouse: http://www.gardenandgreenhouse.net/
- Greenhouse Product News: http://www.gpnmag.com

Lesson 56
DIY approaches to segment research

Presented by
Mark Jewell
@SellingEnergy
info@sellingenergy.com

sellingenergy
Turbocharging Success

Q:

What would a DIY approach to segment-specific research look like?

Where should you start?

- Google and Google Scholar
- Academic clearinghouses
- Trade orgs and bookstores
- Talk to authors of relevant articles
- Chase down the footnotes
- Form 10K filings and earnings calls
- Equity analyst reports on segments
- Access your own Success Story Archive™
- Interview past customers
- Other

Q:

Who is Faith Popcorn?

IDEAS & ACTIONS

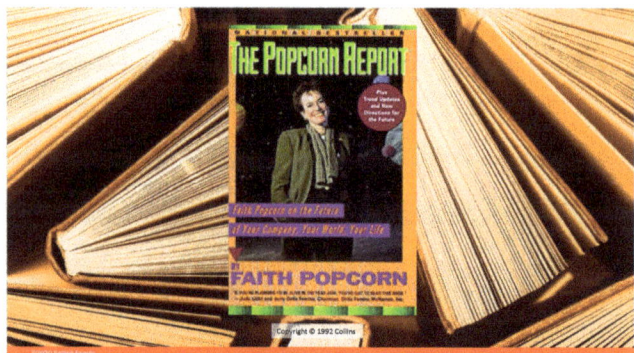

selling in 6™

Lesson 57
Better questions yield better answers

Presented by
Mark Jewell
@SellingEnergy
info@sellingenergy.com

sellingenergy
Turbocharging Success

Are you asking the **right questions?**

Asking the RIGHT questions…

Don't confuse the wisdom of asking the right questions during the meeting…

…with the foolishness of not having done your research on the industry and prospect well in advance of the meeting!

Asking the RIGHT questions…

Never ask a question that could have (should have!) been answered with a little research ahead of time.

There would be no music without silence between the notes.

What 10 seconds of silence sounds like…

Q:
What questions do you normally ask your prospects?

IDEAS & ACTIONS

Why are you interested in our offerings?

1. Saving utilities
2. Reducing carbon
3. Adjunct to planned renewables activity
4. Satisfying sustainability initiatives and/or reporting
5. Improving your ENERGY STAR®, LEED®, or similar rating
6. Improving tenant comfort, convenience
7. Gaining better visibility, control and/or reporting
8. Planning new construction or substantial renovation
9. Demonstrating leadership
10. Emulating best practices seen elsewhere
11. Responding to a mandate (internal or external)
12. Other

Are there particular departments/individuals here that focus on energy efficiency?

How many projects have been proposed in the last "X" years?

- How many have been approved (and why)?
- What has prevented project approvals?

Can you think of any previous capital projects that were particularly gratifying?

What projects or initiatives are on your "wish list"?

What is the process for approving projects here? And then what?

What barriers have you faced in getting projects approved in the past?

- Separation of responsibility for capital and operating budgets
- Lack of staff resources to manage projects
- Lack of reliable info on efficiency measures
- Negative experiences with past efficiency projects
- Lack of funding for studies
- Lack of funding for implementation
- Other

How have you funded efficiency initiatives in the past?

- Self-funded
- Rebates/ incentives
- Grants
- Loans
- Bonds
- Other

IDEAS & ACTIONS

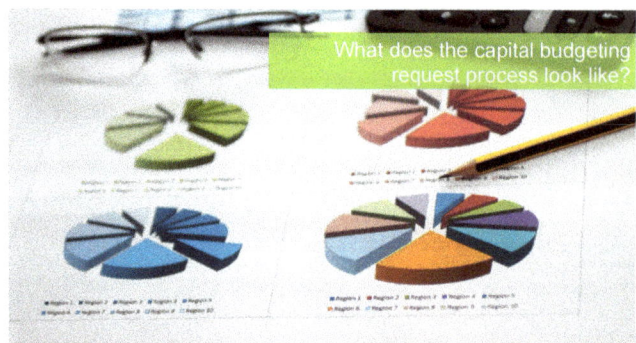

What does the capital budgeting request process look like?

Lesson 58
Revitalizing stalled or rejected proposals

Presented by
Mark Jewell
@SellingEnergy
info@sellingenergy.com

"90% of our roughly $10 million in energy work last year came from **existing customers**."

Q:

Could you drive a segment-specific non-utility-cost financial or non-financial benefit?

Q:

Could you reframe the benefits so they could be measured using your prospect's yardstick?

Q:

Could a Digits-to-Widgets™ calculation help the prospect visualize the true cost of waiting?

Q:

Could you recover from a previous proposal that was "less than concise"?

20% More Light with 40% Lower Energy Cost for the Parking Garage at 123 Market Street
Improving security, saving energy, lowering operating costs, and boosting the ENERGY STAR score

TARGET: TO IMPROVE PARKING-AREA LIGHTING WITH ENERGY-EFFICIENT, LONG-LASTING LED TECHNOLOGY

- To address tenant safety concerns by increasing average lighting levels by 20% and moving to "whiter" light, enhancing visibility for both occupants and security cameras
- To reduce operating and maintenance costs for parking-area lighting by $15,000 the first year (10-year NPV of over $53,000[1])
- To capture $15,400 in Energy Trust incentives, covering 24% of project cost
- To avoid a quarter-million pounds of CO2 emissions annually, boosting the ENERGY STAR score to 70 from 68

Over the last 12 months, 4 of 10 tenants have raised concerns about the lighting in and around the 5-level garage at 123 Market. A qualified lighting contractor has studied the situation and confirmed that the existing inefficient, 14-year-old fixtures deliver inadequate lighting levels. Changing to LED fixtures would increase lighting levels by approximately 20% while reducing annual operating expenses by about 40%. Moreover, LED technology produces "whiter" light, which improves "visibility" for both occupants and security cameras, even at low light levels.

Initially proposing a project…

IDEAS & ACTIONS _____

_____

_____

_____

Could Better Lighting, Pumps and Fans Mean 95,630 Gallons of Milk?
Lower energy and maintenance costs yield higher net profit; better lighting improves milk production as well

TARGET: IMPLEMENT LIGHTING, PUMP AND FAN EFFICIENCY IMPROVEMENTS TO BOOST YOUR PROFITABILITY

- The money you are now wasting in utilities could be better used to feed three more milk-producing cows.
- Studies suggest that you could also see 6% to 8% higher milk production overall by switching to LED lighting.
- At your net profit margin of 5%, saving $1 in energy is equivalent to driving $20 in revenue.
  - $108 per year saved on *each* 400W metal halide to LED upgrade equates to $2,160 in revenue.
  - $1,680 per year saved on free stall fans equates to $33,600 in revenue.
  - Adding variable frequency drives to cooling fans and irrigation pumps further increases your savings.
- Your business pays into the Public Benefits Fund, which entitles you to rebates to help fund your project.
- Since your project also qualifies for On-Bill Financing, any first cost not covered by rebates could be financed by <<Your Utility>> with $0 out of pocket and 0% interest. Your loan would be repaid on your monthly utility bill using a formula that limits the monthly debt service amount to the utility savings generated by the project.
- *This project's payback is less than one year, so you will pay for the project this year whether you do it or not.*

Revitalizing a project…

selling in 6™

Lesson 59
Circling back to expand and extend success

Presented by
Mark Jewell
@SellingEnergy
info@sellingenergy.com

sellingenergy
Turbocharging Success

How much value is hidden in each of your current customers?

Q:
How closely have you evaluated your "cost of customer acquisition" versus the "lifetime value of a customer"?

Q:
Are you maximizing the value of the customer relationships you already have?

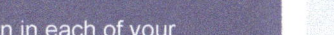

---

1. Are you systematically growing the relationship?

Cross-selling
Up-serving
Referrals

2. Are you systematically mapping your successes with the goal of extending them?

Who are your best customers?
What segments are they in?
What offerings are they buying?
Where are they located?
Who else looks a lot like them?

IDEAS & ACTIONS

www.SellingEnergy.com

3. What are the most obvious extensions of the customers you already have?

Divisions or affiliate companies
Supply chain partners
Customers
Neighbors
Competitors

4. Are you committed to being proactive rather than reactive?

Customer nurturing campaigns
Staying up-to-date on each segment
Offering unsolicited proposals
Warm calls to those extensions (see previous slide)

5. Are you systematically reaching out to non-competitive trade partners?

Exchanging qualification checklists
Lead sharing with the "coopetition"

Lesson 60
Planning your 7 most important things to do

Presented by
Mark Jewell
@SellingEnergy
info@sellingenergy.com

Plan your "7 most important things to do" the night before...

No part of this presentation may be recorded or transferred.

Lesson 61
FINANCIAL ANALYSIS FUNDAMENTALS
Fundamental approaches for energy projects

Presented by
Mark Jewell
@SellingEnergy
info@sellingenergy.com

Most decisions are made *emotionally* and then justified *financially*

IDEAS & ACTIONS

Is your analysis transparent, credible and compelling?

1. Properly timed cash inflows and outflows (no surprises!)
2. Accurately estimated utility savings
3. Reasonably estimated maintenance labor savings
4. Credibly estimated non-utility-cost financial benefits*

*Credible estimates can come from authoritative studies, common sense calculations, pilot measurements, etc.

Is your analysis transparent, credible and compelling?

5. Sensible inflation, discount, finance, reinvestment rates
6. Accurately calculated financial metrics
7. Thoughtful sensitivity analysis involving key variables
8. Careful comparison re: paying all-cash, phasing, or financing

Realize that the person approving the funding may not be as emotionally motivated as your internal champion at the outset.

It's your job to ensure that the approvers see a link between your project and one or more outcomes that they truly value.

And keep it to a single page!

selling in 6™

Lesson 62
FINANCIAL ANALYSIS FUNDAMENTALS
Simple Payback Period (SPP)

Presented by
Mark Jewell
@SellingEnergy
info@sellingenergy.com

selling energy
Turbocharging Success

Simple Payback Period

- "The amount of time it takes to recover your initial investment through savings"
- Generally expressed in years (or months)
- Computed as the ratio of first cost to Year 1 savings
- It does not take into account the time value of money

$$\text{Simple Payback Period} = \frac{\text{First Cost}}{\text{Savings in Year 1}}$$

Simple Payback Period
EXAMPLE #1

- Investment of $10,000 made today
- First-year savings estimated at $2,500
- What is the Simple Payback Period?

IDEAS & ACTIONS

Simple Payback Period
EXAMPLE #1

- Investment of $10,000 made today
- First-year savings estimated at $2,500
- What is the Simple Payback Period?

$$SPP = \frac{\$10,000}{\$2,500} = 4.0 \text{ years}$$

Simple Payback Period
EXAMPLE #2

- Investment of $125,000 made today
- First-year savings estimated at $35,000
- What is the Simple Payback Period?

Simple Payback Period
EXAMPLE #2

- Investment of $125,000 made today
- First-year savings estimated at $35,000
- What is the Simple Payback Period?

$$SPP = \frac{\$125,000}{\$35,000} = 3.57 \text{ years}$$

1. What about the Time Value of Money?

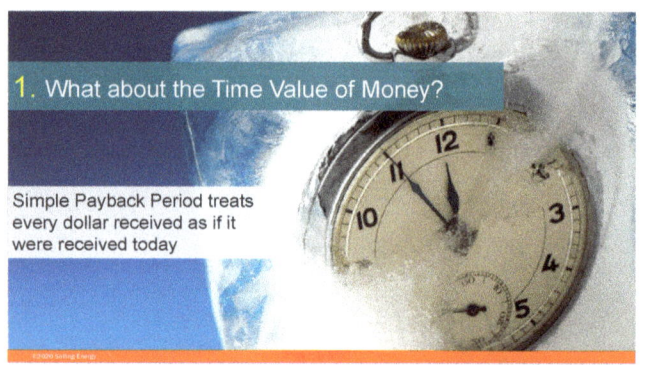

1. What about the Time Value of Money?

Simple Payback Period treats every dollar received as if it were received today

2. What about the period after payback?

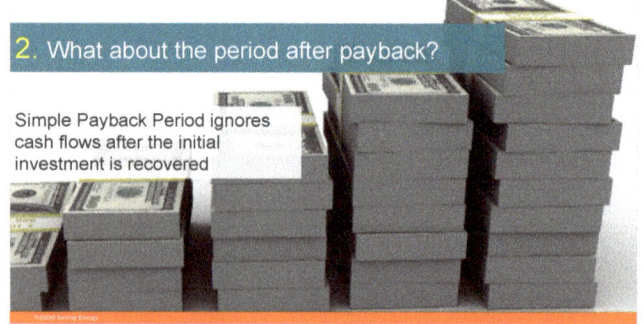

2. What about the period after payback?

Simple Payback Period ignores cash flows after the initial investment is recovered

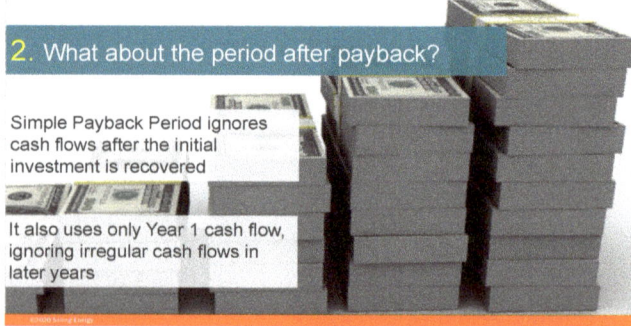

2. What about the period after payback?

Simple Payback Period ignores cash flows after the initial investment is recovered

It also uses only Year 1 cash flow, ignoring irregular cash flows in later years

IDEAS & ACTIONS

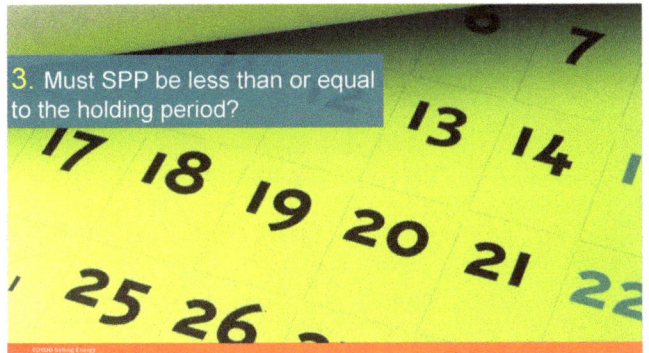

3. Must SPP be less than or equal to the holding period?

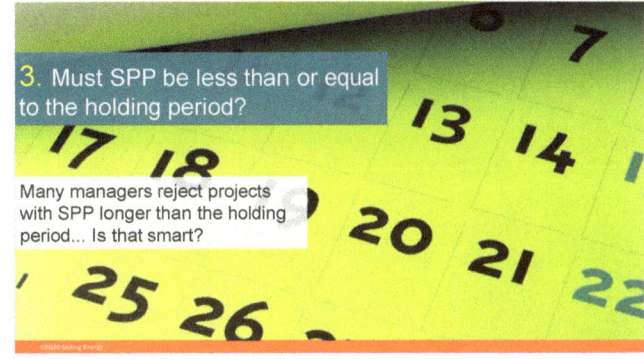

3. Must SPP be less than or equal to the holding period?

Many managers reject projects with SPP longer than the holding period... Is that smart?

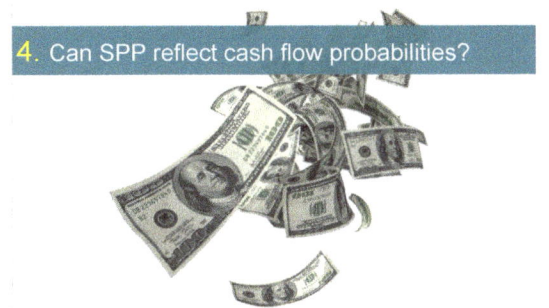

4. Can SPP reflect cash flow probabilities?

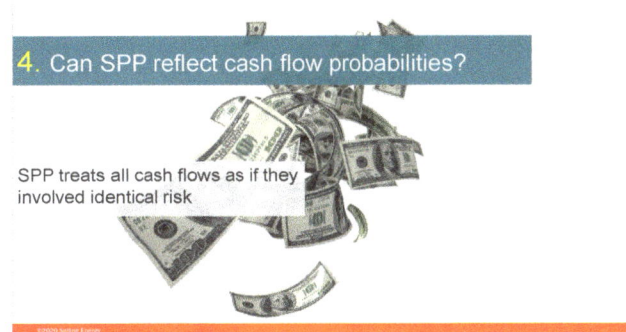

4. Can SPP reflect cash flow probabilities?

SPP treats all cash flows as if they involved identical risk

5. Do SPP rules of thumb make any sense?

5. Do SPP rules of thumb make any sense?

Managers have been clinging to "maximum 2-year payback" for decades, even though the prime rate was 18.75% in 1980 and only 3.25% in 2010.

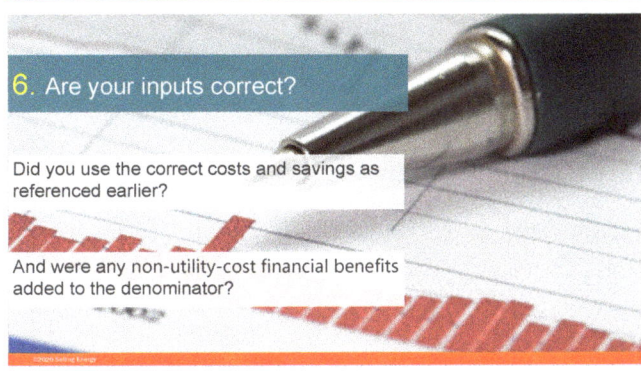

6. Are your inputs correct?

Did you use the correct costs and savings as referenced earlier?

And were any non-utility-cost financial benefits added to the denominator?

7. And whose SPP are you calculating?

IDEAS & ACTIONS

www.SellingEnergy.com

In Landlord/Tenant Settings...

- What are the Landlord's shares of costs and savings?

In Landlord/Tenant Settings...

- Could the Landlord use a "capital expense cost recovery" clause and have the tenants repurpose wasted utility dollars to help improve the building?

In Landlord/Tenant Settings...

- Would the Landlord see a reduction in unreimbursed operating expenses?

In Landlord/Tenant Settings...

- Would lower Op Ex result in higher base rents and/or better tenant retention/attraction?

In Landlord/Tenant Settings...

- Would higher NOI support higher asset value upon refinancing or sale?

Lesson 63
FINANCIAL ANALYSIS FUNDAMENTALS
Cumulative Payback Period (CPB)

Presented by
Mark Jewell
@SellingEnergy
info@sellingenergy.com

Turbocharging Success

Q:

Is there more than one way to calculate "payback period"?

IDEAS & ACTIONS

_____

_____

_____

_____

There are actually 3 types of "payback"

1. Simple Payback Period
2. Cumulative Payback Period
3. Discounted Payback Period

Downsides of Simple Payback Period

1. Ignores Time Value of Money
2. Ignores cash flows occurring after the payback
3. Ignores any irregularity in cash flows after Year 1
4. Discourages project approval if holding period < SPP
5. Does not reflect cash flow probabilities
6. Disregards the economic backdrop of other investments
7. Gets tricky in income-producing property settings

Q:

What is Cumulative Payback Period?

Cumulative Payback Period

- The length of time needed to accumulate sufficient **cash inflows** to recoup the initial investment completely

- Calculated by adding each period's **cash inflow** until the amount of the original investment is reached

- Cumulative Payback Period **does not** compensate for Time Value of Money.

Advantage of Cumulative Payback Period (CPB)

1. Accounts for irregularity in cash flows, *but only until the end of the Cumulative Payback Period*

Lesson 64
FINANCIAL ANALYSIS FUNDAMENTALS
Discounted Payback Period (DPB)

Presented by
Mark Jewell
@SellingEnergy
info@sellingenergy.com

Turbocharging Success

Q:

What is Discounted Payback Period?

IDEAS & ACTIONS

www.SellingEnergy.com

Discounted Payback Period

- The length of time needed to accumulate sufficient discounted cash inflows to recoup the initial investment completely

- Calculated by adding the present value of each period's cash inflow until the amount of the original investment is reached

- Discounted Payback Period does compensate for Time Value of Money (i.e., for cash flows prior to the DPP)

Advantages of Discounted Payback Period (DPB)

1. Accounts for any irregularity in cash flows, *but only until the end of the Discounted Payback Period*
2. Accounts for Time Value of Money, *but only for the cash flows that occur before the end of the Discounted Payback Period*

selling in 6™

Lesson 65
FINANCIAL ANALYSIS FUNDAMENTALS
Return on Investment (ROI)

Presented by
Mark Jewell
@SellingEnergy
info@sellingenergy.com

selling energy
Turbocharging Success

Return On Investment (ROI)

- ROI is sometimes thought of as a **reciprocal** of SPP
  - SPP is first cost divided by YR1 savings
  - ROI is YR1 savings divided by first cost

Assume $100,000 first cost saves $25,000 in YR1

SPP = $100,000 / $25,000 = 4 years
ROI = $25,000 / $100,000 = 25%

Return On Investment (ROI)

- ROI is sometimes thought of as a **reciprocal** of SPP
  - SPP is first cost divided by YR1 savings
  - ROI is YR1 savings divided by first cost
  - Therefore, 1 / SPP = ROI and 1 / ROI = SPP

Assume $100,000 first cost saves $25,000 in YR1

SPP = $100,000 / $25,000 = 4 years
ROI = $25,000 / $100,000 = 25%

However, which "ROI" are you actually referencing?

$$\text{"ROI"} \quad \frac{\text{Current Period Inflow}}{\text{Cumulative Outflow}}$$

$$\text{"Total ROI"} \quad \frac{\text{Cumulative Inflow} - \text{Cumulative Outflow}}{\text{Cumulative Outflow}}$$

$$\text{"Annualized ROI"} \quad \left[\frac{\text{Cumulative Inflow}}{\text{Cumulative Outflow}} \right]^{1/N} - 1$$

NONE OF THESE VERSIONS OF ROI CONSIDERS THE TIME VALUE OF MONEY

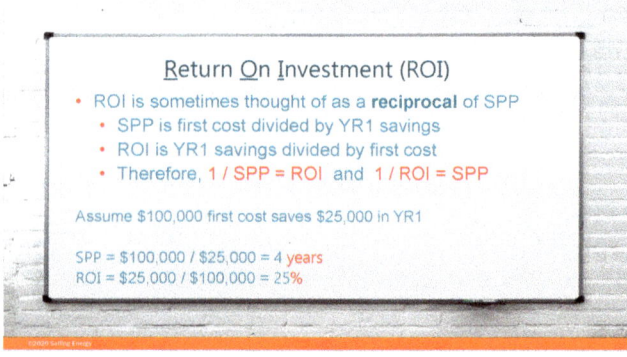

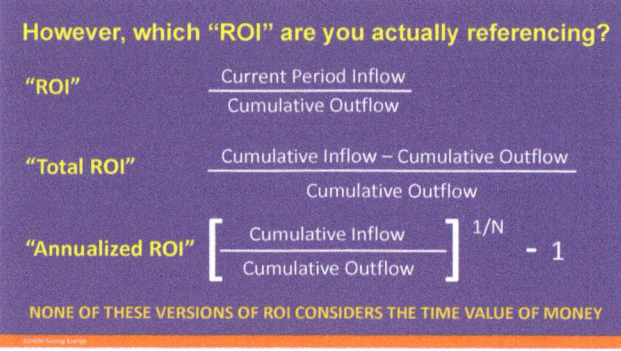

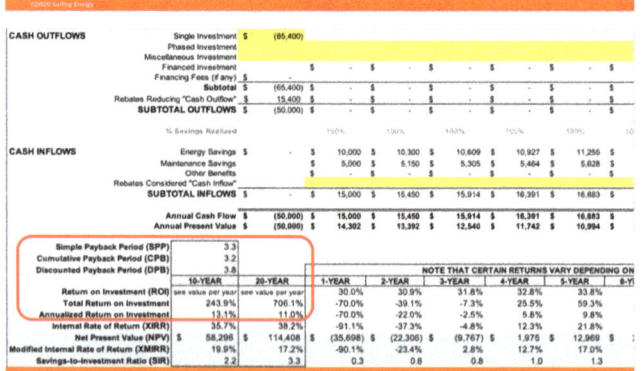

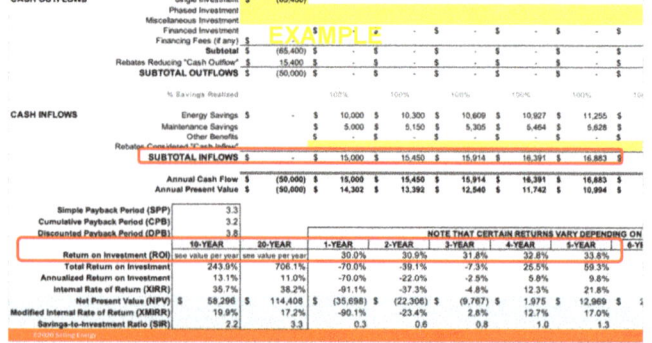

IDEAS & ACTIONS

_____

_____

_____

_____

Lesson 66
FINANCIAL ANALYSIS FUNDAMENTALS
Calculating ROI over multiple years

Presented by
Mark Jewell
@SellingEnergy
info@sellingenergy.com

sellingenergy
Turbocharging Success

Q:

How do "arithmetic mean" and "geometric mean" differ, and why is that difference so important when calculating a multi-period ROI?

Q:

What does "arithmetic mean" actually mean?

"Arithmetic Mean"

The arithmetic mean is the **simple average.**

Year 1   return: 15%
Year 2   return: -10%
Year 3   return: 5%

The simple average is
(15% + -10% + 5%)/3 = 10%/3 = **3.33%**

Adapted from https://www.investopedia.com/articles/08/annualized-returns.asp

---

Q:

What does "geometric mean" actually mean?

"Geometric Mean"

The geometric mean is the **compound average.**

Year 1   return: 15%
Year 2   return: -10%
Year 3   return: 5%

The compound average is 2.81%
[(1 + 15%) * (1 + -10%) * (1 + 5%)] ^ 1/3 = 1.0281

Convert to a percentage by subtracting 1 and
multiplying by 100... **2.81%**

Q:

Do the arithmetic mean and geometric mean get closer to each other or farther away as volatility increases?

Q:

Do the arithmetic mean and geometric mean get closer to each other or farther away as volatility increases?

Farther away... as predicted by a concept called "Jensen's inequality"

IDEAS & ACTIONS

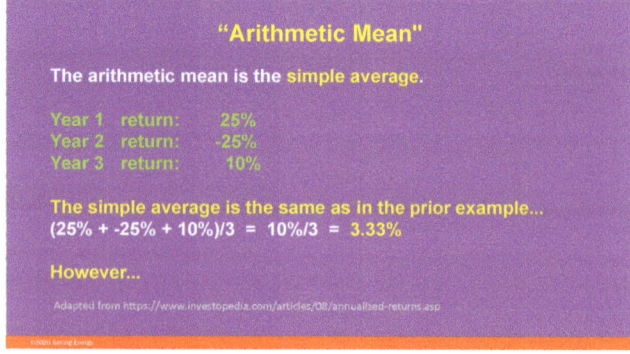

"Arithmetic Mean"

The arithmetic mean is the **simple average**.

Year 1   return: 25%
Year 2   return: -25%
Year 3   return: 10%

The simple average is the same as in the prior example...
(25% + -25% + 10%)/3 = 10%/3 = 3.33%

However...

Adapted from https://www.investopedia.com/articles/08/annualized-returns.asp

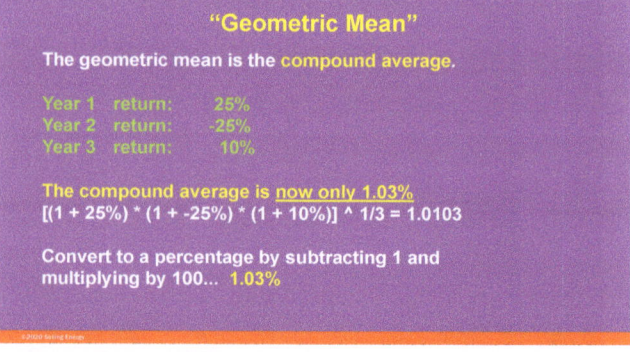

"Geometric Mean"

The geometric mean is the **compound average**.

Year 1   return: 25%
Year 2   return: -25%
Year 3   return: 10%

The compound average is now only 1.03%
[(1 + 25%) * (1 + -25%) * (1 + 10%)] ^ 1/3 = 1.0103

Convert to a percentage by subtracting 1 and
multiplying by 100... 1.03%

Q:

How do you calculate arithmetic mean and geometric mean in Microsoft Excel?

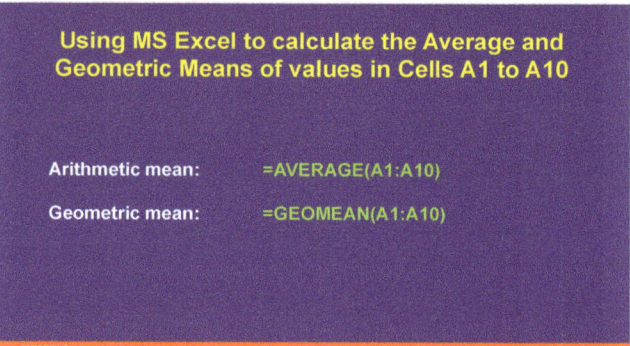

Using MS Excel to calculate the Average and Geometric Means of values in Cells A1 to A10

Arithmetic mean: =AVERAGE(A1:A10)

Geometric mean: =GEOMEAN(A1:A10)

selling in 6™

Lesson 67
FINANCIAL ANALYSIS FUNDAMENTALS
Discount Rate and Time Value of Money (TVM)

Presented by
Mark Jewell
@SellingEnergy
info@sellingenergy.com

sellingenergy
Turbocharging Success

Discount Rate

• The minimum rate of return required by the investor
• Interest rate used in present value calculations

More about discount rates...

• The higher the perceived risk of an investment, the higher the discount rate.
• The higher the discount rate, the lower the present value of any future cash flow.

More about discount rates...

• Discount rate reflects an investor's opportunity cost of money over time and represents the investor's minimum acceptable rate of return.

IDEAS & ACTIONS

2 types of discount rates

- Real discount rates do not include the general rate of inflation
- Nominal discount rates do incorporate inflation

Moving between real and nominal rates

$(1 + \text{Nominal \%}) = (1 + \text{Real \%}) * (1 + \text{Infl.\%})$

$(1 + \text{Real \%}) = (1 + \text{Nominal \%}) / (1 + \text{Infl.\%})$

$(1 + \text{Infl.\%}) = (1 + \text{Nominal \%}) / (1 + \text{Real \%})$

PV of a future cash flow

- The amount of the cash flow
- The timing* of the cash flow
- The investor's discount rate

* The number of compounding periods from today

Setting a discount rate

- Weighted-average cost of capital (WACC)
- Rate of return from a project of similar magnitude, duration, and risk
- Capitalization rate of the income-producing property targeted for the investment
- Other...

Lesson 68

FINANCIAL ANALYSIS FUNDAMENTALS
Present Value (PV) and Net Present Value (NPV)

Presented by
Mark Jewell
@SellingEnergy
info@sellingenergy.com

sellingenergy
Turbocharging Success

Present Value

- What is a particular cash flow worth in today's dollars?
- Based on the concept that money earns interest

Present Value

Determine value of each cash flow at "Date 0" using discount rate, then add them together:

Date 1	$1.00	=	$ .91	at Date 0
Date 2	$1.00	=	$ .83	at Date 0
Date 3	$1.00	=	$ .75	at Date 0
TOTAL		=	$2.49	at Date 0

"Date 0" is today   Assumes 10% discount rate
"Date 1" is the end of Year 1 $PV = \text{Cash Flow} / (1 + \text{Discount Rate})^N$

Net Present Value

Net Present Value	=	PV of the cash inflows	+	PV of the cash outflows*

*NOTE: Keep in mind that PV of the cash outflows is a negative number.

IDEAS & ACTIONS

Lesson 69
FINANCIAL ANALYSIS FUNDAMENTALS
Internal Rate of Return (IRR)

Presented by
Mark Jewell
@SellingEnergy
info@sellingenergy.com

sellingenergy
Turbocharging Success

Internal Rate of Return

$$\text{Net Present Value} = \text{PV of the cash inflows} + \text{PV of the cash outflows*}$$

- As the discount rate increases, the PV of any cash flows after Date 0 decreases
- In a typical upgrade where the only cash outflow occurs at Date 0, a higher discount rate will reduce the NPV

*NOTE: This formula assumes that the PV of the cash outflows is a negative number

---

Internal Rate of Return

$$\text{Net Present Value} = \text{PV of the cash inflows} + \text{PV of the cash outflows*}$$

- IRR is the discount rate that makes the PV of the cash inflows *equal to* the (absolute value of the) PV of the cash outflows, which makes the NPV equal to zero.

*NOTE: This formula assumes that the PV of the cash outflows is a negative number

---

IRR has two shortcomings

1. Multiple changes in sign (i.e., positive to negative or vice versa) in the periodic cash flows opens the door to multiple correct answers for IRR.

IRR has two shortcomings

2. IRR assumes that you can reinvest any cash inflow you receive during the analysis term at the IRR for the entire time between *the date you receive the cash inflow* and *the end of the analysis term*.

Internal rate of return: A cautionary tale

By John C. Kelleher and Justin J. MacCormack

Tempted by a project with a high internal rate of return? Better check those interim cash flows again.

Maybe finance managers just enjoy living on the edge. What else would explain their weakness for using the internal rate of return (IRR) to assess capital projects? For decades, finance textbooks

---

Lesson 70
FINANCIAL ANALYSIS FUNDAMENTALS
Modified Internal Rate of Return (MIRR)

Presented by
Mark Jewell
@SellingEnergy
info@sellingenergy.com

sellingenergy
Turbocharging Success

Modified Internal Rate of Return

1. Also known as "Adjusted Internal Rate of Return"
2. MIRR requires the input of assumptions for finance rate and reinvestment rate to calculate.
3. MIRR has neither of the previously mentioned shortcomings of IRR.

IDEAS & ACTIONS

Lesson 71
FINANCIAL ANALYSIS FUNDAMENTALS
Savings-to-Investment Ratio (SIR)

Presented by
Mark Jewell
@SellingEnergy
info@sellingenergy.com

©2020 Selling Energy

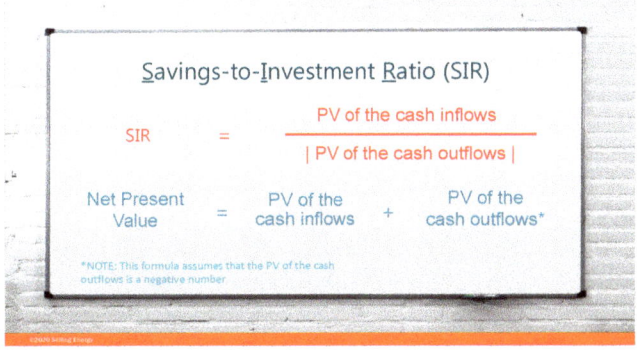

Savings-to-Investment Ratio (SIR)

$$\text{SIR} = \frac{\text{PV of the cash inflows}}{|\text{ PV of the cash outflows }|}$$

$$\text{Net Present Value} = \text{PV of the cash inflows} + \text{PV of the cash outflows*}$$

*NOTE: This formula assumes that the PV of the cash outflows is a negative number.

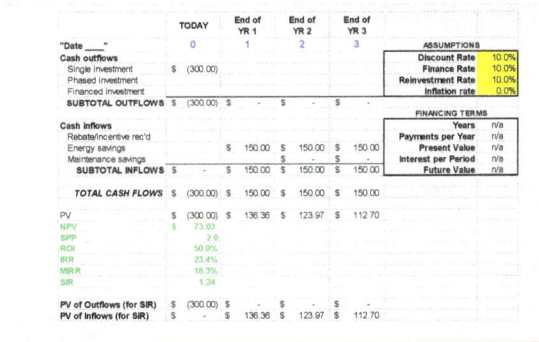

Savings-to-Investment Ratio (SIR)

$$\text{SIR} = \frac{\text{PV of the cash inflows}}{|\text{ PV of the cash outflows }|}$$

$$\text{Net Present Value} = \text{PV of the cash inflows} + \text{PV of the cash outflows*}$$

*NOTE: This formula assumes that the PV of the cash outflows is a negative number.

Lesson 72
FINANCIAL ANALYSIS FUNDAMENTALS
A simple example illustrating various metrics

Presented by
Mark Jewell
@SellingEnergy
info@sellingenergy.com

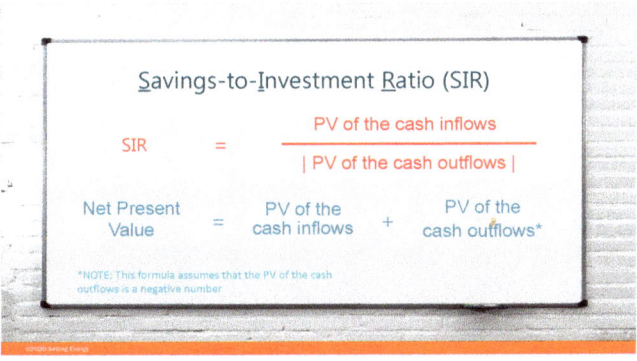

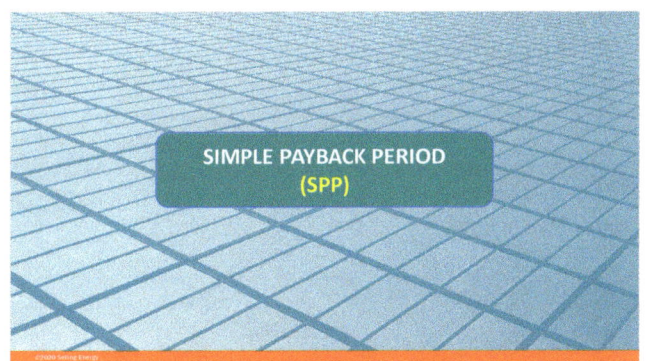

SIMPLE PAYBACK PERIOD
(SPP)

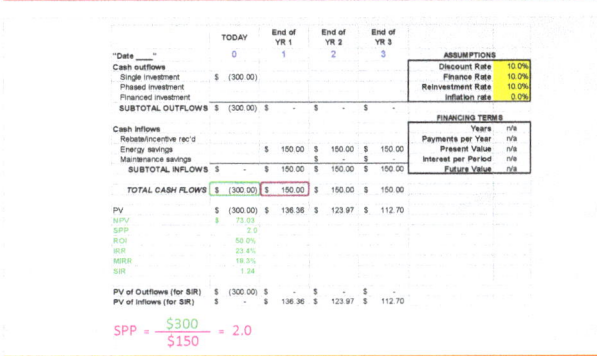

$$\text{SPP} = \frac{\$300}{\$150} = 2.0$$

RETURN ON INVESTMENT
(ROI)

IDEAS & ACTIONS

www.SellingEnergy.com

Slide 1 (spreadsheet)

"Date ____"	TODAY	End of YR 1	End of YR 2	End of YR 3		ASSUMPTIONS	
	0	1	2	3			
Cash outflows						Discount Rate	10.0%
Single investment	$ (300.00)					Finance Rate	10.0%
Phased investment						Reinvestment Rate	10.0%
Financed investment						Inflation rate	0.0%
SUBTOTAL OUTFLOWS	$ (300.00)	$ -	$ -	$ -			
Cash inflows						FINANCING TERMS	
Rebate/incentive rec'd						Years	n/a
Energy savings		$ 150.00	$ 150.00	$ 150.00		Payments per Year	n/a
Maintenance savings		$ -	$ -	$ -		Present Value	n/a
SUBTOTAL INFLOWS	$ -	$ 150.00	$ 150.00	$ 150.00		Interest per Period	n/a
						Future Value	n/a
TOTAL CASH FLOWS	$ (300.00)	$ 150.00	$ 150.00	$ 150.00			
PV	$ (300.00)	$ 136.36	$ 123.97	$ 112.70			
NPV	$ 73.03						
SPP	2.0						
ROI	50.0%						
IRR	23.4%						
MIRR	18.3%						
SIR	1.24						
PV of Outflows (for SIR)	$ (300.00)	$ -	$ -	$ -			
PV of Inflows (for SIR)	$ -	$ 136.36	$ 123.97	$ 112.70			

$$ROI = \frac{\$150}{\$300} = 50\%$$ NOTE: This is "Current Year ROI" rather than Total or Annualized.

Slide 2

PRESENT VALUE (PV)

Slide 3 (spreadsheet, same layout)

$$Present\ Value = \frac{Cash\ Flow}{(1 + Disc.\ Rate)^N}$$

Slide 4 (spreadsheet, same layout)

$$Present\ Value = \frac{Cash\ Flow}{(1 + Disc.\ Rate)^N}$$

Slide 5 (spreadsheet, same layout)

$$Present\ Value = \frac{\$150}{(1 + 10\%)^1} = \$136.36$$

Slide 6 (spreadsheet, same layout)

$$Present\ Value = \frac{\$150}{(1 + 10\%)^2} = \$123.97$$

Slide 7 (spreadsheet, same layout)

$$Present\ Value = \frac{\$150}{(1 + 10\%)^3} = \$112.70$$

Slide 8

NET PRESENT VALUE (NPV)

IDEAS & ACTIONS

_____

_____

_____

_____

Slide 1

"Date ____"	TODAY 0	End of YR 1	End of YR 2	End of YR 3	ASSUMPTIONS	
Cash outflows					Discount Rate	10.0%
Single investment	$ (300.00)				Finance Rate	10.0%
Phased investment					Reinvestment Rate	10.0%
Financed investment					Inflation rate	0.0%
SUBTOTAL OUTFLOWS	$ (300.00)	$ -	$ -	$ -		
Cash inflows					FINANCING TERMS	
Rebate/incentive rec'd					Years	n/a
Energy savings		$ 150.00	$ 150.00	$ 150.00	Payments per Year	n/a
Maintenance savings			$ -	$ -	Present Value	n/a
SUBTOTAL INFLOWS	$ -	$ 150.00	$ 150.00	$ 150.00	Interest per Period	n/a
					Future Value	n/a
TOTAL CASH FLOWS	$ (300.00)	$ 150.00	$ 150.00	$ 150.00		
PV	$ (300.00)	$ 136.36	$ 123.97	$ 112.70		
NPV	$ 73.03					
SPP	2.0					
ROI	50.0%					
IRR	23.4%					
MIRR	18.3%					
SIR	1.24					
PV of Outflows (for SIR)	$ (300.00)	$ -	$ -	$ -		
PV of Inflows (for SIR)	$ -	$ 136.36	$ 123.97	$ 112.70		

Net Present Value = PV of outflows* + PV of inflows
*NOTE: The PV of the cash outflows is a negative number

Slide 2

"Date ____"	TODAY 0	End of YR 1	End of YR 2	End of YR 3	ASSUMPTIONS	
Cash outflows					Discount Rate	10.0%
Single investment	$ (300.00)				Finance Rate	10.0%
Phased investment					Reinvestment Rate	10.0%
Financed investment					Inflation rate	0.0%
SUBTOTAL OUTFLOWS	$ (300.00)	$ -	$ -	$ -		
Cash inflows					FINANCING TERMS	
Rebate/incentive rec'd					Years	n/a
Energy savings		$ 150.00	$ 150.00	$ 150.00	Payments per Year	n/a
Maintenance savings			$ -	$ -	Present Value	n/a
SUBTOTAL INFLOWS	$ -	$ 150.00	$ 150.00	$ 150.00	Interest per Period	n/a
					Future Value	n/a
TOTAL CASH FLOWS	$ (300.00)	$ 150.00	$ 150.00	$ 150.00		
PV	$ (300.00)	$ 136.36	$ 123.97	$ 112.70		
NPV	$ 73.03					
SPP	2.0					
ROI	50.0%					
IRR	23.4%					
MIRR	18.3%					
SIR	1.24					
PV of Outflows (for SIR)	$ (300.00)	$ -	$ -	$ -		
PV of Inflows (for SIR)	$ -	$ 136.36	$ 123.97	$ 112.70		

$$\text{Present Value} = \frac{\text{Cash Flow}}{(1 + \text{Disc. Rate})^N}$$

Slide 3

"Date ____"	TODAY 0	End of YR 1	End of YR 2	End of YR 3	ASSUMPTIONS	
Cash outflows					Discount Rate	10.0%
Single investment	$ (300.00)				Finance Rate	10.0%
Phased investment					Reinvestment Rate	10.0%
Financed investment					Inflation rate	0.0%
SUBTOTAL OUTFLOWS	$ (300.00)	$ -	$ -	$ -		
Cash inflows					FINANCING TERMS	
Rebate/incentive rec'd					Years	n/a
Energy savings		$ 150.00	$ 150.00	$ 150.00	Payments per Year	n/a
Maintenance savings			$ -	$ -	Present Value	n/a
SUBTOTAL INFLOWS	$ -	$ 150.00	$ 150.00	$ 150.00	Interest per Period	n/a
					Future Value	n/a
TOTAL CASH FLOWS	$ (300.00)	$ 150.00	$ 150.00	$ 150.00		
PV	$ (300.00)	$ 136.36	$ 123.97	$ 112.70		
NPV	$ 73.03					
SPP	2.0					
ROI	50.0%					
IRR	23.4%					
MIRR	18.3%					
SIR	1.24					
PV of Outflows (for SIR)	$ (300.00)	$ -	$ -	$ -		
PV of Inflows (for SIR)	$ -	$ 136.36	$ 123.97	$ 112.70		

If the discount rate increases, would the Present Values go up or down?

Slide 4

"Date ____"	TODAY 0	End of YR 1	End of YR 2	End of YR 3	ASSUMPTIONS	
Cash outflows					Discount Rate	15.0%
Single investment	$ (300.00)				Finance Rate	10.0%
Phased investment					Reinvestment Rate	10.0%
Financed investment					Inflation rate	0.0%
SUBTOTAL OUTFLOWS	$ (300.00)	$ -	$ -	$ -		
Cash inflows					FINANCING TERMS	
Rebate/incentive rec'd					Years	n/a
Energy savings		$ 150.00	$ 150.00	$ 150.00	Payments per Year	n/a
Maintenance savings			$ -	$ -	Present Value	n/a
SUBTOTAL INFLOWS	$ -	$ 150.00	$ 150.00	$ 150.00	Interest per Period	n/a
					Future Value	n/a
TOTAL CASH FLOWS	$ (300.00)	$ 150.00	$ 150.00	$ 150.00		
PV	$ (300.00)	$ 130.43	$ 113.42	$ 98.63		
NPV	$ 42.48					
SPP	2.0					
ROI	50.0%					
IRR	23.4%					
MIRR	18.3%					
SIR	1.14					
PV of Outflows (for SIR)	$ (300.00)	$ -	$ -	$ -		
PV of Inflows (for SIR)	$ -	$ 130.43	$ 113.42	$ 98.63		

If the discount rate increases, would the Present Values go up or down?

Slide 5

"Date ____"	TODAY 0	End of YR 1	End of YR 2	End of YR 3	ASSUMPTIONS	
Cash outflows					Discount Rate	15.0%
Single investment	$ (300.00)				Finance Rate	10.0%
Phased investment					Reinvestment Rate	10.0%
Financed investment					Inflation rate	0.0%
SUBTOTAL OUTFLOWS	$ (300.00)	$ -	$ -	$ -		
Cash inflows					FINANCING TERMS	
Rebate/incentive rec'd					Years	n/a
Energy savings		$ 150.00	$ 150.00	$ 150.00	Payments per Year	n/a
Maintenance savings			$ -	$ -	Present Value	n/a
SUBTOTAL INFLOWS	$ -	$ 150.00	$ 150.00	$ 150.00	Interest per Period	n/a
					Future Value	n/a
TOTAL CASH FLOWS	$ (300.00)	$ 150.00	$ 150.00	$ 150.00		
PV	$ (300.00)	$ 130.43	$ 113.42	$ 98.63		
NPV	$ 42.48					
SPP	2.0					
ROI	50.0%					
IRR	23.4%					
MIRR	18.3%					
SIR	1.14					
PV of Outflows (for SIR)	$ (300.00)	$ -	$ -	$ -		
PV of Inflows (for SIR)	$ -	$ 130.43	$ 113.42	$ 98.63		

Higher discount rate lowers the PV in cash flows occurring after Date 0

Slide 6

And if the PV of the cash inflows decreases, NPV also decreases.

Slide 7

"Date ____"	TODAY 0	End of YR 1	End of YR 2	End of YR 3	ASSUMPTIONS	
Cash outflows					Discount Rate	23.4%
Single investment	$ (300.00)				Finance Rate	10.0%
Phased investment					Reinvestment Rate	10.0%
Financed investment					Inflation rate	0.0%
SUBTOTAL OUTFLOWS	$ (300.00)	$ -	$ -	$ -		
Cash inflows					FINANCING TERMS	
Rebate/incentive rec'd					Years	n/a
Energy savings		$ 150.00	$ 150.00	$ 150.00	Payments per Year	n/a
Maintenance savings			$ -	$ -	Present Value	n/a
SUBTOTAL INFLOWS	$ -	$ 150.00	$ 150.00	$ 150.00	Interest per Period	n/a
					Future Value	n/a
TOTAL CASH FLOWS	$ (300.00)	$ 150.00	$ 150.00	$ 150.00		
PV	$ (300.00)	$ 121.58	$ 98.55	$ 79.87		
NPV	$ 0.00					
SPP	2.0					
ROI	50.0%					
IRR	23.4%					
MIRR	18.3%					
SIR	1.00					

And what happens when the discount rate gets even higher?

Slide 8

INTERNAL RATE OF RETURN (IRR)

IDEAS & ACTIONS

www.SellingEnergy.com

The PV of the cash inflows equals the (absolute value of the) PV of the cash outflows…

And at that discount rate (i.e., the Internal Rate of Return), NPV equals 0.

MODIFIED INTERNAL RATE OF RETURN (MIRR)

Modified Internal Rate of Return corrects the shortcomings of IRR

SAVINGS-TO-INVESTMENT RATIO (SIR)

Savings-to-Investment Ratio reflects the PV of cash inflows ÷ |PV of cash outflows|

Discount rate = IRR   NPV = 0   SIR = 1
PV of cash inflows = | PV of cash outflows |

Original discount rate of 10% makes SIR equal to 1.24

IDEAS & ACTIONS

Lesson **73**
FINANCIAL ANALYSIS FUNDAMENTALS
Life-cycle cost analysis

Presented by
Mark Jewell
@SellingEnergy
info@sellingenergy.com

sellingenergy
Turbocharging Success

Life-Cycle Cost Analysis (LCCA)

- Life-Cycle Cost Analysis (LCCA) looks at the total cost of a design choice:
  - First-cost
  - Operation, maintenance and repair costs
  - Financing costs
  - Serviceable life of the design
  - Salvage

Should you use LCCA?

EXAMPLE

Life-Cycle Cost Analysis proves that the option with the higher first cost actually has a lower life-cycle cost over the 15-year analysis term.

OPTION 1
LIFE CYCLE COST OF REPLACING END-OF-LIFE EQUIPMENT "LIKE FOR LIKE"

		Today	Year 1	Year 2	Year 3
First Cost	Costs if done today	$ 348,000			
Annual Energy Cost	$ 33,996		$ 34,676	$ 35,369	$ 36,077
Maintenance Cost A	$ 344		$ 351	$ 358	$ 365
Maintenance Cost B	$ 516		$ 526	$ 537	$ 548
Maintenance Cost C	$ 1,032		$ 1,053	$ 1,074	$ 1,095
Maintenance Cost D	$ 1,032		$ 1,053	$ 1,074	$ 1,095
Maintenance Cost E	$ 344		$ 351	$ 358	$ 365
Maintenance Cost F	$ 2,064		$ 2,105	$ 2,147	$ 2,190
Maintenance Cost G	$ 1,032		$ 1,053	$ 1,074	$ 1,095
Maintenance Cost H	$ 688		$ 702	$ 716	$ 730
Maintenance Cost I	$ 3,840		$ 3,917	$ 3,995	$ 4,075
Maintenance Cost J	$ 1,500		$ 1,530	$ 1,561	$ 1,592
Maintenance Cost K	$ 2,500		$ 2,550	$ 2,601	$ 2,653
Motor Replacement	$ 5,500				
Subtotal of Non-Energy-Related Operating Costs	$ 20,392				
Subtotal by Year		$ 348,000	$ 49,866	$ 50,863	$ 51,880
Present Value by Year		$ 348,000	$ 45,333	$ 42,036	$ 38,978
Life-Cycle Cost for 15 Years	$ 773,079				

OPTION 1
LIFE CYCLE COST OF REPLACING END-OF-LIFE EQUIPMENT "LIKE FOR LIKE"

		Today	Year 1	Year 2	Year 3
First Cost	Costs if done today	$ 348,000			
Annual Energy Cost	$ 33,996		$ 34,676	$ 35,369	$ 36,077
Maintenance Cost A	$ 344		$ 351	$ 358	$ 365
Maintenance Cost B	$ 516		$ 526	$ 537	$ 548
Maintenance Cost C	$ 1,032		$ 1,053	$ 1,074	$ 1,095
Maintenance Cost D	$ 1,032		$ 1,053	$ 1,074	$ 1,095
Maintenance Cost E	$ 344		$ 351	$ 358	$ 365
Maintenance Cost F	$ 2,064		$ 2,105	$ 2,147	$ 2,190
Maintenance Cost G	$ 1,032		$ 1,053	$ 1,074	$ 1,095
Maintenance Cost H	$ 688		$ 702	$ 716	$ 730
Maintenance Cost I	$ 3,840		$ 3,917	$ 3,995	$ 4,075
Maintenance Cost J	$ 1,500		$ 1,530	$ 1,561	$ 1,592
Maintenance Cost K	$ 2,500		$ 2,550	$ 2,601	$ 2,653
Motor Replacement	$ 5,500				
Subtotal of Non-Energy-Related Operating Costs	$ 20,392				
Subtotal by Year		$ 348,000	$ 49,866	$ 50,863	$ 51,880
Present Value by Year		$ 348,000	$ 45,333	$ 42,036	$ 38,978
Life-Cycle Cost for 15 Years	$ 773,079				

OPTION 2
LIFE CYCLE COST OF USING HIGHER-FIRST-COST, PREMIUM-EFFICIENCY EQUIPMENT

		Today	Year 1	Year 2	Year 3
First Cost	Costs if done today	$ 465,880			
Annual Energy Cost	$ 19,450		$ 19,839	$ 20,236	$ 20,640
Maintenance Cost A (now n/a)	$ -				
Maintenance Cost B	$ 516		$ 526	$ 537	$ 548
Maintenance Cost C	$ 1,032		$ 1,053	$ 1,074	$ 1,095
Maintenance Cost D (now n/a)	$ -				
Maintenance Cost E	$ 344		$ 351	$ 358	$ 365
Maintenance Cost F (now n/a)	$ -				
Maintenance Cost G	$ 1,032		$ 1,053	$ 1,074	$ 1,095
Maintenance Cost H	$ 688		$ 702	$ 716	$ 730
Maintenance Cost I	$ 3,840		$ 3,917	$ 3,995	$ 4,075
Maintenance Cost J	$ 1,500		$ 1,530	$ 1,561	$ 1,592
Maintenance Cost K (now n/a)	$ -				
Motor Replacement	$ 1,100				
Subtotal of Non-Energy-Related Operating Costs	$ 10,052				
Subtotal by Year		$ 465,880	$ 28,970	$ 29,549	$ 30,140
Present Value by Year		$ 465,880	$ 26,336	$ 24,421	$ 22,645
Life-Cycle Cost for 15 Years	$ 711,849				

OPTION 2
LIFE CYCLE COST OF USING HIGHER-FIRST-COST, PREMIUM-EFFICIENCY EQUIPMENT

		Today	Year 1	Year 2	Year 3
First Cost	Costs if done today	$ 465,880			
Annual Energy Cost	$ 19,450		$ 19,839	$ 20,236	$ 20,640
Maintenance Cost A (now n/a)	$ -				
Maintenance Cost B	$ 516		$ 526	$ 537	$ 548
Maintenance Cost C	$ 1,032		$ 1,053	$ 1,074	$ 1,095
Maintenance Cost D (now n/a)	$ -				
Maintenance Cost E	$ 344		$ 351	$ 358	$ 365
Maintenance Cost F (now n/a)	$ -				
Maintenance Cost G	$ 1,032		$ 1,053	$ 1,074	$ 1,095
Maintenance Cost H	$ 688		$ 702	$ 716	$ 730
Maintenance Cost I	$ 3,840		$ 3,917	$ 3,995	$ 4,075
Maintenance Cost J	$ 1,500		$ 1,530	$ 1,561	$ 1,592
Maintenance Cost K (now n/a)	$ -				
Motor Replacement	$ 1,100				
Subtotal of Non-Energy-Related Operating Costs	$ 10,052				
Subtotal by Year		$ 465,880	$ 28,970	$ 29,549	$ 30,140
Present Value by Year		$ 465,880	$ 26,336	$ 24,421	$ 22,645
Life-Cycle Cost for 15 Years	$ 711,849				

IDEAS & ACTIONS

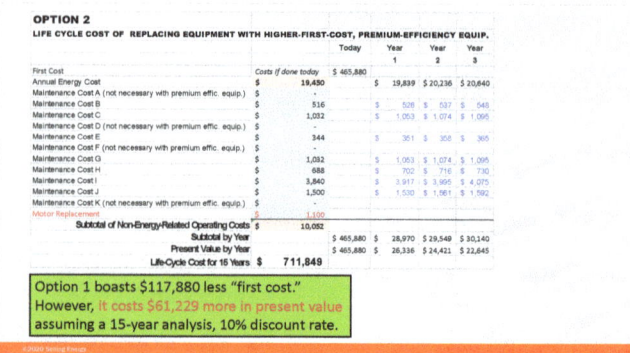

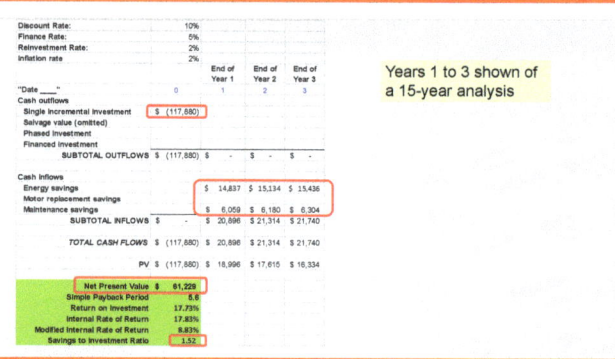

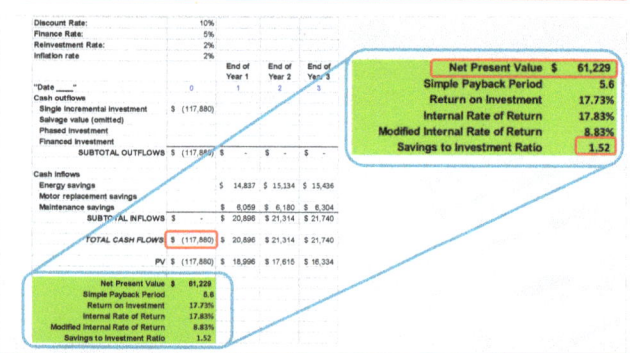

Years 1 to 3 shown of a 15-year analysis

Lesson 74
FINANCIAL ANALYSIS FUNDAMENTALS
Financial analysis in landlord/tenant settings

Presented by
Mark Jewell
@SellingEnergy
info@sellingenergy.com

selling in 6™

selling energy
Turbocharging Success

Owner-occupied properties

More Competitive	More Profitable	More Valuable
Lower occupancy cost enables competitive pricing	Lowering "heat, power and light" improves profitability; reduces risk of price spikes	Lower operating expense increases earnings per share
Sustainability & comfort can help attract or retain employees, investors, and customers	Greater comfort & convenience supports higher productivity	More efficient facilities have higher resale values

Income properties

More Competitive	More Profitable	More Valuable
Lower occupancy cost	Better tenant retention & attraction	Higher rent revenue increases cash flow
Enhanced comfort & productivity	Lower vacancy rates result in higher rent revenue	Lower operating costs increase cash flow
Sustainability that gives marketing advantage	Lower tenant utility bills support higher base rents	Higher net operating income (NOI) supports higher appraisal

IDEAS & ACTIONS

"When you purchase an income-producing property, you get the 'sticks and bricks'… but what you're buying is a box of leases."

What kind of lease did you say it was?

"Fixed-Base"   "Net"   "Rent Inclusion"   "Gross"

"Electric Rent Inclusion Factor"   "Plus Cleans"   "Net of Electric"

"Full Service"   "Plus Electric & Cleaning"

"Plus Electric & Cleans"   "Porter's Wage"

"Plus Lights & Plugs"

"Industrial Gross"   "Triple Net" ("NNN")

"Double Net" ("NN")   "Tenant Electric"

"Plus All Utilities"

"Hybrid"

"Modified Gross"

Graphic excerpted from Jewell-authored leasing brief for BetterBricks

---

Q:

Isn't it really just about who pays and who benefits?

Yes, and the 3 major lease types are…

- Net
- Gross
- Fixed-base*

* Fixed-base leases typically use an "expense-stop" or "base year" to describe the level of expenses included in the rent.

The "fixed-base" lease

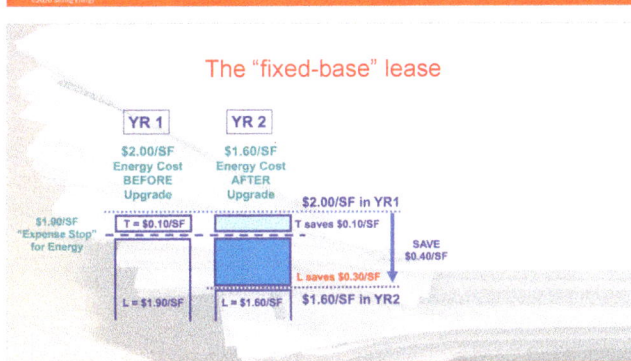

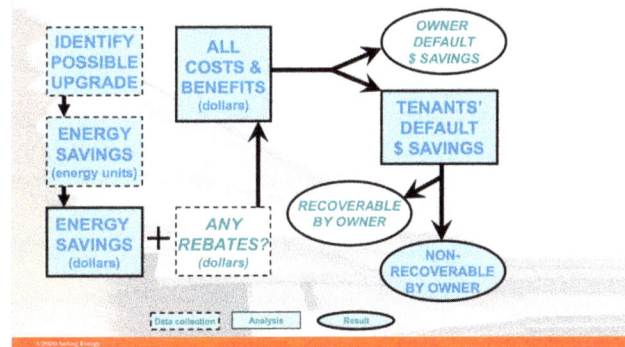

Tips for financial analysis in income property

1. Be sure to view the other lessons in this program related to landlord/tenant settings.

2. Be sure to allocate each cash inflow and outflow, or portions thereof, to the landlord and the appropriate tenant(s) so that you can accurately represent who pays and who benefits.

---

selling in 6™

Lesson 75
OVERCOMING MYTHS AND OBJECTIONS
"My building is already efficient."

Presented by
Mark Jewell
@SellingEnergy
info@sellingenergy.com

Turbocharging Success

IDEAS & ACTIONS

"My building is already energy-efficient."

"My building is already efficient"

- "My building was designed to be efficient."
- "My building was built to code."
- "My building already has an ENERGY STAR® label."
- "My building is LEED®-certified."

Lesson 75.1

OVERCOMING MYTHS AND OBJECTIONS
"My building was designed to be efficient."

Presented by
Mark Jewell
@SellingEnergy
info@sellingenergy.com

Turbocharging Success

"Our design is already efficient."

What does "efficient design" really mean?

1. Do you mean to say that the building was built to code, which you presume was "efficient" at the time, or did the engineering team specify some additional degree of efficiency beyond code?

What does "efficient design" really mean?

2. If the engineering team specified a higher level of efficiency, were they designing to exceed code by a certain %, or perhaps to meet a particular higher benchmark?

What does "efficient design" really mean?

3. Was the building commissioned before occupancy to ensure that the design intent was actually met (e.g., that value engineering and/or contractor substitutions didn't compromise the design)?

What does "efficient design" really mean?

4. Have there been significant changes to the layout, equipment, occupancy profile, etc. since the building was constructed?

IDEAS & ACTIONS

What does "efficient design" really mean?

5. Have you considered the design of all spaces, rather than just the common areas?

What does "efficient design" really mean?

6. Are there building efficiency standards in place to ensure that occupants adhere to efficient design guidelines when doing tenant fit-outs or renovations and/or bringing energy-consuming equipment into the building?

What does "efficient design" really mean?

7. Can you be sure that the current building operators and occupants understand how to maximize efficiency?

What does "efficient design" really mean?

8. Has the building been re-commissioned (or retroactively commissioned) recently to ensure that the design intent is still being satisfied given the current occupancy profile?

What does "efficient design" really mean?

9. Has the building been benchmarked recently using US EPA's Portfolio Manager® software to see how its performance compares with similar buildings on a normalized basis, and if so, what was its score?

What does "efficient design" really mean?

10. If you were to design and build today, would you incorporate a higher level of efficiency into your design (especially given how new technologies have lowered the cost of higher efficiency)?

Lesson 75.2
OVERCOMING MYTHS AND OBJECTIONS
"My building was built to code."

Presented by
Mark Jewell
@SellingEnergy
info@sellingenergy.com

IDEAS & ACTIONS

www.SellingEnergy.com

Does "built to code" really mean "efficient"?

1. What year was the building built*?
2. Do you happen to know what energy efficiency code was in place at that time?

*You could research when the building was built, as well as the vintage of major renovations and additions before your first meeting.

Does "built to code" really mean "efficient"?

3. Are you confident that building was inspected and found to be in compliance with code after it was built?
4. Has the building been benchmarked recently, and if so, how high was the score?

selling in 6™

Lesson 75.3
OVERCOMING MYTHS AND OBJECTIONS
"My building has the ENERGY STAR® label."

Presented by
Mark Jewell
@SellingEnergy
info@sellingenergy.com

sellingenergy
Turbocharging Success

ENERGY STAR

What does this benchmarking really tell us?

1. How recently was the building benchmarked?

What does this benchmarking really tell us?

2. What was its score?

What does this benchmarking really tell us?

3. Were you aware that the US EPA recently changed the baselines for its ratings?

What does this benchmarking really tell us?

4. Were you aware that there is a large difference in energy use between, say, a score of 75 and 99?

IDEAS & ACTIONS

What does this benchmarking really tell us?

5. Were you aware that the ENERGY STAR® score is based on source kBTU rather than site kBTU, and if you use on-site solar/wind, you could have a better score (due to the specially assigned 1:1 multiplier of source-to-site energy) even though you still have plenty of efficiency potential remaining to be harvested?

What does this benchmarking really tell us?

6. Was your building's benchmarking exercise verified by a professional engineer or other licensed building professional?

Lesson 75.4
OVERCOMING MYTHS AND OBJECTIONS
"We're more focused on LEED® certification."

Presented by
Mark Jewell
@SellingEnergy
info@sellingenergy.com

Turbocharging Success

"Our building must be efficient because it is LEED®-certified."

Does LEED® certification imply "efficiency"?

1. Has your building been benchmarked for energy efficiency in particular?

Does LEED® certification imply "efficiency"?

2. Were you aware that many LEED®-certified buildings could not qualify for the ENERGY STAR® label because they were not in the top quartile when rated on efficiency?

Does LEED® certification imply "efficiency"?

3. How long ago did your building attain LEED® status?

How closely is LEED® related to "efficiency"?

4. Have there been changes to the configuration and/or operation of the building since then?

IDEAS & ACTIONS

How closely is LEED® related to "efficiency"?

5. Does it make sense to pursue a rating called "Leadership in Energy and Environmental Design®" without paying close and ongoing attention to the energy resources that the building consumes?

How closely is LEED® related to "efficiency"?

6. And of course, LEED® rewards increasing levels of energy performance, so the higher that performance, the better the LEED® score.

Lesson 76
OVERCOMING MYTHS AND OBJECTIONS
"We're already as efficient as possible."

Presented by
Mark Jewell
@SellingEnergy
info@sellingenergy.com

"We're already as efficient as possible"

- "My building is older, so naturally it's less efficient."
- "It's riskier to build a high-performance building."
- "Landlord/tenant split incentive stymies efficiency."

Lesson 76.1
OVERCOMING MYTHS AND OBJECTIONS
"Our building is older, so naturally it's less efficient."

Presented by
Mark Jewell
@SellingEnergy
info@sellingenergy.com

"Our building is older, so you would expect it to be less energy-efficient."

Does it really matter how old the building is?

1. Did you know that the oldest building to receive the ENERGY STAR® label is more than 100 years old?
2. Many old buildings have replaced their equipment at end of life with more efficient models.

Does it really matter how old the building is?

3. Meanwhile, too many new buildings have been value-engineered with less-efficient equipment.
4. And how much of a building's energy performance is due to how it's operated rather than the age of its energy-consuming equipment?

IDEAS & ACTIONS

Lesson 76.2
OVERCOMING MYTHS AND OBJECTIONS
"It's riskier to build a high-performance building."

Presented by
Mark Jewell
@SellingEnergy
info@sellingenergy.com

"It's riskier to build a high-performance building."

High-performance is the most prudent path

1. Building anything less than a high-performance building exposes the owner and occupants to additional risk...
   - Potential "brown" discounts on appraisals
   - Technological obsolescence
   - Regulatory compliance
   - Exposure to utility price spikes and carbon taxes
   - Tenant attraction/retention difficulties
   - And more.

High-performance is the most prudent path

2. The architectural and engineering (A&E) community has ample experience designing and constructing high-performance buildings.

High-performance is the most prudent path

3. There is growing evidence that high-performance can be attained at the same (or even lower) cost than conventional construction.
4. Moreover, the life-cycle cost of a high-performance building is certainly lower.

Lesson 76.3
OVERCOMING MYTHS AND OBJECTIONS
"Landlord/tenant split incentive stymies efficiency."

Presented by
Mark Jewell
@SellingEnergy
info@sellingenergy.com

Addressing the "split incentive" with landlords/tenants

1. Virtually all lease forms either already contain language or can be amended with language addressing "who pays" and "who benefits" to overcome the split incentive.

IDEAS & ACTIONS

www.SellingEnergy.com

Addressing the "split incentive" with landlords/tenants

2. Harnessing the energy efficiency potential in an income-producing property can raise net operating income (NOI) and asset value.

Addressing the "split incentive" with landlords/tenants

3. Installing efficient equipment that also improves occupant comfort and convenience can drive significant benefits to the occupants as well.

Lesson 77
OVERCOMING MYTHS AND OBJECTIONS
"We're working on efficiency at our own pace."

Presented by
Mark Jewell
@SellingEnergy
info@sellingenergy.com

"We're working on efficiency at our own pace."

- "Our manager knows all about energy efficiency."
- "We've already done the low-hanging fruit."
- "We prefer to phase-in upgrades over time."
- "We wait to upgrade until the end of useful life."
- "We'll wait until we have a bit more cushion."

Lesson 77.1
OVERCOMING MYTHS AND OBJECTIONS
"Our manager knows all about energy efficiency."

Presented by
Mark Jewell
@SellingEnergy
info@sellingenergy.com

"Our 3rd-party manager knows all about energy efficiency."

Is it wise to depend on your manager for this?

1. Do you have your manager do your housekeeping?
2. Do you have your manager do your landscaping?
3. Why not? Because both housekeeping and landscaping require specific skills and tools as well as time...

IDEAS & ACTIONS _____

_____

_____

_____

Is it wise to depend on your manager for this?

4. So, does your property manager have the skills, tools, and time to do justice to this important value-creation activity?
5. Does your manager have the time/inclination to stay up-to-date on all building technologies and efficiency strategies?

Is it wise to depend on your manager for this?

6. Does he have experience with dozens (or hundreds) of similar buildings so he can evaluate your relative performance?
7. Does your manager have access to the most current studies documenting non-utility-cost financial and non-financial savings?

Is it wise to depend on your manager for this?

8. Does your manager tend to evaluate projects based on simple payback period?
9. Is your manager comfortable calculating (and explaining) net present value, savings-to-investment ratio, and life-cycle cost?

And if you own an income-producing property...

10. Has your manager read your leases lately?
11. Do they clearly understand who would pay and who would benefit from efficiency improvements in both the tenant spaces and common areas if you were to proceed with this energy initiative?

And if you own an income-producing property...

12. Have they explained to any vendors that their recommendations need to be delineated based on whether the energy loads are tenant- or landlord-related?

And if you own an income-producing property...

13. Is the manager familiar with the nuances of Capital Expense Cost Recovery?
14. Do they know precisely how the costs and savings of energy efficiency measures would be reflected in the year-end lease accounting?

And if you own an income-producing property...

15. And is your manager comfortable extending the analysis to how the investment would positively impact net operating income (NOI) and asset value?
    - Lower landlord share of operating costs
    - Higher tenant retention/attraction
    - Lower tenant fit-out expenses
    - Less demand on CapEx reserves
    - Potentially lower capitalization rate
    - And more...

And regardless of the type of property...

16. Do your manager's upgrade recommendations communicate the true costs and benefits to the capital budgeting decision-makers?

IDEAS & ACTIONS

And **regardless** of the type of property...

17. Is your manager comfortable preparing and presenting both of the following documents?
- A compelling **one-page narrative proposal** focused on the "why" (with a technical appendix for the what, how, how much and when)
- A **one-page financial analysis** highlighting the proper metrics (MIRR, SIR, NPV, and life-cycle cost if applicable)

Lesson 77.2
OVERCOMING MYTHS AND OBJECTIONS
"We've already done the low-hanging fruit."

 Presented by **Mark Jewell** @SellingEnergy info@sellingenergy.com

"We have already done the low-hanging fruit."

What does "low-hanging fruit" really mean?

1. It had the shortest simple payback period?
2. It could be done by your own staff in their spare time?
3. It didn't require you to go out to bid?
4. It could be done as part of normal replacements?
5. It was limited to lighting measures?
6. It was limited to building common area?
7. It was limited to rebate-eligible measures?
8. It was limited to high-power-cost areas?
9. Etc., etc., etc.

A tip from a seasoned sales professional...

Responding to an objection like this is like frisking a wet seal!

You need to get your arms around what the prospect really meant before you can productively respond.

Lesson 77.3
OVERCOMING MYTHS AND OBJECTIONS
"We prefer to phase-in upgrades over time."

 Presented by **Mark Jewell** @SellingEnergy info@sellingenergy.com

"**Phasing** the measures will be better than doing them all at once."

IDEAS & ACTIONS

How about the downsides of phased upgrades?

1. Delaying the start of savings from some of the work, which could result in significantly lower returns (see following chart for examples)

2. Delaying the start of potential non-utility-cost financial and non-financial benefits, which are often much larger than the utility-cost financial savings

How about the downsides of phased upgrades?

3. Missing the opportunity to get greater economy-of-scale in materials/labor as well as project management

4. Potentially losing the opportunity to collect rebates/incentives in future periods if program qualifications change or available funding is exhausted

"Value is created by the compression of time."
- Peter Drucker

"Value is created by the compression of time"
— Peter Drucker

	Assume 10 upgrade projects (five 4-year SPP & five 2.5-year SPP)	
	Scenario A 10 projects this year	Scenario B 2 projects per year
Total Cap Ex	$1,681,000	$1,764,503
PV of Investment	$1,681,000	$1,241,656
NPV	$1,016,071*	$578,366
NPV of "avoided cost of delay"		$437,705

75% higher NPV helps build shareholder value faster

How about the downsides of phased upgrades?

5. If you need to borrow capital to accelerate the pace of the projects, compare any interest you'll pay to the higher net present value of doing all the projects now.

How about the downsides of phased upgrades?

6. Calculate the NPV of the following 3 scenarios for your project and compare...
   * A: 100% funded at "Date 0" (today) using cash
   * B: 100% funded at "Date 0" using 3-year financing
   * C: 50% funded at "Date 0"; 50% at "Date 1"; using cash

   A's NPV is highest; B's NPV is a close 2nd; C's NPV is significantly lower, mainly because of missing Year 1 savings on the second half of the installation.

How about the downsides of phased upgrades?

7. If you don't have the management bandwidth to implement all the projects this year, think of how much outsourced project management talent you could fund with that same net present value premium.

How about the downsides of phased upgrades?

8. And how soon would you like to begin enjoying the non-utility-cost financial and non-financial benefits?

IDEAS & ACTIONS

Lesson 77.4
OVERCOMING MYTHS AND OBJECTIONS
"We wait to upgrade until the end of useful life."

Presented by
Mark Jewell
@SellingEnergy
info@sellingenergy.com

Turbocharging Success

"It would be a waste to replace the equipment before it stops running."

How about the downsides of waiting?

1. Think of the savings you'll be forgoing while you wait for the present equipment to fail.
2. And does this equipment typically fail in periods of low load or high load?

How about the downsides of waiting?

3. And what happens when it fails at an inopportune time?
   - Interrupting your operations
   - Renting temporary equipment under duress
   - Specifying the quick-ship option with "rush service"
   - Paying overtime labor to replace it

How about the downsides of waiting?

4. And what else happens when it fails at an inopportune time?
   - Likely maroon further savings for another life-cycle of the replacement equipment since the most efficient models are probably not stocked at the distributor, much less part of their "quick-ship" program

Discount Rate 10%
O&M Annual Inflation % 3%

OPTION 1
LIFE-CYCLE COST OF WAITING TO REPLACE EQUIPMENT FOR 5 MORE YEARS

	Today	Year 1	Year 2	Year 3	Year 4	Year 5
	Valued at Date 0					
Equip. Replaced at End of Year 5	$ 20,388					$ 23,636
Annual Energy Cost for Existing Equip.	$ 25,000		25,750	$ 26,523	$ 27,318	$ 28,138	$ 28,982
Annual Maint. for Existing Equip.	$ 3,000		3,090	$ 3,183	$ 3,278	$ 3,377	$ 3,478
Subtotal by Year	$ -	$ 28,840	$ 29,705	$ 30,596	$ 31,514	$ 56,095
Present Value by Year	$ -	$ 26,218	$ 24,550	$ 22,987	$ 21,525	$ 34,831
Life-Cycle Cost for First 5 Years	$ 130,111					

OPTION 2
LIFE-CYCLE COST OF INSTALLING THE NEW EQUIPMENT TODAY

	Today	Year 1	Year 2	Year 3	Year 4	Year 5
Equip. Replaced Now	$ 20,388	$ 20,388					
Annual Energy Cost for New Equip.	$ 18,204		18,750	$ 19,313	$ 19,892	$ 20,489	$ 21,103
Annual Maint. for New Equip.	$ 2,000		2,060	$ 2,122	$ 2,185	$ 2,251	$ 2,319
Subtotal by Year	$ 20,388	$ 20,811	$ 21,436	$ 22,080	$ 22,744	$ 23,427
Present Value by Year	$ 20,388	$ 18,919	$ 17,716	$ 16,589	$ 15,534	$ 14,546
Life-Cycle Cost for First 5 Years	$ 103,693					

Incremental PV Cost of
OPTION 1 $ 26,418

Discount Rate 10%
O&M Annual Inflation % 3%

OPTION 1
LIFE-CYCLE COST OF WAITING TO REPLACE EQUIPMENT FOR 5 MORE YEARS

	Today	Year 1	Year 2	Year 3	Year 4	Year 5
	Valued at Date 0					
Equip. Replaced at End of Year 5	$ 20,388					$ 23,636
Annual Energy Cost for Existing Equip.	$ 25,000		25,750	$ 26,523	$ 27,318	$ 28,138	$ 28,982
Annual Maint. for Existing Equip.	$ 3,000		3,090	$ 3,183	$ 3,278	$ 3,377	$ 3,478
Subtotal by Year	$ -	$ 28,840	$ 29,705	$ 30,596	$ 31,514	$ 56,095
Present Value by Year	$ -	$ 26,218	$ 24,550	$ 22,987	$ 21,525	$ 34,831
Life-Cycle Cost for First 5 Years	$ 130,111					

OPTION 2
LIFE-CYCLE COST OF INSTALLING THE NEW EQUIPMENT TODAY

	Today	Year 1	Year 2	Year 3	Year 4	Year 5
Equip. Replaced Now	$ 20,388	$ 20,388					
Annual Energy Cost for New Equip.	$ 18,204		18,750	$ 19,313	$ 19,892	$ 20,489	$ 21,103
Annual Maint. for New Equip.	$ 2,000		2,060	$ 2,122	$ 2,185	$ 2,251	$ 2,319
Subtotal by Year	$ 20,388	$ 20,811	$ 21,436	$ 22,080	$ 22,744	$ 23,427
Present Value by Year	$ 20,388	$ 18,919	$ 17,716	$ 16,589	$ 15,534	$ 14,546
Life-Cycle Cost for First 5 Years	$ 103,693					

Incremental PV Cost of
OPTION 1 $ 26,418

IDEAS & ACTIONS

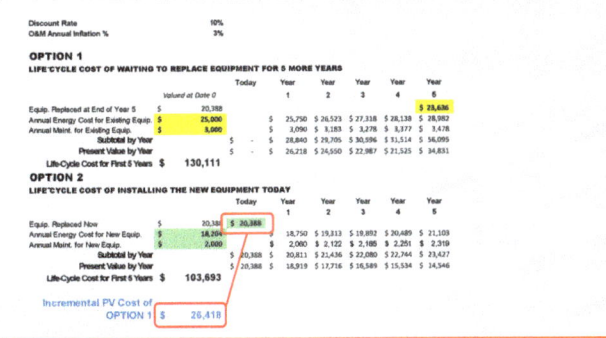

Discount Rate   10%
O&M Annual Inflation %   3%

OPTION 1
LIFE CYCLE COST OF WAITING TO REPLACE EQUIPMENT FOR 5 MORE YEARS

	Today	Year 1	Year 2	Year 3	Year 4	Year 5
	Valued at Date 0					
Equip. Replaced at End of Year 5	20,388					$ 28,636
Annual Energy Cost for Existing Equip.	$ 25,000	$ 25,750	$ 26,523	$ 27,318	$ 28,138	$ 28,982
Annual Maint. for Existing Equip.	$ 3,000	$ 3,090	$ 3,183	$ 3,278	$ 3,377	$ 3,478
Subtotal by Year	$ —	$ 28,840	$ 29,705	$ 30,596	$ 31,514	$ 56,095
Present Value by Year	$ —	$ 26,218	$ 24,550	$ 22,987	$ 21,525	$ 34,831
Life-Cycle Cost for First 5 Years	$ 130,111					

OPTION 2
LIFE CYCLE COST OF INSTALLING THE NEW EQUIPMENT TODAY

	Today	Year 1	Year 2	Year 3	Year 4	Year 5
Equip. Replaced Now	$ 30,388	$ 30,388				
Annual Energy Cost for New Equip.	$ 18,204	$ 18,750	$ 19,313	$ 19,892	$ 20,489	$ 21,103
Annual Maint. for New Equip.	$ 2,000	$ 2,060	$ 2,122	$ 2,185	$ 2,251	$ 2,319
Subtotal by Year	$ 20,388	$ 30,811	$ 21,436	$ 22,080	$ 22,744	$ 23,427
Present Value by Year	$ 20,388	$ 18,919	$ 17,716	$ 16,589	$ 15,534	$ 14,546
Life-Cycle Cost for First 5 Years	$ 103,693					

Incremental PV Cost of OPTION 1 $ 26,418

selling in 6™

Lesson 77.5
OVERCOMING MYTHS AND OBJECTIONS
"We'll wait until we have a bit more cushion."

Presented by
Mark Jewell
@SellingEnergy
info@sellingenergy.com

selling energy
Turbocharging Success

©2020 Selling Energy

"We'll wait until next year when we'll have a little more cushion to afford it."

Let's talk about financial "cushions"...

1. When is the last time you had a surplus in your budget large enough to enable significant discretionary spending?

Let's talk about financial "cushions"...

2. Imagine how much lower your operating expenses would be today if you had already replaced this equipment by repurposing the dollars you were wasting on overly large utility bills...

Let's talk about financial "cushions"...

3. Wouldn't capturing these savings now help you build up an actual financial cushion faster?

Let's talk about financial "cushions"...

4. And remember, whether you do this project or not, you're still paying for it....
   - If you do it, you'll be repurposing dollars you'd be spending on wasted utilities
   - If you don't do it, you'll be paying out those same dollars, but getting nothing in return

---

selling in 6™

Lesson 78
OVERCOMING MYTHS AND OBJECTIONS
"We would prefer to wait to see what's next."

Presented by
Mark Jewell
@SellingEnergy
info@sellingenergy.com

selling energy
Turbocharging Success

©2020 Selling Energy

IDEAS & ACTIONS

"We prefer to wait to see what's next."

- "New technologies would be even more efficient."
- "Upgrades made sense when there were more rebates."
- "We're waiting for a new rebate program to open."

Lesson 78.1
OVERCOMING MYTHS AND OBJECTIONS
"New technologies will be even more efficient."

Presented by
Mark Jewell
@SellingEnergy
info@sellingenergy.com

"New technologies are coming, and they'll be even more efficient."

The **paralysis of waiting** for the next new thing...

1. When the first time you bought a computer? *Why did you buy it then?* They're so much faster and cheaper now!

The **paralysis of waiting** for the next new thing...

2. Technology does improve over time; however, you could probably pay for the current generation of efficient technology through savings way before the new generation becomes available.

Lesson 78.2
OVERCOMING MYTHS AND OBJECTIONS
"Upgrades made sense when there were rebates."

Presented by
Mark Jewell
@SellingEnergy
info@sellingenergy.com

"Energy-efficiency upgrades used to make sense when there were a lot more rebates."

The **perils** of letting rebates drive your timing...

1. While a rebate/incentive can improve the financials, what portion of your project's net present value would it represent?

2. Have you compared the returns your project will generate (even in the absence of rebates or incentives) to alternative investments?

IDEAS & ACTIONS

The **perils** of letting rebates drive your timing...

3. Have you considered the non-utility-cost financial and non-financial benefits to doing the project?
4. Is it worth sacrificing those benefits, waiting for rebates or incentives to return or to become more generous?

Lesson 78.3
OVERCOMING MYTHS AND OBJECTIONS
"We're waiting for a new rebate program to open."

Presented by
Mark Jewell
@SellingEnergy
info@sellingenergy.com

The **perils** of letting rebates drive your timing...

1. While a rebate/incentive can improve a project's financials, what portion of your project's net present value would it represent?
2. Which is larger: the anticipated rebate, or the returns you'll lose while you're waiting for the new rebate program to open?

The **perils** of letting rebates drive your timing...

3. Have you considered the non-utility-cost financial and non-financial benefits to doing the project?
4. Is it worth sacrificing those benefits, plus the utility-cost financial savings, waiting for a new rebate or incentive to arrive?

The **perils** of letting rebates drive your timing...

5. And what if the new rebate or incentive program you're anticipating is delayed... or never comes?

Lesson 79
OVERCOMING MYTHS AND OBJECTIONS
"Upgrading our space doesn't make sense."

Presented by
Mark Jewell
@SellingEnergy
info@sellingenergy.com

"Upgrading our space doesn't make sense."

- "We don't own the building."
- "We may vacate before the upgrade's SPP."
- "We know we're moving this year."

IDEAS & ACTIONS

www.SellingEnergy.com

Lesson 79.1
OVERCOMING MYTHS AND OBJECTIONS
"We don't own the building."

Presented by
Mark Jewell
@SellingEnergy
info@sellingenergy.com

You may not own it, but you do occupy the space

1. Have you considered the non-utility-cost financial and non-financial benefits to doing the project?

You may not own it, but you do occupy the space

2. Would those benefits help you more than recoup the first cost before you vacate, even though you'll likely leave the improvement behind when you do?

You may not own it, but you do occupy the space

3. And what is your share of the utility-cost savings and any rebate/incentive?

You may not own it, but you do occupy the space

4. Have you suggested to the landlord that you use your lease's Capital Expense Cost Recovery language (or add it to the lease) and have the landlord pay for the improvement?

You may not own it, but you do occupy the space

4. Consider the "win-win" results…
   - You would enjoy the non-utility-cost and non-financial benefits immediately.
   - Your landlord repurposes dollars you have been wasting on utility costs to install improvements that will likely outlive your tenancy.
   - If you agree to share (even a portion of) the savings via a permanent rent increase, the Landlord's Net Operating Income would increase, supporting a higher appraised value for the building.

Lesson 79.2
OVERCOMING MYTHS AND OBJECTIONS
"We may vacate before the upgrade's SPP."

Presented by
Mark Jewell
@SellingEnergy
info@sellingenergy.com

IDEAS & ACTIONS

Are you *sure* you're leaving? And what about...

1. Have you considered the non-utility-cost financial and non-financial benefits to doing the project?
2. Would those benefits help you more than recoup the first cost before you vacate, even though you'll likely leave the upgrades behind when you do?

Are you *sure* you're leaving? And what about...

3. And how about your share of the utility-cost savings and any rebate/incentive?
4. And do you have any lease renewals you might exercise?

Are you *sure* you're leaving? And what about...

5. How much have you invested in the fixtures and finishes here?
6. Are your customers in the area? How about your workforce? How likely is it you'll actually leave?

Lesson 79.3
OVERCOMING MYTHS AND OBJECTIONS
"We know we're moving this year."

Presented by
Mark Jewell
@SellingEnergy
info@sellingenergy.com

Where are you moving? And who is taking your space?

1. Great, where are you moving? Let's talk about upgrading that new space, perhaps even in the context of your new landlord's fit-out allowance.

Where are you moving? And who is taking your space?

2. May I please have contact info for your current landlord? Perhaps he or his new tenant would opt to do this upgrade here after you leave.

IDEAS & ACTIONS

www.SellingEnergy.com

Lesson 80
OVERCOMING MYTHS AND OBJECTIONS
"We can't focus on the opportunity right now."

Presented by
Mark Jewell
@SellingEnergy
info@sellingenergy.com

"We can't focus on the opportunity right now."

- "We're busy with other projects now."
- "We don't have the manpower."
- "Energy is not a significant factor in our success."
- "Even if we saved money, we wouldn't see it."

Lesson 80.1
OVERCOMING MYTHS AND OBJECTIONS
"We're busy with other projects now."

Presented by
Mark Jewell
@SellingEnergy
info@sellingenergy.com

"We're busy with other projects now."

What are you working on these days?

1. Do any of the projects you're working on have an energy component?
2. Would you like me to take a look to see if fine-tuning any of your current projects would allow them to be more efficient in the long run?

Lesson 80.2
OVERCOMING MYTHS AND OBJECTIONS
"We don't have the manpower."

Presented by
Mark Jewell
@SellingEnergy
info@sellingenergy.com

"We don't have the manpower."

IDEAS & ACTIONS

How much is needed... And how would you like more?

1. How much manpower do you think you need to support the project we've been discussing? Keep in mind that we are a turn-key operation and will minimize the burden we place on your staff.

How much is needed... And how would you like more?

2. If you're short-staffed, think about how you might repurpose some of these savings to fund additional, *permanent* headcount.

Lesson 80.3
OVERCOMING MYTHS AND OBJECTIONS
"Energy is not a significant factor in our success."

Presented by
Mark Jewell
@SellingEnergy
info@sellingenergy.com

Lesson 80.4
OVERCOMING MYTHS AND OBJECTIONS
"Even if we saved money, we wouldn't see it."

Presented by
Mark Jewell
@SellingEnergy
info@sellingenergy.com

I understand; however, energy's impact can be huge

1. For most of our clients, the energy line item is a small fraction of their profit and loss statement.
2. However, the non-utility-cost financial and non-financial benefits of installing energy upgrades can drive huge benefits for your organization.

I understand; however, energy's impact can be huge

1. For most of our clients, the energy line item is a small fraction of their profit and loss statement, so even if they received the cash savings (and rebate/incentive), it wouldn't be a large sum.

IDEAS & ACTIONS

www.SellingEnergy.com

I understand; however, *energy's impact* can be huge

2. However, the non-utility-cost financial and non-financial benefits of installing energy upgrades can drive huge benefits for your organization, and those you *do* get to keep.

Lesson 81
OVERCOMING MYTHS AND OBJECTIONS
"We can't get energy projects approved."

Presented by
Mark Jewell
@SellingEnergy
info@sellingenergy.com

Turbocharging Success

"We can't get energy projects approved."

- "We don't have the budget."
- "Capital and operating budgets are different silos."
- "We only approve projects with very short SPP."
- "Our CFO doesn't believe in monthly payments."
- "Hurdle rates are higher for non-core projects."
- "Rebates are too difficult to find and capture."
- "Procurement favors value engineering."
- "We need to *lower* our utility spend, not raise it."

Lesson 81.1
OVERCOMING MYTHS AND OBJECTIONS
"We don't have the budget."

Presented by
Mark Jewell
@SellingEnergy
info@sellingenergy.com

Turbocharging Success

"We don't have the budget."

OPERATING BUDGET ITEMS
Expenses that occur within the current fiscal year.

EXAMPLES
Utilities, housekeeping, roads and grounds, repairs and maintenance, security, and administrative.

CAPITAL BUDGET ITEMS
Expenses that involve periods longer than a year and are capitalized, appearing as long-term assets on the balance sheet.

EXAMPLES
Tenant fit-outs, new parking lot, new chiller, etc.

IDEAS & ACTIONS _____

_____

_____

_____

www.SellingEnergy.com

First, clarify the prospect's budget situation...

1. Which budget are you referring to, the Operating budget, or the Capital budget?

First, clarify the prospect's budget situation...

2. If you were speaking of the Operating budget, who drafts it, who approves it, and when?
3. Do you have the ability to move money from the Utilities line item to a new line item called "Debt Service on 3rd-party Financing for Energy Upgrades"?

First, clarify the prospect's budget situation...

4. I bet you have the money needed to accomplish this upgrade (with the help of financing) in your Operating budget, since you're paying your (overly large) utility bills every month, right?

First, clarify the prospect's budget situation...

5. If you were speaking of the Capital budget, who drafts it, who approves it, and when?
6. And how often are adjustments made in the middle of a fiscal year?

First, clarify the prospect's budget situation...

7. Could you borrow the money and then pass along the cost to another party (e.g., Capital Expense Cost Recovery, which would allow you to amortize the principal and perhaps charge interest to the tenant(s) who would benefit from the savings)?

First, clarify the prospect's budget situation...

8. Have you thought about innovative approaches to financing like PACE?

*Property Assessed Clean Energy, available in certain jurisdictions.

---

selling in 6™

Lesson 81.2
OVERCOMING MYTHS AND OBJECTIONS
"Capital and operating budgets are different silos."

Presented by
Mark Jewell
@SellingEnergy
info@sellingenergy.com

sellingenergy
Turbocharging Success

IDEAS & ACTIONS

First, clarify the prospect's budget situation...

1. Have you ever seen those responsible for the Capital and Operating budgets actually collaborate for a common cause?
2. Who oversees both Capital and Operating decision-making?

Appealing to a higher authority...

3. Could emphasizing mission-critical non-utility-cost financial and non-financial benefits to your organization cause that leader to mandate or at least shepherd collaboration between those in charge of the Capital and Operating budgets?

Appealing to a higher authority...

4. Are there any particular acupressure points that could give senior management a strong motivation to cooperate?
   - Making an already anticipated capital project easier or more affordable to implement given advance planning, rebate availability, etc.
   - Addressing safety, regulatory compliance, etc.
   - Other...

Lesson 81.3
OVERCOMING MYTHS AND OBJECTIONS
"We only approve projects with very short SPP."

Presented by
Mark Jewell
@SellingEnergy
info@sellingenergy.com

Turbocharging Success

"Projects must have a simple payback of less than 2 years."

Are you willing to use a better financial metric?

1. Are you aware of the shortcomings of Simple Payback Period?
2. Would you be willing to evaluate the project based on NPV, MIRR, SIR, or life-cycle cost?

Are you using the inputs for the payback calcs?

3. Have you quantified and monetized the non-utility-cost financial benefits (and the non-financial benefits like "safety" that might drive non-utility-cost financial benefits) and added them to the denominator of the SPP calculation?

If it's an income-producing property...

4. Have you considered using Cap Ex Cost Recovery, in which case the SPP matters less since you will be repurposing the tenant's currently wasted utility spend to fund improvements to your building?

IDEAS & ACTIONS

_____

_____

_____

_____

If it's an income-producing property...

5. Did you realize that if your Cap Ex Cost Recovery language allows it, you could earn a "carrying cost" that is many times what you are currently earning on your non-deployed capital?

If it's an income-producing property...

6. Any portion of the savings that accrues to net operating income (NOI) could help you support higher appraised value, an "equity bonus" that should be cherished, even though it won't likely appear in the Simple Payback Period calculation because of its timing.

Lesson 81.4
OVERCOMING MYTHS AND OBJECTIONS
"Our CFO doesn't believe in monthly payments."

Presented by
Mark Jewell
@SellingEnergy
info@sellingenergy.com

You already have monthly payments!

1. You already have monthly payments in the form of an unnecessarily large utility bill!

How about the downside of waiting to have cash?

2. Calculate the NPV of the following 3 scenarios for your project and compare...
   - **A:** 100% funded at "Date 0" (today) using cash
   - **B:** 100% funded at "Date 0" using 3-year financing
   - **C:** 50% funded at "Date 0"; 50% at "Date 1"; using cash

A's NPV is highest; B's NPV is a close 2nd; C's NPV is significantly lower, mainly because of missing Year 1 savings on the last half of the installation.

You already have monthly payments!

3. Whether you do the project now or not, you're still paying for it. You need to partition your current utility spend into two parts:
   - Your new lower utility bill
   - Your payment to a 3rd party who finances the upgrades

Otherwise, you are throwing away that second portion of your payment and receiving nothing in return!

Lesson 81.5
OVERCOMING MYTHS AND OBJECTIONS
"Hurdle rates are higher for non-core projects."

Presented by
Mark Jewell
@SellingEnergy
info@sellingenergy.com

IDEAS & ACTIONS

www.SellingEnergy.com

27% Hurdle rate for "non-core" projects

21% Hurdle rate for "core" projects

Q:

Do "core" or "non-core" projects actually hold the greater potential to deliver surprising benefits for your prospect?

Zeroing in on what "core" really means...

1. Relegating energy projects to "non-core" project status reflects a myopic view of the benefits an energy project can bring to your operations.

Zeroing in on what "core" really means...

2. If we successfully "connect the dots" between our energy project and a core business outcome your organization values, does the energy project become a "core" project?

Lesson 81.6
OVERCOMING MYTHS AND OBJECTIONS
"Rebates are too difficult to find and capture."

Presented by
Mark Jewell
@SellingEnergy
info@sellingenergy.com

Where's all the "free money"?

1. There has never been more transparency in the availability of rebates, incentives, grants, 3rd-party financing and the like...

IDEAS & ACTIONS

Where's all the "free money"?

2. Moreover, virtually none of that is more important than the non-utility-cost financial and non-financial benefits that you are depriving yourself of while you search for some "free money" to help cover your upgrade's first cost.

Lesson 81.7
OVERCOMING MYTHS AND OBJECTIONS
"Procurement favors value engineering."

Presented by
Mark Jewell
@SellingEnergy
info@sellingenergy.com

"Value engineering saves money"

What should "value engineering" really mean?

1. Too many procurement specialists misuse the term "value engineering" to mean removing features at the last minute to reduce first cost.

What should "value engineering" really mean?

2. True value engineering would...
   • Provide a solution that requires lower energy/maintenance costs over time
   • Recommend a model that qualifies for higher rebates/incentives, helping to offset any incremental first cost
   • Support a longer equipment lifetime

Lesson 81.8
OVERCOMING MYTHS AND OBJECTIONS
"We need to *lower* our utility spend, not raise it."

Presented by
Mark Jewell
@SellingEnergy
info@sellingenergy.com

Smart energy technologies could create more value

1. There are situations where increasing electricity use creates value
   • Improving thermal comfort and indoor air quality, attracting/retaining employees and boosting productivity
   • Providing better visibility or control in a manufacturing process, increasing quality while reducing scrap rate
   • Reducing the emissions profile of a facility
   • Adding lighting to outdoor spaces, allowing safe and effective use after dark
   • And many others...

IDEAS & ACTIONS

www.SellingEnergy.com

Lesson 82
OVERCOMING MYTHS AND OBJECTIONS
"Decision-making process is complicated."

Presented by
Mark Jewell
@SellingEnergy
info@sellingenergy.com

"Decision-making process is complicated."

- "Owner is remote, both physically and mentally."
- "Approval requires multiple parties to collaborate."

Lesson 82.1
OVERCOMING MYTHS AND OBJECTIONS
"Owner is remote, both physically and mentally."

Presented by
Mark Jewell
@SellingEnergy
info@sellingenergy.com

Winning sales strategies/tactics know no borders

1. Professional sales strategies/tactics prevail with concise, compelling communication

- Understanding segment-specific benefits
- Using elevator pitches and one-page proposals that evoke emotional responses
- Using one-page financial analyses that allow decision-makers to justify their decisions
- Success stories that build confidence and shorten due diligence periods
- Other

Lesson 82.2
OVERCOMING MYTHS AND OBJECTIONS
"Approval requires multiple parties to collaborate."

Presented by
Mark Jewell
@SellingEnergy
info@sellingenergy.com

IDEAS & ACTIONS

STEP 1: Identify the parties to collaborate...

1. Step #1 is identifying the parties who need to collaborate.
2. Step #2 is determining what each party's values and drivers are.

STEP 1: Identify the parties to collaborate...

3. Step #3 is reframing the proposal to resonate with each decision-maker and influencer, even if it requires multiple one-page proposals, one geared for each stakeholder.

Lesson 83
OVERCOMING MYTHS AND OBJECTIONS
"We focus on reducing our energy cost per unit."

Presented by
Mark Jewell
@SellingEnergy
info@sellingenergy.com

Turbocharging Success

With all due respect...

1. How much better do you feel knowing that all the energy you're now wasting costs a bit less per unit?

With all due respect...

2. Which offers the possibility of the greatest percentage swing in energy expense?
   - Reducing the cost per unit of energy used
   - Reducing the number of energy units used
   - Modifying when those energy units are used

With all due respect...

3. Have you considered all of the non-utility-cost financial and non-financial benefits that you're missing because you haven't addressed your actual energy-consuming systems?

With all due respect...

4. And what happens when the unit cost pendulum swings the other way? Or you miscalculate an energy trade?

IDEAS & ACTIONS

With all due respect...

5. And how quickly do utility price shocks arrive? Could you reduce your consumption quickly enough in reaction to a severe pricing swing?

With all due respect...

6. And what about your ENERGY STAR® score, and any beneficial impact an ENERGY STAR® label could have on your building's competitiveness, profitability and value?

With all due respect...

7. And how about your overall sustainability profile, which will likely become more important as public sentiment regarding climate change converges?

selling in 6™

Lesson 84
OVERCOMING MYTHS AND OBJECTIONS IN INCOME PROPERTIES
"Efficiency is tough in landlord/tenant settings."

Presented by
Mark Jewell
@SellingEnergy
info@sellingenergy.com

sellingenergy
Turbocharging Success

"Efficiency is tough in landlord/tenant settings."

- "Energy costs are a pass-through to tenants."
- "Tough to predict Owner's share of costs/savings."
- "Can't control what the tenants do in their space."
- "It's best to do upgrades as leases roll over."

"Efficiency is tough in landlord/tenant settings."

- "Upgrades don't make sense on smaller projects."
- "Our lease form lacks Capital Expense Cost Recovery."
- "Tenants don't trust our Capital Expense Cost Recovery."
- "Upgrade financing encumbers our building at sale."

"Efficiency is tough in landlord/tenant settings."

- "Appraisers don't value high energy performance."
- "We're not selling the building anytime soon."
- "We are selling the building soon."
- "We're make all of our *new* buildings efficient."
- "Building/buying and selling is more profitable."

IDEAS & ACTIONS

Lesson 84.1
OVERCOMING MYTHS AND OBJECTIONS IN INCOME PROPERTIES
"Energy costs are a pass-through to tenants."

Presented by
Mark Jewell
@SellingEnergy
info@sellingenergy.com

"My tenants pay for energy, so I see no benefit."

Understanding "who pays" and "who benefits"

1. What kind of lease(s) do you use?

Understanding "who pays" and "who benefits"

2. Does your lease form provide for Capital Expense Cost Recovery, in which case you could repurpose your tenants' wasted utility spend and upgrade your building's energy-consuming systems?

Understanding "who pays" and "who benefits"

3. Has anyone examined each lease and calculated who would pay and who would benefit from an expense-reducing capital project?

Understanding "who pays" and "who benefits"

4. Are the tenants paying for *all* energy, only the amount they consume in their spaces, only the amount above a certain base year or expense stop, etc.?

Understanding "who pays" and "who benefits"

5. Could your fixed-base leases be acting like gross leases, in that your exposure to operating expenses may be so high, you would be the ultimate beneficiary of reduced energy bills?

Consider other reasons to upgrade...

6. Are there other reasons to finance energy upgrades, such as convincing tenants to renew, attracting new tenants more easily, or attaining an ENERGY STAR®, LEED®, or other accolade that will generate more interest in your building?

IDEAS & ACTIONS

www.SellingEnergy.com

Lesson **84.2**
OVERCOMING MYTHS AND OBJECTIONS IN INCOME PROPERTIES
"Tough to predict Owner's share of costs/savings."

Presented by
Mark Jewell
@SellingEnergy
info@sellingenergy.com

©2020 Selling Energy

"It's too difficult to predict the owner's share of savings."

©2020 Selling Energy

Understanding "who pays" and "who benefits"

1. What are you using to do the calculations?
   - Upgrade costs and savings by lease and space
   - Discounted cash flow calculations (e.g., Argus models) that allocate expenses by tenant, make assumptions for renewal probability and other factors, and provide estimates of the property's profitability and asset value using various inputs and sensitivity analysis
   - Doing pre- and post-upgrade Argus models can isolate the landlord's share of costs and savings

©2020 Selling Energy

Understanding "who pays" and "who benefits"

2. Would having these figures make it easier to do Cap Ex Cost Recovery?
3. Do you make the calculations a requirement of each capital project?
4. There are at least 5 approaches to dealing with uncertainty when upgrading landlord/tenant spaces (see next slide)

©2020 Selling Energy

Understanding "who pays" and "who benefits"

5. There are at least 5 approaches used by experienced landlords to address this issue.
   - "It's the right thing to do regardless of who benefits."
   - "Given idiosyncrasies of lease accounting, the building owner will get some of the savings."
   - "We're passing through the Cap Ex anyway."
   - "We're installing sub-meters and allocating the savings directly to the tenants where appropriate."
   - "We'll do multiple Argus runs and get it right."

©2020 Selling Energy

Lesson **84.3**
OVERCOMING MYTHS AND OBJECTIONS IN INCOME PROPERTIES
"Can't control what the tenants do in their space."

Presented by
Mark Jewell
@SellingEnergy
info@sellingenergy.com

©2020 Selling Energy

©2020 Selling Energy

Leveraging your economy of scale and influence

1. The best landlords determine the ideal energy solutions for their property and then leverage their economy of scale to make a path for tenants to upgrade their spaces cost-effectively and time-efficiently.

©2020 Selling Energy

IDEAS & ACTIONS

_____

_____

_____

_____

Leveraging your economy of scale and influence

2. Tenant education on energy use goes a long way to reducing expenses and improving landlord/tenant relations.

Lesson 84.4
OVERCOMING MYTHS AND OBJECTIONS IN INCOME PROPERTIES
"It's best to do upgrades as leases roll over."

 Presented by
Mark Jewell
@SellingEnergy
info@sellingenergy.com

"Upgrades in mid-lease won't benefit the owner."

It's smart to do the upgrades as soon as possible

1. Would doing the upgrades now allow the landlord to set a lower base year (or expense stop) for new leases signed?

It's smart to do the upgrades as soon as possible

2. If you're seeking the highest appraisal, it's smart to make sure the landlord's share of operating expenses is lowered at least a year prior to having the building appraised.

It's smart to do the upgrades as soon as possible

3. Would lower operating expenses and/or improved tenant comfort and convenience help with tenant retention/attraction?

It's smart to do the upgrades as soon as possible

4. How many upgrades would need to be done anyway in the context of tenant fit-outs as a condition for signing new leases?

It's smart to do the upgrades as soon as possible

5. Speaking of tenant churn, upgrades help keep tenants happier and better able to pay their rent... Consider the costs you face if the space turns over:
- Lag vacancy (looking for a new tenant)
- Build-out vacancy (configuring the space)
- Free rent period (inducing a longer lease term)
- Tenant fit-out allowance
- Leasing commission
- Legal, accounting and more...

IDEAS & ACTIONS

www.SellingEnergy.com

Lesson 84.5
OVERCOMING MYTHS AND OBJECTIONS IN INCOME PROPERTIES
"Upgrades don't make sense on smaller projects."

Presented by
Mark Jewell
@SellingEnergy
info@sellingenergy.com

"High performance doesn't make sense on smaller projects."

Small projects here and there... Soon it's all done.

1. Think about multi-tenant buildings, where the churning of tenant improvements eventually redefines the entire building's performance.

Small projects here and there... Soon it's all done.

2. Maintaining "attic stock" of efficient equipment facilitates time-efficient installation of the right equipment even in spaces that must turn over quickly.

Lesson 84.6
OVERCOMING MYTHS AND OBJECTIONS IN INCOME PROPERTIES
"Our lease form lacks Cap Ex Cost Recovery."

Presented by
Mark Jewell
@SellingEnergy
info@sellingenergy.com

That's what a lease amendment is for...

1. Lease modifications are common.
2. Mutually beneficial language should not be difficult to add mid-lease.

That's what a lease amendment is for...

3. Modifying existing lease forms (and renewals) to include Capital Expense Cost Recovery language will avoid the need for amendments in the future.

IDEAS & ACTIONS _____

_____

_____

_____

Lesson 84.7
OVERCOMING MYTHS AND OBJECTIONS IN INCOME PROPERTIES
"Tenants don't trust our CapEx cost recovery."

Presented by
Mark Jewell
@SellingEnergy
info@sellingenergy.com

The Energy Aligned Lease* solves this issue...

1. Consider using a modified cost-recovery formula that allows the landlord to pass-through only 80% of the projected savings in the form of Cap Ex Cost Recovery.

*See "Energy Aligned Lease" developed by the former New York City Mayor Bloomberg's task force.

The Energy Aligned Lease* solves this issue...

2. This gives the tenants headroom so that even if the engineering projections were overstated, the recovery will not exceed the energy savings realized from the upgrade.

*See "Energy Aligned Lease" developed by the former New York City Mayor Bloomberg's task force.

Lesson 84.8
OVERCOMING MYTHS AND OBJECTIONS IN INCOME PROPERTIES
"Upgrade financing encumbers our building at sale."

Presented by
Mark Jewell
@SellingEnergy
info@sellingenergy.com

Think about the whole cycle...

1. You borrow money to improve the building's energy profile.
2. Lower energy costs help the landlord, the tenants, or both.
3. The value of the building goes up.

Think about the whole cycle...

4. When the building is sold, the capitalized value of the landlord's share of the savings is more than the loan principal outstanding.
5. The loan is handily repaid with the incrementally higher sales price, even after subtracting any incrementally higher real estate sales commission.

IDEAS & ACTIONS

www.SellingEnergy.com

Lesson 84.9
OVERCOMING MYTHS AND OBJECTIONS IN INCOME PROPERTIES
"Appraisers don't value high energy performance."

Presented by
Mark Jewell
@SellingEnergy
info@sellingenergy.com

Turbocharging Success

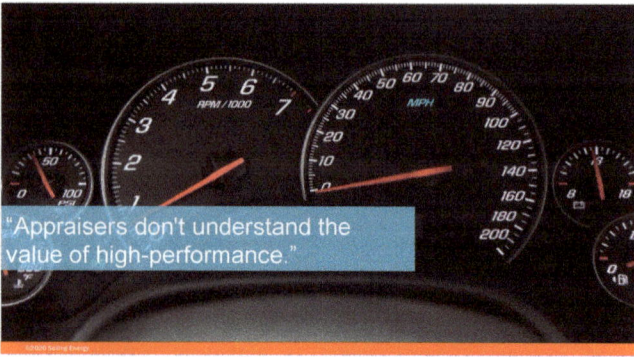

"Appraisers don't understand the value of high-performance."

Understanding the appraisal process...

1. In owner-occupied property, the appraiser can be educated on features that make the building more attractive, which may help support a higher appraisal using either the Cost Approach or the Market Comparison Approach to appraisal.

Understanding the appraisal process...

1. In income-producing properties, the Income Approach to Appraisal is key. Appraisers seek Net Operating Income (NOI), which can be improved by
   - Higher occupancy percentage
   - Higher rent per square foot (or higher percentage rent)
   - Lower landlord share of operating expenses
   - Other factors

Understanding the appraisal process...

2. Higher NOI should support a higher appraisal, all other factors held constant.
3. The technology that drove the NOI improvement is less important.

Lesson 84.10
OVERCOMING MYTHS AND OBJECTIONS IN INCOME PROPERTIES
"We're not selling the building anytime soon."

Presented by
Mark Jewell
@SellingEnergy
info@sellingenergy.com

Turbocharging Success

"We're not selling the building anytime soon, so increases in appraised value aren't important."

Higher valuation is beneficial even without a sale...

1. Selling the building is not the only way to benefit from increased appraised value.
2. Refinancing the property allows the owner to pull equity from the property, and when refinancing, the higher the appraisal, the better.
3. Periodic portfolio evaluations also benefit from higher appraised values.

IDEAS & ACTIONS

Lesson 84.11
OVERCOMING MYTHS AND OBJECTIONS <u>IN INCOME PROPERTIES</u>
"We are selling the building soon."

Presented by
Mark Jewell
@SellingEnergy
info@sellingenergy.com

"We are selling the building soon, so upgrading it now doesn't make sense."

Efficiency can help prime a building for sale...

1. Lowering the owner's share of operating expenses raises the building's appraised value.
2. Ideal to incorporate this and similar approaches to increasing Net Operating Income (NOI) at least a year prior to appraising the building for sale.

Lesson 84.12
OVERCOMING MYTHS AND OBJECTIONS <u>IN INCOME PROPERTIES</u>
"We're making all of our *new* buildings efficient."

Presented by
Mark Jewell
@SellingEnergy
info@sellingenergy.com

"We are making all of our *new* buildings efficient."

The difference between "stock" and "flow"

1. If a real estate portfolio has many more buildings in it than the number of buildings added to it in any given year, doesn't it make sense to focus on the "stock" and not just the "flow"?

The difference between "stock" and "flow"

2. The larger the portfolio, the less significant an impact any single new efficient structure will have on portfolio-wide average efficiency.

Lesson 84.13
OVERCOMING MYTHS AND OBJECTIONS <u>IN INCOME PROPERTIES</u>
"Building/buying and selling is more profitable."

Presented by
Mark Jewell
@SellingEnergy
info@sellingenergy.com

IDEAS & ACTIONS

www.SellingEnergy.com

Build/buy and sell OR upgrade your portfolio?

1. Which approach requires more capital?
2. Which approach results in greater diversity?
3. Which approach takes longer to complete?
4. Which approach involves more market risk?
5. Which gives a higher return on invested capital?

Build/buy and sell OR upgrade your portfolio?

6. Which approach has the risk of investing in an inflated real estate market?
7. Which approach has the potential for other parties to bear some or all of the cost (rebates, tenant cost recoveries)?

Build/buy and sell OR upgrade your portfolio?

8. Which approach has the potential to support higher asset value across the broader portfolio?

Lesson 85
OVERCOMING OBJECTIONS TO YOUR PROPOSAL
Listening to and carefully addressing concerns

Presented by
Mark Jewell
@SellingEnergy
info@sellingenergy.com

Overcoming objections to your proposal...

- "I don't understand what you're selling."
- "I'm concerned about service after the sale."
- "It's not worth the effort."
- "Your price is too high."
- "Is this your best price?"

Lesson 85.1
OVERCOMING OBJECTIONS TO YOUR PROPOSAL
"I don't understand what you're selling."

Presented by
Mark Jewell
@SellingEnergy
info@sellingenergy.com

IDEAS & ACTIONS

www.SellingEnergy.com

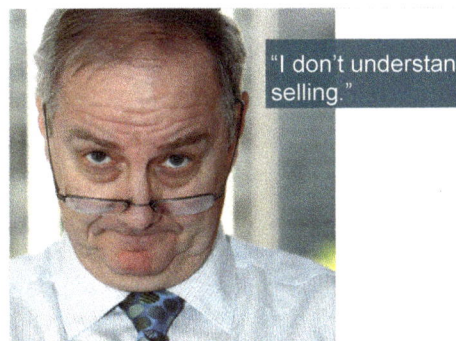

"I don't understand what you are selling."

Are you spending too much time on tech talk?

1. Are you planting seeds of confusion as you focus on the "bits, bytes, and blinking lights" technical aspects of your offering?
2. Have you reframed your benefits so that they "connect the dots" in a segment-specific, prospect-sensitive way?

Lesson 85.2
OVERCOMING OBJECTIONS TO YOUR PROPOSAL
"I'm concerned about service after the sale."

Presented by
Mark Jewell
@SellingEnergy
info@sellingenergy.com

Have you built a good foundation of trust?

1. 39% of business-to-business (B2B) buyers select a vendor according to the skills of the salesperson rather than price, quality or service.*
2. Have you included stories of other similar clients who have benefited from your offering?

*Harvard Business Review

Have you built a good foundation of trust?

3. Have you visualized (and telegraphed through your professionalism) a long and mutually prosperous relationship rather than simply a transaction?

Lesson 85.3
OVERCOMING OBJECTIONS TO YOUR PROPOSAL
"It's not worth the effort."

Presented by
Mark Jewell
@SellingEnergy
info@sellingenergy.com

"It's not worth the effort"

IDEAS & ACTIONS

www.SellingEnergy.com

Have you made it emotionally compelling?

1. Most decisions are made emotionally, and then justified financially.
2. You need to paint a picture of an emotionally compelling result that resonates with your prospect.

Lesson 85.4
OVERCOMING OBJECTIONS TO YOUR PROPOSAL
"Your price is too high."

Presented by
Mark Jewell
@SellingEnergy
info@sellingenergy.com

Turbocharging Success

"The price is too high"

"We may be able to get the same thing less expensively somewhere else"

"The unassailable value equation"

"VALUE = BENEFITS MINUS COSTS"

Adapted from *Escaping the Price-Driven Sale* by Tom Snyder and Kevin Kearns

---

"The unassailable value equation"
"VALUE = BENEFITS - COSTS"

BENEFITS

"**INSIGHT** and **DISCOVERY** that the customer receives from the buying experience"

Adapted from *Escaping the Price-Driven Sale* by Tom Snyder and Kevin Kearns

---

"The unassailable value equation"
"VALUE = BENEFITS - COSTS"

COSTS

"Not just price – from the standpoint of the buying experience itself, it is the **TIME and EFFORT** that the customer is devoting to being SOLD TO"

Adapted from *Escaping the Price-Driven Sale* by Tom Snyder and Kevin Kearns

---

"The *actual* unassailable value equation"

VALUE	equals	BENEFITS INSIGHT DISCOVERY	minus	COSTS TIME EFFORT

Adapted from *Escaping the Price-Driven Sale* by Tom Snyder and Kevin Kearns

---

IDEAS & ACTIONS

Take price off the table by...

revealing an unrecognized problem...
finding an unanticipated solution...
creating/revealing an unseen opportunity...

If your prospect wants a better deal, add more value rather than lower your price.

You may think you lost a deal based on "price."

In reality, you probably lost on "value."

"The quality of your outcome is directly related to the quality of the evaluations you're prepared to make."

- Anthony Robbins

It's not about price; it's about perceived value.

1. You need to understand both the segment and the prospect well enough to "connect the dots" between your offering and what that prospect values.

It's not about price; it's about perceived value.

2. You need to help that prospect make a more refined evaluation that allows them to appreciate your differentiation so that they find your price to be a bargain rather than a premium.

selling in 6™

Lesson 85.5
OVERCOMING OBJECTIONS TO YOUR PROPOSAL
"Your simple payback period is too long."

Presented by
Mark Jewell
@SellingEnergy
info@sellingenergy.com

sellingenergy
Turbocharging Success

IDEAS & ACTIONS

www.SellingEnergy.com

Are you willing to consider a better financial metric?

1. Are you aware of the shortcomings of Simple Payback Period?
   - Ignores Time Value of Money
   - Ignores cash flows occurring after the payback
   - Ignores any irregularity in cash flows after Year 1
   - Discourages project approval if holding period is longer than the SPP
   - Does not reflect cash flow probabilities
   - Disregards the economic backdrop of other investments
   - Gets tricky in income-producing property settings

Are you willing to consider a better financial metric?

2. Would you be willing to evaluate the project based on NPV, MIRR, SIR, or life-cycle cost?

Are you using the inputs for the payback calcs?

3. Have you quantified and monetized the non-utility-cost financial benefits (and the non-financial benefits like "safety" that might drive non-utility-cost financial benefits) and added them to the denominator of the SPP calculation?

If it's an income-producing property...

4. Have you considered using Capital Expense Cost Recovery, in which case the SPP matters less since you will be repurposing the tenant's currently wasted utility spend to fund improvements to your building.

If it's an income-producing property...

5. Did you realize that if your Cap Ex Cost Recovery language allows it, you could earn a "carrying cost" that is many times what you are currently earning on your non-deployed capital?

If it's an income-producing property...

6. Any portion of the savings that accrues to net operating income (NOI) could help you support higher appraised value, an "equity bonus" that should be cherished, even though it won't likely appear in the Simple Payback Period calculation.

Lesson 85.6
OVERCOMING OBJECTIONS TO YOUR PROPOSAL
"Is this your best price?"

Presented by
Mark Jewell
@SellingEnergy
info@sellingenergy.com

Turbocharging Success

IDEAS & ACTIONS

It had better be your best price!

1. If you offer a lower price when asked for one, you have lost the respect of the prospect and are now on a very slippery slope.

However, there are ways to lower the price...

2. A correct response might be, "This is absolutely my best price for this configuration. If you'd like to explore a lower price we could do 1 of 2 things:
   • Reduce the scope of this project
   • Increase the project scope to include more buildings so that I could explore the potential of compensating you for reducing our marketing costs, etc."

Another option...

3. If needed, you could offer something of high perceived value and low marginal cost to you (e.g., product customization, extended warranty).

Lesson 86
OVERCOMING VAGUE OBJECTIONS
Why prospects resist

Presented by
Mark Jewell
@SellingEnergy
info@sellingenergy.com

Why people resist

Acknowledge the resistance

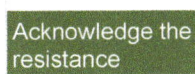

Don't assume the worst

Comfort zone

IDEAS & ACTIONS

_____

_____

_____

_____

Fear

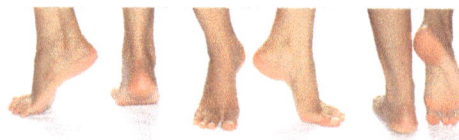

Vulnerabilities

Misunderstanding

Lesson 86.1
OVERCOMING VAGUE OBJECTIONS
"I have to take a look at the numbers."

Presented by
Mark Jewell
@SellingEnergy
info@sellingenergy.com

sellingenergy
Turbocharging Success

"I have to take another look at the numbers."

It would be helpful to know which numbers...

1. "So let me ask you this... Which numbers are you most interested in... the costs, the estimated savings, your budget...?"

selling in 6™

Lesson 86.2
OVERCOMING VAGUE OBJECTIONS
"The benefits are likely impossible to quantify."

Presented by
Mark Jewell
@SellingEnergy
info@sellingenergy.com

sellingenergy
Turbocharging Success

IDEAS & ACTIONS

There's almost always a way to quantify value...

1. Even in complicated, multi-tenant buildings with widely varying expense-sharing clauses, lease terms, etc., running multiple scenarios through industry-standard income-property modeling software can determine the shares of costs and savings for the landlord and each tenant.

There's almost always a way to quantify value...

2. In some cases, doing a simple exercise on a calculator, appealing to common sense, easily proves the point.

- Assume the savings is $10K per year for a 2-year SPP
- You need $10K more in savings to make it a 1-year SPP
- What is the average salary and benefits per worker?
- How many workers are there?
- What is the total payroll each year?
- What percentage of that payroll is $10K?
- How many more minutes of productivity per worker is that?
- Is it obvious that your upgrade will sufficiently improve comfort and convenience to support that many minutes of additional productivity per worker per day?

- Assume the savings is $10K per year for a 2-year SPP
- You need $10K more in savings to make it a 1-year SPP
- What is the average salary and benefits per worker? $50K
- How many workers are there? 50
- What is the total payroll each year? $2.5M
- What percentage of that payroll is $10K? 0.4%
- How many more minutes of productivity per worker is that? (0.4% x 8 hours x 50 minutes per hour = 1.6 minutes)
- Is it obvious that your upgrade will sufficiently improve comfort and convenience to support 1.6 minutes of additional productivity per worker per day?

There's almost always a way to quantify value...

4. In other cases, it pays to bring studies that document impressive results in similar settings.

There's almost always a way to quantify value...

5. If necessary, feel free to reduce those findings down to a small fraction of what was found, illustrating for your prospect how much "cushion" they have in case those studies don't exactly mirror the application under consideration.

Lesson 86.3
OVERCOMING VAGUE OBJECTIONS
"I need to think about it."

Presented by
Mark Jewell
@SellingEnergy
info@sellingenergy.com

IDEAS & ACTIONS

www.SellingEnergy.com

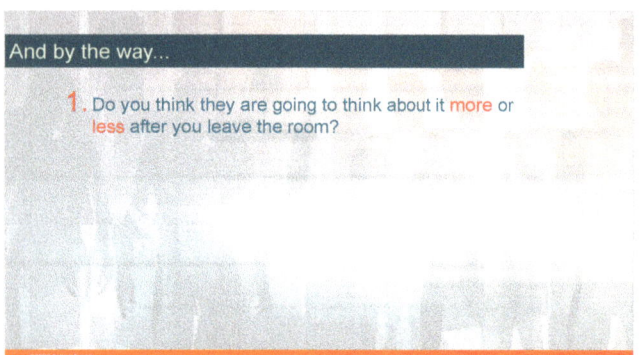

Most
decisions
are made
emotionally
and then
justified
financially

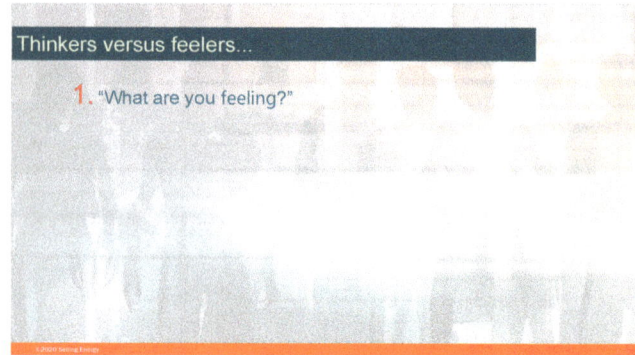

Thinkers versus feelers...

1. "What are you feeling?"

And by the way...

1. Do you think they are going to think about it more or less after you leave the room?

selling
in 6™

Lesson 86.4
OVERCOMING VAGUE OBJECTIONS
"We decided to go a different route."

Presented by
Mark Jewell
@SellingEnergy
info@sellingenergy.com

sellingenergy
Turbocharging Success

"We decided to go a different route"

Leveraging an "exit interview" into opportunity

1. "I respect your decision. So I can be of greater service next time to you and others like you, could you please share with me why you decided to pursue a different path?"

selling
in 6™

Lesson 87
MYTHS PERPETUATED BY SALESPEOPLE
"Knowledge is power."

Presented by
Mark Jewell
@SellingEnergy
info@sellingenergy.com

sellingenergy
Turbocharging Success

"Knowledge is power."

IDEAS & ACTIONS

_____

_____

_____

_____

"This project has an ROI of 2 years."

Lesson 88
MYTHS PERPETUATED BY SALESPEOPLE
"This project is a no-brainer."

Presented by
Mark Jewell
@SellingEnergy
info@sellingenergy.com

"Energy efficiency is a no-brainer."

Lesson 89
MYTHS PERPETUATED BY SALESPEOPLE
"The prospect will buy if I give them a free audit."

Presented by
Mark Jewell
@SellingEnergy
info@sellingenergy.com

"The prospect will buy if I can give them a free audit to show them what I can do first."

Lesson 90
MYTHS PERPETUATED BY SALESPEOPLE
"No need to complicate matters with a rebate."

Presented by
Mark Jewell
@SellingEnergy
info@sellingenergy.com

IDEAS & ACTIONS

Q:

What's the EBITDA margin of a grocery store?

*EBITDA is Earnings Before Interest, Taxes, Depreciation, and Amortization. EBITDA margin is calculated as EBITDA/Revenue

Q:

How many boxes of Cheerios* did that grocery store have to sell at $3.25 each to make the equivalent of that rebate that you're tempted to dismiss?

*For this example, we employ a simplifying assumption that the margin of a box of Cheerios is the same as the margin for a typical enterprise in the Grocery segment.

At an assumed EBITDA margin of 8%...

$$\frac{\$10,000 \text{ rebate}}{8\% \text{ EBITDA margin}} \longleftrightarrow \$125,000 \text{ revenue}$$

Q:

How many boxes of Cheerios* did that grocery store have to sell at $3.25 each to make $125,000 in sales last year?

*For this example, we employ a simplifying assumption that the margin of a box of Cheerios is the same as the margin for a typical enterprise in the Grocery segment.

At an assumed EBITDA margin of 8%...

$$\frac{\$125,000 \text{ revenue}}{\$3.25 \text{ per Cheerios box}} \longleftrightarrow 38,460 \text{ boxes of Cheerios}$$

Perhaps a *full tractor trailer load* of Cheerios?

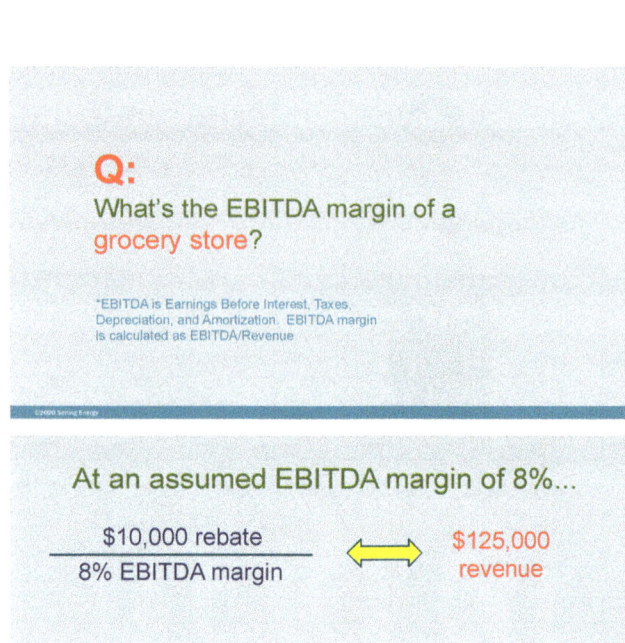

Lesson 91
MYTHS THAT CAN HINDER SALES PERFORMANCE
Professionalism and diligence drive success

Presented by
Mark Jewell
@SellingEnergy
info@sellingenergy.com

"Energy efficiency is the right thing to do, it doesn't need to be sold."

IDEAS & ACTIONS _____

_____

_____

_____

Nothing happens until something is sold.

"I don't have 'Sales' in my title, so I don't need to know how to sell."

Guiding Principles

Energy-related products, services and programs all require effective selling.

Guiding Principles

Professional sales skills make you more successful at advancing any energy-related initiative, regardless of your role in the process.

Guiding Principles

You need to think of yourself as a sales professional even if your job title does not include the word "sales."

"I'm too busy with the day-to-day pressures of making my numbers to spend time developing my sales skills."

IDEAS & ACTIONS

www.SellingEnergy.com

"I can wing it."

Without practice, you can't expect to be good.

"I've got too many plates in the air to be out networking and generating leads."

Dig your well before you're thirsty.

"I can't tell a potential customer 'no'."

Don't waste time spinning your wheels on bad prospects.

"If the prospect really wants to buy what we are offering, they will call back."

IDEAS & ACTIONS

Hot can turn cold.

"I went to school for engineering. If I wanted to write, I'd have gone to school for English."

Unless you can effectively communicate your idea, you might as well not have had it.

"I need to negotiate terms up front."

No, you don't. And if you try to, you will be negotiating price, not terms.

"They call it 'closing' because it's the end of the deal."

Closing is just the beginning.

"Success happens overnight with little or no effort."

IDEAS & ACTIONS

Success takes hard work and focus.

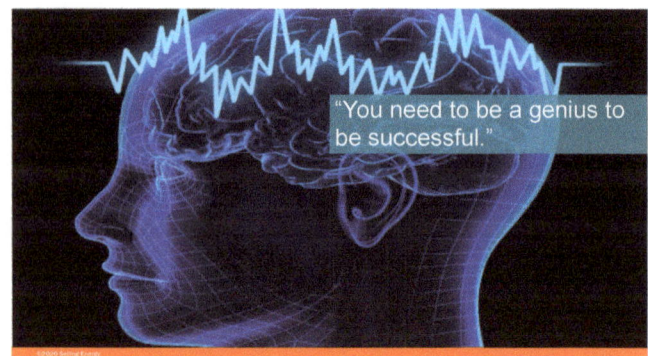

"You need to be a genius to be successful."

Most successful people aren't geniuses... However, they are personable and smart.

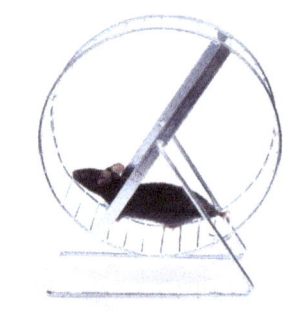

"Never give up."

Know when to move on.

"I am driven by fear."

What would you attempt to do if you knew you could not fail?

- Robert Schuller

"I need to go with the flow."

IDEAS & ACTIONS

Lesson 92
FINDING THE RIGHT DECISION-MAKERS AND INFLUENCERS
Defining and building your brand

Presented by
Mark Jewell
@SellingEnergy
info@sellingenergy.com

Why you matter

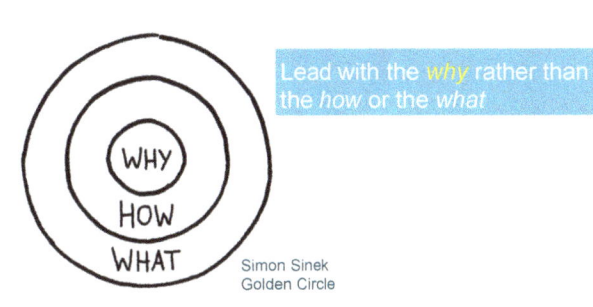

Lead with the *why* rather than the *how* or the *what*

Simon Sinek
Golden Circle

Establishing yourself as an expert enhances both visibility and credibility

Share your expertise... in-person or via webinars

Write articles

Participate in online forums

IDEAS & ACTIONS

www.SellingEnergy.com

IDEAS & ACTIONS

"Arsenal of Competitive Advantage"

Sales team	Trust, differentiation, strategy, linkage, expert product/industry knowledge, exec presence, strategic literacy
Industry focus	Industry expertise & network, market share, tailored solutions
Product/solution	Functionality, features, technology, quality, value, ease of use, availability, brand loyalty, advertising, price, speed
Service	Service, responsiveness, people, customer satisfaction, results, performance
Company	Brand loyalty, financial stability, reputation, quality, other products, experience

Adapted from "Hope is Not a Strategy" by Rick Page; ©2003 McGraw-Hill Education; based on Michael Porter's work at Harvard

How to determine your competitive advantage

Analyze your competition. What are they doing and not doing?

What are they known for... Good and bad?

You can be a hero by helping your prospects solve their puzzles...

HOPE IS NOT A STRATEGY
The 6 Keys to Winning the Complex Sale
RICK PAGE

selling in 6™

Lesson 94
FINDING THE RIGHT DECISION-MAKERS AND INFLUENCERS
Targeting key markets and ideal customers

Presented by
Mark Jewell
@SellingEnergy
info@sellingenergy.com

sellingenergy
Turbocharging Success

Find your focus

IDEAS & ACTIONS

www.SellingEnergy.com

Clearly articulate your target market

No niche is too small

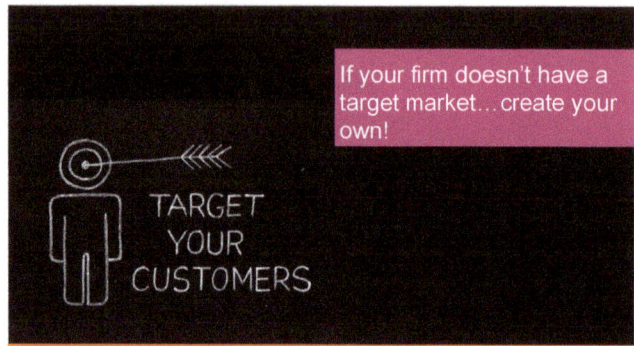

If your firm doesn't have a target market…create your own!

TARGET YOUR CUSTOMERS

It's OK if you don't know who to target

Those with a high likelihood of closing

DONE

Those that you can close quickly

The biggest and most visible that are likely to influence others

The not-so-big that want to be the biggest

IDEAS & ACTIONS

_____

_____

_____

_____

The ones that are the easiest to work with

The stretch goal

The ones that are easiest to commute to

The ones with the best reputations

The ones with corporate "green" goals

selling in 6™

Lesson 95
FINDING THE RIGHT DECISION-MAKERS AND INFLUENCERS
Creating customer profiles

Presented by
Mark Jewell
@SellingEnergy
info@sellingenergy.com

sellingenergy
Turbocharging Success

Establish an ideal customer profile

What your customer profile should not look like...

- "They need what we offer."
- "They're ready to buy."
- "They really want to work with us."
- "They don't panic when we say how much it costs."
- "They appreciate the kind of work we do."

IDEAS & ACTIONS

What your customer profile **should** look like

Start by creating **your own company's** profile...

1. What are your company's strengths, weaknesses, systems and capabilities?
2. What competitive advantages differentiate your company from others in your industry?

Who are your best customers currently?

3. Who are your best current customers?
4. How large or small are they, as measured by revenues, number of locations, employees, customers, etc.?
5. What segments do they hail from?
6. Do they tend to belong to the same association(s)?

Why are they your best customers?

7. What expressed and implied needs did they have when you first encountered them?
8. How were you able to clarify and address those needs?
9. What have they said they've enjoyed about using your offerings, including any unanticipated benefits they've enjoyed as a result of using you?

Who are the **decision-makers** and **influencers**?

10. Who were the decision-makers and influencers in each current customer's buying process?
11. What are the various personas among those decision-makers and influencers, and how could your offering ideally resonate with each persona?

Leveraging that to create your buyer **personas**...

12. Factors to consider when developing your buyer personas:
    - Roles or titles
    - Goals and motivations
    - Challenges they typically experience
    - Language they use to describe them
    - Where they get their info
    - Best ways to reach them
    - What might cause them to engage
    - Their level of *need, desire, authority and ability* to actually purchase your offering

---

Then analyze your most promising **target markets** and your ideal **customer profiles.** Ask yourself...

What specific need do they have that your offering can fill?

IDEAS & ACTIONS

_____

_____

_____

_____

www.SellingEnergy.com

What appeals to them?

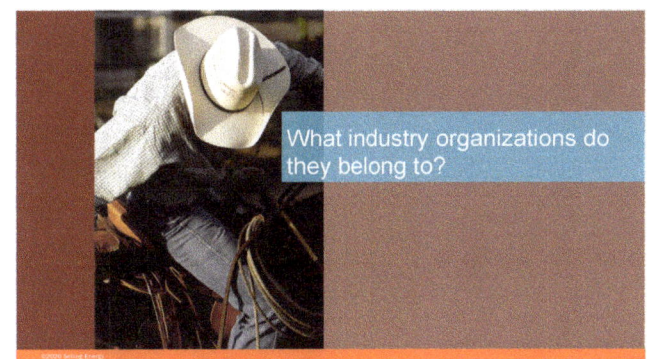

What industry organizations do they belong to?

Where are their headquarters located?

How do they make purchasing decisions?

Who are their current suppliers?

Who are *their* customers?

What are their budget cycles... and what metrics, if any, do they use for purchasing?

"The quality of your outcome is directly related to the quality of the evaluations you're prepared to make."

- Anthony Robbins

IDEAS & ACTIONS

_____

_____

_____

_____

Lesson 96
FINDING THE RIGHT DECISION-MAKERS AND INFLUENCERS
Finding and courting all the right stakeholders

Presented by
Mark Jewell
@SellingEnergy
info@sellingenergy.com

Turbocharging Success

Which stakeholders matter the most?

Which stakeholders do you target?

"
Decision-makers make the budget. Non-decision-makers spend the budget.
"

- Anthony Parinello

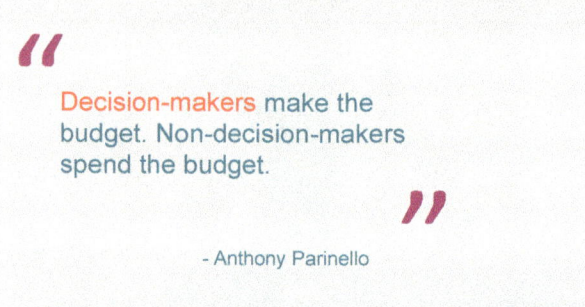

Contact the company's gatekeeper

A **3-sentence solicitation** that gets the conversation started...

We have had the privilege of installing our <<offering>> in "x" buildings within "y" miles of your facility.

I was speaking with <<so and so>> the other day and learned that your physical plant uses the same technology that we replaced in every one of those buildings, at an average energy savings of "z" %.

I'm wondering who the right person would be to explore extending the success we've had with those other buildings to your facility?

Use the Power of 12

12

IDEAS & ACTIONS

_____

_____

_____

_____

Working as a team

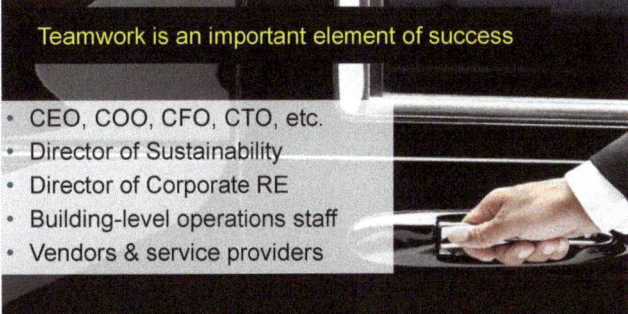

Teamwork is an important element of success

- CEO, COO, CFO, CTO, etc.
- Director of Sustainability
- Director of Corporate RE
- Building-level operations staff
- Vendors & service providers

Asset manager
Property manager
Tenant
Chief engineer
Building engineer
Portfolio manager
Vendors & service providers

selling in 6™

Lesson 97
FINDING THE RIGHT DECISION-MAKERS AND INFLUENCERS
Identifying influencers

Presented by
Mark Jewell
@SellingEnergy
info@sellingenergy.com

sellingenergy
Turbocharging Success

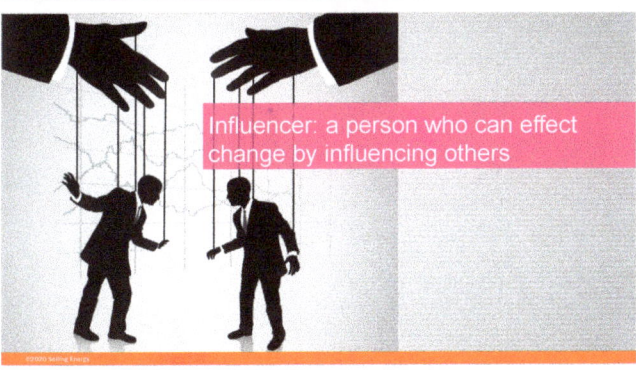

Influencer: a person who can effect change by influencing others

Targeting influencers is about creating advocacy for your products or services

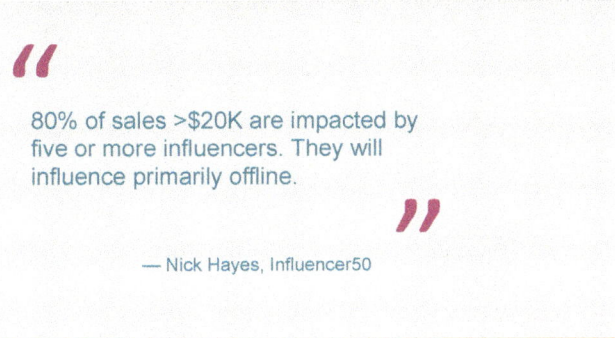

" 80% of sales >$20K are impacted by five or more influencers. They will influence primarily offline. "

— Nick Hayes, Influencer50

Who are the key influencers in your prospect's organization?

IDEAS & ACTIONS

www.SellingEnergy.com

Internal influencer characteristics...

1. A job title that is relevant to the area that your offering addresses
2. A position on the org chart that is relevant

Internal influencer characteristics...

3. A history of being a successful leader within the organization and implementing similar projects
4. A reputation for being closely bound to others in the organization "by mutual advantage"

Potential external influencers...

1. Retailers, manufacturers, customers, etc.
2. Added-value influencers
3. Journalists, industry analysts, professional advisors

Types of influencers

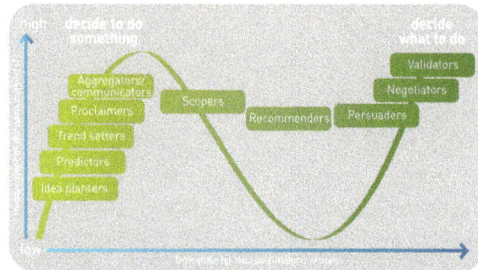

© Influencer50 from http://en.wikipedia.org/wiki/File:Influencer_Roles.jpg

You can market *to* influencers, to increase awareness of the firm within the influencer community

Marketing *through* influencers, using influencers to increase market awareness of the firm in target markets

Marketing *with* influencers, turning influencers into advocates of the firm

Lesson 98
FINDING THE RIGHT DECISION-MAKERS AND INFLUENCERS
Creating influencer maps

Presented by
Mark Jewell
@SellingEnergy
info@sellingenergy.com

IDEAS & ACTIONS _____

_____

_____

_____

Create an influencer map

Map the relationships between players

Ranking influencers in order of importance

1. Market reach
2. Independence
3. Frequency of impact
4. Expertise
5. Persuasiveness
6. Thoroughness of role

What is their influence over *your* project?

Navigate the map to create support

How do you reach the influencer?

Where do they get *their* industry insights?

1. Online and in-person networking
2. Influencers of influencers
3. Other ways...

selling in **6**™

Lesson 99
FINDING THE RIGHT DECISION-MAKERS AND INFLUENCERS
Motivating the players

Presented by
Mark Jewell
@SellingEnergy
info@sellingenergy.com

selling**energy**
Turbocharging Success

IDEAS & ACTIONS

_____

_____

_____

_____

www.SellingEnergy.com

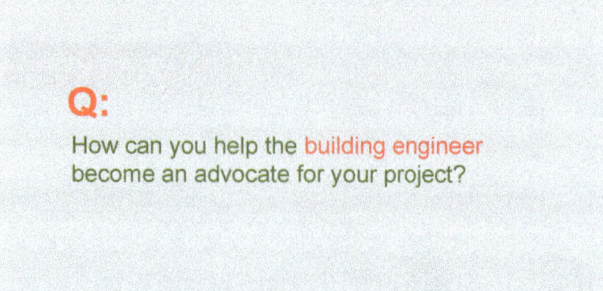

Q:

How can you help the building engineer become an advocate for your project?

Q:

What aspects of your project could you leverage to get your prospects more excited about it?

What is the building engineer thinking?

1. Is their main goal to stop hot/cold calls?
2. Understand the building systems they already have?
3. Have time to consider changing?
4. Would their boss allow them the time to do it?
5. Would they sabotage your pilot or undermine a proposal?
6. Would you make their job easier?
7. Do they know (and understand) financial metrics?
8. Do they know their manager's "yield requirements"?

Would your proposed solution...

1. Minimize complaints from occupants?
2. Reduce costs?
3. Help the engineer cope with understaffing?
4. Free up time to do preventive maintenance?
5. Increase the life of the physical plant?
6. Help the building win an ENERGY STAR® or LEED® certification?

How else could you help the engineer become an advocate for your solution?

Q:

What motivates the property manager to become interested in energy projects?

What does the property manager see as his or her role?

What does the manager see as his/her role?

1. Proud to keep all the plates spinning
2. Performing the role of tenant concierge
3. Keeping the building leased
4. Maintaining a safe and profitable asset
5. Addressing tenant requests for evidence of sustainability

IDEAS & ACTIONS

_____

_____

_____

_____

Q:

Would your solution support the property manager in being more successful?

Making the property manager more successful

1. How significant is energy as an element of the property's income statement?
2. If the manager focused on "green" initiatives, where do they see energy fitting in that agenda?

Making the property manager more successful

3. Could you emphasize the link between your energy solutions and higher tenant retention and attraction?

Making the property manager more successful

4. Could you reframe your solution as the route to the benefits that managers seek (higher occupancy and base rents, lower vacancy and operating expenses, lower capitalization rates)?

Making the property manager more successful

5. Would your offering make the property safer?
6. Could they position your offering as an "upgrade" or "amenity" to generate tenant goodwill and additional broker attention?

Making the property manager more successful

7. Could you help the manager prepare more accurate budgets?
8. Could you help the manager sell the proposal to all three of these stakeholders?
   - Tenants
   - Capital budgeting folks
   - Building staff

How else could you help the property manager become an advocate of your solution?

Q:

What motivates the asset manager to become interested in energy projects?

IDEAS & ACTIONS

www.SellingEnergy.com

The mindset of the asset manager...

1. Needs to meet/exceed the yield requirements
2. Only approves "highest and best use of capital"
3. Must reduce risk, and maximize risk-adjusted return

The mindset of the asset manager...

4. Needs to understand which energy technologies actually work as promised, how they compare, and which are the most appropriate for which properties

The mindset of the asset manager...

5. May be hesitant to interfere with hired 3rd-party managers in the field by mandating changes
6. May assume that the manager is handling it

How else could you help the asset manager become an advocate for your solution?

Q:

What motivates the CFO to become interested in energy projects?

The mindset of the CFO...

1. Concerned about the timeline of cash inflows and outflows
2. Wants as much certainty as possible about total costs, projected savings, projected expenses
3. What could go wrong?

The mindset of the CFO...

4. What about non-utility-cost financial and non-financial benefits (or impacts)?
5. How does this compare with similar projects?
6. What are the short- and long-term implications of various funding options?

Pay particular attention to the CFO...

1. "Put the last slide first!"
2. Make the cash flows and timeline crystal clear
3. Calculate all financial metrics transparently
4. Disclose what could go wrong
5. Offer "what if" analyses

IDEAS & ACTIONS

Pay particular attention to the CFO...

6. Specify the non-utility-cost financial benefits clearly and have a credible basis for their valuation in your projections
7. Preemptively address any other potential impacts on the prospect's operations

Pay particular attention to the CFO...

8. Describe the short- and long-term consequences of various funding options
9. Take the time to understand the Cap Ex approval process
10. Highlight the cost of delay, including the delayed enjoyment of any non-utility-cost financial and non-financial benefits

How else could you help the CFO become an advocate for your solution?

Q:

In any given selling situation, have you taken the time to consider what issues matter to each of the stakeholders, decision-makers and influencers?

Be genuinely helpful and create value

Consider giving a trial offer

Use a time constraint

Convey the cost of delay

IDEAS & ACTIONS
_____
_____
_____
_____

Play to their desires

Show time efficiencies

Help them justify the purchase

selling in 6™

Lesson 100
FINDING THE RIGHT DECISION-MAKERS AND INFLUENCERS
Qualifying your prospects

Presented by
Mark Jewell
@SellingEnergy
info@sellingenergy.com

Turbocharging Success

You want quality over quantity

Why quality is more important than quantity

Indicators of a solid prospect

1. Must be in need of your offering
2. Must have the desire to purchase your offering
3. Must have the means to purchase your offering
4. Must have the authority/ability to make the decision to buy

If you don't have all four, you aren't selling your offering, you are selling one (or more) of the four.

IDEAS & ACTIONS

_____

_____

_____

_____

Lesson 101
FINDING THE RIGHT DECISION-MAKERS AND INFLUENCERS
Selling to the C-Suite effectively

Presented by
Mark Jewell
@SellingEnergy
info@sellingenergy.com

Turbocharging Success

How comfortable are you selling to the "C-Suite"?

"The higher up the corporate ladder you get, the less price matters."

"Decision-makers make the budget. Non-decision-makers spend the budget."

Adapted from Anthony Parinello, Selling to VITO

"Place the last slide first"

Adapted from Anthony Parinello, Selling to VITO

"Do not dive too deeply into the how"

Adapted from Anthony Parinello, Selling to VITO

"Stay away from your product"

Adapted from Anthony Parinello, Selling to VITO

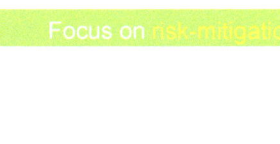

Focus on risk-mitigation

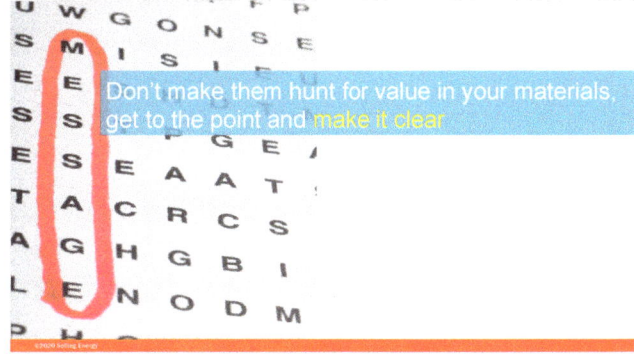

Don't make them hunt for value in your materials; get to the point and make it clear

IDEAS & ACTIONS

www.SellingEnergy.com

Use name-dropping carefully

Lesson 102

Harnessing the power of in-person networking

Presented by
Mark Jewell
@SellingEnergy
info@sellingenergy.com

Networking is the cultivating of mutually beneficial, give-and-take, win-win relationships.

—Bob Burg

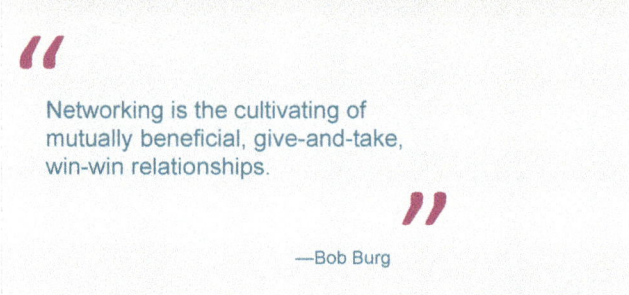

Networking is like dating

The goal is to get them to know, like, and trust you

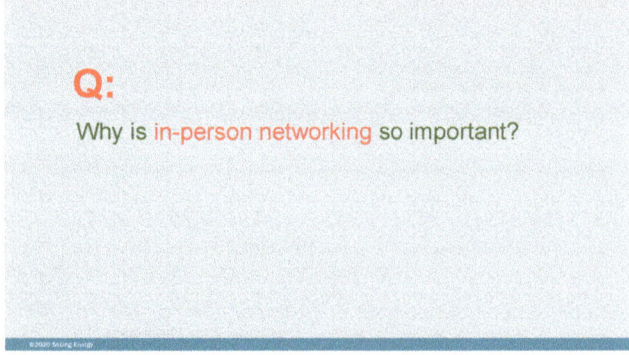

Q:

Why is in-person networking so important?

Why in-person networking is so important...

1. Easier to build lasting relationships face-to-face
2. Great way to build your reputation since you'll be seen as being consistent

IDEAS & ACTIONS _____

_____

_____

_____

Why in-person networking is so important...

3. Time-efficient way to reconnect with people you already know while meeting those you don't know
4. Great place to practice your elevator pitch

Q:

So what are some steps to mastering in-person networking?

Steps to mastering in-person networking...

4. Get a plan together and determine when and where.
5. Master your elevator pitch.
6. Prepare ahead of time, researching likely fellow attendees online or through colleagues.

Why in-person networking is so important...

5. Strong relationships start with shared experiences.
6. People are more relaxed and have their guard down.
7. Others are there to network too, so you aren't "bugging them."

Steps to mastering in-person networking...

1. Network as often as possible.
2. Don't think of networking events as boring.
3. Be willing to dedicate the time to mastering in-person networking skills.

Q:

Where do you go to network?

Where do you go to network...

1. Your industry events
2. Your prospects' industry events
3. Formal networking events, parties, etc.

IDEAS & ACTIONS

www.SellingEnergy.com

Target at least **4** events a month
1. _____
2. _____
3. _____
4. _____

Don't wait to follow up

Always say "thank you"

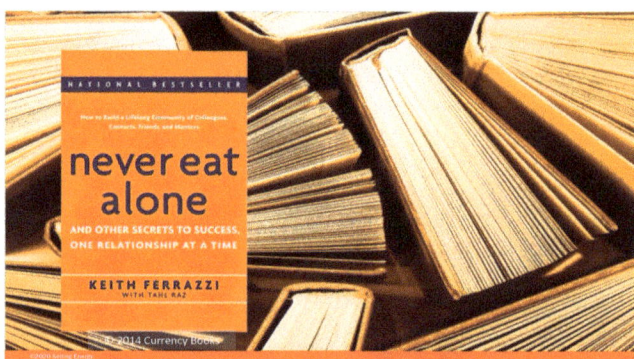

IDEAS & ACTIONS

_____
_____
_____
_____

Lesson 103
Preparing to network more effectively

 Presented by
Mark Jewell
@SellingEnergy
info@sellingenergy.com

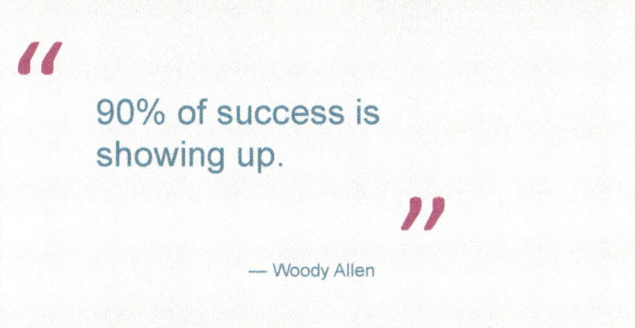

90% of success is showing up.

— Woody Allen

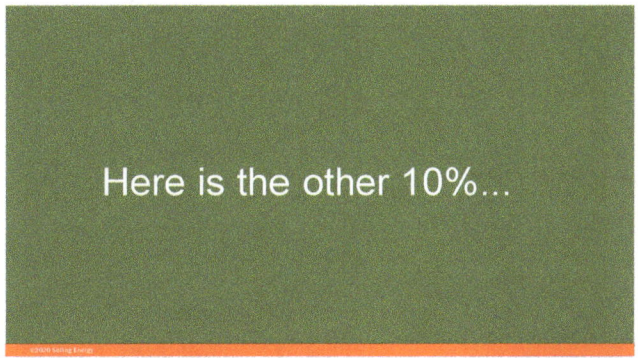

Here is the other 10%...

Visualize your dream prospect...

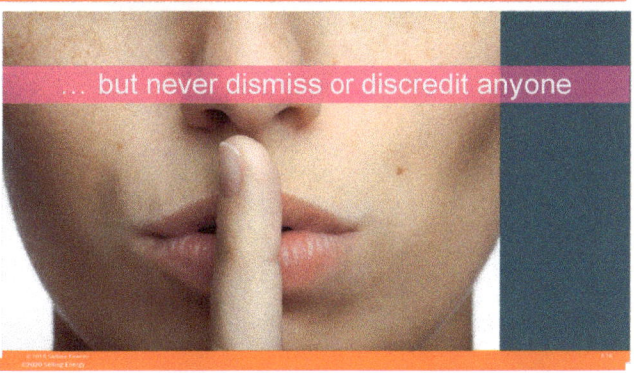

... but never dismiss or discredit anyone

Prepare for and focus on those you want to meet

Know what you want out of the relationship

IDEAS & ACTIONS

www.SellingEnergy.com

Stay up-to-date on current events

Have your pick-up lines memorized

Set an ambitious goal

Bring a notebook and a pen

And carry plenty of business cards!

Make at least 4 notes on the back of each prospect's card...

1. Where did you meet?
2. When did you meet?
3. What is the next step?
4. What sound bite will help continue the dialogue?

BONUS TIP:
Always carry a silver-ink Sharpie and/or Post-It notes to annotate cards with no open space (or surfaces too slick to write on)!

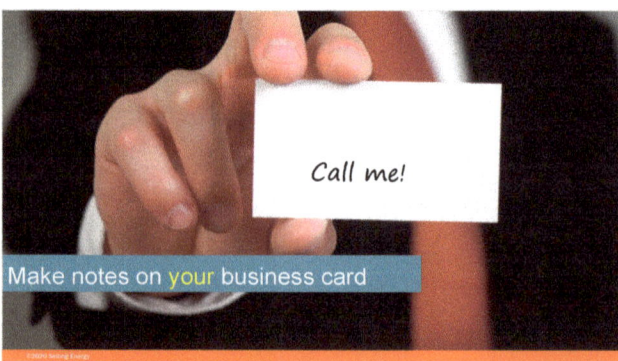

Call me!

Make notes on your business card

Find something that distinguishes you...

IDEAS & ACTIONS

... but always dress for success

Lesson 104
Maximizing the value of a networking event

Presented by
Mark Jewell
@SellingEnergy
info@sellingenergy.com

> Get face to face first.
> Networking eliminates cold calling.
> Networking leads to referrals.

—Jeffrey Gitomer

Be the first one to arrive and the last to leave. The middle gets crowded.

Spend 75% of the time with people you don't know

Be absolutely confident and cheerful

Don't be creepy

Don't get drunk

IDEAS & ACTIONS

www.SellingEnergy.com

Don't be aggressive

Don't just use people

Make sure you get their name

selling in 6™

Lesson 105
Paying close attention to what is actually said

Presented by
Mark Jewell
@SellingEnergy
info@sellingenergy.com

sellingenergy
Turbocharging Success

Don't talk about yourself the entire time

Don't start with your pitch

Listen and remember

Pay attention to non-verbal clues

IDEAS & ACTIONS

Avoid "risky" topics

Read between the lines

No forcing, tricking, pressuring, or guilt-tripping

Get them excited!

Leave them with a "hook"… Remember, you want a "second date"

selling in 6™

Lesson 106
Mastering the art of conversation

Presented by
Mark Jewell
@SellingEnergy
info@sellingenergy.com

sellingenergy
Turbocharging Success

Does the thought of tackling a crowded room full of people you don't know make you nervous or even afraid?

You can decide to replace those emotions with absolute confidence and curiosity…

You can decide to reframe the whole experience… For you, this is now an exciting and profitable treasure hunt!

IDEAS & ACTIONS

Q:

So how do you broadcast your willingness to make some new friends?

Make eye contact, smile, and laugh

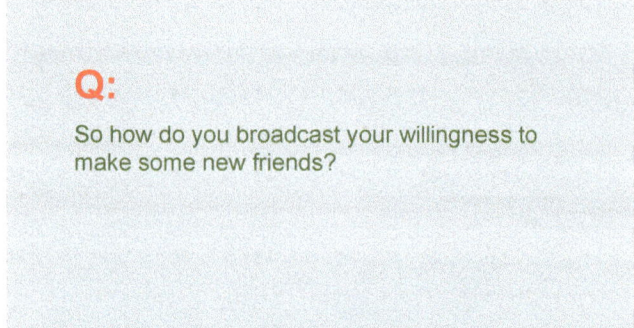

HELLO
my name is

Write a question or statement on your name badge that sparks a conversation.

Booths are great places to start conversations... they give you something to talk about.

Know when to use your "wingman"

Check out the tweets of those you want to meet... and use them to start an in-person conversation

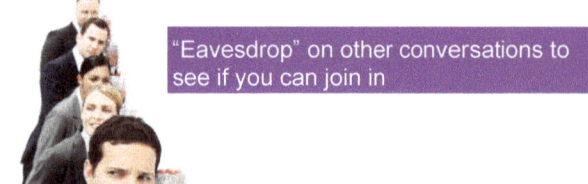

"Eavesdrop" on other conversations to see if you can join in

Have a few one-liners

IDEAS & ACTIONS

PUT YOUR PHONE AWAY!

Keep an open stance that invites others to join the conversation

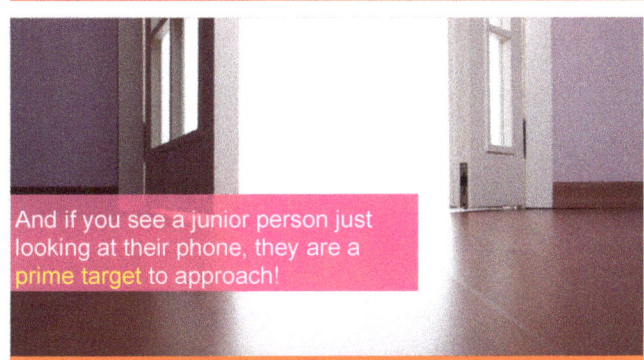

And if you see a junior person just looking at their phone, they are a prime target to approach!

Join a group that has someone you know… they will likely introduce you to everyone else

PERFECT PHRASES for PROFESSIONAL NETWORKING

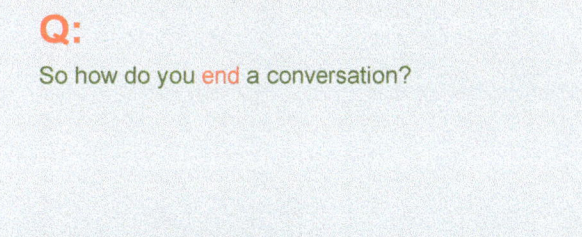

Q:

So how do you end a conversation?

Don't scan the room for someone more interesting

"Please excuse me, I need to use the restroom"

IDEAS & ACTIONS

www.SellingEnergy.com

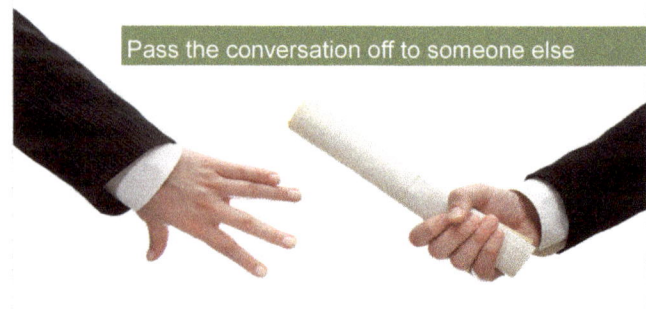

Have your wingman "tap you out"

Pass the conversation off to someone else

Lesson 107
Calling the best prospects... the "60/30/10" rule

Presented by
Mark Jewell
@SellingEnergy
info@sellingenergy.com

selling**energy**
Turbocharging Success

60%

30%

10%

Adapted from Scott Channell

60%   Who you call

30%   What you say

10%   Everything else

Adapted from Scott Channell

Lesson 108
Cold-calling and warm-calling

Presented by
Mark Jewell
@SellingEnergy
info@sellingenergy.com

selling**energy**
Turbocharging Success

"
Cold calling is not dead,
it's the approach that has
changed.
"

—Jill Konrath

Different opinions on cold calling

Cold calling destroys your status as a business equal.

For those of you who want to succeed, know that selling on the telephone works.

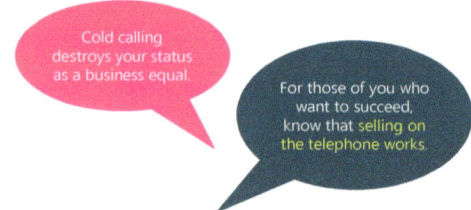

IDEAS & ACTIONS _____

_____

_____

_____

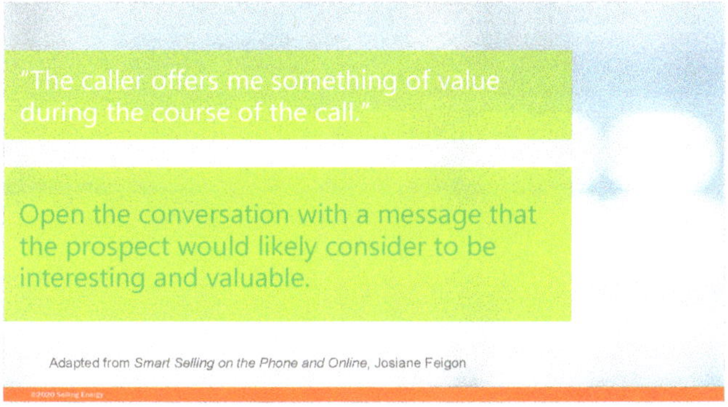

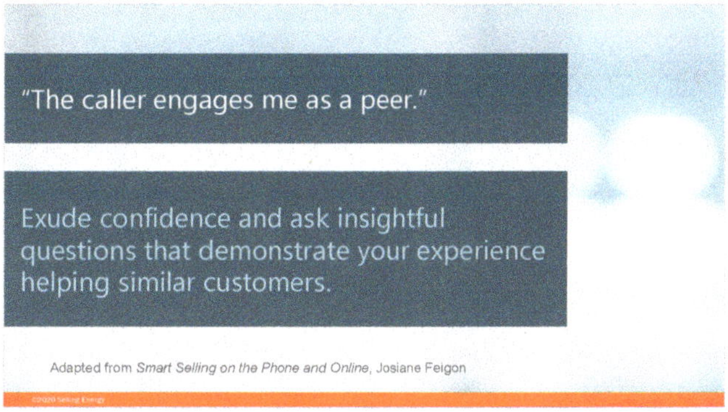

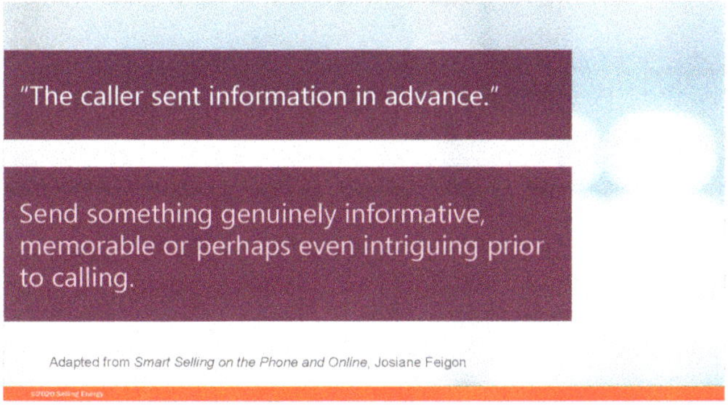

Focus on why you're calling

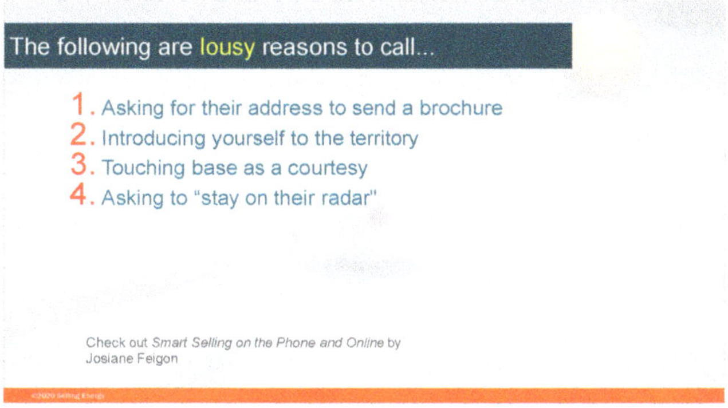

The following are **lousy** reasons to call...

1. Asking for their address to send a brochure
2. Introducing yourself to the territory
3. Touching base as a courtesy
4. Asking to "stay on their radar"

Check out *Smart Selling on the Phone and Online* by Josiane Feigon

Ask yourself, "What kind of cold call would I be willing to receive?"

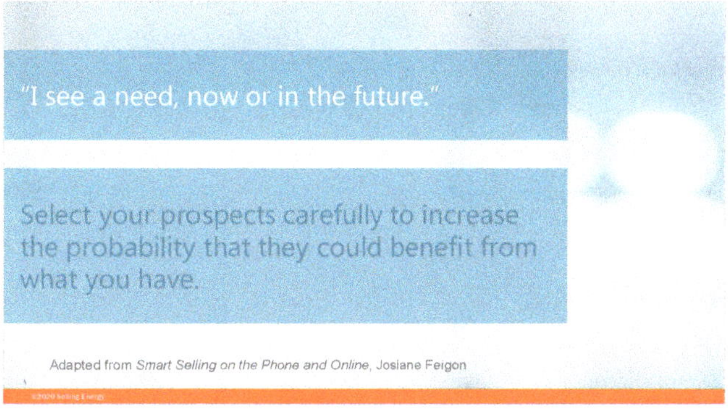

"I see a need, now or in the future."

Select your prospects carefully to increase the probability that they could benefit from what you have.

Adapted from *Smart Selling on the Phone and Online*, Josiane Feigon

"The caller offers me something of value during the course of the call."

Open the conversation with a message that the prospect would likely consider to be interesting and valuable.

Adapted from *Smart Selling on the Phone and Online*, Josiane Feigon

"The caller engages me as a peer."

Exude confidence and ask insightful questions that demonstrate your experience helping similar customers.

Adapted from *Smart Selling on the Phone and Online*, Josiane Feigon

"The caller sent information in advance."

Send something genuinely informative, memorable or perhaps even intriguing prior to calling.

Adapted from *Smart Selling on the Phone and Online*, Josiane Feigon

Plenty of other **great** prospecting strategies...

IDEAS & ACTIONS

_____

_____

_____

_____

Plenty of other great prospecting strategies...

1. "Best practice" approach
2. "Straight results" approach
3. "New idea" approach
4. "New and different" approach

Check out *Rainmaking Conversations* by Mike Schultz and John Doerr

Plenty of other great prospecting strategies...

5. "First step" approach
6. "Can you help me?" approach
7. "What's in it for me?" approach

Check out *Rainmaking Conversations* by Mike Schultz and John Doerr

Cold-calling success tips...

Cold-calling success tips...

1. Stand while cold-calling.
2. Visualize that you know the person you're calling.
3. Follow any answer you give to a gatekeeper's question with "Thank you."

Cold-calling success tips...

4. Research the pronunciation of your prospect's name.
5. Never read from a script.
6. Imagine you're calling to return their wallet that you found in the back of a taxi.

Cold-calling success tips...

7. Remember Scott Channell's 60/30/10 rule.
8. Make sure the info you provide is useful to them.
9. Do your homework.

Cold-calling success tips...

10. Mention clients in the same industry or situation that you've helped.
11. Ask questions that demonstrate that you know the space.
12. Keep smiling – literally – as much as you can throughout the call.

Cold-calling success tips...

13. You worked on your elevator pitch for in-person interactions... You can use elements of it here as well.
14. A thoughtfully crafted 3-sentence solicitation works well in cold-calling situations.
15. Remember it's a numbers game, and every rejection gets you closer to your goal... Stay positive!

IDEAS & ACTIONS

7 more cold-calling success tips...

7 more cold-calling success tips...

1. Opening impressions are important.
2. After you deliver the opener, make the prospect think.
3. Get to the point fast.
4. If you are asked for a price, give it immediately.

Adapted from *The Sales Bible* by Jeffrey Gitomer

7 more cold-calling success tips...

5. Determine what your prospect needs as quickly as possible.
6. They may resist you – it can take 7 impressions – so don't let the next salesperson claim the customer.
7. They will buy to solve a problem or satisfy a need.

Adapted from *The Sales Bible* by Jeffrey Gitomer

Should you leave voicemails?

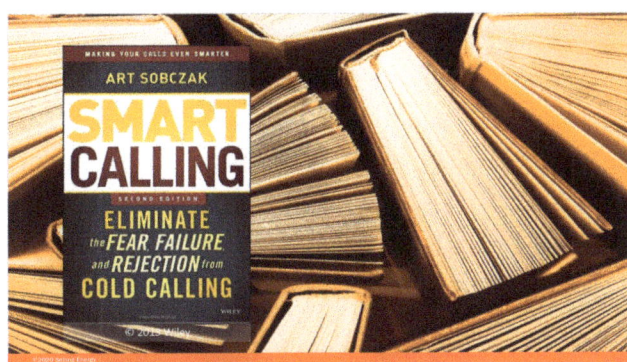

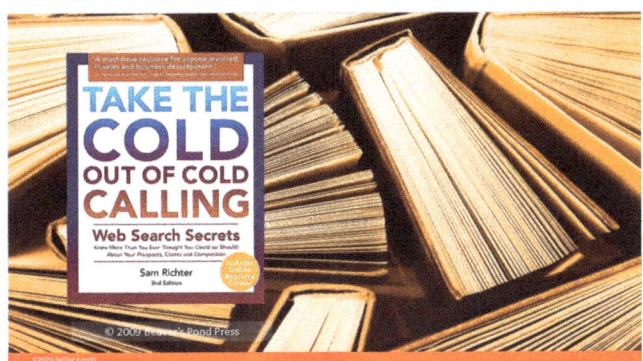

IDEAS & ACTIONS

Lesson 109
Fine-tuning for personalities and decision trees

Presented by
Mark Jewell
@SellingEnergy
info@sellingenergy.com

Q:

How many personality types are there, and how do you best approach each one?

One approach is noticing whether your prospect...

Asks or **Tells?**
Emotes or **Controls Emotion?**

- ANALYTICAL: Controls Emotions and Asks
- DRIVER: Controls Emotions and Tells
- AMIABLE: Emotes and Asks
- EXPRESSIVE: Emotes and Tells

ANALYTICAL
Controls Emotions and Asks

Motivated by logic, accuracy and risk avoidance

- Emphasize accuracy in your presentation
- Share supporting case studies or statistics
- Remain professional rather than getting personal

DRIVER
Controls Emotions and Tells

Motivated by power and respect

- Be concise
- Share tangible results that can be proven
- Avoid emotional arguments
- Offer options to select from
- Focus on the big picture rather than the details

AMIABLE
Emotes and Asks

Motivated by stability and cooperation

- Establish and maintain good rapport
- Present information systematically
- Highlight team-related benefits
- Listen carefully and agree often

IDEAS & ACTIONS

EXPRESSIVE
Emotes and Tells

Motivated by recognition and approval

- Develop a personal relationship
- Reframe offerings as boosting image
- Tell stories of your offering in use elsewhere
- Being personable is better than giving statistics

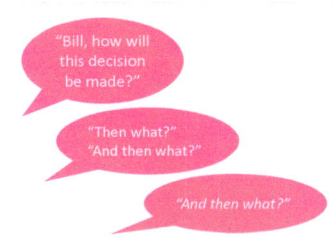

"Bill, how will this decision be made?"

"Then what?"
"And then what?"

"And then what?"

Assess the decision-making chain by asking, "And then what?"

Adapted from *The Little Red Book of Selling* by Jeffrey Gitomer

---

How do you know you are talking to the real decision-maker?

selling in 6™

Lesson 110
Making prospects confident enough to buy

Presented by
Mark Jewell
@SellingEnergy
info@sellingenergy.com

sellingenergy
Turbocharging Success

39%

The percentage of B2B buyers who select a vendor according to the **skills of the salesperson** rather than price, quality or service.

Guiding Principles

Energy-related products, services and programs all require effective selling.

Guiding Principles

Professional sales skills make you more successful at advancing any energy-related initiative, regardless of your role in the process.

Guiding Principles

You need to think of yourself as a sales professional even if your job title does not include the word "sales."

IDEAS & ACTIONS

_____

_____

_____

_____

www.SellingEnergy.com

Be completely prepared

Involve the prospect early in the presentation

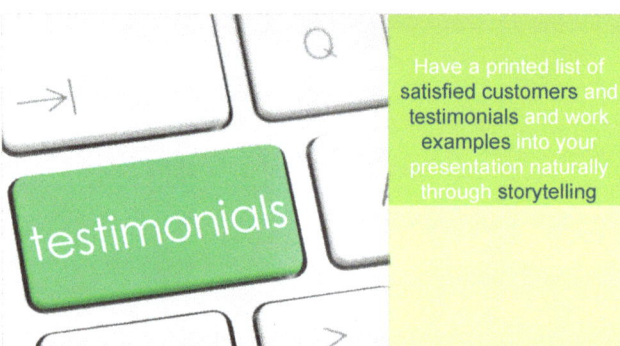

testimonials

Have a printed list of satisfied customers and testimonials and work examples into your presentation naturally through storytelling

Tell a story about helping another customer

Use a referral source if possible

Drop names of larger customers or the buyer's competitors*

*carefully

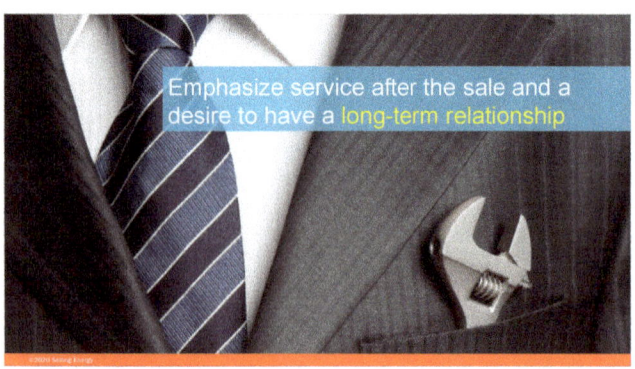

Emphasize service after the sale and a desire to have a long-term relationship

Sell to help, not for commissions

IDEAS & ACTIONS

Ask the **right** questions. Not the ones you should know the answers to.

Pay attention to your prospect's **decision-making** process.

Many ways to characterize "decision-making"

1. Rational vs. irrational
2. Logic vs. reason vs. emotion
3. Voluntary vs. deliberate
4. Democratic vs. autocratic
5. Collective participation vs. consensus

Most decisions are made unconsciously

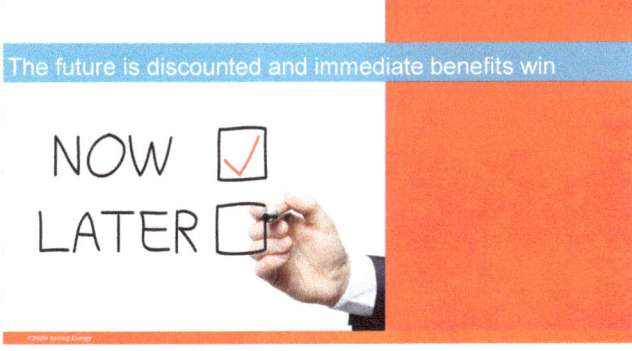

The future is discounted and immediate benefits win

NOW ☑
LATER ☐

Most people stop searching for alternatives once they make a choice

Confirmation bias

IDEAS & ACTIONS

www.SellingEnergy.com

Some morals to the story (with more to come later)...

1. First impressions and professionalism matter a lot
2. People make emotional decisions, perhaps even without knowing it

Some morals to the story (with more to come later)...

3. Help your prospect visualize future success so that they can experience the future benefit vividly enough to be motivated to take action now

Some morals to the story (with more to come later)...

4. The sooner they make a decision, the fewer alternatives they'll need to evaluate.

Some morals to the story (with more to come later)...

5. Once they make a decision, they'll likely continue to believe it was the right one (if only because they don't want to admit they were wrong in their initial evaluation).

selling in 6

Lesson 111
Focusing on losses avoided versus savings gained

Presented by
Mark Jewell
@SellingEnergy
info@sellingenergy.com

People perceive losses and gains differently

Tales of gains and losses...

1. Most prospects will make a greater effort to avoid a loss than to acquire a gain.
2. If that's the case, perhaps you should focus your value proposition around "avoiding waste" rather than "capturing savings"...

selling in 6

Lesson 112
People make comparisons rather than decisions

Presented by
Mark Jewell
@SellingEnergy
info@sellingenergy.com

IDEAS & ACTIONS

Most people don't actually make **decisions**.

They make **comparisons**.

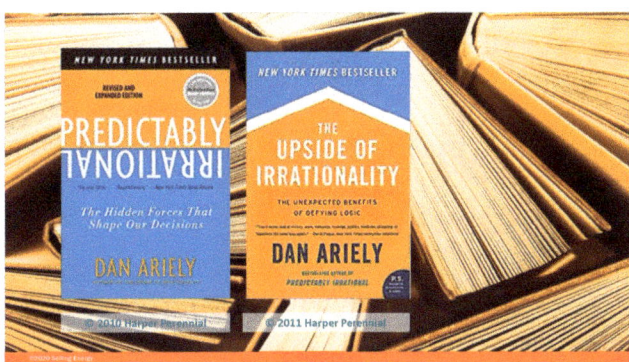

Lesson 113
Leveraging the power of "best, better, good"

Presented by
Mark Jewell
@SellingEnergy
info@sellingenergy.com

Turbocharging Success

The framing effect

Lesson 114
Handling prospects who say "No" or just go silent

Presented by
Mark Jewell
@SellingEnergy
info@sellingenergy.com

Turbocharging Success

There are plenty of great approaches to handling myths and objections either **preemptively** and **reactively**.*

*Refer to Selling in 6™ Lessons on Myths and Objections

The prospect's stated reason for buying or not buying may or may not be the real reason.

Q:

And what if a prospect with whom you have been enjoying regular back-and-forth emails, phone calls, etc. all of sudden goes silent?

IDEAS & ACTIONS

"Are you OK?"

Lesson 115
The art and science of active listening

Presented by
Mark Jewell
@SellingEnergy
info@sellingenergy.com

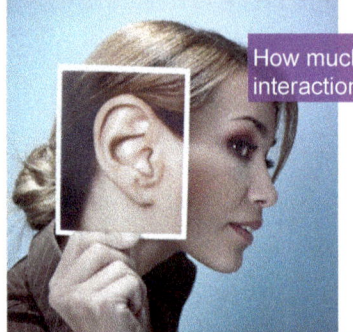

How much of your last sales interaction was spent listening?

Listen with an open mind

"The quality of your life is directly related to the quality of the questions you ask."
- Anthony Robbins

"The quality of your outcome is directly related to the quality of the evaluations you're prepared to make."
- Anthony Robbins

"A good listener has the ability to better understand and process information."
- Christopher Pappas

"A great listener has the ability to use this information to negotiate, influence, and avoid misunderstandings and conflicts."
- Christopher Pappas

IDEAS & ACTIONS

1. Are you properly prepared to listen actively?

Preparing yourself to listen actively...

1. Be fully in the moment.
2. Listen at least 75% of the time.
3. Stay calm, resourceful and flexible.
4. Maintain a sense of curiosity to support discovery and learning.

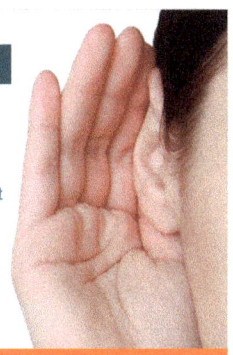

Preparing yourself to listen actively...

5. Nurture the silence.
6. Resist the urge to be composing your response rather than listening.
7. Never multitask.

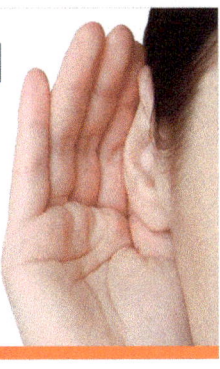

If you don't understand something, wait until the speaker has finished speaking, and *then* ask a qualifying question.

Consider asking the speaker for examples that demonstrate what they have just said.

Q:

What other observations might help you enhance the meaning of the words that you're hearing?

- Gestures
- Facial expressions
- Body language
- Volume
- Tone

IDEAS & ACTIONS

www.SellingEnergy.com

Q:

But what if you're speaking on the phone and you are unable to observe the speaker?

Q:

When you're speaking on the phone, could closing your eyes make you a better listener?

- Volume
- Tone
- Breathing
- Communication lags

2. How can you ensure that the speaker feels as if they are being heard?

Q:

First of all, are you taking notes, and if so, how and at what level of detail?

"What I'm hearing you say is…"
"Help me understand…"
"What I think I heard you say is…"
"Let me be sure I've recorded this properly…"

Q:

What other ways could you ensure that the speaker feels as if you're really listening?

"Uh huh…"
"I see…"
"Tell me more…"
"Hmmm…that's strange…"

IDEAS & ACTIONS _____

_____

_____

_____

If you choose to repeat, be sure to paraphrase rather than simply parrot what you heard.

Perhaps share a personal experience that echoes the speaker's observation or point of view without dominating the conversation.

Consider switching from "we" to "I" to help demonstrate your personal commitment to the customer's success.

Take careful notes on (and remember) any particular anecdotes the speaker has shared so that you can reference them later in the conversation or relationship.

Q:

Realizing that restating what the speaker has just said indicates that you've heard them, what if they say something negative?

3. How important is securing agreement, and how soon might that happen in a conversation?

Q:

How early in the relationship could you secure agreement?

Q:

Could humor relieve stress and encourage the speaker to venture beyond their comfort zone?

IDEAS & ACTIONS

www.SellingEnergy.com

Q:
Could emphasizing areas of agreement set a foundation upon which further agreement could be built?

4. Are you prepared to ask the tough questions right up front to avoid wasting time?

5. Are you prepared to listen for what is not being said?

- What is missing?
- What the speaker values are and/or what they should be concerned about?
- Is there a question behind the question?

- Any changes in the speaker's level of disclosure and/or tone when addressing certain topics or colleagues
- Gap between what the speaker has now and what he/she wants to (or should want to) have going forward

6. Are you listening for key words that could be used to build rapport by mirroring those words later?

Listen for repetition

- Is your speaker's primary modality (as per neuro-linguistic programming or NLP) visual, auditory, or kinesthetic?

IDEAS & ACTIONS _____

_____

_____

_____

- Does your speaker favor certain turns of phrase or metaphors that you could repurpose in your own presentation (or in follow-up correspondence) to gain additional rapport?

Success tips to remember about listening actively...

1. Prime the conversation prior to talking tech.
2. Get out of your comfort zone and into theirs.

Success tips to remember about listening actively...

3. Pace and mirror your prospect.
4. Know that music requires silence between the notes.

Success tips to remember about listening actively...

5. At least 75% of the conversation should be listening.
6. Humor relieves anxiety.

Success tips to remember about listening actively...

7. Stories sell, not brochures or technical specifications.
8. Make sure your prospect's eyes are shining throughout.

Success tips to remember about listening actively...

9. Take great notes to guide the conversation.
10. Be clear about next steps and be sure to follow through.

selling in 6™

Lesson 116
Taking, indexing and archiving great notes

Presented by
Mark Jewell
@SellingEnergy
info@sellingenergy.com

sellingenergy
Turbocharging Success

IDEAS & ACTIONS

Q:
First of all, is it better to take handwritten or typed notes?

Selected realities of handwritten vs. typed notes...

1. Many people type faster than they write.
2. Notetaking can be even faster if you populate a pre-typed form that mirrors your agenda.
3. Some people type without fully processing what they are hearing, which actually *decreases* comprehension.

Selected realities of handwritten vs. typed notes...

4. Some people say typing on a laptop during a meeting is impersonal.
5. Most people don't take the time to re-type their handwritten notes.
6. Some tech exists for handwriting recognition, etc.
7. Consider supplementing with recorded notes after the meeting.

The bottom line...

1. You need to take accurate notes that are archived and searchable later.
2. You need to transfer your and your prospect's To Do items easily and accurately to meeting minutes, work schedules, and calendars.

The bottom line...

3. No one system will be perfect for every professional.
4. You need to try various approaches, settling on the one that keeps you up-to-date, in control, and effective.

Fast Company's advice: "Think like a student!"

1. Start before the meeting
   • Attendees, agenda items, goals
   • Questions that need to be answered
2. Don't transcribe; write in your own words
3. Review what you wrote immediately
   • Observations, more detail, action items

SOURCE: "How to Master the Art of Taking Notes," *Fast Company* magazine

Fast Company's advice: "Think like a student!"

4. Revisit your notes to track progress
5. Save calendar invites for follow-up meetings that justify all of this careful note-taking by continuing to move the ball forward!

SOURCE: "How to Master the Art of Taking Notes," *Fast Company* magazine

IDEAS & ACTIONS

My approach to notes, in case you want to try it...

1. Create Client folder and Client Excel workbook.
2. Keep a shortcut to the workbook on my desktop.
3. All Client folders are sync'd to archive right away.
4. Use noise-canceling headset when typing.
5. Create a new tab for each call, meeting, etc.
6. List name, date, time, all parties meeting.
7. Use **red bold** and red to flag To Do items.
8. Immediately copy actions into my To Dos.
9. Copy/paste highlights into meeting minutes.

Lesson 117
Making better use of calls and voicemails

Presented by
Mark Jewell
@SellingEnergy
info@sellingenergy.com

To call or not to call

Schedule a time in advance

Know when it makes the most sense to call

Should you leave a voicemail?

Leaving a voicemail worth returning...

1. Plan your voicemail *before* you dial any call, to avoid fumbling for what to say in case the call goes to voicemail.
2. Plan each voicemail to be less than 30 seconds long.

Leaving a voicemail worth returning...

3. Don't leave technical details in voicemails.
4. Slowly say your number at both the beginning and end of your (brief!) voicemail.

IDEAS & ACTIONS

www.SellingEnergy.com

After the call...

Used properly, the phone can supercharge success...

1. Plan and prioritize every sales-related call.
2. Protect your "prime calling time."
3. Stand and smile when calling.

Used properly, the phone can supercharge success...

4. Review your prior call notes before dialing.
5. Take good notes on every call (and archive).
6. Notice the length of every call and voicemail.

Used properly, the phone can supercharge success...

7. Track calling activity as well as results.
8. Do as much work by phone as possible.
9. Close your eyes while on the phone.*

*Unless you're driving or doing anything else that
requires you to keep your eyes open!

selling in 6™

Lesson 118
Maximizing the impact of your emails

Presented by
Mark Jewell
@SellingEnergy
info@sellingenergy.com

sellingenergy
Turbocharging Success

Don't forget that email is often your first impression

Don't hit "Send" until you review:

recipients... subject line... attachments... message...

They need to be enticed to open it

Then you need them to read it...

IDEAS & ACTIONS

_____

_____

_____

_____

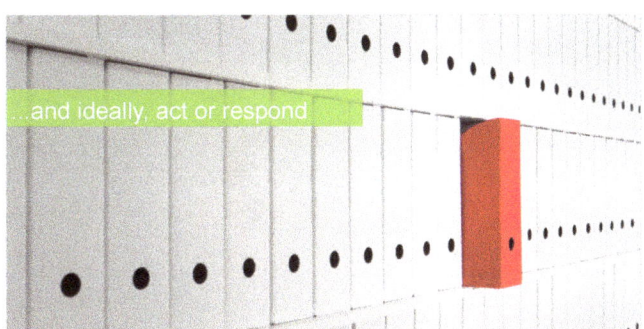

...and ideally, act or respond

How long should it be?

And should really be an attachment?

A dozen useful tips...

12 Tips for maximizing the effectiveness of your emails

1. Think carefully re: "To" vs. "CC" and "BCC."
2. Be especially careful using "Reply All."

12 Tips for maximizing the effectiveness of your emails

3. Write a meaningful subject line.
   - Especially the first 3 and last 3 words!
   - Know your reader; focus on benefits to them
   - Make sure it correctly corresponds to your reply
4. Keep a singular message; get to the point.

12 Tips for maximizing the effectiveness of your emails

5. Include a brief summary at the top and indicate the action required.
6. Be direct, deleting adjectives/adverbs.

12 Tips for maximizing the effectiveness of your emails

7. Consider writing a beginning, middle and end.
   - Greeting (and brief summary statement)
   - Explanation
   - Action steps
8. Use lists/bullets to satisfy scanners.

IDEAS & ACTIONS

www.SellingEnergy.com

12 Tips for maximizing the effectiveness of your emails

9. Diligently proofread prior to pressing Send.
10. Avoid attachments if possible.
11. Ensure any attachments are correct and open.
12. Preview important emails on your phone.

Email Etiquette

THE HAMSTER REVOLUTION

selling in 6™

Lesson 119
Maximizing the effectiveness of meetings

Presented by
Mark Jewell
@SellingEnergy
info@sellingenergy.com

selling energy
Turbocharging Success

How to get a client meeting?

Make it obvious that they will gain useful insights from your meeting regardless of whether you wind up doing business together.

Q:

How long should the meeting be?

Q:

How long should the meeting be?
It depends...

IDEAS & ACTIONS

Q:

How do we make sure every meeting is absolutely as productive as it can be?

Q:

Are there really **24** steps to ensuring that your meeting is productive?

Q:

Are there really **24** steps to ensuring that your meeting is productive?

Yes... **24**.

Ensuring every meeting is a productive meeting...

1. Know the goals of the meeting ahead of time and agree on the ideal agenda.
2. Ensure that the right stakeholders, decision-makers and influencers are invited to attend.

Ensuring every meeting is a productive meeting...

3. Confirm the meeting setting.
   - Audience size vs. room size
   - Audiovisual requirements and capabilities
   - Catering, if needed
   - Time constraints (entering/exiting)

Plan the logistics carefully...

4. Send meeting reminders the day before.
5. Arrive at the meeting venue early.
   - Weather, traffic, parking
   - Security sign-in
   - Audiovisual equipment set-up and testing
   - Visualize a positive outcome, including specific next steps that you expect to be approved.

And once you arrive at the meeting venue...

6. Begin promptly, and thank your host for assembling all parties for this date/time.
7. Be sure you know everyone present, making introductions and collecting contact info as needed.*

*Use a sheet of paper (or a grouping of cells in your Excel worksheet) to simulate the conference table and record where various attendees are sitting for your reference during both the meeting and any post-meeting debriefing.

IDEAS & ACTIONS

www.SellingEnergy.com

And once you arrive at the meeting venue...

8. Do a time check right up front... "Will anyone have to leave early?"
9. Circulate a printed agenda and ensure no items were omitted (or erroneously included).
10. Establish who will be taking meeting notes.

At the beginning of the meeting...

11. Agree on the ground rules before presenting.
    - "We have 'x' minutes to meet..."
    - "My presentation is planned for about 'x' minus 'y' minutes..."
    - "We should have plenty of time for questions ('y' minutes)..."
    - "Spontaneous questions are welcome (or not)."

At the beginning of the meeting...

11. Agree on the ground rules before presenting. (cont'd)
    - "Any off-topic items will be recorded on a 'parking lot' flip pad..."
    - "After the meeting we'll set the date/time for the next..."
    - "And we'll circulate minutes w/each party's action items..."
    - "Who here volunteers to be the scribe?"

Throughout the meeting...

12. Ensure you (and/or colleagues) take detailed notes.
    - You can also dictate details into your smartphone immediately after leaving the building to ensure all nuances and next steps were captured.
    - Transcribe verbal notes later or forward the voice file to yourself with the meeting name/date/time in the email subject line.

Throughout the meeting...

13. Ensure that when a party agrees to do something, it is noted and highlighted (e.g., **red bold** for your To Dos and red for theirs) so that it can be summarized, confirmed before the meeting adjourns, and added to the meeting minutes.

At the end of your presentation...

14. "Does anyone have questions?"
15. "If you *did* have a question, what would it be?" ☺
16. If there are no further audience questions, feel free to reclaim your presentation time with, "One of the questions I usually get asked is..."

At the end of the meeting...

17. Review the "To Do" items (the **red bold** first, and then the red) and secure commitment as well as a timeline for completing each item.
18. Confirm the location, date, time, and desired invitees for the next meeting in everyone's calendar.

IDEAS & ACTIONS

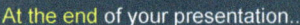

At the end of the meeting...

19. Reiterate that you will be sending meeting minutes (another opportunity to get everyone's contact info).
20. Thank them for a great meeting, and graciously depart.
    - Did the meeting progress as expected?
    - Are they happy with the outcome?
    - Any "off the record" recommendations?
    - Again, thank them for their coordination
    - And offer to take your glassware to the kitchen...

Immediately after the meeting...

23. Ensure that the minutes are shared as well as archived where you (and your clients and colleagues) can easily search/retrieve them later.
24. Be sure to follow through on all of your **red bold** items as promised!

Q:

How about meetings that you don't host?

Q:

And noticing that the table on the previous slide had 8 seats, how many people can meet at one time and still be effective?

Immediately after the meeting...

21. Copy/paste your **red bold** To Do items into your work schedule.
22. Copy/paste the next meeting into your calendar.

Be ready to act on whatever was agreed upon

Get the right people a seat at the table... including you!

Are there too many people in your meeting?

"The 8-18-1800 Rule"

- 8 people can solve a problem or make a decision
- 18 people can brainstorm, but don't expect consensus
- 1,800 people can gather for a motivational speech, new product introduction, etc.

SOURCE: "How to Know if There Are Too Many People in Your Meeting," Harvard Business Review, 2015

IDEAS & ACTIONS

_____

_____

_____

_____

www.SellingEnergy.com

Lesson 120
Deciding to become a better writer

Presented by
Mark Jewell
@SellingEnergy
info@sellingenergy.com

The first step to becoming a better business writer is committing to being a better writer overall.

Concise ideas.
Complete sentences.
Good vocabulary.
Accurate spelling.
Proper punctuation.
Clean formatting.

Review and revise

Focus on "clean lines"... If removing a word doesn't change the meaning, remove it.

Accuracy is essential in both content & form

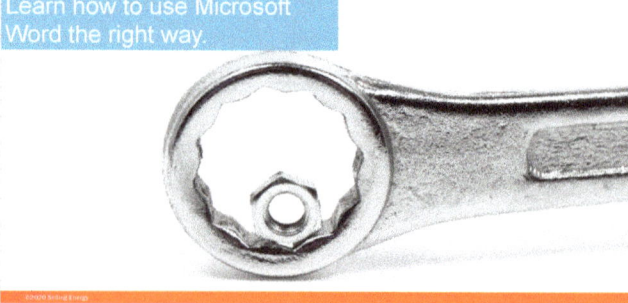

Learn how to use Microsoft Word the right way.

IDEAS & ACTIONS

_____

_____

_____

_____

Use a style guide

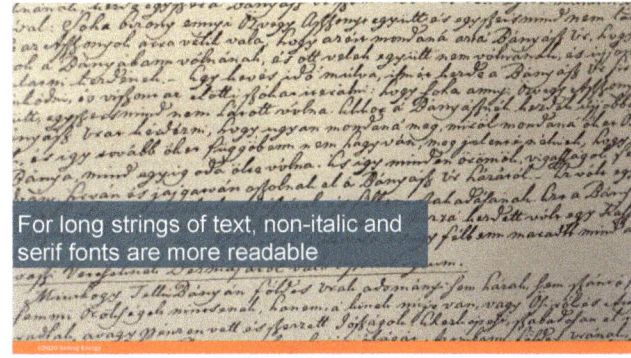

For long strings of text, non-italic and serif fonts are more readable

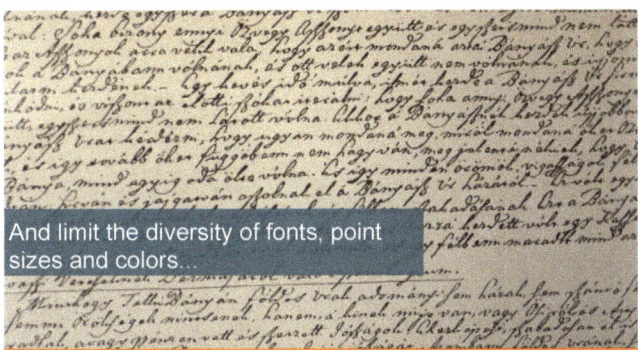

And limit the diversity of fonts, point sizes and colors...

Use the right method of communication

Emails should motivate action.

"Let's bring back the memo."

Proposals should be plans, not boring reports.

Proposals should be plans, not boring reports.

The word "proposal" means you are "proposing" something.

You need to be persuasive.

You need to focus on "WHY."

IDEAS & ACTIONS

_____

_____

_____

_____

www.SellingEnergy.com

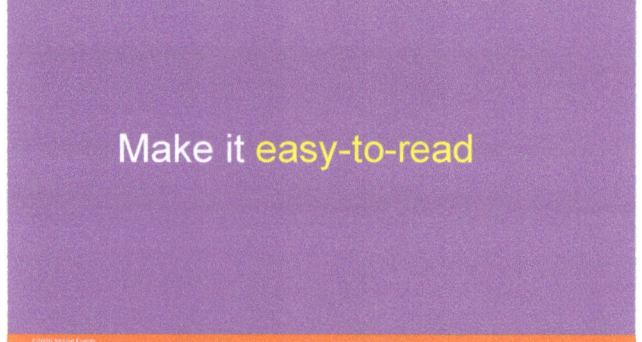

Make it easy-to-read

People are focused on "what about me" and "what do I get"

Make it about your prospect, not your company

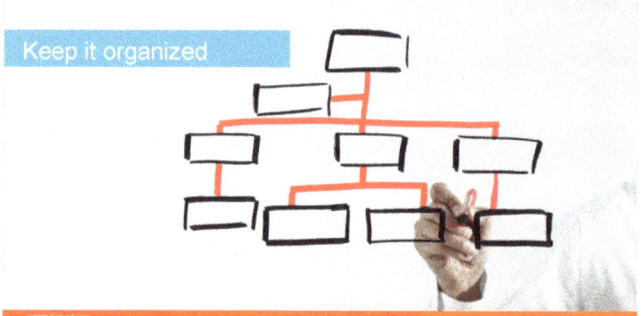

Keep it organized

Focus on results, not methods/processes

Be generous with innovative ideas

Keep your writing action-oriented

Think through any objections and address them squarely

IDEAS & ACTIONS

Keep it simple

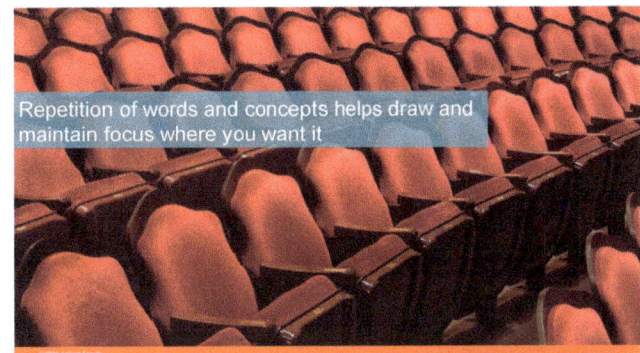

Repetition of words and concepts helps draw and maintain focus where you want it

Proofread your document, have someone else **proofread** it, and then **proofread** it again.

Re-read it the next day before sending it out

Your proposal will either get approved, be sent back for more work... or get rejected, forgotten, or just ignored

You don't get a second chance to make a first impression

Make sure your LinkedIn profile is accessible and complete, including a photo of yourself.

IDEAS & ACTIONS

www.SellingEnergy.com

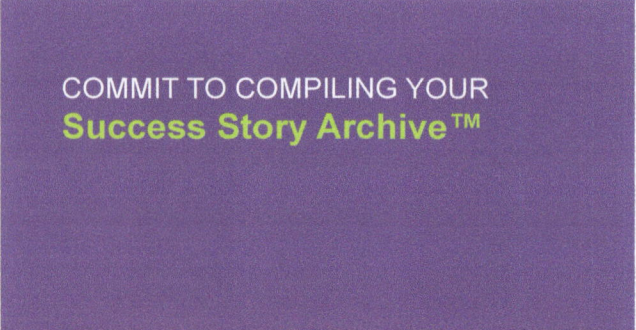

IDEAS & ACTIONS

_____

_____

_____

_____

IDEAS & ACTIONS

Lesson 180
SUCCESS TIPS FROM SALES ROCK STARS
"I visualize successful outcomes before/after sleep."

Presented by
Mark Jewell
@SellingEnergy
info@sellingenergy.com

" I visualize successful outcomes both before I go to sleep and as soon as I wake up. "

Lesson 181
SUCCESS TIPS FROM SALES ROCK STARS
"I deputize everyone on my payroll to sell."

Presented by
Mark Jewell
@SellingEnergy
info@sellingenergy.com

" I deputize everyone on my payroll to sell. "

Lesson 182
SUCCESS TIPS FROM SALES ROCK STARS
"I partner with vendors that I can make into heroes."

Presented by
Mark Jewell
@SellingEnergy
info@sellingenergy.com

" I partner with vendors that I can make into heroes. "

Lesson 183
GETTING IN THE MINDSET FOR SUCCESS
Personality traits of successful sales professionals

Presented by
Mark Jewell
@SellingEnergy
info@sellingenergy.com

Q:
What traits do you associate with a successful sales professional?

IDEAS & ACTIONS

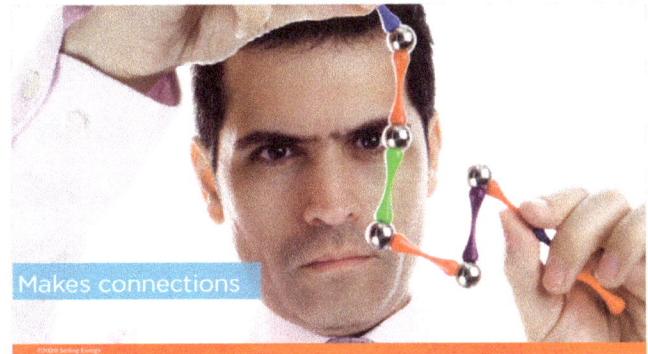
Makes connections

Professional

Knowledgeable

Focused

Perceptive

A good communicator

Persistent

Persistent

IDEAS & ACTIONS

www.SellingEnergy.com

Smart worker

Hard worker

Curious

"I have no special talents. I am only passionately curious."
—Albert Einstein

Interested in others

Confident.

"With confidence, you have won before you have started."

—Marcus Garvey

Available

Trustworthy

Friendly

If you would win a man to your cause, first convince him that you are his sincere friend.

– Abraham Lincoln

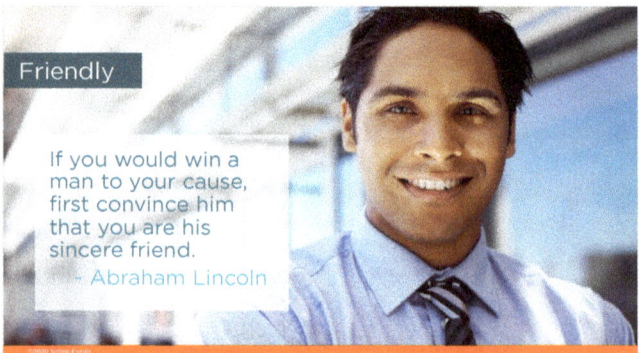

IDEAS & ACTIONS

IDEAS & ACTIONS

Set big goals and get out of your comfort zone.

Have a plan...

... and be biased toward action.

Get and stay organized.

Master your craft.

Be prepared.

Be a giver.

Make it easy to do business with you.

IDEAS & ACTIONS

Follow through on your commitments.

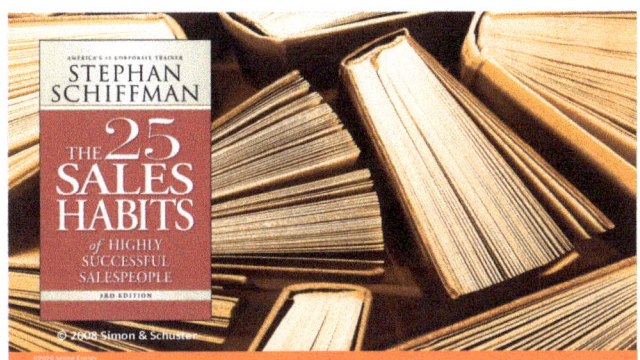

Lesson **185**
GETTING IN THE MINDSET FOR SUCCESS
Setting yourself up for success

Presented by
Mark Jewell
@SellingEnergy
info@sellingenergy.com

See, taste, hear, smell, and feel success.

Work your personal and
professional life in tandem.

Get help and support.

Preserve your energy
for success creation.

Sleep, stay in shape, eat well

IDEAS & ACTIONS

Tony Robbins – Success Principles

- Everything happens for a reason and a purpose, and it serves us.
- There is no such thing as failure. There are only results.
- Whatever happens, take responsibility.

Tony Robbins – Success Principles (cont'd)

- It's not necessary to understand everything to be able to use everything.
- People are your greatest resource.
- Work is play.
- There's no abiding success without commitment.

Ultimate Success Formula

- Formulate a precise definition of yourself and what you wish to achieve.
- Take massive action.
- Gauge or measure the success of your actions.
- Fine-tune your approach and your procedures until you reach your goal.

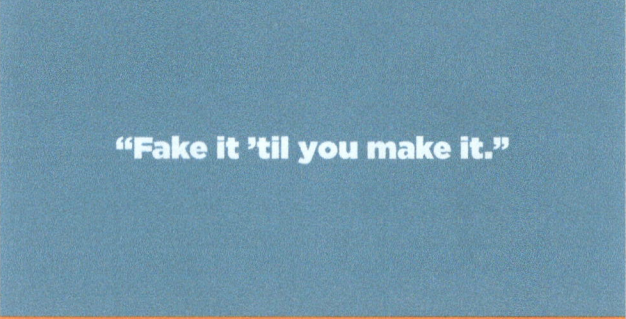

"Fake it 'til you make it."

Now what?

IDEAS & ACTIONS

Have a vision.

Set your goals as the person you want to be, not as the person you are.

Find people who you consider successful and emulate them.

Act and dress for the part.

Sound successful in your communications

- Grammar
- Writing style
- Consistency in terminology
- Spelling
- Formatting
- Tone
- Clarity
- Organization
- The details

Adapted from *Selling to Big Companies* by Jill Konrath

Be and act confident.

Hang around successful people.

Set your goals high, even if you don't always achieve them

IDEAS & ACTIONS

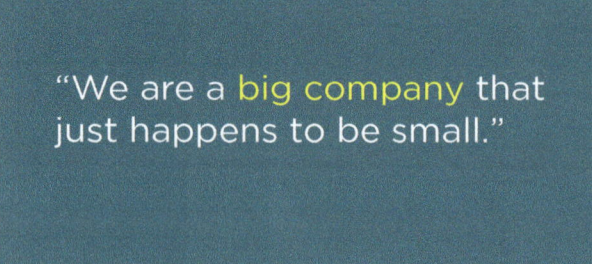

"We are a **big company** that just happens to be small."

Lesson 186
GETTING IN THE MINDSET FOR SUCCESS
Avoiding pitfalls

Presented by
Mark Jewell
@SellingEnergy
info@sellingenergy.com

Avoiding pitfalls...

Why customers might dislike salespeople

- Not listening
- Talking too much
- Lack of knowledge
- Lack of follow-up
- Lying
- Failing to understand their needs
- Refusal to take "no" for an answer

Adapted from *The Secrets of Power Selling*, Kelly Robertson

Embrace success.

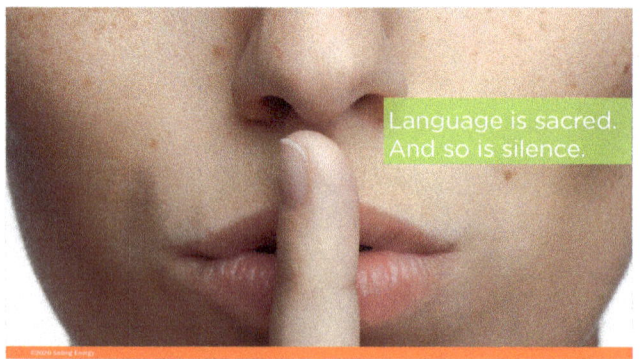

Language is sacred.
And so is silence.

Proceed with a sense of positive expectancy.

IDEAS & ACTIONS

_____

_____

_____

_____

Use your time wisely... focus on your vision.

Maintain your integrity.

Don't get complacent.

> " If you think you can
> or think you cannot,
> you are correct. "
>
> — Henry Ford

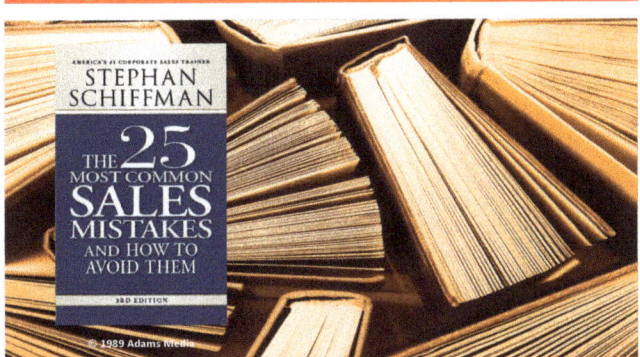

STEPHAN SCHIFFMAN
THE 25 MOST COMMON SALES MISTAKES AND HOW TO AVOID THEM
3RD EDITION
© 1989 Adams Media

selling in 6™

Lesson 187
GETTING IN THE MINDSET FOR SUCCESS
Setting goals and staying motivated

Presented by
Mark Jewell
@SellingEnergy
info@sellingenergy.com

selling energy
Turbocharging Success

> " Setting goals is the
> first step in turning
> the invisible into the
> visible. "
>
> — Tony Robbins

> " The reason that most of us
> are unhappy most of the time
> is that we set our goals not
> for the person we're going to
> be when we reach them... we
> set our goals for the person
> we are when we set them. "
>
> — Jim Coudal (lifehacker.com)

IDEAS & ACTIONS

_____

_____

_____

_____

IDEAS & ACTIONS

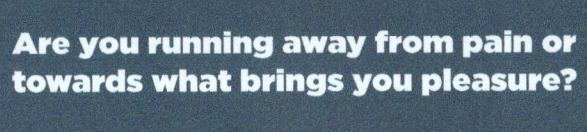
Are you running away from pain or towards what brings you pleasure?

Focus on the positive and make it fun.

Take time for yourself during the day.

Reflect on accomplishments.

EXTRA! EXTRA! READ ALL ABOUT IT! GOOD NEWS!!
Start and end the day with something positive... and avoid negativity.

Focus on how you will feel when you finish.

Overcoming failure and rejection...

"
Our greatest glory is not in never failing, but in rising every time we fall.
"
— Confucius

IDEAS & ACTIONS

www.SellingEnergy.com

Stay confident, don't take it personally.

Everyone gets rejected at some point.

Sometimes rejection is a blessing in disguise

Learn from rejection. What was the reason? Ask for feedback.

Keep trying!

More precisely...
Take massive action...
Measure your results...
Modify your approach...

Take massive action...
Measure your results...
Modify your approach...

Know your sales ratio

Reward your success.

IDEAS & ACTIONS

_____

_____

_____

Lesson 188
GETTING IN THE MINDSET FOR SUCCESS
Planning values/purpose/mission and then goals

Presented by
Mark Jewell
@SellingEnergy
info@sellingenergy.com

Successful people focus on being congruent.

1. Destiny is the by-product of thousands of decisions.
2. Decision-making patterns form self-reinforcing habits.
3. Values drive decision-making.
4. Values inform life purpose.

Successful people focus on being congruent.

5. Life purpose informs life mission.
6. Life mission informs goals.
7. Goals (and accountability) determine actions.
8. Values >>> Purpose >>> Mission >>> Goals

Lesson 189
GETTING IN THE MINDSET FOR SUCCESS
Planning activity-based metrics and tracking them

Presented by
Mark Jewell
@SellingEnergy
info@sellingenergy.com

"You can't manage what you don't measure."

1. Do you set goals in terms of end results or activities?
2. What type of activities would you track?
3. Calculate the number of calls, proposals, wins needed.
4. Granular tracking maximizes the % of time you're on-course.

So what activities should you be tracking?

1. Leads identified
2. Referrals requested
3. Referrals granted
4. Leads contacted
5. Leads requesting proposals

So what activities should you be tracking?

6. Presentations generated
7. Presentations given
8. Immediate wins
9. Size of overall pipeline, probability-weighted
10. Ratios involving all previously mentioned metrics

IDEAS & ACTIONS

Lesson 190
GETTING IN THE MINDSET FOR SUCCESS
Planning your activities to avoid sales slumps

Presented by
Mark Jewell
@SellingEnergy
info@sellingenergy.com

Turbocharging Success

"You can't manage what you don't measure."

1. Do you set goals in terms of results or activities?
2. What type of activities would you track?
3. Calculate the number of calls, proposals, wins needed.
4. Granular tracking maximizes the % of time you're on-course.
5. Consider extrapolating daily productivity into yearly figures.

Do the math and you'll have fewer surprises!

1. How many calls do you need to make a proposal?
2. How many proposals do you need to make a sale?
3. How large is your average sale?
4. How many sales are needed to make your annual goal?

Do the math and you'll have fewer surprises!

5. How many average sales are needed for your income goal?
6. What weeks are suboptimal for prospecting/selling?
7. How much more selling has to occur in the "prime weeks"?
8. The best time to make a sale is when you just made one!

Lesson 191
GETTING IN THE MINDSET FOR SUCCESS
Strategies and tactics of the best sales managers

Presented by
Mark Jewell
@SellingEnergy
info@sellingenergy.com

Turbocharging Success

Top producers are not necessarily the best managers.

1. Large % of sales staff turnover is directly related to mgmt.
2. Top managers inspire and empower the salespeople.

What does effective sales management look like?

1. Value proposition and credible targets are clear.
2. Salespeople are given training and coaching.
3. Territory selection and compensation are rational.
4. Ongoing coaching is available.
5. Managers lobby for marketing and operational support.

Lesson 192
OPTIMIZING YOUR WORKPLACE AND HABITS
Setting yourself up to be more productive

Presented by
Mark Jewell
@SellingEnergy
info@sellingenergy.com

Turbocharging Success

IDEAS & ACTIONS

Q:

What are some of the most important dimensions of "being most productive"?

1. Apply best practices for organizing your workspace and your mind space.

2. Behave in ways that empower massive action, honest and conscious assessment of results, and continuous improvement in approach.

" I get up every morning determined to change the world and have one hell of a good time. Sometimes this makes planning my day difficult. "

— E.B. White

Prep yourself to be productive...

Correlate your big goals to daily activities.

Quiet Area

Work in a place where you are most productive.

Optimize your work station.

IDEAS & ACTIONS

www.SellingEnergy.com

Tips for having (and keeping) an organized desk...

1. Get rid of pens and pencils you don't need.
2. Set up proximity-based frequency of use.
3. Hide electronics you don't need to see.
4. Manage your cords.

Tips for having (and keeping) an organized desk...

1. Scan and then toss papers (receipts, notes, flyers, *everything!*).
2. Have a scratch notepad for stuff you write down but don't need to keep.
3. Recycle stuff you print. It's already electronic!
4. Don't eat at your desk.

Find and leverage your most productive time...

1. Find your most productive time and work on the most challenging tasks then.
2. Make time for reaching out to prospects when they are available.
3. Work on tedious stuff when you have no mental capacity left for the hard stuff.
4. Do things first that others can then keep moving.

Stay hydrated!

Q: Are you more productive in the morning or the evening?

Q: And if you're more productive in the evening, why are you clocking out at 5PM?

Q: If you are trying to capture New York City prospects, why is your day starting in San Francisco at 9AM?

Keep all your To-Dos in one place.

IDEAS & ACTIONS

Get rid of Post-It notes!

Keep an inspirational image in view.

Set yourself up for success Friday afternoon.

selling in 6™

Lesson 193
OPTIMIZING YOUR WORKPLACE AND HABITS
Getting things done

Presented by
Mark Jewell
@SellingEnergy
info@sellingenergy.com

sellingenergy
Turbocharging Success

Getting things done...

Getting Things Done
the art of stress-free productivity
from the New York Times bestselling author
David Allen
A brand new edition for 2015
© 2015 Platkus

The "2-minute rule": Do it now.

Get everything out of your head... write it down.

IDEAS & ACTIONS

_____

_____

_____

_____

Have a trusted organizational system.

Adapted from *Getting Things Done*

Have a trusted organizational system...

1. A list of active tasks
2. A list of active projects
3. A calendar
4. A someday/maybe list
5. Reference files
6. A capture device

Adapted from *Getting Things Done*

Use specific action verbs when writing your To-Do list.

"Call Mark at ABC Corp. to confirm Q2 training."
versus
"ABC Training"

The 5 phases of effective work

- **Collect.** Gather inputs, resources, knowledge, and tasks
- **Process.** Examine your inputs
- **Organize.** Process and put the info into systems (to-do lists, future projects lists, trackers)
- **Do.** Work through the tasks you can accomplish now
- **Review.** Examine results, revise strategy, improve your systems

Adapted from *Getting Things Done*

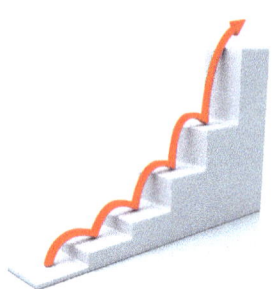

Focus on the next step.

Don't worry... you won't get it right the first time.

Getting *more* things done...

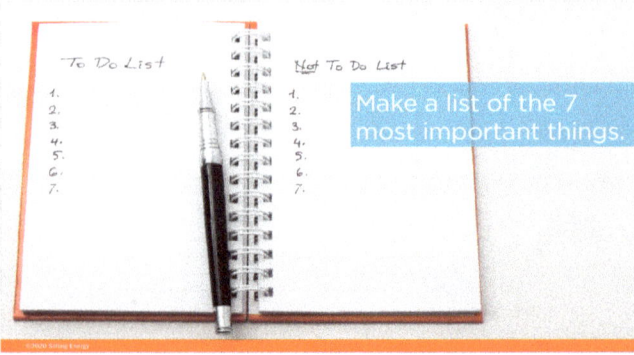

Make a list of the 7 most important things.

IDEAS & ACTIONS

Minimize interruptions...

1. Screen phone calls.
2. Set aside time for email and turn it off the rest of the time.
3. Block out "getting things done" time as you do with meetings... And make it non-negotiable.

Avoid procrastination...

1. Do the task that you don't want to do first.
2. Reward yourself when you complete a task, not as a way of delaying doing a task.
3. Make a schedule and stick to it.
4. Add the date you put something on your To-Do list.

Figure out where you are wasting time... and keep a big clock nearby.

Don't waste time waiting.

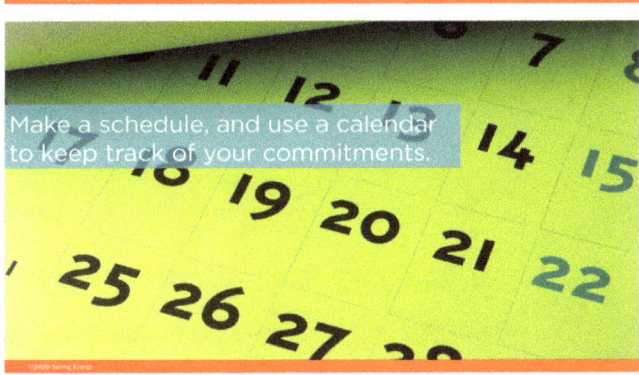

Make a schedule, and use a calendar to keep track of your commitments.

Learn to say "no".

Q:

What is the #1 thing stopping you from getting stuff done?

Getting organized!!!

IDEAS & ACTIONS

_____

_____

_____

_____

www.SellingEnergy.com

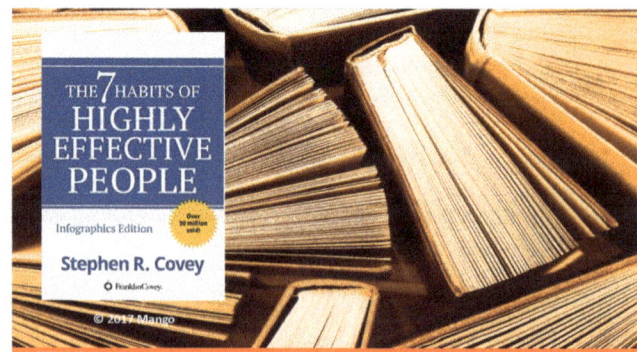

Lesson 194
OPTIMIZING YOUR WORKPLACE AND HABITS
Getting and staying organized

Presented by
Mark Jewell
@SellingEnergy
info@sellingenergy.com

> If your day-to-day life is out of control, it's almost impossible to think strategically or plan effectively.
>
> — David Allen

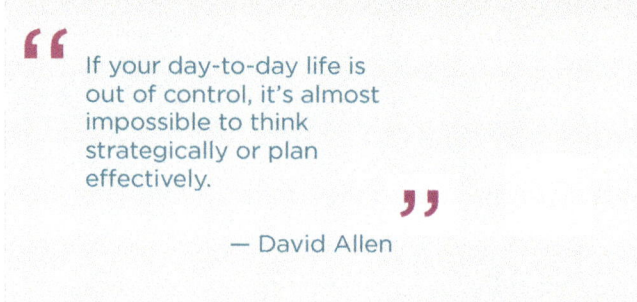

Q:

What are some of the areas where you spend too much time because you aren't organized?

You ALWAYS have enough time to get organized.

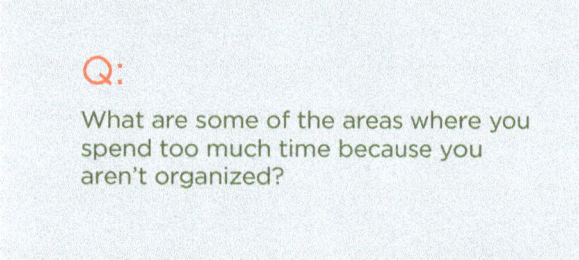

Set aside non-negotiable organizational time.

Get your business cards organized.

IDEAS & ACTIONS

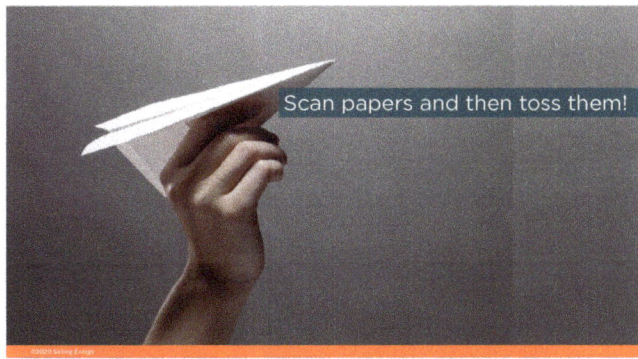

Scan papers and then toss them!

Q:

What are some of your best organization tips?

Several tips to consider adopting immediately...

1. Have a designated place for biz cards, receipts, etc.
2. Only touch each item once.
3. Abide by the "two-minute rule."
4. Look at your goals, tasks and scorecard constantly.

Several tips to consider adopting immediately...

5. Keep only active projects in your visual field at work.
6. Break projects into tasks and schedule those tasks.
7. Focusing on the results makes even boring tasks motivating.
8. Revisit your goals often to ensure that your activities matter.

© 2009 Penguin Books

© 2004 Penguin Books

Lesson **195**
OPTIMIZING YOUR WORKPLACE AND HABITS
Work smarter, not just harder

Presented by
Mark Jewell
@SellingEnergy
Info@sellingenergy.com

Turbocharging Success

Improve your everyday efficiency.

IDEAS & ACTIONS

Get the proper training in software you use everyday.

Don't reinvent the wheel.

Outsource what you can.

Be dedicated to organization.

If you think there is an easier way, there usually is.

Create templates for things you use everyday.

Recognize the point of diminishing returns – go home before you crash.

IDEAS & ACTIONS

Q:
What if you worked smart **and** hard?

Q:
But how do you balance the **short term** with the **long term**?

"
On average, a plane will be off-course 95% of its flight.

"
— J.S. Gilbert

Keep your eyes on **where you are going** while your head is down **getting stuff done.**

Long-term projects get sidetracked more easily but are usually more important.

Plan your time carefully...

Break big projects into small chunks.

Last in, first out is for logistics, not operations.

EFFICIENCY

DELEGATE

TO DO LIST

ORGANIZE

TIME MANAGEMENT

FOCUS

PRIORITIZE

PROACTIVE

PROJECTS

IDEAS & ACTIONS

And remember, you don't have to be **perfect** all the time.

Lesson 196
PRESENTATION EXCELLENCE
Making great first and lasting impressions

Presented by
Mark Jewell
@SellingEnergy
info@sellingenergy.com

Focus on your first impression...

You don't get a second chance to make a first impression.

Eat it? Mate with it? Kill it?

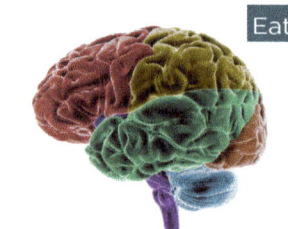

Q:

Who has made a great first impression on you, and why?

People make a decision about you in 2 seconds.

IDEAS & ACTIONS

Be early... always.

Dress appropriately.

Remember to smile!

Be and stay confident.

Be human... and interesting.

Do something crazy every once in a while.

Talk more about the other person than yourself.

Use the other person's name.

IDEAS & ACTIONS

_____

_____

_____

_____

Be positive... always.

Demonstrate your sense of humor.

Find a connection.

blink

Malcolm Gladwell

© 2007 Back Bay Books

And leave a great impression...

Thank you
Send a thank-you note.

Deliver what you promised in a timely manner.

IDEAS & ACTIONS

Keep a database of contacts.

Regularly touch base with your contacts.

Send newsletters & surveys.

selling in 6™

Lesson 197
PRESENTATION EXCELLENCE
Focusing on clear communication

Presented by
Mark Jewell
@SellingEnergy
info@sellingenergy.com

sellingenergy
Turbocharging Success

Unless you are able to communicate your ideas effectively, you might as well not have had them.

Just because you didn't go to school for English

doesn't mean you don't need to know how to write.

People who write well do well. You have to be an effective and persuasive communicator in order to make something happen.

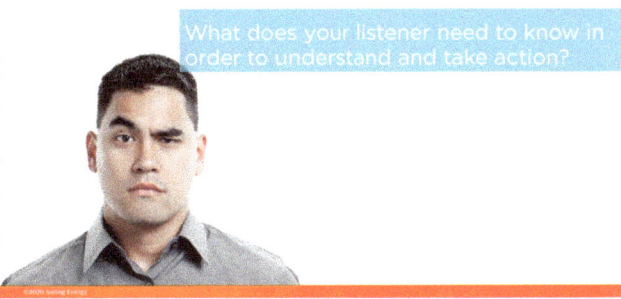

What does your listener need to know in order to understand and take action?

IDEAS & ACTIONS

Keep it simple.

Get to *their* point.

Make sure you have said what you wanted to say after you think you have said it.

The details count.

When it has to go long...

Formatting matters.

Lesson **198**
PRESENTATION EXCELLENCE
Becoming genuinely persuasive

Presented by
Mark Jewell

@SellingEnergy
info@sellingenergy.com

The **easiest** thing to buy is nothing.

IDEAS & ACTIONS

Don't ignore the current state.

To accept something new, something old has to be given up.

Acknowledge the sacrifice of change.

Acknowledge the risk of change.

Not wanting to give up the old is a barrier to making the sale.

In order to progress, you have to break down the old before you build up the new.

Make the case for immediate change.

Q:

Assuming your "proposal" is actually "proposing" something, it's vital that you are persuasive, right?

IDEAS & ACTIONS

www.SellingEnergy.com

What it means to be persuasive

You need to be persuasive to make things happen.

The Greeks outlined all of the tactics used to persuade:

Logos: logic
Ethos: character
Pathos: emotion

You need to connect with the people you are communicating with.

Be passionate about what you are proposing.

I believe all people should have the right to laugh.
I believe all people should have the right to laugh.
I believe all people should have the right to laugh.
I believe all people should have the right to laugh.
I believe all people should have the right to laugh.
I believe all people should have the right to laugh.
I believe all people should have the right to laugh.

Focus on where you are placing your emphasis.

Be confident in your language

Avoid vague adjectives and adverbs.

IDEAS & ACTIONS

_____

_____

_____

_____

Use stories that your listener can relate to as you convey your ideas.

RAINMAKING CONVERSATIONS

© 2011 John Wiley & Sons

HOW TO WIN FRIENDS & INFLUENCE PEOPLE
The Only Book You Need to Lead You to Success
Dale Carnegie

© 1998 Pocket Books

TALK LESS, SAY MORE
3 Habits to Influence Others and Make Things Happen
CONNIE DIEKEN

© 2009 Wiley

Yes!
50 Scientifically Proven Ways to Be Persuasive
Noah J. Goldstein, Steve J. Martin, and Robert B. Cialdini
Bestselling Author of Influence

© 2009 Free Press

Lesson 199
PRESENTATION EXCELLENCE
Knowing and applying proper business etiquette

Presented by
Mark Jewell
@SellingEnergy
info@sellingenergy.com

selling energy
Turbocharging Success

What is etiquette?

Make an excellent impression within the context of manners, dress code, dining, gift-giving, conversation topics, job-site behavior, **and more...**

IDEAS & ACTIONS

www.SellingEnergy.com

Etiquette is not...

1. A set of rigid rules
2. Something only for the wealthy
3. A thing of the past
4. Snobbishness

Adapted from Emily Post's Etiquette, 17th Edition

Roadmap for your professional interaction

Etiquette in email...

1. Read your emails aloud to ensure that the tone and content are appropriate.
2. Use spell check.
3. Start and end with salutations.
4. If the information is ambiguous or easily misinterpreted, consider making a phone call instead.

Adapted from Emily Post's Etiquette, 17th Edition

Etiquette on the phone...

1. Always ensure you are calling at an appropriate time.
2. Use "please" and "thank you" as you interact with receptionists.
3. Limit or encourage small talk as appropriate.
4. Never multitask.
5. Never interrupt.
6. Ask questions one at a time.
7. Listen for signs of stress; suggest calling back if appropriate.

Don't prioritize "tech" over presence.

PERFORM LIKE A ROCK STAR
AND STILL HAVE TIME FOR LUNCH

ORNA W. DRAWAS

© 2010 ROI Marketing

Who would you rather do business with?

Etiquette in person...

1. Always be early... "on-time" is too close to "late."
2. Use breath mints.
3. Sport a genuine smile! (Think of something that makes you *genuinely* happy.)
4. Know your meeting objectives and pursue them diligently and gently.
5. Switch your mobile phone to silent or even "do not disturb."

IDEAS & ACTIONS

Introductions

Etiquette upon first meeting...

1. Always address the person of highest authority first, and ensure everyone is introduced.
2. Extend a warm and dry hand, and remember to remove your glove if you're wearing one.
3. Be firm but gentle – no bone-crushing handshakes!
4. Match palm-to-palm rather than grasping fingers!
5. May wish to avoid pressing palms together on a mixed-gender handshake.

Some things are better left unsaid.

Sincerely ask, "How are you?" and pay close attention to the answer.

Attitude and courtesy for all.

Dining etiquette

Who pays?

Gift giving

IDEAS & ACTIONS

Thank you

Etiquette in the global economy

When in doubt – mirror!

Etiquette extends into *every corner of business...*

1. Resolving conflicts with courtesy and respect...
2. Knowing when and how to take responsibility for mistakes...
3. Avoiding harassment in the workplace...
4. Being ethical in all professional dealings...
5. Respecting the privacy of both colleagues, prospects and clients...
6. Social media dos and don'ts...
7. And more...

Lesson **200**
PRESENTATION EXCELLENCE
Breaking bad communication habits

Presented by
Mark Jewell
@SellingEnergy
Info@sellingenergy.com

IDEAS & ACTIONS

Multitasking while on the phone with someone

Interrupting others

Dominating discussions

Too much text

Starting conversations with what matters most to you

Rambling and taking too much time to get to the point

Using one method of communication... the one that you like most

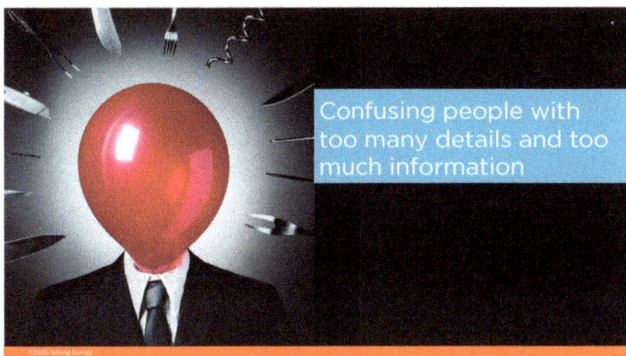

Confusing people with too many details and too much information

IDEAS & ACTIONS

Focusing on technology, not people

Lesson 201
SELLING TO HUMAN BEINGS
Body language

Presented by
Mark Jewell
@SellingEnergy
info@sellingenergy.com

4 Approaches worth mastering...

1. Body language
2. Microfacial expressions
3. Neuro-linguistic programming (NLP)
4. Active listening

What is your
prospect **thinking**?

Body language...

Q:

How adept are you at evaluating body language...

...both yours and your prospect's?

POSITIVE EVALUATION
Rubbing eyebrows
Scratching eyebrows
Scratching part of the forehead above eyebrows
Pushing eyeglasses back in place

NEGATIVE EVALUATION
Touching the nose
Scratching the nose

Shift to another point to move away from the negative evaluation.

IDEAS & ACTIONS

DEFENSIVE POSITION
Folding the arms
Crossing the legs

Try to be more flexible.

TILTED HEAD
Listener is interested in what he is hearing.

Keep talking;
Look for additional signs of interest.

CONFIDENCE
Clasping hands behind the back
Clasping hands in front of the body

Avoid debate; customer likely
knows a lot about the topic.
Change the topic/point until
customer releases his/her hands.

BODY ORIENTATION
Customer's shoulders are not
parallel to yours.

Customer may be in a hurry or
want to leave the conversation.

HIDING THE MOUTH
Reflects doubt

Customer needs reassurance in
order to be convinced.

ANXIETY
Cannot be identified by a single
position or gesture; look for 3 or more:
Fingernail biting; fidgeting; tapping
fingers or heels; jiggling contents of
pockets; whistling

Probe for the source of anxiety and
alleviate accordingly.

CONFIDENCE
Fingertips touching (done when
the customer feels confident
about the topic s/he is
discussing and/or believes s/he
knows much about the topic
s/he is listening to)

DOMINANT SITTING
Alpha monkey behavior (taking up
a lot of space while sitting with
hands clasped behind the head and
ankle crossed on opposite knee)
signals confidence.

IDEAS & ACTIONS

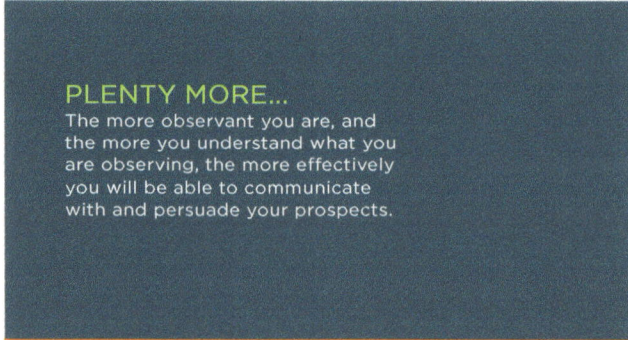

Lesson 202
SELLING TO HUMAN BEINGS
Microfacial expressions

Presented by
Mark Jewell
@SellingEnergy
info@sellingenergy.com

Microfacial expressions...

Paul Ekman

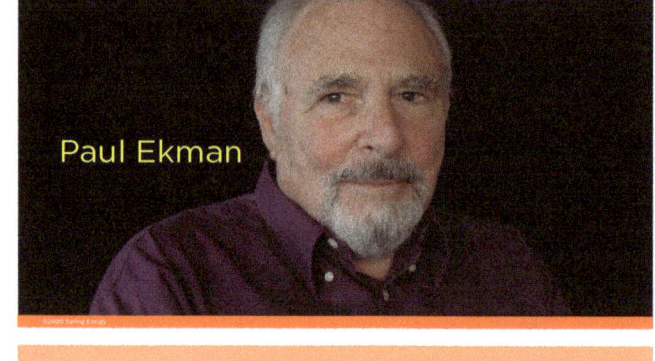

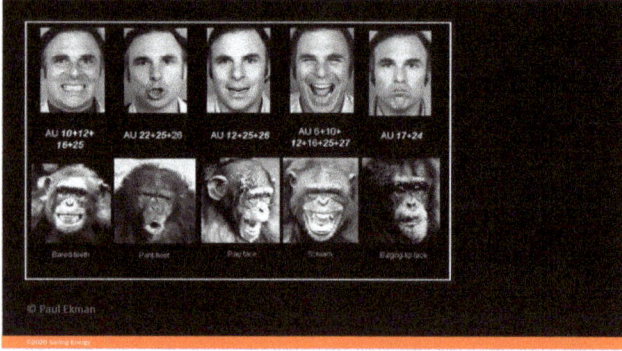

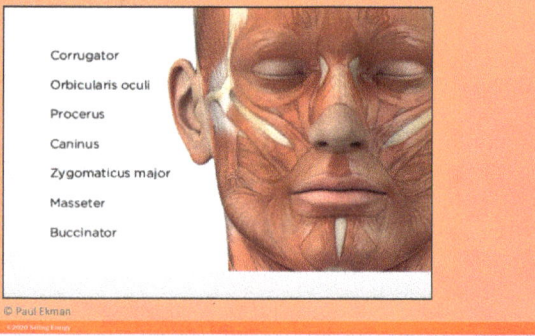

Corrugator

Orbicularis oculi

Procerus

Caninus

Zygomaticus major

Masseter

Buccinator

© Paul Ekman

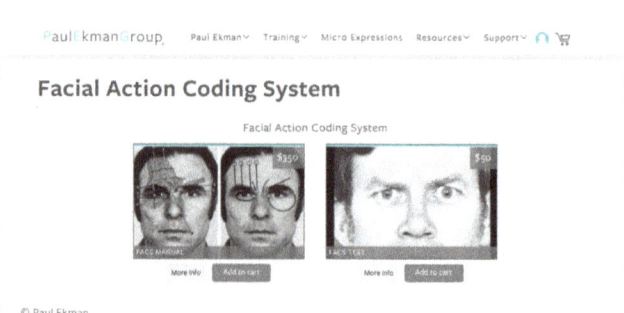

Facial Action Coding System

© Paul Ekman

Lesson 203
SELLING TO HUMAN BEINGS
Neuro-linguistic programming (NLP)

Presented by
Mark Jewell
@SellingEnergy
info@sellingenergy.com

IDEAS & ACTIONS

_____

_____

_____

_____

Neuro-linguistic programming...

Anthony Robbins

How significant is rapport in making the sale?

How do you know if you have genuine rapport with your prospect?

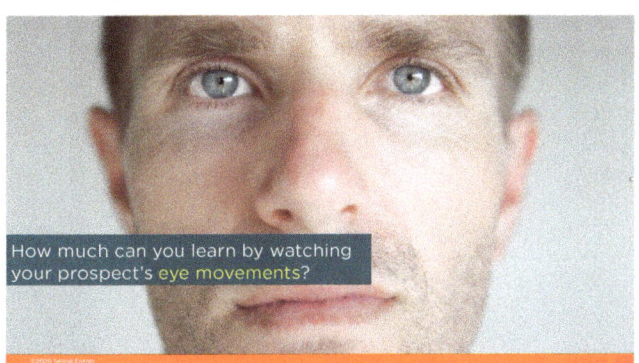

How much can you learn by watching your prospect's eye movements?

What can we learn from NLP?

1. Visual, auditory and kinesthetic modalities
2. The value of watching eye movements
3. What are your prospect's values?
4. How does your value proposition map into those values?
5. The importance of pacing and mirroring

IDEAS & ACTIONS

What can we learn from NLP?

1. Building rapport by delivering information at the appropriate pace
2. Language is sacred... Ensure positive self-talk.
3. The quality of your communication is your responsibility.
4. Always maintain a sense of positive expectancy.
5. Visualize the 5 senses of success before the sale.

See, taste, hear, smell, and feel success

Lesson 204
PRESENTATION EXCELLENCE
Knowing when (and when not) to use slides

Presented by
Mark Jewell
@SellingEnergy
info@sellingenergy.com

Turbocharging Success

What circumstances justify the use of slides?

1. Large speaking venue, where the slides are the backdrop for the performance
2. Any performance where visuals are necessary to enhance comprehension and/or persuasion
3. Be sure to distinguish between the need for "slides" versus "handouts" and if using both, they should not necessarily be the same.

What are the downsides of using slides?

1. The audience may become preoccupied with the visuals (and/or read ahead if given hard copies).
2. The presenter may rely too heavily on the slides, becoming a narrator rather than a compelling speaker.
3. Any visual presentation could be compromised by room configuration, audience seating, equipment issues, etc.

Lesson 205
PRESENTATION EXCELLENCE
Transforming your ideas into a presentation

Presented by
Mark Jewell
@SellingEnergy
info@sellingenergy.com

Turbocharging Success

Transforming your idea into reality...

Don't start with PowerPoint.

IDEAS & ACTIONS

_____

_____

_____

_____

Know who your audience is.

"Educating causes people to think; persuading motivates them to act."

Decide on the end goal.

Identify your one primary intention.

Illustrate and support your intention.

Identify three or four key messages.

Understand your presentation's context.

Aristotle's outline for persuasive arguments...

1. Deliver a story or statement that arouses the audience's interest.
2. Pose a problem or question that has to be solved or answered.
3. Offer a solution to the problem you raised.
4. Describe specific benefits for adopting the course of action set forth in your solution.
5. State a call to action.

IDEAS & ACTIONS

Carefully contemplate the ways in which your audience might resist.

Determine the reward that would resonate most with them.

Position the reward for the individual, the organization, and for mankind.

Structuring your presentation...

A presentation is not a report.

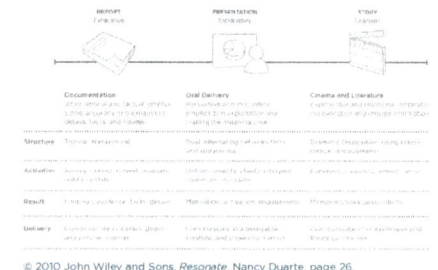

© 2010 John Wiley and Sons, *Resonate*, Nancy Duarte, page 26.

Most presentations are dreadfully boring, don't let yours be one of them.

Structure of an effective presentation

Keep it focused.

IDEAS & ACTIONS

Make it interesting.

Don't be afraid to make it personal.

Use storytelling.

Resonate p. 17, Nancy Duarte

Develop for a shorter presentation.

Keep the language natural.

Practice your presentation.

selling in 6™

Lesson 206
PRESENTATION EXCELLENCE
Developing your slide deck

Presented by
Mark Jewell
@SellingEnergy
info@sellingenergy.com

sellingenergy
Turbocharging Success

Developing your slide deck...

IDEAS & ACTIONS

www.SellingEnergy.com

And remember... don't start with PowerPoint!

Leverage the power of visuals.

Your slides need to support you (but not steal the show)!

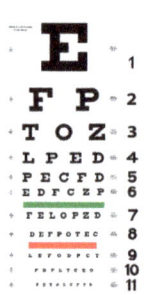

Design for the last row... in your audience, not on this eye chart!

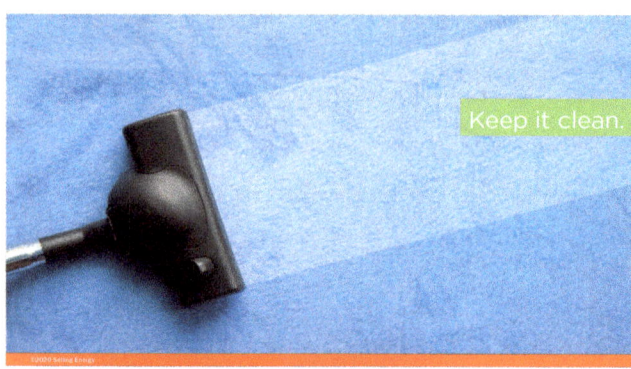

Keep it clean.

Use images and color to reinforce your message.

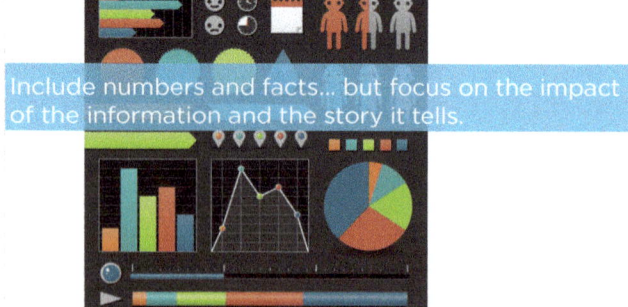

Include numbers and facts... but focus on the impact of the information and the story it tells.

Use charts or graphs if it makes the message clearer

IDEAS & ACTIONS

Less is more

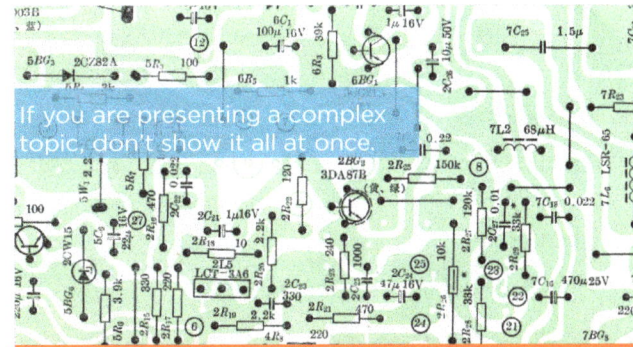

If you are presenting a complex topic, don't show it all at once.

Lesson 207
PRESENTATION EXCELLENCE
Presenting your proposal

Presented by
Mark Jewell
@SellingEnergy
info@sellingenergy.com

IDEAS & ACTIONS

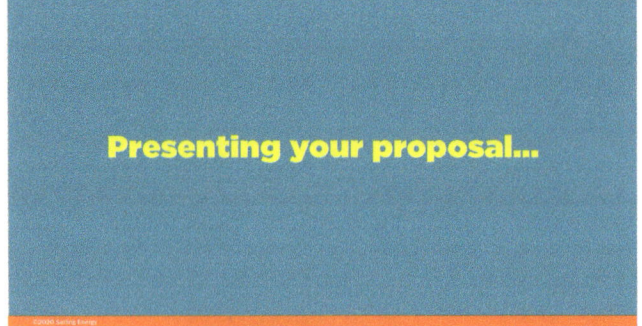

Presenting your proposal...

Make an immediate personal connection.

Keep the audience focused on you, the speaker, not on your presentation.

Audiences are selfish.

Know your content inside and out.

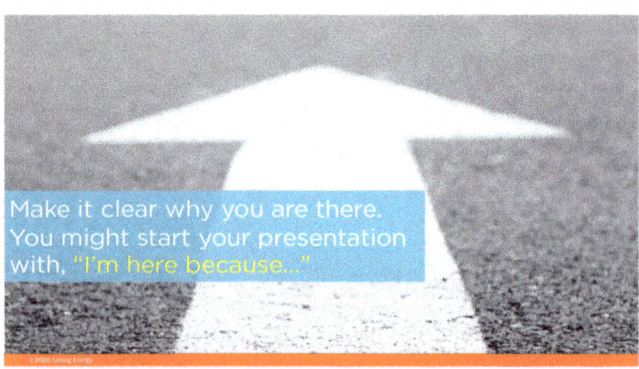

Make it clear why you are there. You might start your presentation with, "I'm here because..."

Other presentation tips...

Why I am here...

IDEAS & ACTIONS

Don't go over your allotted time, and *always* leave time for Q&A

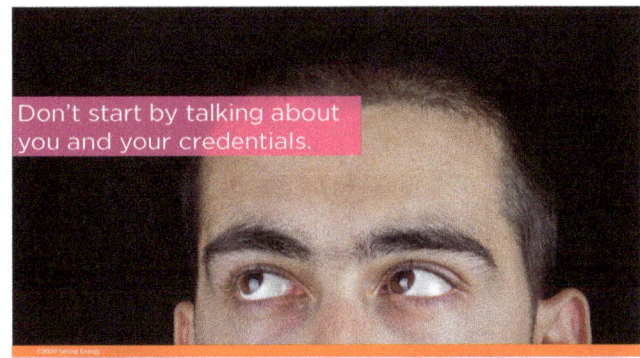

Don't start by talking about you and your credentials.

To read or not to read.

Face the audience.

Get your audience to interact.

Your audience should be the hero, not you.

selling in 6™

Lesson **208**
PRESENTATION EXCELLENCE
Tips for anyone who hates public speaking

Presented by
Mark Jewell
@SellingEnergy
info@sellingenergy.com

sellingenergy
Turbocharging Success

In case you "hate" public speaking...

IDEAS & ACTIONS

Prepare, prepare, prepare.

Take a deep breath.

You are not as bad as you think you are.

This will not affect your career in any way.

A little anxiety is good because it means you care.

Be confident. Recognize that you are there to offer them something that they need.

If you have severe anxiety, you can always get professional help.

Toastmasters...
Rotary International...
Lions International...
and more...

IDEAS & ACTIONS

Use the nervous energy to your advantage.

Lesson **209**
PRESENTATION EXCELLENCE
Making the delivery count

Presented by
Mark Jewell
@SellingEnergy
info@sellingenergy.com

Making the delivery count...

Keep your energy level high

Remember to smile.

Use shorter sentences.

Use emphasis to your advantage.

Use pauses to signal that what you just said or are about to say is important.

IDEAS & ACTIONS

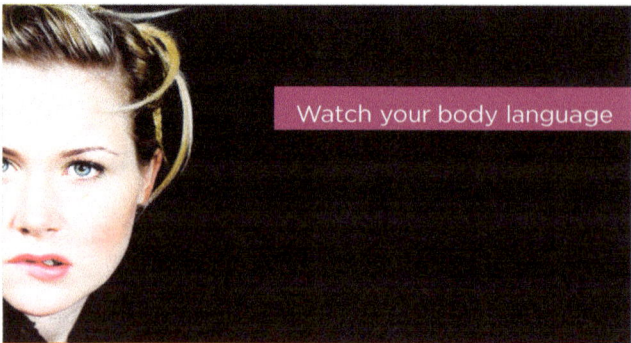

Watch your body language

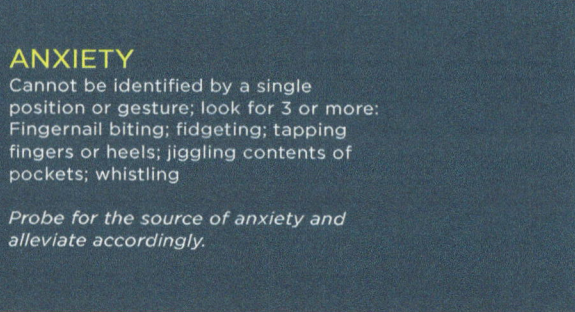

ANXIETY
Cannot be identified by a single position or gesture; look for 3 or more: Fingernail biting; fidgeting; tapping fingers or heels; jiggling contents of pockets; whistling

Probe for the source of anxiety and alleviate accordingly.

If you are standing, look relaxed but in charge.

"Resonate" with your audience.

Have a face-to-face conversation.

Targeted message

Answer client questions immediately.

Adjust to the frequency of your audience.

IDEAS & ACTIONS

_____

_____

_____

_____

Don't overwhelm.

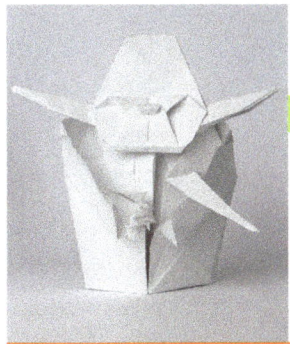

What would Yoda do?

Recognize the doers, suppliers, influencers, and innovators.

What would Yoda do?

1. Be mindful.
2. Stop focusing on the negative and commit.
3. You are not a psychic. Quit trying to predict your fate and bend it to your will.
4. Who's in charge of your future? YOU.

SOURCE: https://www.starwars.com/news/8-great-life-teachings-from-yoda

What would Yoda do?

5. Quit being so selfish and impulsive.
6. Learn to let go.
7. Don't make rash decisions.
8. Be patient.

SOURCE: https://www.starwars.com/news/8-great-life-teachings-from-yoda

© 2010 John Wiley and Sons

© 2007 Harvard Business Review Press

© 2005 Oxford University Press

IDEAS & ACTIONS

www.SellingEnergy.com

And what are those 9 mistakes according to Sjodin?

1. "Winging it instead of preparing thoroughly;
2. Being overly informative instead of persuasive;
3. Misusing allocated time;
4. Providing inadequate support;
5. Failing to close the deal;
6. Being boring;
7. Relying too heavily on visual aids;
8. Using distracting gestures or body language;
9. Wearing inappropriate clothing."

Excerpted from Publishers Weekly review of *New Sales Speak*.
© Reed Business Information, a division of Reed Elsevier Inc.

Lesson 210
PRESENTATION EXCELLENCE
Making the most of time allotted to audience Q&A

Presented by
Mark Jewell
@SellingEnergy
info@sellingenergy.com

Success strategies for handling the inevitable Q&A

1. If you value "active listening," you need Q&A.
2. It's OK if the questions don't come immediately.
3. "What if you did have a question, what would it be?"
4. Reclaim your time by asking your own questions.

You could take either or both of these approaches:

1. "One of the questions I normally get asked is..."
2. "I actually have a few questions for *you*..."

Suggestions for questions to ask your audience...

1. "Has anyone here had experience with a similar initiative?"
2. "What aspect of this initiative is <<most desirable, most daunting>>?"
3. "If you were to proceed with this initiative, how do you think your organization would reinvest the savings?"

Suggestions for questions to ask your audience...

4. "We talked about several 'non-utility-cost financial' and 'non-financial' benefits. Which one(s) did you find most interesting or valuable to your operation?"
5. "How soon would you like to begin enjoying them?"

IDEAS & ACTIONS

Lesson **211**
CAPTURING MORE BUSINESS
Appreciating the importance of referrals

Presented by
Mark Jewell
@SellingEnergy
Info@sellingenergy.com

Q:
So how important are referrals?

Q:
And what do typical organizations do to maximize the quantity of referrals that they receive?

63%

80%

Realities of referrals

Why are referrals so important?

Why don't all salespeople ask for referrals?

Use a referral network

Focus on new interpretations of collaboration

IDEAS & ACTIONS

Lesson **212**
CAPTURING MORE BUSINESS
Asking for referrals at every turn

Presented by
Mark Jewell
@SellingEnergy
info@sellingenergy.com

Q:

So how many ways are there to ask for a referral?

Asking for referrals is not begging!

Referrals can work whether or not the source is revealed.

IDEAS & ACTIONS

Q:

So when are the best times to ask for a referral?

---

6 of the **best opportunities** to ask for a referral...

1. When customer voluntarily suggests that your product is incredible
2. When customer sends an unsolicited testimonial
3. When a customer refers someone – that's right, now is the time to ask for more
4. When a customer admits you've saved their rear end
5. When a strategic partner tells you about an association they've joined
6. When you complete a project for a customer

Lesson 213
CAPTURING MORE BUSINESS
Cloning your best customers and firing the others

 Presented by
Mark Jewell
@SellingEnergy
info@sellingenergy.com

Turbocharging Success

Q:

So how do you clone your best customers?

Analyze your best customers and clone them.

Rank your existing customers.

Most profitable
Least profitable

Best revenue
Worst revenue

Easiest to do business with
Hardest to do business with

Evaluate attributes of each company.

IDEAS & ACTIONS

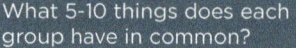

What 5-10 things does each group have in common?

These become your ideal and not so ideal customer profiles

Target new customers matching your ideal profile...

... and drop the ones that are not your ideal customers.

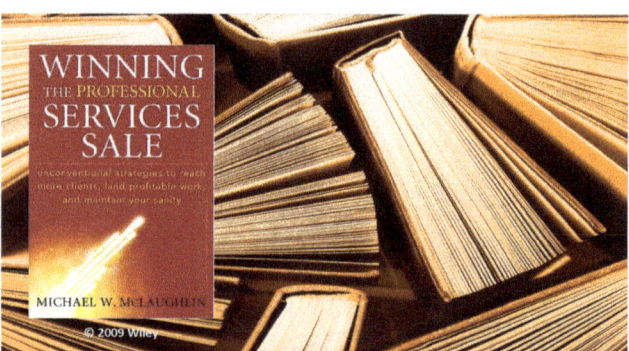

WINNING THE PROFESSIONAL SERVICES SALE

MICHAEL W. McLAUGHLIN

© 2009 Wiley

selling in 6™

Lesson **214**
CAPTURING MORE BUSINESS
Making an effort to partner with the "co-opetition"

Presented by
Mark Jewell
@SellingEnergy
info@sellingenergy.com

sellingenergy
Turbocharging Success

Q:

Why do all of your lead generation by yourself?

" Partnerships are a "win-win promotion between salespeople, merchants, or professionals who are trying to reach the same customers. "

—Bob Berg

IDEAS & ACTIONS

Q:
So who are your best prospects to begin partnering with?

Partnering starts at "home."

Get others to help you identify leads.

... but watch your reputation.

Find ways to cross-promote.

How could a commercial plant maintenance vendor get new customers without knocking on doors and getting thrown out of buildings by security?

Perhaps by partnering with a commercial spring water vendor who is already servicing those office suites?

selling in 6™

Lesson 215
CAPTURING MORE BUSINESS
Organizing events that facilitate lead swapping

Presented by
Mark Jewell
@SellingEnergy
info@sellingenergy.com

selling energy
Turbocharging Success

IDEAS & ACTIONS

Tips for organizing "lead swapping" events...

1. Ensure that everyone realizes it's a "win-win."
2. Invite trade professionals from various fields.
3. Affix colored badge stickers to denote each field.
4. Draw for prizes from a fishbowl of "stapled card pairs."
5. Suggest that players give provide qualifying questions.

Lesson 216
CAPTURING MORE BUSINESS
Designing lead-swapping programs around quality

Presented by
Mark Jewell
@SellingEnergy
info@sellingenergy.com

Quality is the touchstone for all parties involved.

1. Prospects place a high value on the quality of a referral.
2. Trade pros referred should be vetted thoroughly.
3. Prospects should be vetted with qualifying questions.
4. Everyone should value cross-selling and up-serving.
5. Timing is everything – referrals must be pursued ASAP.
6. Ideally all players should "sing from the same songbook."

Lesson 217
MARKETING TO WIN
Coordinating your marketing and sales teams

Presented by
Mark Jewell
@SellingEnergy
info@sellingenergy.com

How to ensure Marketing and Sales are partners...

1. Make sure both groups truly embrace the mission.
2. Engage in collaborative research and planning.
3. Sales team members become skilled using marketing tools.
4. Weekly updates are a no-exceptions best practice.

How to ensure Marketing and Sales are partners...

5. Monthly check-ins support higher-level progress.
6. Quarterly reviews are shared with the C-suite.
7. Successes are celebrated and emulated.

Lesson 218
MARKETING TO WIN
Setting the stage for an effective marketing effort

Presented by
Mark Jewell
@SellingEnergy
info@sellingenergy.com

Q:

Why do you need marketing?

IDEAS & ACTIONS

_____

_____

_____

_____

Q:

What are you doing to market your business now?

Q:

How much do you rely on others to bring you leads?

Q:

Have you been tracking the costs and results of your marketing efforts?

Q:

Have you calculated an ROI for your investments in marketing?

Q:

How many leads do you need to produce one proposal?

Q:

How many proposals do you need to generate one sale?

Q:

Assume your leads-to-proposal ratio is 10:1, and your proposal-to-close ratio is 2:1.

How many leads do you need to generate to get each closed deal?

Q:

So where are you going to get all of those leads?

IDEAS & ACTIONS

Q:

And by the way, do you want to...

...get more leads,
...write more proposals,
...get to yes more often,
...or do all three?

Lesson **219**
MARKETING TO WIN
26 Tips for maximizing online reach

Presented by
Mark Jewell
@SellingEnergy
info@sellingenergy.com

selling energy
Turbocharging Success

97% of consumers use the Internet when researching local services.

88% of consumers trust online reviews as much as personal recommendations.

Approximately 50% of SMBs have invested in a website.

30% of small businesses without a website cite cost as the main factor.

98% of searchers choose a business that is on page one of the results.

Almost 90% of marketers say their social marketing efforts have increased exposure for their business, and 75% say they've increased traffic.

Q:

So what do the pros suggest for effective B2B marketing?

IDEAS & ACTIONS

1. Don't spread yourself too thin.
2. Use press releases to promote new projects.
3. Use non-competing businesses for referrals.
4. Manage your social media wisely.
5. Focus on a niche.
6. Be recognizable with a custom logo.

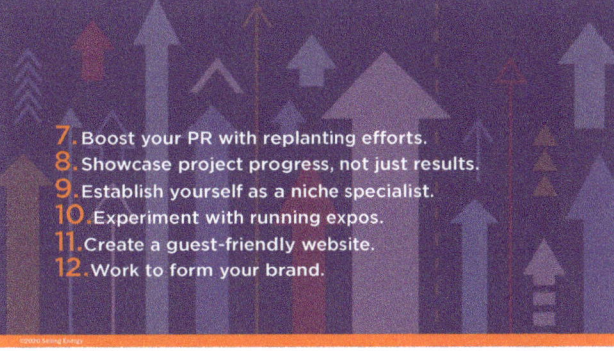

7. Boost your PR with replanting efforts.
8. Showcase project progress, not just results.
9. Establish yourself as a niche specialist.
10. Experiment with running expos.
11. Create a guest-friendly website.
12. Work to form your brand.

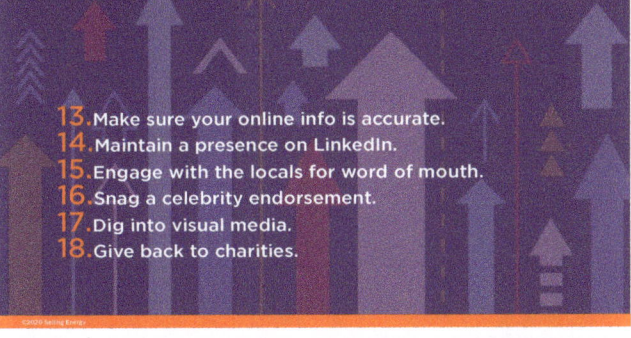

13. Make sure your online info is accurate.
14. Maintain a presence on LinkedIn.
15. Engage with the locals for word of mouth.
16. Snag a celebrity endorsement.
17. Dig into visual media.
18. Give back to charities.

19. Produce content that can be sourced to Wikipedia.
20. Utilize direct mail marketing.
21. Run a Facebook promotion.
22. Solicit customer reviews.

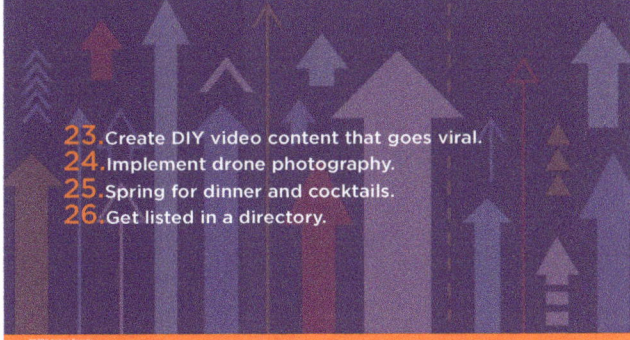

23. Create DIY video content that goes viral.
24. Implement drone photography.
25. Spring for dinner and cocktails.
26. Get listed in a directory.

SOURCE:
https://fitsmallbusiness.com/construction-marketing-ideas/

selling in 6™

Lesson **220**
MARKETING TO WIN
Additional tips to consider from marketing pros

Presented by
Mark Jewell
@SellingEnergy
Info@sellingenergy.com

sellingenergy
Turbocharging Success

Q:
What do other leading experts recommend as their "Top 5" or "Top 10" marketing tips?

IDEAS & ACTIONS

www.SellingEnergy.com

Another "Top 5 Proven Marketing Ideas…"

1. Focus on one market.
2. Create engaging content (photos, consumer awareness guides, case studies, videos).
3. Analyze your website.
4. Create marketing campaigns, not just ads.
5. Engage with previous clients and prospects.

SOURCE: https://contractordynamics.com/proven-construction-marketing-ideas/

And *another* "Top 10 Proven Marketing Ideas…"

1. Develop a sharp, functional website.
2. Consider Google Local Service Ads.
3. Get more reviews and manage your reputation.
4. Create a video commercial.
5. Do search engine optimization (SEO).

SOURCE: https://www.marketing360.com/smb-marketing-verticals/contractor-marketing-ideas-tips-and-strategies-for-2018-this-is-how-you-get-more-contractor-leads/

And *another* "Top 10 Proven Marketing Ideas…"

6. Use social media.
7. Have a strong lead intake process.
8. Have a client retention strategy.
9. Develop a specialization.
10. Use marketing automation software.

SOURCE: https://www.marketing360.com/smb-marketing-verticals/contractor-marketing-ideas-tips-and-strategies-for-2018-this-is-how-you-get-more-contractor-leads/

**They're all good ideas…
…now you just have to start!**

Lesson 221
MARKETING TO WIN
Distinguishing "marketing" from "communications"

Presented by
Mark Jewell
@SellingEnergy
info@sellingenergy.com

Turbocharging Success

Q:

First, what's the difference between **Marketing** and **Communications**?

The "4 Ps" of
Product Marketing

The "7 P's" of
Services Marketing

Product
Price
Place
Promotion
Physical Environment
Process
People

IDEAS & ACTIONS

Lesson 222
MARKETING TO WIN
14 Steps to a fully featured marketing plan

Presented by
Mark Jewell
@SellingEnergy
info@sellingenergy.com

14 Steps to a fully featured marketing plan...

1. Conducting market research
2. Identifying target markets
3. Analyzing the competition
4. Evaluating competitive advantage and value proposition
5. Defining a business strategy or statement of intent

14 Steps to a fully featured marketing plan...

6. Defining your brand
7. Setting marketing goals
8. Planning your marketing strategies
9. Designing your sales plan
10. Setting pricing strategies and any promotions

14 Steps to a fully featured marketing plan...

11. Planning customer support after the sale
12. Agreeing on a marketing budget
13. Using "Return on Marketing Investment" (ROMI)
14. Fine-tuning based on your efforts and outcomes

Lesson 223
MARKETING TO WIN
1. Conducting market research

Presented by
Mark Jewell
@SellingEnergy
info@sellingenergy.com

1. Conducting market research

IDEAS & ACTIONS

www.SellingEnergy.com

Questions to consider in market research...

1. What market dynamics influence your customers?
2. Which peers/competitors are worth emulating?
3. Where do you see unmet or underserved needs?
4. What are current sales and at what fragmentation?

Questions to consider in market research...

5. What industry benchmarks might you track?
6. What partners might you consider enlisting?
7. Are there any significant barriers to entry?
8. And others...

Lesson 224
MARKETING TO WIN
2. Identifying target markets

Presented by
Mark Jewell
@SellingEnergy
info@sellingenergy.com

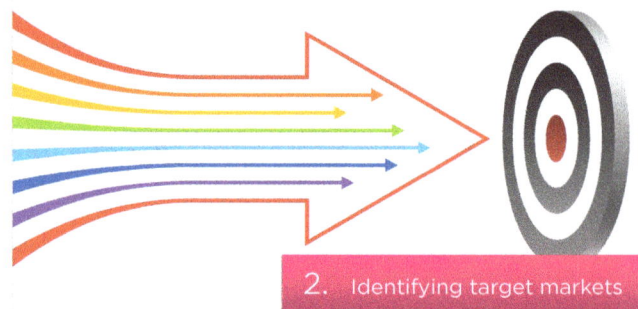

2. Identifying target markets

Q:

What are some of the best ways to target prospective customers?

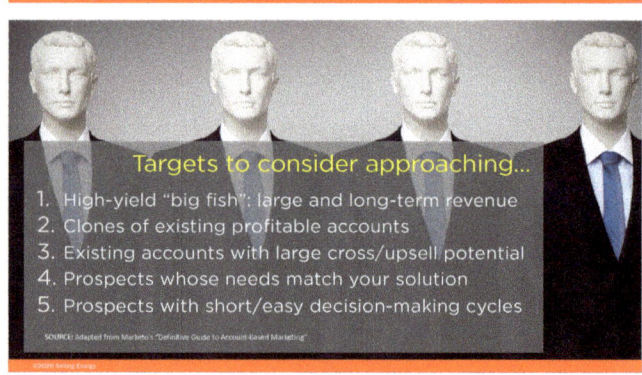

Targets to consider approaching...

1. High-yield "big fish": large and long-term revenue
2. Clones of existing profitable accounts
3. Existing accounts with large cross/upsell potential
4. Prospects whose needs match your solution
5. Prospects with short/easy decision-making cycles

SOURCE: Adapted from Marketo's "Definitive Guide to Account-Based Marketing"

Targets to consider approaching...

6. Big dogs other prospects would wish to emulate
7. Prospects that fall in particular sales territories
8. Competitors' educated customers (easy to convert)
9. Prospects on the Sales team's wish list
10. And others...

SOURCE: Adapted from Marketo's "Definitive Guide to Account-Based Marketing"

Lesson 225
MARKETING TO WIN
3. Analyzing the competition

Presented by
Mark Jewell
@SellingEnergy
info@sellingenergy.com

IDEAS & ACTIONS

3. Analyzing the competition

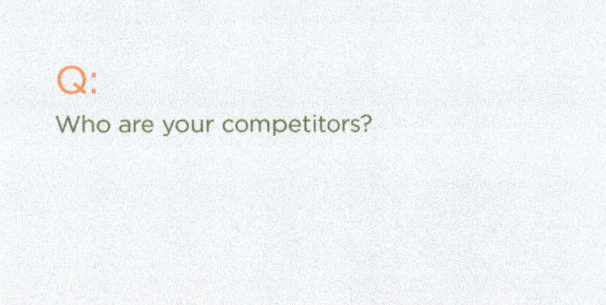

Q:
Who are your competitors?

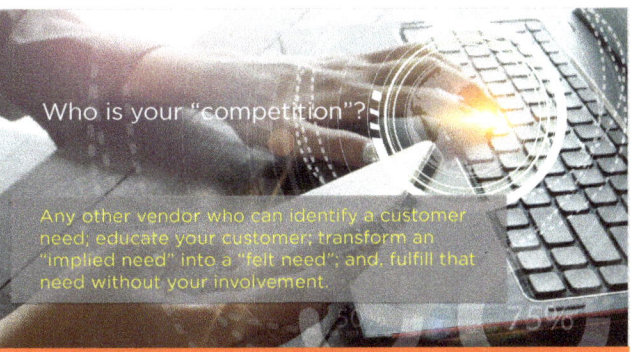

Who is your "competition"?

Any other vendor who can identify a customer need; educate your customer; transform an "implied need" into a "felt need"; and, fulfill that need without your involvement.

selling in 6™

Lesson **226**
MARKETING TO WIN
4. Competitive advantage and value proposition

Presented by
Mark Jewell
@SellingEnergy
info@sellingenergy.com

sellingenergy
Turbocharging Success

4. Distilling your competitive advantage and your unique value proposition

Q:
What can you advance as your competitive advantages and/or unique value propositions?

Sales team	Trust, differentiation, strategy, linkage, expert product/industry knowledge, exec presence, strategic literacy
Industry focus	Industry expertise & network, market share, tailored solutions
Product/solution	Functionality, features, technology, quality, value, ease of use, availability, brand loyalty, advertising, price, speed
Service	Service, responsiveness, people, customer satisfaction, results, performance
Company	Brand loyalty, financial stability, reputation, quality, other products, experience

Adapted from "Hope is Not a Strategy" by Rick Page, based on the work of Michael Porter of Harvard Univ.

Given the opportunity, most of your customers would prefer to have their trusted incumbent vendor provide or endorse a solution.

IDEAS & ACTIONS

www.SellingEnergy.com

Lesson 227
MARKETING TO WIN
5. Defining a business strategy or statement of intent

Presented by
Mark Jewell
@SellingEnergy
info@sellingenergy.com

5. Defining your business strategy or statement of intent

Q:

Can you express your business strategy or marketing intent in a few sentences?

Perhaps a 3-sentence mission statement?

1. Who you are selling to
2. What you have to offer
3. Your unique value proposition

Puget Power. 1988.

Puget Power's
Marketing Mission Statement
(1988)

"To provide services and products that improve our customers' lives and make their businesses more profitable."

Puget Power's
Corporate Mission Statement
(1988)

"Puget Sound Power & Light Company is an investor-owned public service company committed to being financially sound and responsive to our customers' needs by providing electric power and related services in an increasingly competitive environment. We fulfill this mission through teamwork, with pride in our performance and integrity."

Puget Power's
4 Marketing Goals
(1988)

"Energy efficiency is central for all products and services.

"Puget Power is the energy supplier of choice.

"Strong revenues are the key to stable rates.

"Excellent customer service is the cornerstone of Puget Power."

IDEAS & ACTIONS

Lesson 228
MARKETING TO WIN
6. Defining your brand

Presented by
Mark Jewell
@SellingEnergy
Info@sellingenergy.com

6. Defining your brand

IDENTITY

VALUE

MARKETING

ADVERTISING

DESIGN

STRATEGY

BRAND

TRUST

Q:

What exactly is a "brand"?

The world's best brands...

1. Are not logos or slogans
2. Offer more than their product (e.g., Apple, Nike)
3. Seek models to emulate outside their own space
4. Gravitate to controlling more mindshare and spend
5. Use leverage (e.g., incumbent relationship or big data)
6. Look at demographics and far beyond
7. Shift their focus to a customer of one
8. Engage all stakeholders, not just the customer

*Customers or members, *plus* investors, employees and any other parties who are affected by their business

---

Lesson 229
MARKETING TO WIN
7. Setting marketing goals

Presented by
Mark Jewell
@SellingEnergy
Info@sellingenergy.com

7. Setting marketing goals

Q:

What are some quantifiable goals to consider establishing at the outset?

Set quantifiable goals up front...

1. Gain at least "a" new customers or revenues?
2. Expand the average offerings per customer to "b"?
3. Deliver at least "c" new installations this year?
4. Increase the quantity of inbound leads to "d"?
5. See at least "e" percent of prospects sign up for an offer?
6. Or any of the dozens of other marketing metrics...

IDEAS & ACTIONS

_____

_____

_____

_____

www.SellingEnergy.com

Lesson **230**
MARKETING TO WIN
8. Planning your marketing strategies

Presented by
Mark Jewell
@SellingEnergy
info@sellingenergy.com

MARKETING STRATEGY

8. Planning your marketing strategies

Q:

How much have marketing strategies really changed over the years?

A richer (and more interconnected) world!

- Online
- Direct mail
- Email
- Mobile
- Video
- Print

- Social media*
- Display
- Phone
- Blogs
- Search
- Events

*Social media: Some of the most popular social media websites are Baidu Tieba, Facebook (and its associated Facebook Messenger), Gab, Google+, MySpace, Instagram, LinkedIn, Pinterest, Reddit, Tumblr, Twitter, Viber, VK, WeChat, Weibo, WhatsApp, Wikia, Snapchat, and YouTube. These social media websites have more than 100,000,000 registered users.

SOURCE: Wikipedia

Social media landscape is huge!

 Some of the most popular social media websites: Baidu Tieba, Facebook (and its associated Facebook Messenger), Gab, Google+, MySpace, Instagram, LinkedIn, Pinterest, Reddit, Snapchat, Tumblr, Twitter, Viber, VK, WeChat, Weibo, WhatsApp, Wikia, and YouTube. **Each has more than 100,000,000 registered users.**

SOURCE: Wikipedia

Successful combinations vary widely...

1. Publish monthly magazine or newsletter.
2. Be active on social media.

1. Blog tells human-interest customer or employee story.
2. Announce new YouTube "tips" video or upcoming event.

1. Email debuts social media links.
2. Join our Facebook page, take a survey, enter a drawing.
3. Follow-up email announces online billing.
4. YouTube video teaches customer how to use app.
5. App ensures ongoing mobile engagement.

Lesson **231**
MARKETING TO WIN
9. Designing your sales plan

Presented by
Mark Jewell
@SellingEnergy
info@sellingenergy.com

9. Designing your sales plan

IDEAS & ACTIONS _____

_____

_____

_____

Fine-tune 4 ways to support Sales...

1. TARGET
- Segment
- Prospect's goals
- Competitive landscape

3. PERSONA
- CEO, COO, etc.
- Middle management
- End-user

2. SALES CYCLE STAGE
- Pre-sales-cycle
- Early
- Middle
- Late

4. SOLICIT FEEDBACK

Q:

Can you diagram how your Sales team will interact with and leverage all of the channels and materials that Marketing has developed?

Q:

And do you have the Sales team's buy-in at every step of that diagram?

Lesson **232**
MARKETING TO WIN
10. **Setting pricing strategies and any promotions**

Presented by
Mark Jewell
@SellingEnergy
info@sellingenergy.com

10. Setting your pricing strategy and any promotions

Q:

Have you been careful to engage all stakeholders in this process?

Q:

And what happens if the marketing campaign achieves a higher level of interest than expected/budgeted?

Lesson **233**
MARKETING TO WIN
11. **Planning customer support after the sale**

Presented by
Mark Jewell
@SellingEnergy
info@sellingenergy.com

IDEAS & ACTIONS

11. Planning customer support after the sale

Q:

How can Marketing continue to support Sales after the deal is done?

Lesson 234
MARKETING TO WIN
12. Agreeing on a marketing budget

Presented by
Mark Jewell
@SellingEnergy
info@sellingenergy.com

12. Agreeing on a marketing budget

Q:

Have you developed a month-by-month schedule of what you plan to spend on marketing activities?

Q:

Do you have a plan for conducting monthly cost/benefit analysis for each marketing activity and reallocating resources as needed?

Lesson 235
MARKETING TO WIN
13. Using "Return on Marketing Investment" (ROMI)

Presented by
Mark Jewell
@SellingEnergy
info@sellingenergy.com

13. Monitoring results

IDEAS & ACTIONS

Q:

How many different ways are there to monitor your results?

Q:

How many different ways can you measure "Return on Marketing Investment"?

Short-term ROMI (quick and dirty approach)

$$ROMI = \frac{\text{Incremental Revenue Attributed to Marketing Spending (\$)}}{\text{Marketing Spending (\$)}}$$

EXAMPLE:
Assume $100K campaign delivers $500K in incremental revenue attributed to that campaign.

$$ROMI = \frac{\$500K}{\$100K} = 5$$

Short-term ROMI (more realistic approach*)

$$ROMI = \frac{\text{Incremental Contribution Margin Attrib. to Mktg. (\$)} - \text{Marketing Spending (\$)}}{\text{Marketing Spending (\$)}}$$

EXAMPLE:
Assume $100K campaign delivers $300K in incremental contribution margin, of which $100K pays for the campaign.

$$ROMI = \frac{\$300K - \$100K}{\$100K} = 2$$

This approach is more realistic because 1) it uses incremental contribution margin rather than top-line revenue; and, 2) it includes the marketing spending itself in the calculation.

Long-term ROMI...

1. Used to determine less tangible effects
2. Considers increased brand awareness, consideration or purchase intent
3. Often incorporates Customer Lifetime Value, Incremental Customer Acquisition, or Churn
4. Sometimes incorporates Marketing Mix Modeling and/or Brand Valuation analysis
5. Digital marketing metrics can simulate ROMI using pre- and post-campaign metrics.

Plenty of sources of customer feedback to consult...

1. Surveys
2. Online polls
3. Blogs
4. Database management tools
5. Feedback from Customer Service or Techs
6. Feedback from the Sales team
7. Other

Digital marketing metrics

- Average Time on Page
- Bounce Rate
- Click-Through Rate
- Content Downloads
- Cost Per Action
- Cost Per Lead
- Customer Acquisition Cost
- Customer Attrition
- Customer Lifetime Value
- Customer Share by Category
- Dormancy Rate
- External Website Links
- Funnel Conversion Rate
- Incremental Sales

Digital marketing metrics (cont'd)

- Keyword Ranking Performance
- Lead Conversion Rate
- Lifetime Value/Customer Acquisition Cost
- Marketing Originated Customers
- New Leads Generated
- Online Conversions Metric
- Pageviews Per Session
- Referral Traffic
- Response Rate
- Sessions by Device Type
- Total Visits
- Unique Visitors
- Web Traffic Concentration
- Website Traffic Lead Ratio

IDEAS & ACTIONS

Email marketing metrics

- Recipients
- Delivered
- Opens
- Unique Opens
- Clicks
- Bounces
- Forwards
- Unsubscribes

Gain additional insights over time

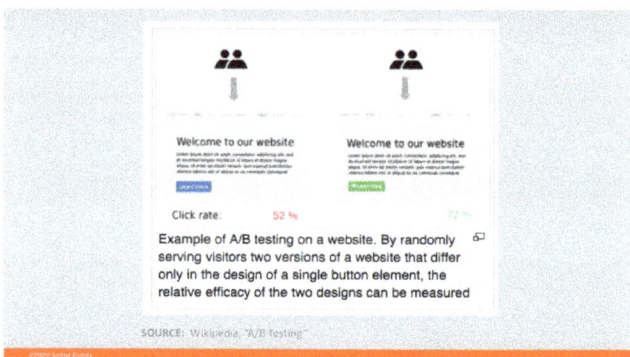

	ACTIVE SUBSCRIBERS	UNSUBSCRIBERS	BOUNCES
TOTAL	124,566	1,340	1,045
TODAY	180	15	11
THIS MONTH	977	46	56

Using A/B testing...

1. Two versions of a marketing piece ("A" and "B") are compared for effectiveness.
2. Copy text, layouts, images and colors are typically tested.
3. A/B testing can be performed continuously with marketing automation software.

Example of A/B testing on a website. By randomly serving visitors two versions of a website that differ only in the design of a single button element, the relative efficacy of the two designs can be measured

SOURCE: Wikipedia, "A/B testing"

Lesson 236
MARKETING TO WIN
14. Fine-tuning based on your efforts and outcomes

Presented by
Mark Jewell
@SellingEnergy
info@sellingenergy.com

Learn from the Past   Think of the Future

14. Fine-tuning the plan based on previous efforts and outcomes

Q:

Are you committed to a no-exceptions best practice of taking massive action, measuring your results, adjusting as needed, and then taking more action?

Lesson 237
MARKETING TO WIN
6 Key ways that Marketing can support Sales

Presented by
Mark Jewell
@SellingEnergy
info@sellingenergy.com

IDEAS & ACTIONS

Q:

How many ways can Marketing help the Sales effort?

Lesson **238**
MARKETING TO WIN
1. Demand generation

Presented by
Mark Jewell
@SellingEnergy
Info@sellingenergy.com

Turbocharging Success

Marketing can help Sales in at least 6 ways...

1. Demand generation
2. Inbound marketing
3. Content marketing
4. Product marketing
5. Customer marketing
6. Customer operations

MARKETING ROLE #1:
Demand Generation

Q:

How do you generate demand?

Generating demand...

1. Filling the top of the funnel with prospects predisposed to become interested in your solution
2. Lead nurturing to ensure they become customers
3. Analyzing what prospects really want

Generating demand...

4. Components of "demand generation" are varied, from cold calls to direct mailings to email newsletters to webinars.
5. Some say "demand generation" can create demand for your solution even without capturing contact info to produce a "lead."

Lesson **239**
MARKETING TO WIN
2. Inbound marketing

Presented by
Mark Jewell
@SellingEnergy
info@sellingenergy.com

Turbocharging Success

IDEAS & ACTIONS

www.SellingEnergy.com

MARKETING ROLE #2:
Inbound Marketing

Q:

What exactly is "inbound marketing"?

According to Hubspot, its creator...

"Sharing is caring and inbound is about creating and sharing content with the world. By creating content specifically designed to appeal to your dream customers, inbound attracts qualified prospects to your business and keeps them coming back for more."

Inbound marketing uses content marketing...

1. Content marketing attracts the best prospects and facilitates their journey down the sales funnel.
2. Inbound is facilitated with a marketing software solution.
3. Inbound includes all of the different forms of content that marketers use to attract prospects and engage leads (e.g., blogs, e-newsletters, white papers, social media posts, video content, podcasts, etc.).

Lesson 240
MARKETING TO WIN
3. Content marketing

Presented by
Mark Jewell
@SellingEnergy
info@sellingenergy.com

MARKETING ROLE #3:
Content Marketing

So what exactly is "content marketing"?

1. A subset of inbound marketing
2. Often uses digital channels, but could also entail speaking events, demonstrations, etc.
3. Content marketing helps generate demand ("demand generation"), attract prospects ("inbound marketing"), and drives sales.

Q:

How do you know if you're creating the right content?

IDEAS & ACTIONS

_____

_____

_____

_____

What's the best content to create?

1. Valuable and educational content
2. Has to attract attention
3. Has to keep the prospect engaged from initial interest, through the evaluation stage, and into the final decision-making process

Q:

Should content be geared to segment, account, persona, sales cycle stage, or all of the above?

Two very important tips...

1. Pay attention to offering precisely appropriate content at each stage so as not to interrupt "the conversation."
2. Develop and adhere to a master calendar of content to avoid chaos.

All of the above, and perhaps more!

Lesson 241
MARKETING TO WIN
4. Product marketing

Presented by
Mark Jewell
@SellingEnergy
Info@sellingenergy.com

Turbocharging Success

MARKETING ROLE #4:
Product Marketing

What is "product marketing"?

1. The "product" is not the same as the "brand."
2. Product marketing supplies the content and materials needed for deal support and sales enablement.

Q:

How does "marketing" differ from "product marketing"?

IDEAS & ACTIONS

_____

_____

_____

_____

Lesson 242
MARKETING TO WIN
5. Customer marketing

Presented by
Mark Jewell
@SellingEnergy
info@sellingenergy.com

MARKETING ROLE #5:
Customer Marketing

Q:

What is "customer marketing" and why is it so important?

What is "customer marketing"?

1. Successful customers breed further successes via relationship expansion, cross-selling and up-serving.
2. Happy customers also exude the trust that give new prospects the confidence to engage.
3. Marketing should create and implement systematic approaches for capturing and leveraging success stories, testimonials and referrals.

Lesson 243
MARKETING TO WIN
6. Customer operations

Presented by
Mark Jewell
@SellingEnergy
info@sellingenergy.com

MARKETING ROLE #6:
Customer Operations

Q:

Is it helpful for Marketing to monitor the quality, progress and outcome of any leads generated?

Absolutely!

1. Marketing needs to ensure that its efforts are producing the right quality and quantity of leads.
2. Each generated lead should be carefully evaluated to ensure that Sales has properly prioritized it.

IDEAS & ACTIONS

_____

_____

_____

_____

You cannot manage what you do not measure.

1. Key metrics should be continuously collected and evaluated (e.g., account penetration, frequency of contact, closing ratios, sales cycle length, and sales magnitude and frequency).
2. Marketing approaches should be optimized as needed, particularly if Sales needs help penetrating particular segments or accounts.

"No" or "Not yet" does not mean "Never."

1. Marketing and Sales should collaborate to ensure that any generated lead that is not ready to buy now is sufficiently "nurtured" to maximize the propensity to buy later.

Q:

Does the role of Marketing end when the deal is signed?

Marketing stays involved.

1. Marketing should continue to monitor client relationships for satisfaction, testimonials, unanticipated benefits realized, etc.
2. Marketing should also coordinate closely with Sales to ensure messaging is not only consistent, but also reflects the most up-to-date versions of the organization's competitive advantage, track record, market share, etc.

Q:

Can Marketing and Sales accomplish such hand-in-glove collaboration?

How to ensure Marketing and Sales are partners...

1. Make sure both groups truly embrace the mission.
2. Engage in collaborative research and planning.
3. Sales team members become skilled using marketing tools.
4. Weekly updates are a no-exceptions best practice.

How to ensure Marketing and Sales are partners...

5. Monthly check-ins support higher-level progress.
6. Quarterly reviews are shared with the C-suite.
7. Successes are celebrated and emulated.

Lesson 244
MARKETING TO WIN
8 Key success tools that Marketing should create

Presented by
Mark Jewell
@SellingEnergy
info@sellingenergy.com

IDEAS & ACTIONS

www.SellingEnergy.com

Q:

What are the principal success tools that Marketing can provide to Sales?

---

8 Success tools Marketing should provide to Sales

1. Market insight cards
2. Thought leadership content
3. Pitch materials
4. Email templates
5. Recorded training
6. Customer journey fodder
7. LinkedIn profile template
8. Newsletter template

Lesson 245
MARKETING TO WIN
1. Market insight cards

Presented by
Mark Jewell
@SellingEnergy
info@sellingenergy.com

Market Insight Cards

Q:

What are the principal elements of an effective Market Insight Card*?

*AKA "sales enablement resource" or "cheat sheet"

Marketplace conditions	Target segments, customers and opportunities	Product features
Elevator Pitch	Frequently asked questions	Non-utility-cost & non-financial benefits
Competitor analysis	Customer segment-specific propositions	Excerpts from the Objections Archive™
High-value questions isolating need or pain	Excerpts from the Success Story Archive™	Additional insights

---

Q:

What is "account profiling" and how detailed should it get?

The more granular the profiling, the better...

1. Who are the key decision-making personas?
2. What are their pain points?
3. Where do they seek information?
4. What types of content work best?

IDEAS & ACTIONS

_____

_____

_____

_____

The more granular the profiling, the better...

5. Who are their influencers and where do they get *their* information?
6. Are there any potential blockers and where do they get *their* information?
7. An average of 5.4 people have to sign off formally on each B2B purchase* – and you need to reach them.

*CEB study, as cited by Marketo

Lesson 246
MARKETING TO WIN
2. Thought leadership content

Presented by
Mark Jewell
@SellingEnergy
info@sellingenergy.com

MARKETING SUCCESS TOOL #2
Thought Leadership Content

Q:

What thought leadership could a vendor offer its customers using internal talent?

Q:

What thought leadership could a vendor offer its customers using external talent?

Q:

What thought leadership could a vendor offer its customers using insight gleaned from customer peer groups?

Lesson 247
MARKETING TO WIN
3. Pitch materials

Presented by
Mark Jewell
@SellingEnergy
info@sellingenergy.com

MARKETING SUCCESS TOOL #3
Pitch Materials

IDEAS & ACTIONS

www.SellingEnergy.com

Q:

How many varieties of pitch materials does Sales need?

Effective pitch materials run the gamut...

1. Elevator pitch and 3-sentence solicitation
2. Persona descriptions, with sales guidance for each
3. Guidance on initiating or revitalizing conversations
4. Success Story Archive™
5. Objections Archive™

Effective pitch materials run the gamut...

6. Segment-specific "sound bites" and referral paths
7. Guidance on conducting effective calls and meetings
8. Templates for meeting agendas and minutes
9. PowerPoint slide templates (design well; use sparingly)
10. Financial return calculators and reporting templates
11. RFP generators
12. And undoubtedly a lot more!

Lesson **248**
MARKETING TO WIN
4. Email templates

 Presented by
Mark Jewell
@SellingEnergy
info@sellingenergy.com

MARKETING SUCCESS TOOL #4
Email Templates

Q:

What are the ideal length and optimal structure of an effective email?

Q:

What are examples of email topics that would spur a conversation?

Lesson **249**
MARKETING TO WIN
5. Recorded training

 Presented by
Mark Jewell
@SellingEnergy
info@sellingenergy.com

IDEAS & ACTIONS

MARKETING SUCCESS TOOL #5
Recorded Training

Q:

How many opportunities are there for Marketing to produce recorded trainings for prospects, customers and/or the Sales team themselves?

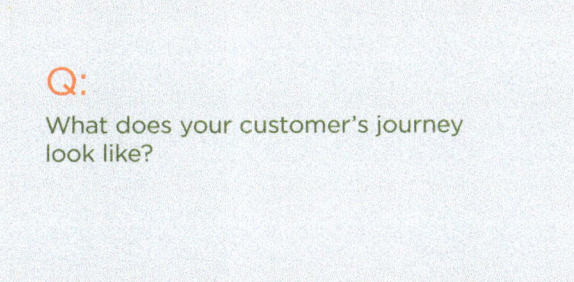

selling in 6™

Lesson **250**
MARKETING TO WIN
6. Customer journey fodder

Presented by
Mark Jewell
@SellingEnergy
info@sellingenergy.com

sellingenergy
Turbocharging Success

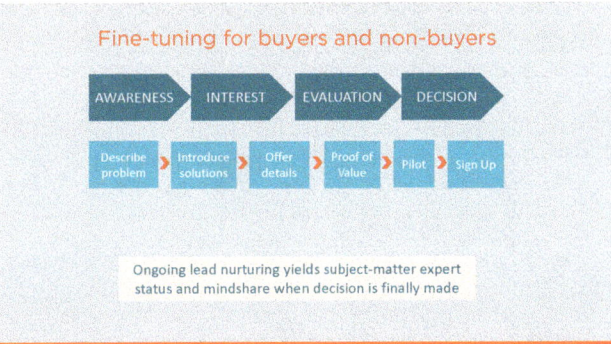

MARKETING SUCCESS TOOL #6
Customer Journey Fodder

Q:

What does your customer's journey look like?

Fine-tuning for buyers and non-buyers

AWARENESS → INTEREST → EVALUATION → DECISION

| Describe problem | Introduce solutions | Offer details | Proof of Value | Pilot | Sign Up |

Ongoing lead nurturing yields subject-matter expert status and mindshare when decision is finally made

Messaging tactics for lead nurturing

EMAIL NEWSLETTERS	57%
SALES CALLS	41%
WHITEPAPERS	35%
THOUGHT LEADERSHIP ARTICLES	35%
WEBINARS	30%
BLOG POSTS	29%
DIRECT MAIL	25%
RESEARCH-BASED CONTENT	25%
TELEPROSPECTING CALLS	18%
SELF-PROMOTIONAL CONTENT	16%
INFOGRAPHICS	8%
PODCASTS	6%

selling in 6™

Lesson **251**
MARKETING TO WIN
7. LinkedIn profile template

Presented by
Mark Jewell
@SellingEnergy
info@sellingenergy.com

sellingenergy
Turbocharging Success

IDEAS & ACTIONS

MARKETING SUCCESS TOOL #7
LinkedIn Profile Template

Q:
How closely does everyone's LinkedIn profile mirror the organization's overall vision and mission, etc.?

Q:
Does everyone have a consistent professional headshot?

Lesson **252**
MARKETING TO WIN
8. Newsletter template

Presented by
Mark Jewell
@SellingEnergy
info@sellingenergy.com

MARKETING SUCCESS TOOL #8
Newsletter Template

Q:
Could the organization provide templates for newsletters and similar outreach vehicles?

Lesson **253**
MARKETING TO WIN
Understanding and optimizing the buyer's journey

Presented by
Mark Jewell
@SellingEnergy
info@sellingenergy.com

Q:
Are you using the traditional sales and marketing "funnel" or an account-based marketing approach?

IDEAS & ACTIONS

Traditional sales and marketing funnel

AWARENESS/INTEREST	EVALUATION	DECISION
Prospect realizes they may have a need	Prospect defines the perceived need and begins considering potential solutions	Prospect selects a solution and becomes a customer

Traditional sales and marketing funnel

AWARENESS/INTEREST	EVALUATION	DECISION
Prospect realizes they may have a need	Prospect defines the perceived need and begins considering potential solutions	Prospect selects a solution and becomes a customer
How do they describe their goals or challenges?		
Are there myths to be addressed?		
What is the price of inaction?		
How is finding a solution prioritized?		

Traditional sales and marketing funnel

AWARENESS/INTEREST	EVALUATION	DECISION
Prospect realizes they may have a need	Prospect defines the perceived need and begins considering potential solutions	Prospect selects a solution and becomes a customer
	What types of solutions are investigated?	
	Where do they seek answers or advice?	
	What are the pros and cons being weighed?	
	What determines the urgency of the solution?	

Traditional sales and marketing funnel

AWARENESS/INTEREST	EVALUATION	DECISION
Prospect realizes they may have a need	Prospect defines the perceived need and begins considering potential solutions	Prospect selects a solution and becomes a customer
		What criteria are at work in the decision-making?
		What do they like/dislike about your solution?
		What parties are involved in the decision?
		Are there additional factors to be considered?

How can Marketing help at each stage?

AWARENESS/INTEREST	EVALUATION	DECISION
Prospect realizes they may have a problem	Prospect defines the perceived problem and begins considering potential solutions	Prospect becomes a Customer by selecting a solution
Create awareness of the problem so that your prospect can self-identify		
Content should focus on the pain points, not a brand-specific solution		
Begin tracking prospect downloads & preferences, and capturing contact info		
NOTE: *72% of prospects will turn to Google for their initial research*		

How can Marketing help at each stage?

AWARENESS/INTEREST	EVALUATION	DECISION
Prospect realizes they may have a problem	Prospect defines the perceived problem and begins considering potential solutions	Prospect becomes a Customer by selecting a solution
	Provide resources your prospect would find useful	
	Educational content is very helpful at this stage	
	Provide a stream of value-added content in a lead-nurturing campaign	

How can Marketing help at each stage?

AWARENESS/INTEREST	EVALUATION	DECISION
Prospect realizes they may have a problem	Prospect defines the perceived problem and begins considering potential solutions	Prospect becomes a Customer by selecting a solution
		Prospects typically dive deeply into the research after narrowing choices
		Ensure that your resources are both easy to find and compelling
		Help shorten due diligence by making solution comparisons easy
		NOTE: *70% of prospects return to Google 2-3 times during this vetting stage*

How can Marketing help at each stage?

AWARENESS/INTEREST	EVALUATION	DECISION
Prospect realizes they may have a problem	Prospect defines the perceived problem and begins considering potential solutions	Prospect becomes a Customer by selecting a solution
Create awareness of the problem so that your prospect can self-identify	*Provide resources your prospect would find useful*	*Prospects typically dive deeply into the research after narrowing choices*
Content should focus on the pain points, not a brand-specific solution	*Educational content is very helpful at this stage*	*Ensure that your resources are both easy to find and compelling*
Begin tracking prospect downloads & preferences, and capturing contact info	*Provide a stream of value-added content in a lead-nurturing campaign*	*Help shorten due diligence by making solution comparisons easy*
NOTE: *72% of prospects will turn to Google for their initial research*		***NOTE:*** *70% of prospects return to Google 2-3 times during this vetting stage*

IDEAS & ACTIONS

www.SellingEnergy.com

Lesson **254**
MARKETING TO WIN
Fine-tuning for buyers and non-buyers

Presented by
Mark Jewell
@SellingEnergy
info@sellingenergy.com

Fine-tuning for buyers and non-buyers

AWARENESS → INTEREST → EVALUATION → DECISION

Describe problem → Introduce solutions → Offer details → Proof of Value → Pilot → Sign Up

Ongoing lead nurturing yields subject-matter expert status and mindshare when decision is finally made

Lesson **255**
MARKETING TO WIN
Traditional versus account-based marketing funnels

Presented by
Mark Jewell
@SellingEnergy
info@sellingenergy.com

Q:

So how does the "account-based marketing" approach differ?

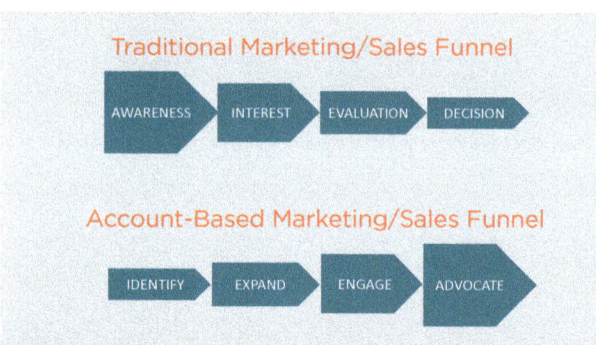

Traditional Marketing/Sales Funnel

AWARENESS → INTEREST → EVALUATION → DECISION

Account-Based Marketing/Sales Funnel

IDENTIFY → EXPAND → ENGAGE → ADVOCATE

Lesson **256**
MARKETING TO WIN
Ensuring that content tracks the buyer's journey

Presented by
Mark Jewell
@SellingEnergy
info@sellingenergy.com

Get ready for "The Omnichannel," the convergence of physical, digital and mobile marketing.

Content should track the buyer's journey

AWARENESS/INTEREST	EVALUATION	DECISION
Blogs, surveys, ebooks, research data, infographics, webinars, in-person events, newsletters, podcasts, videos, LinkedIn groups, etc.		

IDEAS & ACTIONS

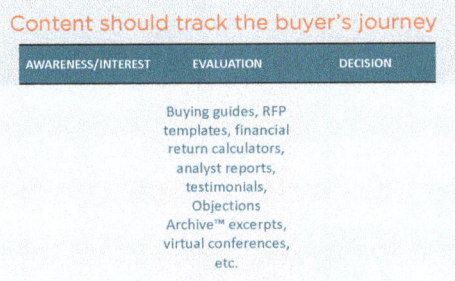

Content should track the buyer's journey

AWARENESS/INTEREST	EVALUATION	DECISION
	Buying guides, RFP templates, financial return calculators, analyst reports, testimonials, Objections Archive™ excerpts, virtual conferences, etc.	

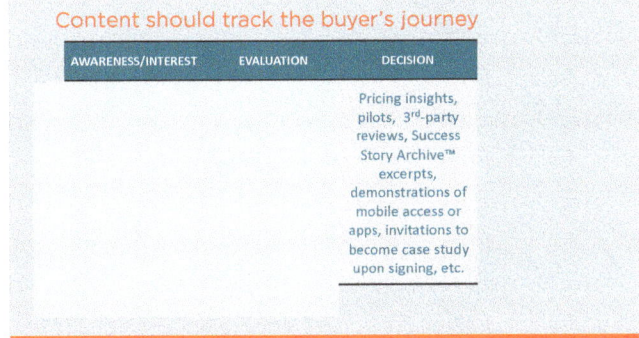

Content should track the buyer's journey

AWARENESS/INTEREST	EVALUATION	DECISION
		Pricing insights, pilots, 3rd-party reviews, Success Story Archive™ excerpts, demonstrations of mobile access or apps, invitations to become case study upon signing, etc.

Content should track the buyer's journey

AWARENESS/INTEREST	EVALUATION	DECISION
Blogs, surveys, ebooks, research data, infographics, webinars, in-person events, blogs, newsletters, podcasts, videos, LinkedIn groups, etc.	Buying guides, RFP templates, financial return calculators, analyst reports, testimonials, Objections Archive™ excerpts, virtual conferences, etc.	Pricing insights, pilots, 3rd-party reviews, Success Story Archive™ excerpts, demonstrations of mobile access or apps, invitations to become case study upon signing, etc.

And remember to consider every relevant persona at each stage: **Initiator, Gatekeeper, Influencer, Decision-maker, End-User, and Purchasing**

Lesson 257
MARKETING TO WIN
Sample marketing campaigns

Presented by
Mark Jewell
@SellingEnergy
info@sellingenergy.com

Q:

What are some examples of typical campaigns for existing customers?

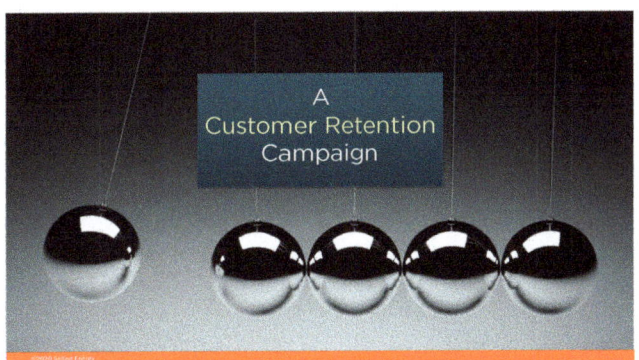

A Customer Retention Campaign

A Customer Retention Campaign

Provide an existing customer with the motivation and resources needed for success; help ensure a long and mutually prosperous relationship.

1. Personalized email #1 from their Account Manager welcoming them aboard, with web personalization featuring content, alerts or other messages
2. Personalized email #2 featuring tips on how to get started or how to get the most value from the offering
3. Surveys, calling, etc. prior to renewal to identify/fix issues to maximize renewal probability
4. Ongoing nurturing emails re: help desk, users group, etc.

A Cross-sell/Up-serve Campaign

IDEAS & ACTIONS

The Cross-sell/Up-serve Campaign

Maximize the lifetime value of each customer by identifying opportunities to satisfy additional needs that the customer could have the desire, authority and ability to satisfy

1. Personalized email from their Account Manager citing examples of similar customers who have found value in additional solutions
2. Email nurturing campaign featuring educational content pinpointing circumstances that would suggest the need for those additional solutions
3. Invitations to specific in-person, online or online/on-demand events to encourage timely action

A Customer Advocacy Campaign

Reach out to contacts within existing accounts who are particularly enthusiastic about your offerings and have derived great value to date

1. Personalized email #1 from their Account Manager personally recognizing their success using your offerings and your appreciation for their patronage
2. Personalized email #2 from a C-level executive inviting them to participate in an appreciation event, advisory group, media opportunity or other VIP activity
3. Ongoing outreach offering complimentary service upgrades, prioritized access to technical support or early adopter testing, invitations to conference panels and events that prospective customers may attend, etc.

A Customer Advocacy Campaign

Lesson 258
MARKETING TO WIN
25 Steps to creating engaging marketing copy

Presented by
Mark Jewell
@SellingEnergy
info@sellingenergy.com

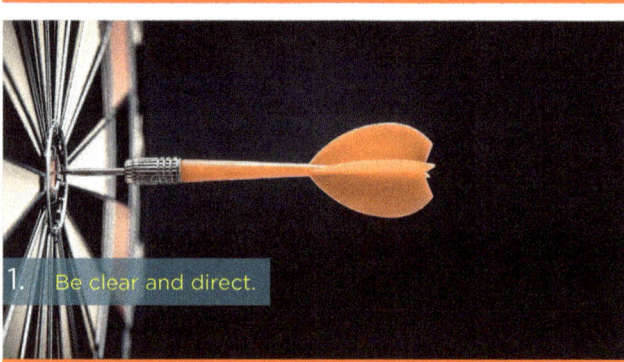

1. Be clear and direct.

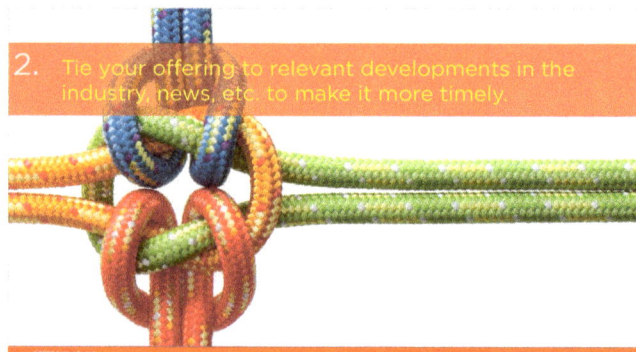

2. Tie your offering to relevant developments in the industry, news, etc. to make it more timely.

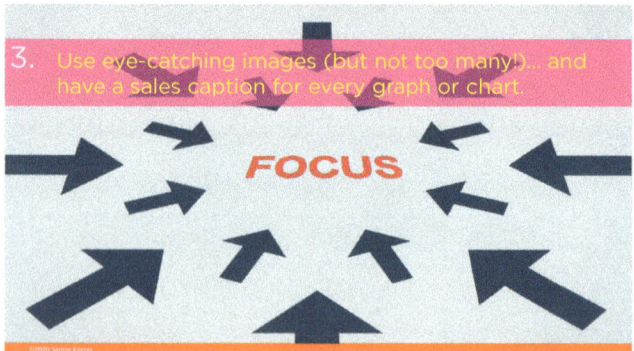

3. Use eye-catching images (but not too many!)... and have a sales caption for every graph or chart.

FOCUS

4. Keep it mobile-friendly* and ideally responsive... and test it on multiple devices!

*Single-column, readable font, most important content first, responsive for varied viewing formats, etc.

IDEAS & ACTIONS

5. Use "fascination" points.

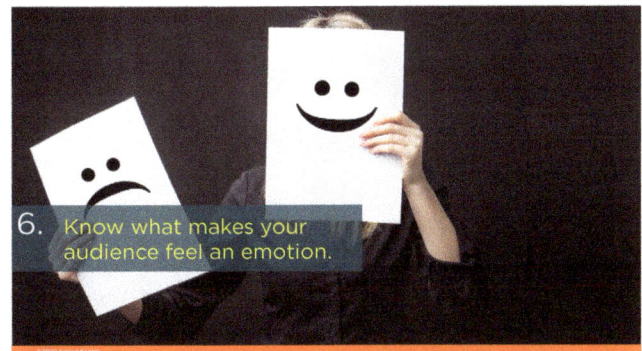

6. Know what makes your audience feel an emotion.

7. Find your tribe and consistently write for it.

8. Be sure to use "you" and "yours" liberally.

9. Stick to your "one big idea."

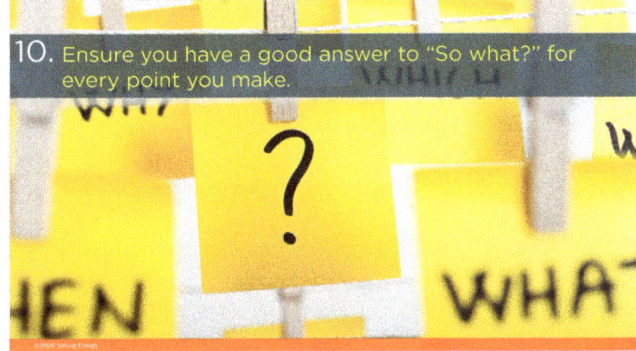

10. Ensure you have a good answer to "So what?" for every point you make.

11. Realize when it makes sense to make the piece long or short.

12. Write the **subheads** first... ...since most readers are actually scanners.

IDEAS & ACTIONS

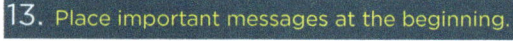
13. Place important messages at the beginning.

14. Use short and broken sentences.

15. Use sensory words.

16. Use analogies.

17. Enhance credibility with technical details.

18. Focus on quantitative benefits wherever possible.

19. Make it more memorable with sound bites.

20. Remove all unnecessary sentences, adverbs, adjectives, and any other fluff... as in poetry!

IDEAS & ACTIONS

_____

_____

_____

_____

www.SellingEnergy.com

21. Tell a story... ideally a memorable and repeatable one.

Everyone has a story...

22. Proof it on paper, real it aloud, and read it again later.

23. Lower the perceived risk...
an overwhelming value prop, guarantee, or both!

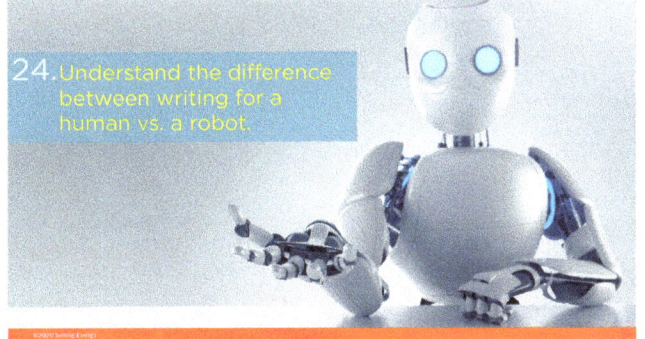

24. Understand the difference between writing for a human vs. a robot.

25. Test it!

selling in 6™

Lesson 259
MARKETING TO WIN
Placing the most important messages at the top

Presented by
Mark Jewell
@SellingEnergy
info@sellingenergy.com

selling energy
Turbocharging Success

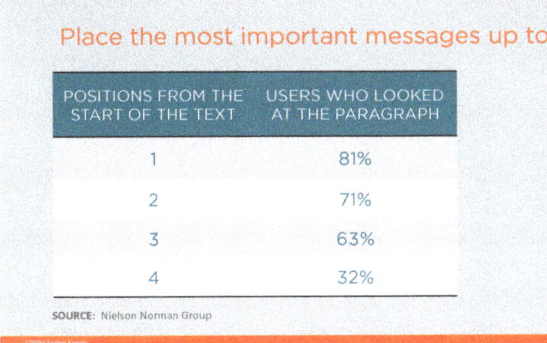

Place the most important messages up top!

POSITIONS FROM THE START OF THE TEXT	USERS WHO LOOKED AT THE PARAGRAPH
1	81%
2	71%
3	63%
4	32%

SOURCE: Nielsen Norman Group

Realize that many readers read in an "F" pattern.

F

IDEAS & ACTIONS

Lesson 260
MARKETING TO WIN
25 Essential elements of an effective website

Presented by
Mark Jewell
@SellingEnergy
info@sellingenergy.com

Turbocharging Success

Q:

What are the ingredients of an effective website?

---

25 Essentials of an effective website...

1. Showcase "who" and "what" up front.
2. Make contact info immediately obvious.
3. Have a response time of 3 seconds or less.

Adapted from Forbes "The Little Black Book of Billionaire Secrets" and other resources

---

25 Essentials of an effective website...

4. Design the experience around repeat visits.
5. Provide one or more genuinely useful tools.
6. Use intuitive navigation, ideally limited to 3 clicks.

Adapted from Forbes "The Little Black Book of Billionaire Secrets" and other resources

---

25 Essentials of an effective website...

7. Feature robust content as well as design elements.
8. Focus attention on the best highlights.
9. Feature content that resonates with the need, not the sell.

Adapted from Forbes "The Little Black Book of Billionaire Secrets" and other resources

---

25 Essentials of an effective website...

10. Maintain fresh content, which keeps humans and search engine robots happy.
11. Minimizes bounces, maximize time on site and page visits, and conversions.
12. Use a maximum of 3 typefaces (ideally sans serif) in a maximum of 3 point sizes.

Adapted from Forbes "The Little Black Book of Billionaire Secrets" and other resources

---

25 Essentials of an effective website...

13. Select colors carefully, with vibrant colors driving emotion or action steps (e.g., clicks).
14. Realize how humans read ("F" pattern); place most important content appropriately.
15. Keep the content concise, easy to scan, and objective

    (see quote on following slide)

Adapted from Forbes "The Little Black Book of Billionaire Secrets" and other resources

---

"Studies of how users read on the Web found that they do not actually read: instead, they scan the text. A study of five different writing styles found that a sample Web site scored 58% higher in measured usability when it was written concisely, 47% higher when the text was scannable, and 27% higher when it was written in an objective style instead of the promotional style used in the control condition and many current Web pages. Combining these three changes into a single site that was concise, scannable, and objective at the same time resulted in 124% higher measured usability."

SOURCE: Concise, Scannable, and Objective: How to Write for the Web", Nielsen & Morkes, 1997.

IDEAS & ACTIONS

_____

_____

_____

_____

25 Essentials of an effective website...

16. Maintain readability with enough white space.
17. Select pictures, infographics, videos and graphics to drive messages better than text.
18. Require minimal scroll; use links from main page.

Adapted from Forbes "The Little Black Book of Billionaire Secrets" and other resources

25 Essentials of an effective website...

19. Use consistent layout, with repeated elements.
20. Maximize the value of your "above the fold" real estate.
21. Long link text is easier and more searchable.

Adapted from Forbes "The Little Black Book of Billionaire Secrets" and other resources

25 Essentials of an effective website...

22. Back links maintain a sense of place/direction.
23. Site should work with Internet Explorer, Safari, and Firefox and look good at various typical screen resolutions (e.g., 1024-768).

Adapted from Forbes "The Little Black Book of Billionaire Secrets" and other resources

25 Essentials of an effective website...

24. Use plenty of written content in HTML; use keywords frequently; minimize the use of tables; and, use clutter-free code.
25. Leverage your links by making them descriptive and use keywords in the link text.

Adapted from Forbes "The Little Black Book of Billionaire Secrets" and other resources

Lesson 261
MARKETING TO WIN
The importance of "visual hierarchy"

Presented by
Mark Jewell

@SellingEnergy
Info@sellingenergy.com

Q:
What is "visual hierarchy" and why is it so important?

"Visual hierarchy refers to the arrangement or presentation of elements in a way that implies importance.[1] In other words, visual hierarchy influences the order in which the human eye perceives what it sees. This order is created by the visual contrast between forms in a field of perception. Objects with highest contrast to their surroundings are recognized first by the human mind. The term visual hierarchy is used most frequently in the discourse of the visual arts fields, notably so within the field of graphic design."

SOURCE: Wikipedia

"The concept of visual hierarchy is based in Gestalt psychological theory, an early 20th-century German theory that proposes that the human brain has innate organizing tendencies that "structure individual elements, shapes or forms into a coherent, organized whole." [2] The German word Gestalt translates into "form," "pattern," or "shape" in English.[3] When an element in a visual field disconnects from the 'whole' created by the brain's perceptual organization, it "stands out" to the viewer. The shapes that disconnect most severely from their surroundings stand out the most."

SOURCE: Wikipedia

IDEAS & ACTIONS

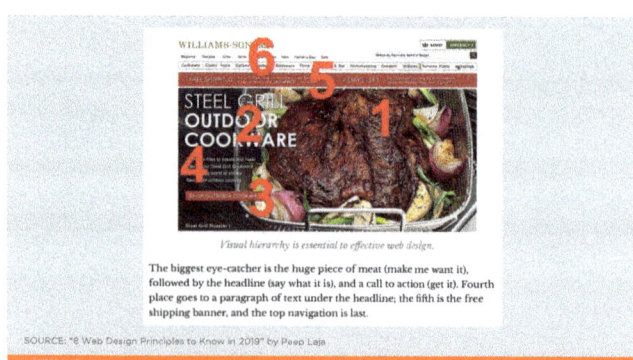

Visual hierarchy is essential to effective web design.

The biggest eye-catcher is the huge piece of meat (make me want it), followed by the headline (say what it is), and a call to action (get it). Fourth place goes to a paragraph of text under the headline; the fifth is the free shipping banner, and the top navigation is last.

SOURCE: "8 Web Design Principles to Know in 2019" by Peep Laja

---

The importance of "visual hierarchy" in design...

1. Size
2. Color
3. Contrast
4. Alignment
5. Repetition
6. Proximity
7. Density
8. Whitespace
9. Style
10. Texture

Adapted from "Understanding Visual Hierarchy in Web Design" by Brandon Jones and other resources

---

Test your own website for adherence to hierarchy...

1. List the information that your visitors are likely seeking.
2. Rank them in likely importance to your visitors.
3. List the informational ingredients on your own website.
4. Rank them in importance using visual hierarchy principles.
5. Compare your results.

Adapted from "Understanding Visual Hierarchy in Web Design" by Brandon Jones and other resources

---

selling in 6™

Lesson 262
MARKETING TO WIN
The importance of Search Engine Optimization (SEO)

Presented by
Mark Jewell
@SellingEnergy
info@sellingenergy.com

selling energy
Turbocharging Success

Q:

What is Search Engine Optimization (SEO) and why is it so important?

SEO: The process of getting traffic to your site from the "free," "organic," "editorial," or "natural" search results on search engines.

SOURCE: Search Engine Land

---

selling in 6™

Lesson 263
MARKETING TO WIN
Maximizing the effectiveness of social media

Presented by
Mark Jewell
@SellingEnergy
info@sellingenergy.com

selling energy
Turbocharging Success

Q:

Why all the fuss about social media?

IDEAS & ACTIONS

Social media landscape

Some of the most popular social media websites: Baidu Tieba, Facebook (and its associated Facebook Messenger), Gab, Google+, MySpace, Instagram, LinkedIn, Pinterest, Reddit, Snapchat, Tumblr, Twitter, Viber, VK, WeChat, Weibo, WhatsApp, Wikia, and YouTube **Each has more than 100,000,000 registered users.**

SOURCE: Wikipedia

Tips for maximizing social media...

1. Sell at the right time.
2. Always be genuine and post with a purpose.
3. Start with a goal and consider the networks.

Tips for maximizing social media...

4. Ask yourself, "Would I click on this?"
5. Be sure your headline is strong.*
6. Focus on the content, not the marketing.

*For both humans and robots.

Tips for maximizing social media...

7. Make it easy to read.
8. Add shared content.
9. Build curiosity.

Tips for maximizing social media...

10. Include a call to action.
11. Keep a consistent voice.

Please also review the Social Media appendix for best practices using selected platforms like Facebook, LinkedIn and Twitter

Lesson 264
MARKETING TO WIN
Maximizing the effectiveness of LinkedIn

 Presented by
Mark Jewell
@SellingEnergy
info@sellingenergy.com

Tips for leveraging LinkedIn...

1. Look for company characteristics.
2. Look for buyer characteristics.
3. Look for situational characteristics.

IDEAS & ACTIONS

www.SellingEnergy.com

Tips for leveraging LinkedIn...

4. Search for customers' colleagues.
5. Search for customers' connections.
6. Carefully review suggested similar connections.
7. Notice organizations and industry groups.

And thoughtfully craft your own profile...

1. Choose a professional photo.
2. Write a good profile summary.
3. Include work experience, skills, endorsements, etc. from others in your network.
4. Request recommendations (employers, clients, colleagues, etc.).
5. Send messages and invitations to connect.

And here are tips from LinkedIn re: marketing...

1. Optimize your own profile.
2. Create an effective LinkedIn company page.
3. Define your audience and goals.
4. Optimize your company page for search (insert keywords, insert links to your company page on your website, blog, etc.)
5. Ensure employees' pages are up-to-date.
6. Share relevant content.
7. And a lot more... See LinkedIn for more details.

Lesson 265
MARKETING TO WIN
Measuring outcomes, analyzing and optimizing

Presented by
Mark Jewell
@SellingEnergy
info@sellingenergy.com

Turbocharging Success

Appropriate and timely measurement

EARLY	MIDDLE	LATE
Increase in targeted accounts visiting website; or opening and clicking emails		
New contacts within targeted accounts (completing org chart)		
New targeted accounts accepting website offers		
Begin tracking prospect downloads & preferences, and capturing contact info		

Appropriate and timely measurement

EARLY	MIDDLE	LATE
	Addition to the Success Story Archive™ as proof	
	Quantity of connections with targeted contacts	
	Quantity of meetings within targeted accounts	
	Quantity of genuinely qualified leads within targeted accounts	

Appropriate and timely measurement

EARLY	MIDDLE	LATE
		Quantity of opportunities within targeted accounts
		Quantity of first meetings on those opportunities
		Quantity of multiple meetings and/or stakeholders
		Quantifiable pipeline identified by Sales with high % probabilities

Appropriate and timely measurement

EARLY	MIDDLE	LATE
Increase in targeted accounts visiting website; or opening and clicking emails	Addition to the Success Story Archive™ as proof	Quantity of opportunities within targeted accounts
New contacts within targeted accounts (completing org chart)	Quantity of connections with targeted contacts	Quantity of first meetings on those opportunities
New targeted accounts accepting website offers	Quantity of meetings within targeted accounts	Quantity of multiple meetings and/or stakeholders
Begin tracking prospect downloads & preferences, and capturing contact info	Quantity of genuinely qualified leads within targeted accounts	Quantifiable pipeline identified by Sales with high % probabilities

IDEAS & ACTIONS

5 Marketing KPIs to impress the C-suite

1. Value of all opportunities sourced by Marketing
2. % of customers directly sourced by Marketing
3. Ratio of sales pipeline to Marketing spend
4. Customer acquisition cost
5. % of customers influenced by Marketing.

Lesson 266
MARKETING TO WIN IN THE UTILITY SECTOR
Harnessing marketing to overcome challenges

Presented by
Mark Jewell
@SellingEnergy
info@sellingenergy.com

Turbocharging Success

Q:

Why do utilities need marketing?

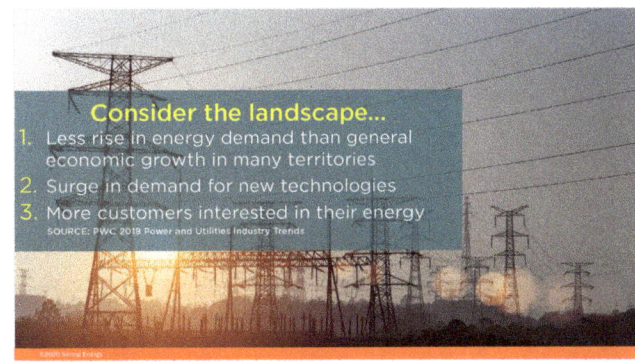

Consider the landscape...

1. Less rise in energy demand than general economic growth in many territories
2. Surge in demand for new technologies
3. More customers interested in their energy

SOURCE: PWC 2019 Power and Utilities Industry Trends

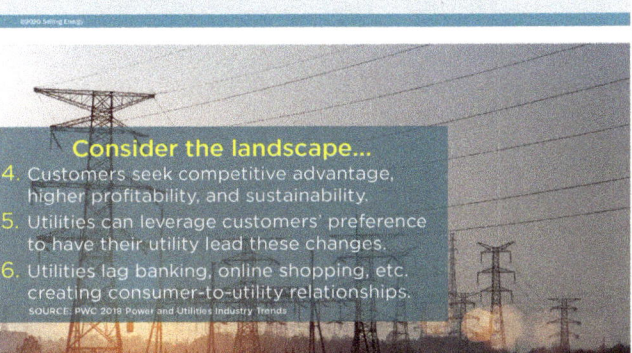

Consider the landscape...

4. Customers seek competitive advantage, higher profitability, and sustainability.
5. Utilities can leverage customers' preference to have their utility lead these changes.
6. Utilities lag banking, online shopping, etc. creating consumer-to-utility relationships.

SOURCE: PWC 2019 Power and Utilities Industry Trends

Customer Experience

"The most important marketing priority, above new product innovation, branding, or content creation."

SOURCE: 2014 Forbes Insight / EY Study. "US Utilities: time to get smart about marketing", study surveyed 300 US senior executives across all industries

Challenges to optimizing that experience

Most customers don't choose their utility providers.
Most customers take their utility for granted.
Most customer interactions are focused on the negative (outages, billing issues, rate hikes).

SOURCE: 2014 Forbes Insight / EY Study

Overcoming those challenges...

STEP #1:
Marketing to build trust & expand utility offerings

SOURCE: 2014 Forbes Insight / EY Study

IDEAS & ACTIONS

www.SellingEnergy.com

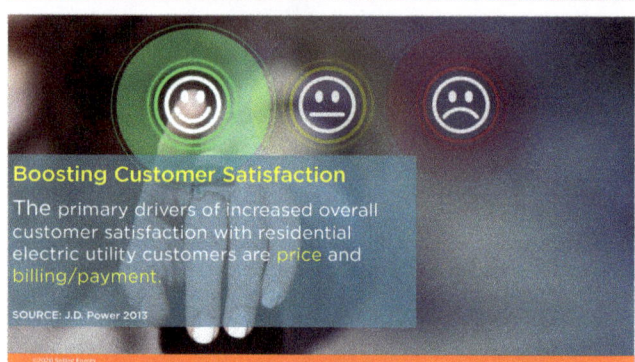

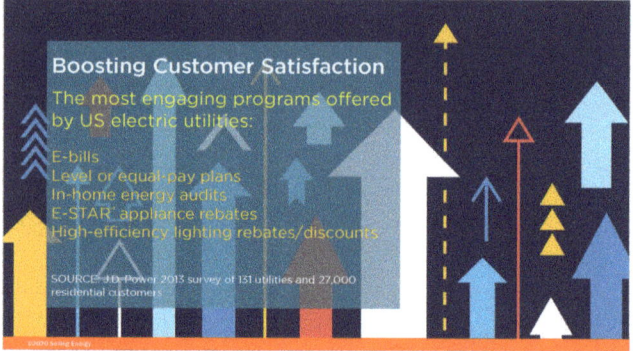

Lesson **267**

MARKETING TO WIN IN THE UTILITY SECTOR
Opportunities with non-residential customers

Presented by
Mark Jewell
@SellingEnergy
info@sellingenergy.com

Q:

Would non-residential customers have similar opinions?

"Utilities are really beginning to understand the importance of engagement with their business customers, which is reflected in increased communication."

SOURCE: John Hazen, director in the utility and infrastructure practice at J.D. Power, January 2017, citing data from the "J.D. Power 2016 Calendar-Year Electric Utility Business Customer Satisfaction Study."

IDEAS & ACTIONS

"Business customers expect their utility to do more than just keep the lights on. In the absence of communication, which creates a void of critical information such as the status of outages, customers may not recognize the good things their utility is doing for the economy, the community and the environment. Proactive engagement creates awareness, which leads to higher satisfaction."

SOURCE: John Hazen, director in the utility and infrastructure practice at J.D. Power, January 2017, citing data from the "J.D. Power 2016 Calendar-Year Electric Utility Business Customer Satisfaction Study."

"It's remarkable how utilities have improved as an industry in understanding the importance of being customer-focused." Hazen said. "In doing so, they hope to not only improve their financial performance, but also to be viewed more favorably by regulators."

SOURCE: John Hazen, director in the utility and infrastructure practice at J.D. Power, January 2017, citing data from the "J.D. Power 2016 Calendar-Year Electric Utility Business Customer Satisfaction Study."

"Furthermore, business customers are also more supportive of the investment plans utilities have in such projects as updating or developing their infrastructure."

SOURCE: John Hazen, director in the utility and infrastructure practice at J.D. Power, January 2017, citing data from the "J.D. Power 2016 Calendar-Year Electric Utility Business Customer Satisfaction Study."

"The study finds that 52% of business customers recall at least one communication from their utility in the past six months, up from 49% last year. The topics of those communications range from billing to energy conservation tips to customer service, and the delivery method varies from direct mail to in-person visits from a utility representative."

SOURCE: John Hazen, director in the utility and infrastructure practice at J.D. Power, January 2017, citing data from the "J.D. Power 2016 Calendar-Year Electric Utility Business Customer Satisfaction Study."

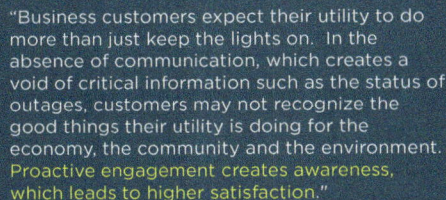

Lesson 268
MARKETING TO WIN IN THE UTILITY SECTOR
Optimizing utility marketing yields many benefits

 Presented by Mark Jewell
@SellingEnergy
info@sellingenergy.com

Q:
What are some of the other reasons that utilities need to optimize their marketing?

Becoming the "Utility of Tomorrow"

Need to become a trusted partner for beneficial electrification, energy efficiency, and other energy initiatives

Reducing regulatory intervention

Satisfied customers who trust your brand are less likely to call for more regulation

IDEAS & ACTIONS

www.SellingEnergy.com

Insulating against negative events

Satisfied customers who trust their utility partner are more forgiving of rate increases, outages due to force majeure or other factors, etc.

Improving uptake of utility programs

Customers who are more engaged and informed about utility offerings have greater participation in them...

...and they serve as better advocates in the marketplace, further enhancing uptake.

Improving communication

Stronger customer engagement supports...

...greater willingness to be contacted
...greater attention to utility communications
...better recall of key messages*

*particularly if marketing messages arrive through multiple channels

Advancing utility goals

Robust customer engagement better positions the utility to meet beneficial electrification or efficiency goals, address peak loads or other distribution issues, or implement new rate designs.

Q:

What are some baby steps to becoming a better utility marketer?

Assemble "benefit bundles"

Most customers would resonate with a "convenience bundle" including electronic bill, auto-deduction, and fixed-bill services in the same package.

Formalize the onboarding process

Organize the business to enroll customers in a host of relevant offerings immediately. Studies show that customers fall victim to "inertia" once they've been with the utility for 3+ years.

Lesson **269**
SUCCESSFUL SELLING IN RESIDENTIAL PROPERTIES
Helping homeowners get excited about energy

Presented by
Mark Jewell
@SellingEnergy
info@sellingenergy.com

IDEAS & ACTIONS

Q:
Why might your residential prospect be interested in your solutions?

Saving energy

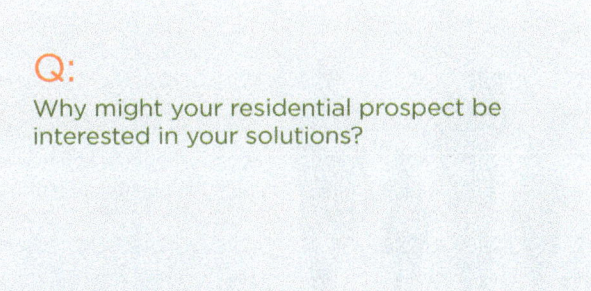
Saving money

Q:
How often does the prospect of saving money actually drive decisions?

How often does the promise of "saving money" drive decisions?

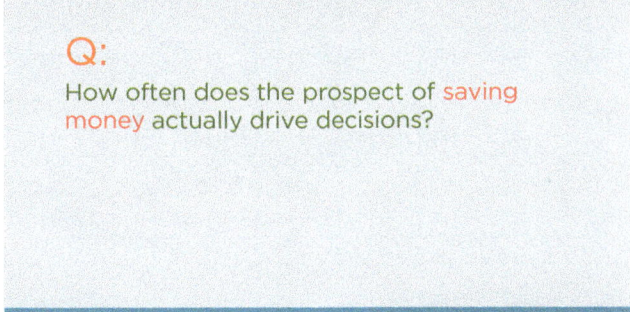

Q:
Could financial savings be reframed to be even more compelling?

"I have a friend who is saving "$x" each month on his utility bill and he's using that savings to…"

IDEAS & ACTIONS

Saving money to fund educational expenses

More discretionary income for the family

Using utility bill savings to afford more leisure

Using utility bill savings to do more good work

Using utility bill savings to buy school supplies.

Using utility bill savings to fund sports activities

Using utility bill savings to spoil the grandkids!

selling in 6™

Lesson **270**
SUCCESSFUL SELLING IN RESIDENTIAL PROPERTIES
What's more important than saving energy or money?

Presented by
Mark Jewell
@SellingEnergy
info@sellingenergy.com

sellingenergy
Turbocharging Success

IDEAS & ACTIONS

_____

_____

_____

_____

Q:
What could be even more important than saving energy or even money?

Enhancing comfort

Hedging against utility price spikes

Supporting an easier sale and/or higher price

Maintaining a healthy home

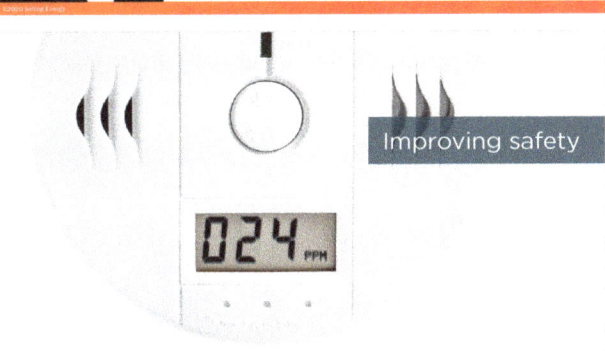
Improving safety

Reducing carbon emissions

Pride of ownership

IDEAS & ACTIONS

Providing green and/or high-performance "badge value"

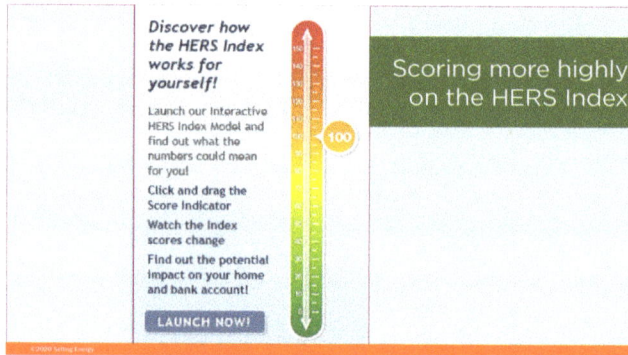

Scoring more highly on the HERS Index

Discover how the HERS Index works for yourself!

Launch our Interactive HERS Index Model and find out what the numbers could mean for you!

Click and drag the Score Indicator

Watch the Index scores change

Find out the potential impact on your home and bank account!

LAUNCH NOW!

Social norm... the neighbors are doing it.

Q:

How many home efficiency solutions have you already installed in your prospect's neighborhood?

HERE'S WHAT TOPS CONSUMERS' LISTS FOR THE MOST DESIRED SMART HOME DEVICES:

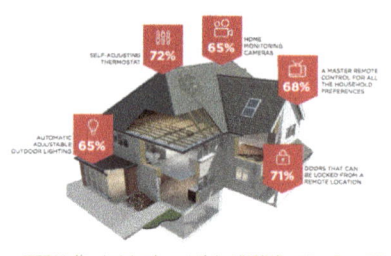

SOURCE: http://www.icontrol.com/wp-content/uploads/2015/06/Smart_Home_Report_2015.pdf

selling in 6™

Lesson 271
SUCCESSFUL SELLING IN RESIDENTIAL PROPERTIES
Personally attesting to the value of upgrading

Presented by
Mark Jewell
@SellingEnergy
Info@sellingenergy.com

sellingenergy
Turbocharging Success

Q:

Do you believe that your offering creates genuine value?

Q:

Have you personally installed the solution(s) you are recommending so that you can personally attest to their value?

IDEAS & ACTIONS

Q:

Remember, your persona is "the energy expert," and wouldn't experts have these solutions installed in their own homes?

Q:

Given all the different behavior motivators mentioned herein, how do you know what your prospect most values?

Lesson 272
SUCCESSFUL SELLING IN RESIDENTIAL PROPERTIES
Knowing what *your* prospect most values

Presented by
Mark Jewell
@SellingEnergy
info@sellingenergy.com

Turbocharging Success

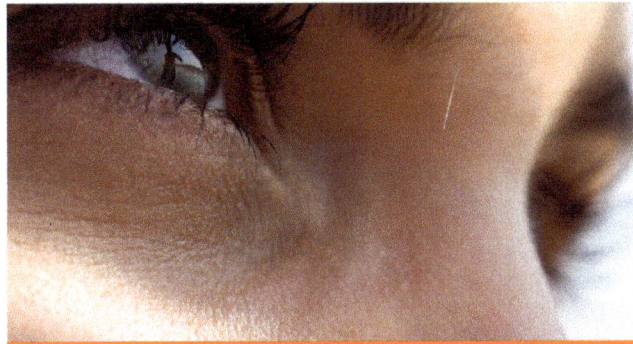

"
The quality of your life is directly related to the quality of the questions you ask.
"

— Anthony Robbins

...and when you ask those high-quality questions...

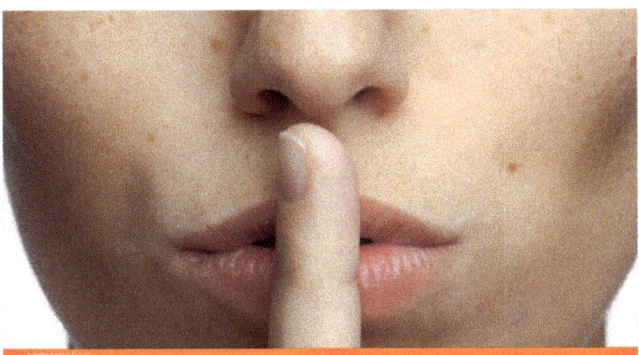

Q:

What questions do you typically ask when you're in someone's home doing your work?

IDEAS & ACTIONS

You need to ask **intelligent** questions.

You need to understand the **homeowner** as well as the home.

Perceived problems.
Financial issues.
Priorities.
Decision-making process.

Begin by discovering **what has changed** that caused the homeowner to get involved in the program at this time.

"How long have you lived in this house?"

"What has changed for you since you moved into this house?"

"May I ask what **motivated** you to sign up for this program?"

or...

"May I ask you, what aspect of this program was **most attractive** to you?"

Asking follow-up questions that delve into **impacts** provides insight into **what the homeowner truly values**.

"How comfortable is this house in the summer (or winter)?"

"And what impact does that have on your family?"

IDEAS & ACTIONS

Additional questions about what the homeowner has done (or considered doing) about the problem can also give **insight into how the homeowner thinks.**

Starting with a statement and **asking a question to secure agreement** can be particularly effective.

"Many folks who have this kind of cooling system have difficulty getting every room in the house comfortable.

"Has that been your experience?"

Remember, most decisions are **made emotionally...**

...and then **justified financially.**

You need to discover which **emotions** will actually **motivate** this homeowner.

Would you pay into Social Security your entire career and then forget to file for benefits?

Imagine getting a $1,200/year *after-tax* salary increase just by saving $100 per month on your utility bill.

selling in 6™

Lesson 273
SUCCESSFUL SELLING IN RESIDENTIAL PROPERTIES
Research findings that help shape the message

Presented by
Mark Jewell
@SellingEnergy
info@sellingenergy.com

sellingenergy
Turbocharging Success

IDEAS & ACTIONS

www.SellingEnergy.com

RESEARCH FINDING #1

Homeowners typically believe their homes are already as efficient as they can be.

51% agree/strongly agree with this statement
Another 35% were neutral on this statement

RESEARCH FINDING #2

Bundling measures allows customers to enjoy deeper savings by reframing the decision and making the benefits of greater change more obvious.

RESEARCH FINDING #3

Expressing benefits in five-year rather than monthly terms drives higher adoption rates.

RESEARCH FINDING #4

Customers respond to energy efficiency messages as they relate to thermal comfort.

51% ranked "making my home more comfortable" as a very important energy efficiency program feature (Cadmus test branding survey)

RESEARCH FINDING #5

Cost is a barrier, but rebates can be an incentive

* 60% said cost was biggest barrier
* 58%: "availability of rebates" as very important
* 55% ranked "audit is low-cost" as very important feature
* 62% cited "financial barrier" as primary reason for not making EE improvements

RESEARCH FINDING #6

There is a need for personalized assistance and guidance

* Post-service surveys, customers ranked "one-on-one counseling" and "personal energy action plan" as the two most valuable features of the (REAP) program

RESEARCH FINDING #7

Customers don't make decisions....they make comparisons.

(A vital part of your job is framing the comparison properly.)

RESEARCH FINDING #8

Homeowners determine the value of solving problems they want solved.

(Energy efficiency is merely an after-effect of these upgrades, if they are well-designed and implemented.)

SOURCE: Greentip, "How to make energy efficiency programs grab consumers." Aug. 20, 2015

IDEAS & ACTIONS

Lesson 274
SUCCESSFUL SELLING IN RESIDENTIAL PROPERTIES
12 Field-tested tips for successful in-home selling

Presented by
Mark Jewell
@SellingEnergy
Info@sellingenergy.com

Tips for successful
in-home selling...

1. Never underestimate first impressions.

2. Make a proper introduction.

3. Break the ice with a little humor.

4. Show your credentials up front.

5. Establish a "base camp" for all discussions.

6. Keep it simple.

IDEAS & ACTIONS

7. Introduce the prospect of greater savings up front.

8. Include a step-by-step review of the process.

9. Keep an eye on the clock.

10. Include the homeowner throughout the process.

11. Be clear about next steps.

12. Commit to next steps... and follow through!

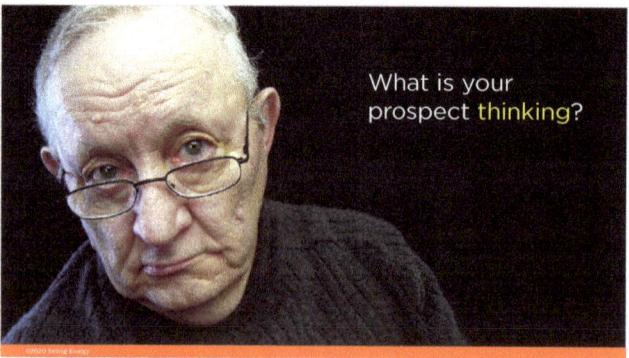

What is your prospect thinking?

Lesson **275**
SUCCESSFUL SELLING IN RESIDENTIAL PROPERTIES
How many times have you pressed the olive?

Presented by
Mark Jewell
@SellingEnergy
info@sellingenergy.com

IDEAS & ACTIONS _____

_____

_____

_____

Understand what your customers are trying to achieve...

...create offerings that really complement each other...

...and partner with like-minded non-competitive vendors.

Capitalize on cross-selling & upselling potential during the initial interaction.

Keep your eyes and ears open for additional needs while you're in the customer's home.

Q:

What offerings make sense to consider cross-selling or upselling to your customers?

1. Energy assessments
2. HVAC diagnostics
3. LED replacements
4. Furnace filters
5. AC coil wraps

6. Duct sealing
7. Water heaters
8. Smart thermostats
9. Insulation
10. Heat pumps

Q:

If your prospect's energy upgrade potential were an olive, how many times would you be pressing it?

IDEAS & ACTIONS

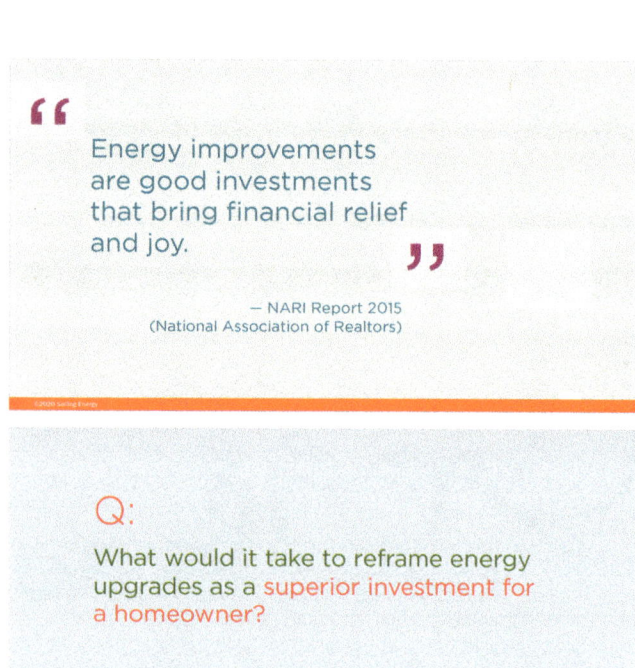

"
Energy improvements are good investments that bring financial relief and joy.
"

— NARI Report 2015
(National Association of Realtors)

Lesson 276
SUCCESSFUL SELLING IN RESIDENTIAL PROPERTIES
Showcasing the financial benefits to homeowners

Presented by
Mark Jewell
@SellingEnergy
Info@sellingenergy.com

Turbocharging Success

Q:

What would it take to reframe energy upgrades as a superior investment for a homeowner?

Most people don't make **decisions**...
...they make **comparisons**.

Q:

How do utilities compare with other out-of-pocket expenses that homeowners might spend more time thinking about?

"On average, **energy costs** are higher than either **property tax** or **insurance** for U.S. homes at $2,506 per year."

SOURCE: U.S. Census

And by the way, even when people do make decisions...

...they usually make emotional decisions first, and then they justify them financially.

Q:

How do investments in energy efficiency compare with other investments?

IDEAS & ACTIONS

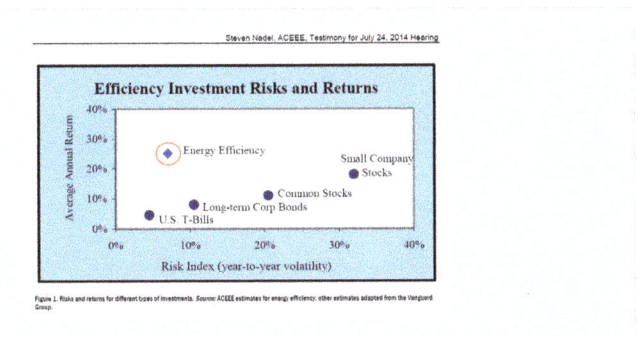

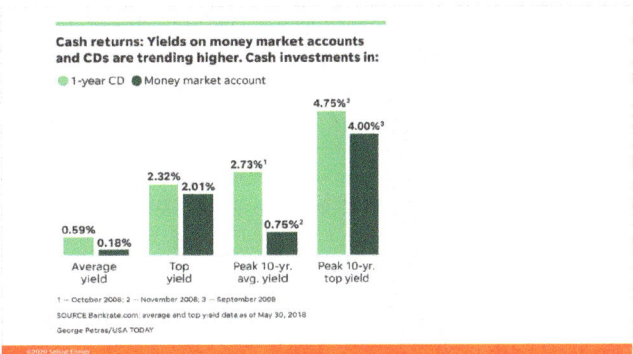

Cash returns: Yields on money market accounts and CDs are trending higher. Cash investments in:
● 1-year CD ● Money market account

~2%
20%
25%
33%
50%

~2% 5-year CD
20% 5-year payback
25% 4-year payback
33% 3-year payback
50% 2-year payback

NOTE: One can express ROI as the "reciprocal of payback"; however, an annualized ROI over time yields lower results.

Q:

What does "ROI" really mean, and how many kinds of ROI are there?

Return On Investment (ROI)

- ROI is the reciprocal of SPP
  - SPP is first cost divided by YR1 savings
  - ROI is YR1 savings divided by first cost
- Therefore, 1 / SPP = ROI and 1 / ROI = SPP

Assume $100,000 first cost saves $25,000 in YR1

SPP = $100,000 / $25,000 = 4 years
ROI = $25,000 / $100,000 = 25%

Which "ROI" are you actually referencing?

"ROI"
$$\frac{\text{Current Period Inflow}}{\text{Cumulative Outflow}}$$

"Total ROI"
$$\frac{\text{Cumulative Inflow} - \text{Cumulative Outflow}}{\text{Cumulative Outflow}}$$

"Annualized ROI"
$$\left[\frac{\text{Cumulative Inflow}}{\text{Cumulative Outflow}}\right]^{1/N} - 1$$

NOTE: No version of ROI incorporates the Time Value of Money.

CASH OUTFLOWS								
Single Investment	$	(65,400)						
Phased Investment								
Miscellaneous Investment								
Financed Investment		$	-	$	-	$	-	$
Financing Fees (if any)	$	-						
Subtotal	$	(65,400)	$	-	$	-	$	-
Rebates Reducing "Cash Outflow"	$	15,400	$	-	$	-	$	-
SUBTOTAL OUTFLOWS	$	(50,000)	$	-	$	-	$	-

| % Savings Realized | | | 100% | | 100% | | 100% | | 100% | | 100% |

CASH INFLOWS									
Energy Savings	$	-	$	10,000	$	10,300	$	10,609	$	10,927	$	11,255
Maintenance Savings	$	-		5,000		5,150		5,305		5,464		5,628
Other Benefits										
Rebates Considered "Cash Inflow"										
SUBTOTAL INFLOWS	$	-	$	15,000	$	15,450	$	15,914	$	16,391	$	16,883

| Annual Cash Flow | $ | (50,000) | $ | 15,000 | $ | 15,450 | $ | 15,914 | $ | 16,391 | $ | 16,883 |
| Annual Present Value | $ | (50,000) | $ | 14,302 | $ | 13,392 | $ | 12,540 | $ | 11,742 | $ | 10,994 |

	10-YEAR	20-YEAR	1-YEAR	2-YEAR	3-YEAR	4-YEAR	5-YEAR	6-YR
Simple Payback Period (SPP)	3.3							
Cumulative Payback Period (CPB)	3.2							
Discounted Payback Period (DPB)	3.8							
Return on Investment (ROI)	see value per year	see value per year	30.0%	30.9%	31.8%	32.8%	33.8%	
Total Return on Investment	243.9%	706.1%	-70.0%	-39.1%	-7.3%	25.5%	59.3%	
Annualized Return on Investment	13.1%	11.0%	-70.0%	-22.0%	-2.5%	5.8%	9.8%	
Internal Rate of Return (XIRR)	35.7%	38.2%	-91.1%	-37.3%	-4.8%	12.3%	21.8%	
Net Present Value (NPV)	$ 58,296	$ 114,408	$ (35,698)	$ (22,306)	$ (9,767)	$ 1,975	$ 12,969	$
Modified Internal Rate of Return (XMIRR)	19.9%	17.2%	-90.1%	-23.4%	2.8%	12.7%	17.0%	
Savings-to-Investment Ratio (SIR)	2.2	3.3	0.3	0.6	0.8	1.0	1.3	

NOTE THAT CERTAIN RETURNS VARY DEPENDING ON

IDEAS & ACTIONS

Q:

But wait... Is comparing "bank interest" and "utility bill savings" an "apples-to-apples" comparison?

Lesson **277**
SUCCESSFUL SELLING IN RESIDENTIAL PROPERTIES
Comparing before-tax and after-tax returns

Presented by
Mark Jewell
@SellingEnergy
info@sellingenergy.com

Q:

Understanding that an energy upgrade could deliver much higher annual returns than a CD, how and when do you recover the "principal" invested in the upgrade?

Q:

Perhaps more importantly, are the utility savings taxed the same way as interest paid by a bank?

HINT:

Does a homeowner pay the utility bill with before-tax or after-tax dollars?

Unlike most other investments, a homeowner's efficiency investment yields an **after-tax return** since utility bills are paid with after-tax dollars.

IDEAS & ACTIONS _____

Unlike most other investments, a homeowner's efficiency investment yields an **after-tax return** since utility bills are paid with after-tax dollars.

$$\frac{\text{After-tax \% return}}{(1 - \text{marginal tax rate})} = \text{Equivalent before-tax \% return}$$

5-year-payback energy upgrade assuming homeowner has a **40%** combined* marginal tax bracket

*Combined tax bracket implies federal, state and local marginal income tax rates

---

5-year-payback energy upgrade assuming homeowner has a **40%** combined* marginal tax bracket

$$\frac{20\%^* \text{ annual return}}{} =$$

*Combined tax bracket implies federal, state and local marginal income tax rates

---

5-year-payback energy upgrade assuming homeowner has a **40%** combined marginal tax bracket

$$\frac{20\%^* \text{ annual return}}{(1 - 40\% \text{ marginal tax})} =$$

*Combined tax bracket implies federal, state and local marginal income tax rates

---

5-year-payback energy upgrade assuming homeowner has a **40%** combined* marginal tax bracket

$$\frac{20\% \text{ annual return}}{(1 - 40\% \text{ marginal tax})} = \text{33.3\% equivalent before-tax return}$$

*Combined tax bracket implies federal, state and local marginal income tax rates

---

4-year-payback energy upgrade assuming homeowner has a **40%** combined* marginal tax bracket

*Combined tax bracket implies federal, state and local marginal income tax rates

---

4-year-payback energy upgrade assuming homeowner has a **40%** combined* marginal tax bracket

$$\frac{25\% \text{ annual return}}{} =$$

*Combined tax bracket implies federal, state and local marginal income tax rates

---

4-year-payback energy upgrade assuming homeowner has a **40%** combined* marginal tax bracket

$$\frac{25\% \text{ annual return}}{(1 - 40\% \text{ marginal tax})} =$$

*Combined tax bracket implies federal, state and local marginal income tax rates

---

IDEAS & ACTIONS

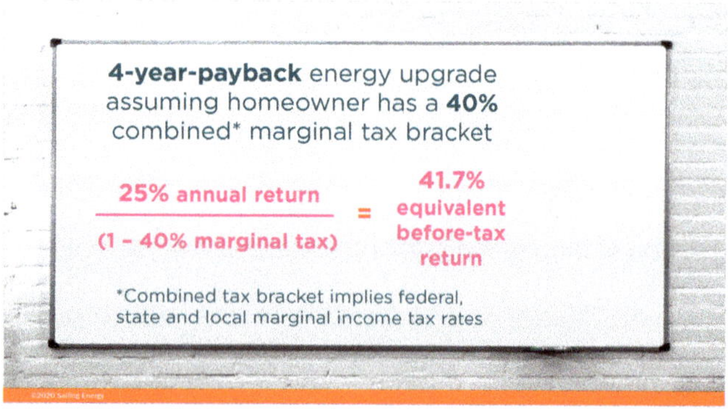

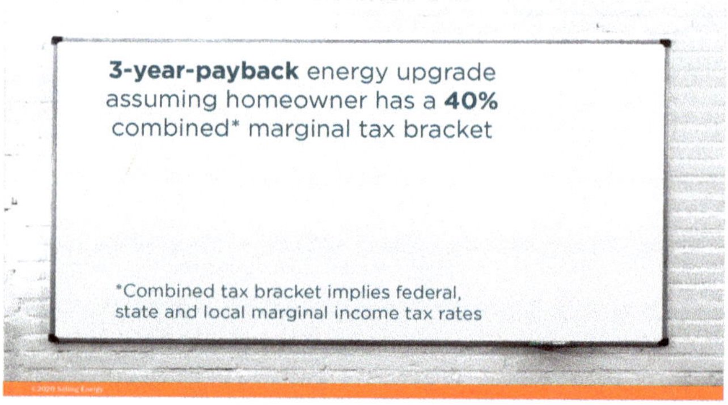

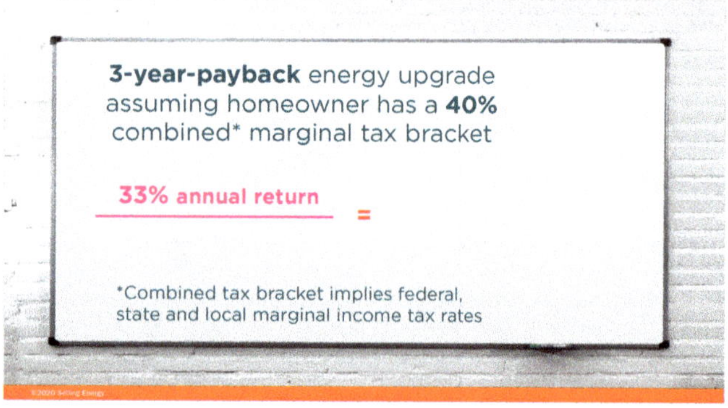

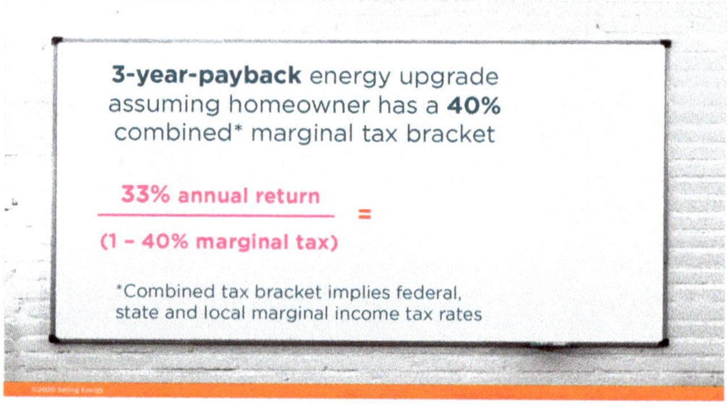

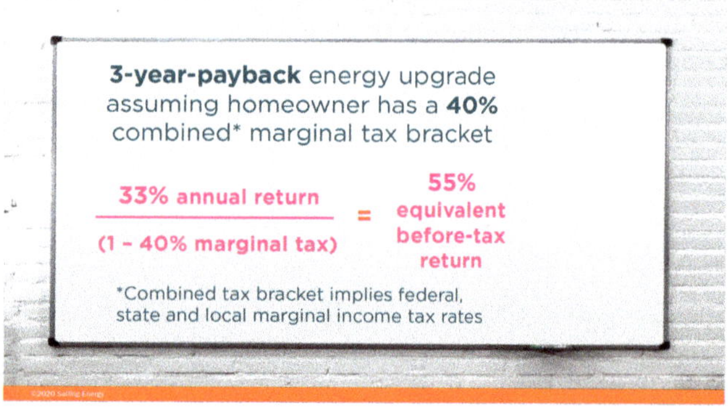

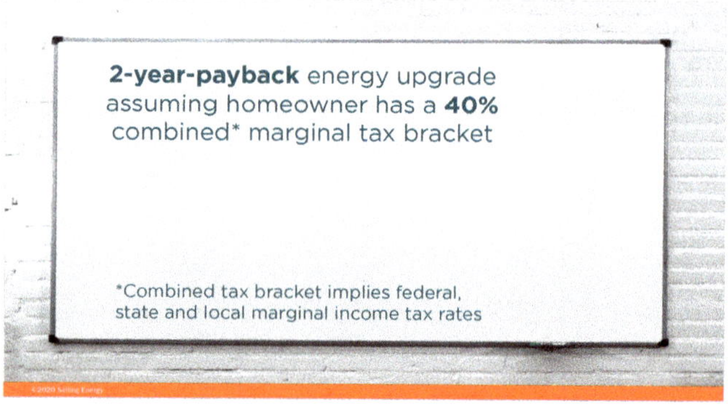

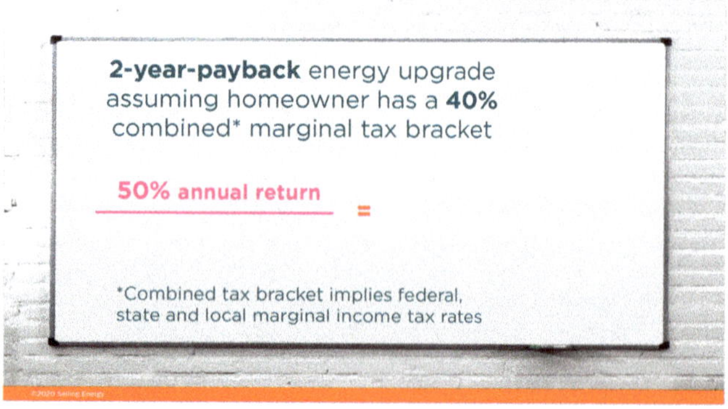

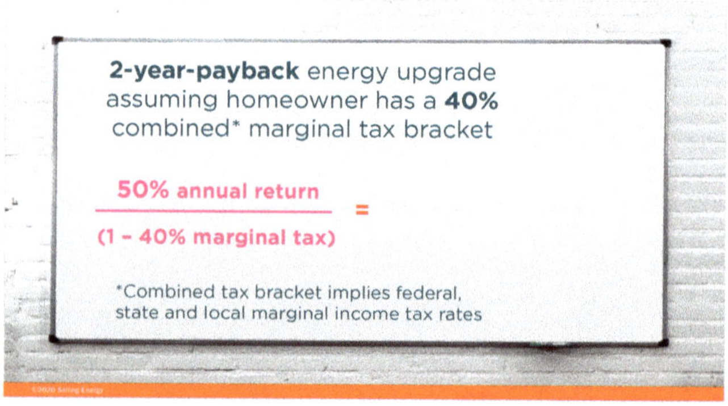

4-year-payback energy upgrade assuming homeowner has a **40%** combined* marginal tax bracket

$$\frac{25\% \text{ annual return}}{(1 - 40\% \text{ marginal tax})} = \begin{array}{c} \textbf{41.7\%} \\ \textbf{equivalent} \\ \textbf{before-tax} \\ \textbf{return} \end{array}$$

*Combined tax bracket implies federal, state and local marginal income tax rates

---

3-year-payback energy upgrade assuming homeowner has a **40%** combined* marginal tax bracket

*Combined tax bracket implies federal, state and local marginal income tax rates

---

3-year-payback energy upgrade assuming homeowner has a **40%** combined* marginal tax bracket

$$33\% \text{ annual return} =$$

*Combined tax bracket implies federal, state and local marginal income tax rates

---

3-year-payback energy upgrade assuming homeowner has a **40%** combined* marginal tax bracket

$$\frac{33\% \text{ annual return}}{(1 - 40\% \text{ marginal tax})} =$$

*Combined tax bracket implies federal, state and local marginal income tax rates

---

3-year-payback energy upgrade assuming homeowner has a **40%** combined* marginal tax bracket

$$\frac{33\% \text{ annual return}}{(1 - 40\% \text{ marginal tax})} = \begin{array}{c} \textbf{55\%} \\ \textbf{equivalent} \\ \textbf{before-tax} \\ \textbf{return} \end{array}$$

*Combined tax bracket implies federal, state and local marginal income tax rates

---

2-year-payback energy upgrade assuming homeowner has a **40%** combined* marginal tax bracket

*Combined tax bracket implies federal, state and local marginal income tax rates

---

2-year-payback energy upgrade assuming homeowner has a **40%** combined* marginal tax bracket

$$50\% \text{ annual return} =$$

*Combined tax bracket implies federal, state and local marginal income tax rates

---

2-year-payback energy upgrade assuming homeowner has a **40%** combined* marginal tax bracket

$$\frac{50\% \text{ annual return}}{(1 - 40\% \text{ marginal tax})} =$$

*Combined tax bracket implies federal, state and local marginal income tax rates

---

IDEAS & ACTIONS

2-year-payback energy upgrade assuming homeowner has a **40%** combined* marginal tax bracket

$$\frac{\text{50\% annual return}}{\text{(1 – 40\% marginal tax)}} = \begin{array}{c}\textbf{83.3\%}\\\textbf{equivalent}\\\textbf{before-tax}\\\textbf{return}\end{array}$$

*Combined tax bracket implies federal, state and local marginal income tax rates

---

Q:

But what if the homeowner is in a lower tax bracket?

5-year-payback energy upgrade assuming homeowner has a **25%** combined* marginal tax bracket

*Combined tax bracket implies federal, state and local marginal income tax rates

---

5-year-payback energy upgrade assuming homeowner has a **25%** combined* marginal tax bracket

$$\frac{\text{20\% annual return}}{\text{(1 – 25\% marginal tax)}} = \begin{array}{c}\textbf{26.7\%}\\\textbf{equivalent}\\\textbf{before-tax}\\\textbf{return}\end{array}$$

*Combined tax bracket implies federal, state and local marginal income tax rates

---

4-year-payback energy upgrade assuming homeowner has a **25%** combined* marginal tax bracket

*Combined tax bracket implies federal, state and local marginal income tax rates

---

4-year-payback energy upgrade assuming homeowner has a **25%** combined* marginal tax bracket

$$\frac{\text{25\% annual return}}{\text{(1 – 25\% marginal tax)}} = \begin{array}{c}\textbf{33.3\%}\\\textbf{equivalent}\\\textbf{before-tax}\\\textbf{return}\end{array}$$

*Combined tax bracket implies federal, state and local marginal income tax rates

---

3-year-payback energy upgrade assuming homeowner has a **25%** combined* marginal tax bracket

*Combined tax bracket implies federal, state and local marginal income tax rates

---

3-year-payback energy upgrade assuming homeowner has a **25%** combined* marginal tax bracket

$$\frac{\text{33\% annual return}}{\text{(1 – 25\% marginal tax)}} = \begin{array}{c}\textbf{44\%}\\\textbf{equivalent}\\\textbf{before-tax}\\\textbf{return}\end{array}$$

*Combined tax bracket implies federal, state and local marginal income tax rates

---

IDEAS & ACTIONS

2-year-payback energy upgrade assuming homeowner has a **25%** combined* marginal tax bracket

*Combined tax bracket implies federal, state and local marginal income tax rates

2-year-payback energy upgrade assuming homeowner has a **25%** combined* marginal tax bracket

$$\frac{50\%^* \text{ annual return}}{(1 - 25\% \text{ marginal tax})} = \begin{array}{c} 66.6\% \\ \text{equivalent} \\ \text{before-tax return} \end{array}$$

*Combined tax bracket implies federal, state and local marginal income tax rates

Q:

And by the way, what about the increases in after-tax utility bill savings due to inflation?

Q:

Bottom line, while an energy upgrade may be initiated in an effort to improve comfort, where else could the homeowner get better after-tax financial returns …and with such little risk?

Q:

Is there an even easier way to describe this before-tax, after-tax scenario to a homeowner?

Imagine getting a $1,200/year *after-tax* salary increase just by saving $100 per month on your utility bill.

Q:

How many hours did your customer have to work last year to earn enough money after-tax to pay the wasted portion of their utility bill?

Assume $100 per month in utility savings…
That's $1,200 per year in utility savings…
And since utilities are not deductible…
That's $1,200 in after-tax return…

Assume 40% combined marginal tax bracket…
$1,200 / (100% minus 40%) = $2,000.

$2,000 pre-tax equates to
50 hours of work @ $40/hour!

IDEAS & ACTIONS

Lesson 278
SUCCESSFUL SELLING IN RESIDENTIAL PROPERTIES
Projecting the recovery of an upgrade's first cost

Presented by
Mark Jewell
@SellingEnergy
info@sellingenergy.com

Q:
But what about the return of the principal that was invested in doing the upgrade?

Q:
How confident can a homeowner be that the increased value upon sale will be enough to recoup the first cost of an energy upgrade?

Q:
Is there evidence supporting sales price premiums associated with particular upgrades?

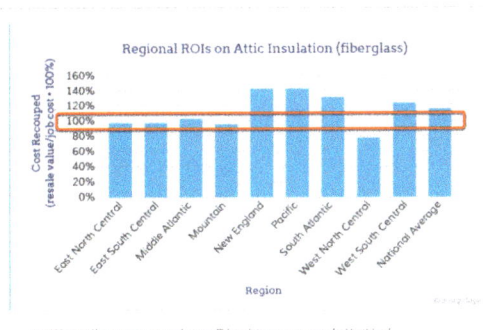

SOURCE: https://www.energysage.com/energy-efficiency/why-conserve-energy/residential-ee/

Q:
And how much higher would that "ROI" be if the upgrade cost that the homeowner paid was actually lower thanks to a rebate or incentive?

Q:
How much evidence exists to support price premiums and other financial benefits associated with overall superior efficiency?

Studies Nationwide Show Energy Efficient Homes Sell for More, Faster

IDEAS & ACTIONS

www.SellingEnergy.com

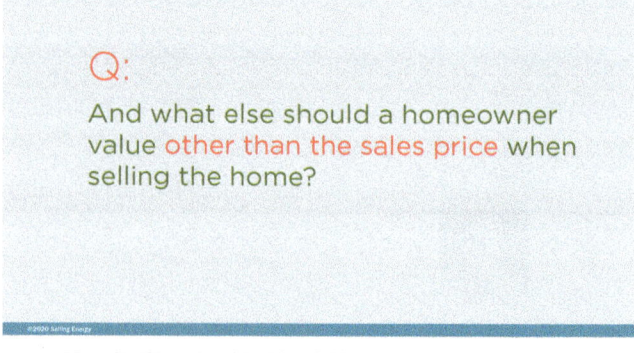

Q:

And what else should a homeowner value other than the sales price when selling the home?

selling in 6™

Lesson 279
SUCCESSFUL SELLING IN RESIDENTIAL PROPERTIES
Linking "green attributes" to beneficial financing

Presented by
Mark Jewell
@SellingEnergy
info@sellingenergy.com

sellingenergy
Turbocharging Success

Q:

Could "green attributes" also lead to more attractive financing?

Lenders care about default risk...

Default risks are on average 32 percent lower in energy-efficient homes, controlling for other loan determinants.

SOURCE:
http://www.imt.org/uploads/resources/files/IMT_UNC_HomeEEMortgageRisksfinal.pdf

Lenders care about loan prepayment...

Borrowers in ENERGY STAR® homes are one-quarter less likely to prepay the mortgage.

SOURCE:
http://www.imt.org/uploads/resources/files/IMT_UNC_HomeEEMortgageRisksfinal.pdf

EE FHA mortgages use better ratios...

Mortgage Type	"Front-end ratio"	"Back-end ratio"
Conventional	28%	36%
FHA mortgage	31%	43%
EE FHA mortgage	33%	45%

"Front-end ratio": divide monthly *principal, interest,* property *taxes,* and *insurance* payments (PITI) and any housing association or condo fees.

"Back-end ratio": divide all recurring monthly payments on debt by a household's gross monthly income.

SOURCE: https://www.fool.com/mortgages/2017/04/14/2836-rule-how-it-affects-your-mortgage-approval.aspx

IDEAS & ACTIONS

Lesson 280
SUCCESSFUL SELLING IN RESIDENTIAL PROPERTIES
Repurposing utility payments as mortgage payments

Presented by
Mark Jewell
@SellingEnergy
info@sellingenergy.com

Q:

How much more house could you afford if utility savings were reallocated to higher mortgage payments?

~$78/month utility savings services $15K more in loan principal...

...before even considering tax benefits of the mortgage interest deduction!

% Down	Loan Amount	Loan Type	Credit Score	Mo. Pmt.
20%	$200K	30-yr. fixed.	740+	$1,043.29
20%	$215K	30-yr. fixed.	740+	$1,121.54

SOURCE: https://www.fool.com/mortgages/compare-mortgage-rates/, assuming 4.75% interest rate

---

Q:

How much more quickly could you pay off your mortgage if you voluntarily increased your monthly mortgage payments by the amount of your monthly utility savings?

$78/month utility savings can accelerate the repayment of a mortgage

Assume the homeowner described on the previous slide is already 5 years into a 30-year mortgage.

Paying an extra $78 toward the monthly mortgage payment would save over $18,000 in interest and eliminate the last 37 payments (i.e., the loan payoff would be 3 years and 1 month sooner).

SOURCE: https://www.bankrate.com/calculators/home-equity/additional-mortgage-payment-calculator.aspx

---

Mortgage Payoff Summary	
Original term	30 Years
Remaining	25 Years
Annual interest rate	4.75%
Additional principal payment	$78 per month
Normal payment (PI)	$1,043
Accelerated payment (PI)	$1,121
Total scheduled payments	$375,588
Total accelerated payments	$357,353
Savings	$18,235
Mortgage shortened by	3 years, 1 months

SOURCE: https://www.bankrate.com/calculators/home-equity/additional-mortgage-payment-calculator.aspx

---

Lesson 281
SUCCESSFUL SELLING IN RESIDENTIAL PROPERTIES
7 Approaches to showcasing the value of efficiency

Presented by
Mark Jewell
@SellingEnergy
info@sellingenergy.com

Q:

Which are the most compelling ways to reframe efficiency as an excellent financial proposition?
• comparatively higher after-tax return
• potential to recover the first cost at sale
• potential for a higher sales price
• potential for a faster sale
• easier mortgage qualification
• ability to service higher debt
• ability to pay off the mortgage sooner

IDEAS & ACTIONS

www.SellingEnergy.com

Lesson 282
SUCCESSFUL SELLING IN RESIDENTIAL PROPERTIES
Focusing on the "why" to make a compelling case

Presented by
Mark Jewell
@SellingEnergy
info@sellingenergy.com

You have to focus on the **"why"** to make your most compelling case.

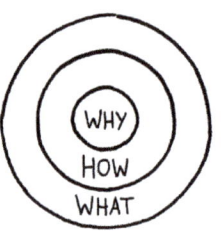

Simon Sinek's
Golden Circle

Focus on the *why* before the *how* or the *what*

Q:
Why would someone want a smart thermostat?

Why would someone want a smart thermostat?

1. Reduce the utility bill
2. Greater security of maintained thermal comfort when away from home (especially with children, elderly, pets)
3. Convenient way to ensure that the HVAC is throttled back after running to work or as children come and go

---

Why would someone want a smart thermostat?

4. Participate in Community Energy Events
5. Enhance the efficiency of the AC systemn
6. And more...

Q:
Why would someone want an energy assessment?

Why would someone want an energy assessment?

1. Reduce the utility bill
2. Independent opinion on the magnitude of potential savings and how to capture it
3. Expert linkage to available rebates and incentives

IDEAS & ACTIONS

Why would someone want an energy assessment?

4. Calculation of equivalent carbon footprint reduction
5. And more...

Q:

Why would someone want an AC diagnostic tune-up?

Why would someone want an AC diagnostic/tune-up?

1. Reduce the utility bill
2. A 10% undercharge of refrigerant could raise the energy use by 20%.
3. Low refrigerant could also lead to frozen coils.

Why would someone want an AC diagnostic/tune-up?

4. Dirty AC coils can raise a home's AC costs by 20%; lead to system freeze-up; and, affect air quality.
5. Lubrication can reduce system noise.

Why would someone want an AC diagnostic/tune-up?

6. Optimized AC also lasts longer because there is less wear on critical components like the compressor.
7. Optimized AC is more efficient at dehumidification.
8. And more...

Q:

Why would someone want an LED lighting retrofit?

Why would someone want an AC diagnostic/tune-up?

1. Reduce the utility bill
2. Significant energy savings
3. Potentially more or better quality light

Why would someone want an AC diagnostic/tune-up?

4. Dimmable, unlike some of the lamps they may be replacing
5. Longer-lived lamps are more convenient, especially in high-ceiling applications.
6. Less ambient heat
7. And more...

IDEAS & ACTIONS

Q:

Why would someone want an new furnace filters?

Why would someone want new furnace filters?

1. Reduce the utility bill (with less resistance in the airstream)
2. Indoor fan motor lasts longer.
3. Controller board may last longer.

Why would someone want new furnace filters?

4. Better airflow throughout the home
5. Healthier indoor air
6. And more...

Q:

Why would someone want a "smart home"?

Why would someone want a "smart home"?

1. Reduce the utility bill
2. Convenience
3. Control
4. Security
5. And more...

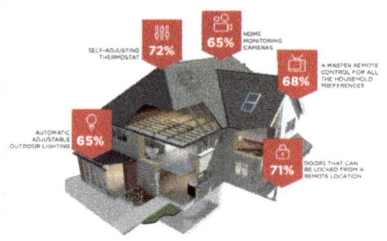

HERE'S WHAT TOPS CONSUMERS' LISTS FOR THE MOST DESIRED SMART HOME DEVICES:

SOURCE: http://www.icontrol.com/wp-content/uploads/2015/06/Smart_Home_Report_2015.pdf

"70% [of consumers] report excitement around the cost savings and related energy efficiency that come from a smart home."

SOURCE: 2016 NAHB International Builders' Show

Q:

Why would someone want better insulation?

IDEAS & ACTIONS _____

_____

_____

_____

Q:

Why would someone want a heat pump?

Q:

Why would someone want solar panels?

Q:

Why would someone want battery storage?

Q:

Perhaps most importantly, why would a customer appreciate having more than one offering suggested and delivered?

Lesson 283
SUCCESSFUL SELLING IN RESIDENTIAL PROPERTIES
Preparing in advance of an in-home visit

Presented by
Mark Jewell
@SellingEnergy
Info@sellingenergy.com

Turbocharging Success

1. **Never underestimate first impressions.**

How do you make a great impression in nanoseconds?

Blink: The Power of Thinking Without Thinking, Copyright 2005, Malcolm Gladwell

IDEAS & ACTIONS

Q:

What do customers tend to complain about the most?

HINT:
It's not about work quality or technical issues...

Most complaints address basic customer service issues:

Scheduling
Timeliness
Etiquette

Be sensitive to myths and fears regarding "contractors"

Q:

So what does a successful engagement look like?

Prep in advance...

Prep in advance...

1. Install these measures in your own home.
2. Assemble a "Story Archive" of others.
3. Set and track your own performance goals.

Prep in advance...

4. Ensure you are well-groomed.
5. Ensure your vehicle and tools are neat.
6. Consider sending a headshot/bio in advance.

IDEAS & ACTIONS

Prep in advance...

7. Look up house details on the assessor's page.
8. Download the customer's utility bill if possible.
9. Look up previous work done on the house.

Prep in advance...

10. Smile prior to calling.
11. What else?

Lesson 284
SUCCESSFUL SELLING IN RESIDENTIAL PROPERTIES
Arriving and excelling while inside the home

Presented by
Mark Jewell
@SellingEnergy
info@sellingenergy.com

Turbocharging Success

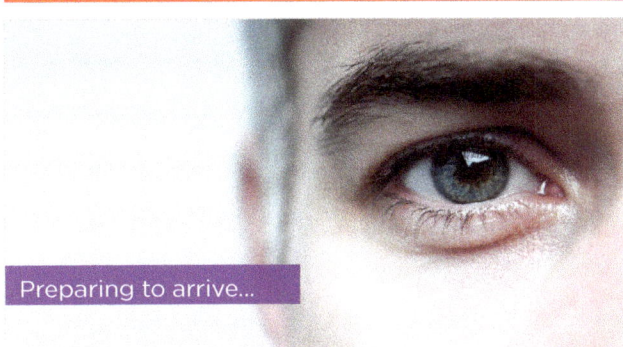

Preparing to arrive...

Preparing to arrive...

1. Call 30 minutes ahead.
2. Look at their paperwork to know the name.
3. Realize that this is when you start "selling."

Preparing to arrive...

4. Arrive in a clean vehicle, inside and out.
5. Have paperwork, tools, and equipment ready.
6. Don't linger in the car outside.

Preparing to arrive...

7. Park close with your logo facing the house.
8. Don't block any driveway.
9. Place safety cones appropriately.

Preparing to arrive...

10. Be careful unloading ladders, etc.
11. And what else?

IDEAS & ACTIONS

At the door...

At the door...

1. Make a great impression in nanoseconds.
2. Visualize placing your hand on the door.
3. Visualize customer praise after the visit.

At the door...

4. Knock on the door rather than ringing.
5. Step at least 6 feet back from the doorway.
6. Look somewhere other than the peephole.

At the door...

7. Ensure your badge is clearly visible.
8. Have 2 biz cards in left hand; shake with right.
9. Properly introduce yourself and your mission.

At the door...

10. Offer to remove shoes or wear booties.
11. Establish a "base camp" for discussions.
12. And what else?

Inside the home...

Inside the home...

1. Set out a clear agenda and timeline.
2. Set the stage for cross-selling.
3. Avoid jargon; keep it human and friendly.

Inside the home...

4. Look for signs of communication style.
5. Explain every step if they follow you around.
6. Lay down mat to protect wherever you work.

IDEAS & ACTIONS

Inside the home...

7. Build trust as a foundation for advice later.
8. Never show any sign of frustration.
9. Look around for other opportunities.

Inside the home...

10. Save additional recommendations for later.
11. And what else?

Etiquette while in the home

Etiquette while in the home...

1. Handshake firmness should mirror your customer's – and no bone-crushing, please!
2. And speaking of hands, clean hands and fingernails are a must.

Etiquette while in the home...

3. Ask before using the bathroom; however, try to take care of those needs before you arrive (and leave the bathroom spotless afterwards if you do have to use it).
4. You can accept a (non-alcoholic) beverage if offered; however, try to bring your own (and take the container with you).

Etiquette while in the home...

5. It's OK to take breaks, ideally away from the premises, provided the customer knows when you plan to return.
6. It's OK to enter private areas if given permission, provided you give occupants sufficient advance notice prior to entering.

Etiquette while in the home...

7. Carefully avoid leaving dust, debris, footprints, fingerprints, or other unwelcome evidence of your work.
8. Carefully interact with pets if invited to do so by the homeowner.

Etiquette while in the home...

9. Avoid conversation topics of a personal nature, politics or religion. Politely listen or change the subject.
10. Smoking (including electronic cigarettes) should be done far off-site, ideally with breath control afterwards.

IDEAS & ACTIONS

Etiquette while in the home...

11. Speaking of breath control, if you had alcohol the night before, be sure you don't still smell like alcohol. The customer may assume you've been drinking on the job.
12. And speaking of smells, avoid both body odor and strongly scented deodorant, after-shave or colognes since some customers may have allergies.

Etiquette while in the home...

13. Profanity, racial references, and any other offensive language are strictly prohibited.
14. Timeliness is imperative throughout the engagement, including your promised arrival time, how long you estimate the visit to take, and when you expect to be leaving the premises.

Etiquette while in the home...

15. Throughout the visit, limit mobile phone use to calls regarding that particular customer's needs and absolute emergencies.
16. Always remember than your customer may be scrutinizing every action while you're in their home, and that you are "selling" both your "brand" and your company's brand with everything you say and do.

Etiquette while in the home...

17. Avoid inappropriate interactions.
18. Emphasize no need for the customer to give you their passwords or additional compensation for your services.
19. If threatened verbally or physically, retreat.
20. And what else?

Before you leave...

Etiquette while in the home...

1. Ensure the customer knows what was done.
2. Ensure the customer knows how to use it.
3. Ensure the customer can log on him/herself.

Etiquette while in the home...

4. Ask if their business or employer would benefit.
5. Ask if they know others; offer business cards.
6. Leave door hangers on 10 nearby houses.

Etiquette while in the home...

7. Encourage them to take an online survey.
8. Tell them how to reach you w/any concerns.
9. Explore all potential cross-selling opportunities prior to leaving the home.

IDEAS & ACTIONS

Etiquette while in the home...

10. Remember that your shirt's brand follows you off the property.
11. And what else?

Lesson 285
SUCCESSFUL SELLING IN RESIDENTIAL PROPERTIES
4 Additional insights to consider re: in-home selling

Presented by
Mark Jewell
@SellingEnergy
info@sellingenergy.com

3 Insights to consider

INSIGHT #1
Most customers are not used to empathetic technicians who are adept at communicating.

Provided you converse effectively, keeping in mind communication strategies that are informed by NLP and body language (see next section), you'll be seen as extraordinary.

INSIGHT #2
Servicing, advising, fixing *and selling* are very similar activities if done properly.

Field techs are naturally suited to "sales" in that it is just another form of helping the customer solve a problem or capture a benefit that in many cases the customer was not even aware of...

INSIGHT #3
Field techs have to ask intelligent questions to gain information and establish credibility.

Communicating what they are doing and why, and the benefit the customer will derive, builds trust and respect. This creates the foundation for cross-selling recommendations later on.

You need to understand the **homeowner** at least as well as you understand the **home**.

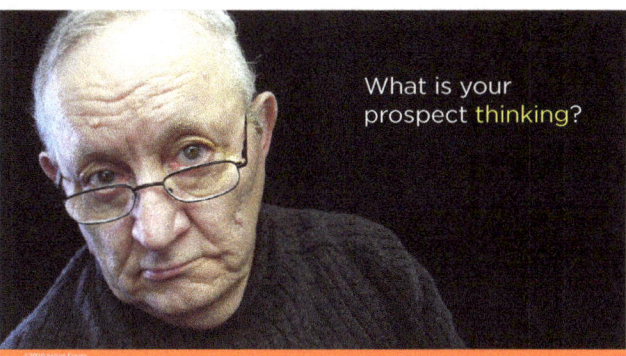

What is your prospect **thinking**?

IDEAS & ACTIONS

www.SellingEnergy.com

4 Approaches worth mastering...

1. Body language
2. Microfacial expressions
3. Neuro-linguistic programming (NLP)
4. Active listening

Lesson 286
SUCCESSFUL SELLING IN MULTI-FAMILY RESIDENTIAL PROPERTIES
Highlighting benefits for condos and coops

Presented by
Mark Jewell
@SellingEnergy
Info@sellingenergy.com

Who are the stakeholders?

1. Owner-occupant
2. Owner-landlord
3. Tenant/occupant
4. Community Association – officers and other members
5. Property manager (in-house or outsourced)
6. Facilities staff (in-house or outsourced)
7. Other influencers (e.g., volunteer committees)

What is the Occupant's "why"?

1. Greater comfort, convenience, control
2. Less deferred maintenance
3. Greater reliability, fewer surprises
4. Lower costs, fewer special assessments
5. Hedge against utility price spikes
6. Insulation against regulatory compliance issues
7. Green halo (or hedge against "brown discount")

What is the Landlord's "why"?

1. Attracting/retaining higher-quality tenants
2. Higher rent
3. Higher asset value if NOI is higher

What is the Community Association's "why"?

1. Manage common areas
2. Manage property interest of owners
3. Provide services for owners
4. Develop sense of community through social activities and/or amenities
5. Address regulatory concerns
6. Handle disputes between neighbors
7. And much more...

What is the Property Manager's "why"?

1. Ensure happy client (Association)
2. Fine-tune and adjust the Reserve Study
3. Support contract renewal
4. Applying best practices portfolio-wide could become a competitive advantage in securing new assignments.
5. And much more...

What is the Facility Staff's "why"?

1. Minimizing recurring complaints/service issues
2. Freeing up time for preventive maintenance
3. Accelerating equipment retirement to reduce uncertainty while gaining higher NPV than phasing in the new when the old equipment fails
4. And much more...

IDEAS & ACTIONS

Lesson 287
SUCCESSFUL SELLING IN <u>RESIDENTIAL INCOME PROPERTIES</u>
Focusing on the "why" to make a compelling case

Presented by
Mark Jewell
@SellingEnergy
Info@sellingenergy.com

How is the sales approach different for multifamily income property?

"The quality of your life is directly related to the quality of the questions you ask."
- Anthony Robbins

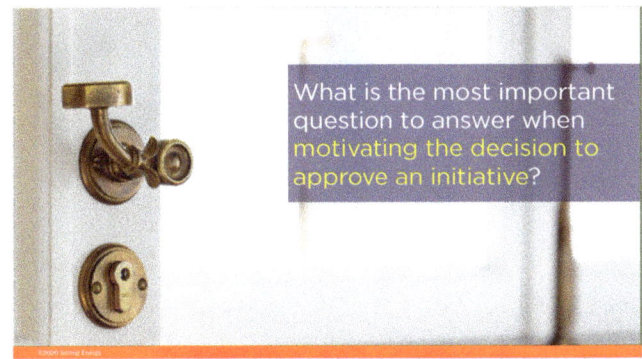

What is the most important question to answer when motivating the decision to approve an initiative?

You have to focus on the "why" to make your most compelling case.

Focus on the why before the how or the what

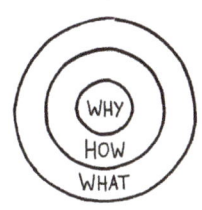

Simon Sinek's Golden Circle
As cited in his 2009 TED Talk

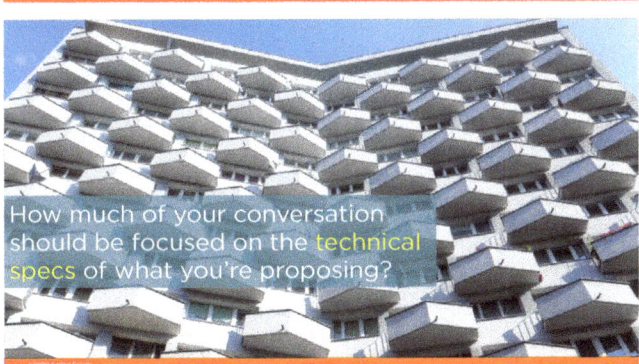

How much of your conversation should be focused on the technical specs of what you're proposing?

How many of your conversations are with the right execs, rather than their technical lieutenants?

IDEAS & ACTIONS

www.SellingEnergy.com

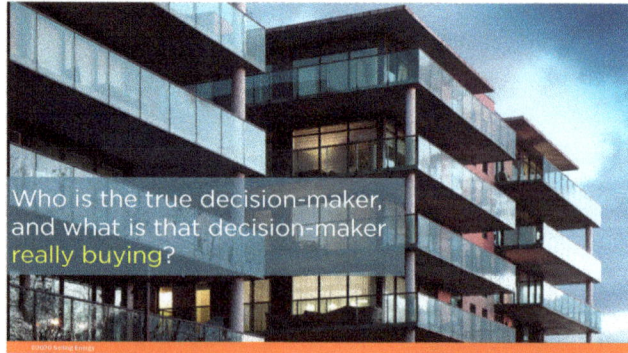

Who is the true decision-maker, and what is that decision-maker really buying?

What if you started talking business outcomes with the actual decision-makers with the budget to spend?

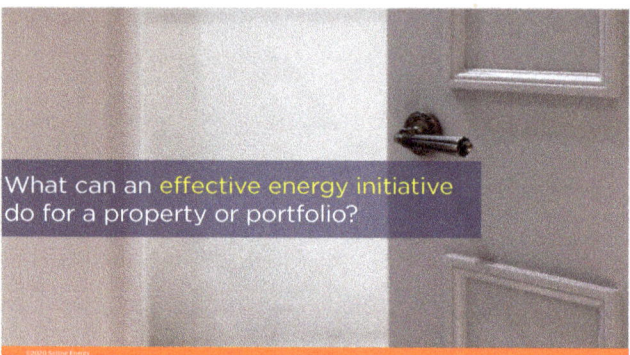

What can an effective energy initiative do for a property or portfolio?

Moving beyond utility-cost savings...

1. Utility-cost financial benefits
2. Non-utility-cost financial benefits
3. Non-financial benefits

selling in 6™

Lesson 288
SUCCESSFUL SELLING IN RESIDENTIAL INCOME PROPERTIES
Focusing on non-utility-cost financial benefits

Presented by
Mark Jewell
@SellingEnergy
info@sellingenergy.com

selling energy
Turbocharging Success

Moving beyond utility-cost savings...

1. Utility-cost financial benefits
2. Non-utility-cost financial benefits
3. Non-financial benefits

What about those non-utility-cost financial benefits?

Financial stability...

1. Differentiating the property
2. Improving cash flow
3. Lowering vacancy
4. Improving asset value
5. Enhancing the image for investors/lenders

IDEAS & ACTIONS

Lesson 289
SUCCESSFUL SELLING IN <u>RESIDENTIAL INCOME PROPERTIES</u>
Focusing on non-financial benefits

Presented by
Mark Jewell
@SellingEnergy
info@sellingenergy.com

Moving *beyond* utility-cost savings...

1. Utility-cost financial benefits
2. Non-utility-cost financial benefits
3. Non-financial benefits

And how many "non-financial benefits" actually drive non-utility-cost financial benefits in the end?

Tenant satisfaction...

1. Upgrading the property's "look and feel"
2. Increasing thermal comfort
3. Improving indoor air quality (IAQ)
4. Reducing exposure to pests/allergens
5. Enhancing security

Tenant satisfaction...

6. Improving affordability
7. Reducing complaints and service requests
8. Showcasing professional management
9. Enabling positive social media (both organic and planned)

Property condition...

1. Addressing deferred maintenance
2. Reducing risk of technological obsolescence
3. Reducing regulatory exposure
4. Insulating against utility price spikes

Property condition...

5. Boosting safety
6. Improving the morale of on-site staff
7. Enhancing the sustainability profile
8. Earning environmental accolades

"Embrace your inner sales professional."

1. How does your proposed initiative produce benefits that can be measured with the yardsticks that ownership is already using to measure their own success?
2. How does your proposal make the property more valuable or easier to manage?
3. How does your proposal compare with other capital requests that ownership may be evaluating?

IDEAS & ACTIONS

Lesson 290
SUCCESSFUL SELLING IN <u>RESIDENTIAL INCOME PROPERTIES</u>
Focusing on the right financial metrics

Presented by
Mark Jewell
@SellingEnergy
info@sellingenergy.com

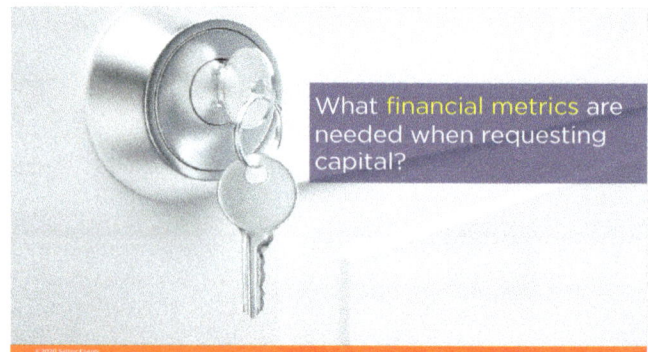

What financial metrics are needed when requesting capital?

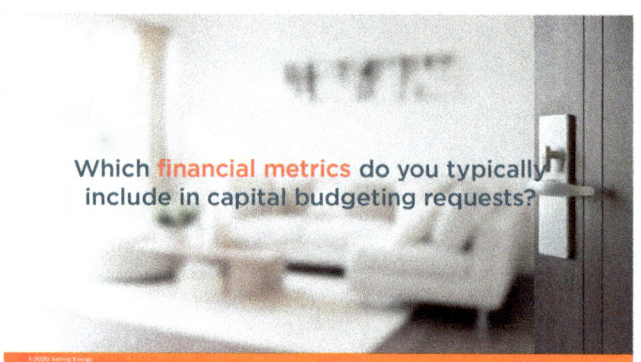

Which financial metrics do you typically include in capital budgeting requests?

Op Ex savings   Rebates or incentives
Simple Payback Period (SPP)   Cumulative Payback Period (CPB)
            Discounted Payback Period (DPB)
Internal Rate of Return (IRR)   Return on Investment (ROI)

      Modified Internal Rate of Return (MIRR)
Savings-to-Investment Ratio (SIR)   Net Present Value (NPV)
      Non-utility-cost financial benefits

And do you focus on minimizing
first cost or **life-cycle cost**?

And do you consider what impact **higher net operating income** and/or **lower capitalization rate** would have on **asset value**?

Sources and benefits of higher
Net Operating Income (NOI)

$$\frac{\text{Net operating income}}{\text{Capitalization rate}} = \text{Asset value}$$

- Higher rent
- Lower vacancy
- Lower landlord share of operating expenses

More efficient equipment in
income-producing property

Energy savings
Maintenance savings
Improved equipment longevity and control
Better look and feel of the space
Better tenant attraction and retention
Higher net operating income
Higher asset value

IDEAS & ACTIONS _____

How prepared are you to incorporate *non-utility-cost financial** and **non-financial benefits**?

*Try to "quantify" and "monetize" as many of these compelling benefits as possible!

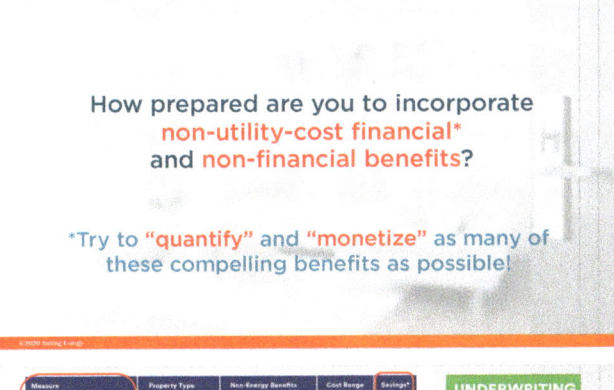

Simple Upgrade

Stewardship
Affordability
Comfort
Performance
Safety
Quality
Health
Value
Risk Mitigation

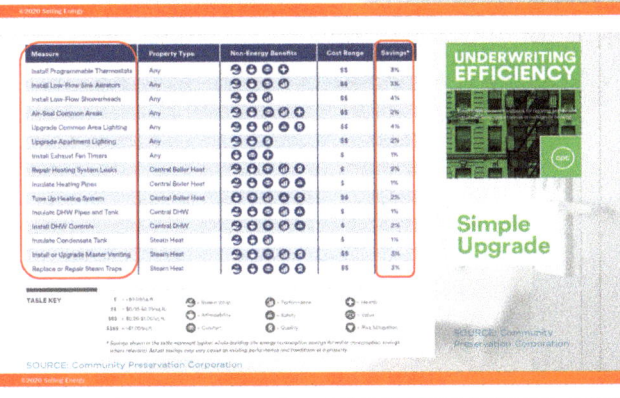

Moderate Renovation

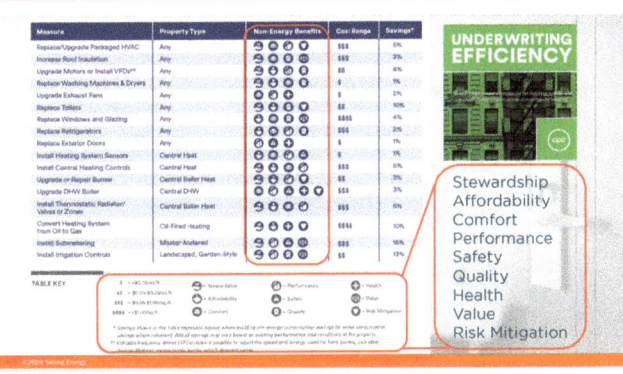

Stewardship
Affordability
Comfort
Performance
Safety
Quality
Health
Value
Risk Mitigation

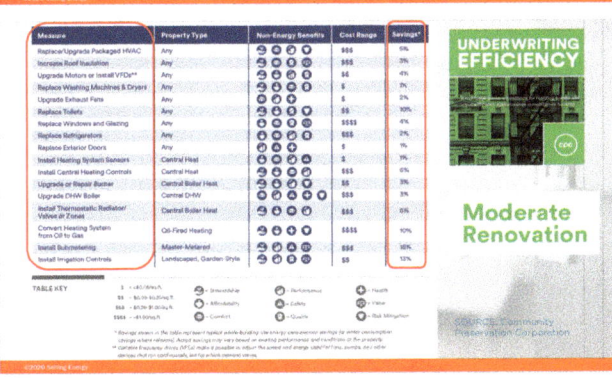

Substantial Improvements

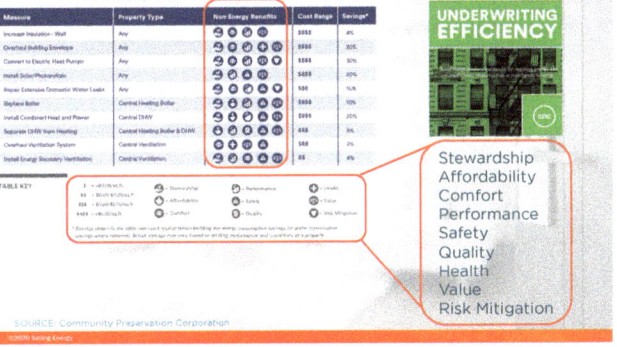

Stewardship
Affordability
Comfort
Performance
Safety
Quality
Health
Value
Risk Mitigation

IDEAS & ACTIONS

Lesson 291
SUCCESSFUL SELLING IN <u>RESIDENTIAL INCOME PROPERTIES</u>
Providing evidence to support suggested benefits

Presented by
Mark Jewell
@SellingEnergy
info@sellingenergy.com

Turbocharging Success

What evidence do you have to support the benefits of your proposed initiative?

Evidence to consider including in your proposal...

1. Similar initiatives successfully completed elsewhere
2. Tenant feedback (both compliments and complaints)
3. Media attention
4. ENERGY STAR® Label activity nearby
5. Crime statistics at both your and neighboring properties
6. Other...

Making a case with familiar yardsticks...

1. Measuring the frequency of service calls pre- and post-upgrade
2. Equating the reduction in Op Ex to higher rent and/or occupancy
3. Correlating new electric vehicle (EV) chargers to durable increases in occupancy
4. Exploring impact of reduced risk on cap rates and asset value
5. Other...

Lesson 292
SUCCESSFUL SELLING IN <u>RESIDENTIAL INCOME PROPERTIES</u>
Reframing benefits to resonate with landlord & tenants

Presented by
Mark Jewell
@SellingEnergy
info@sellingenergy.com

Turbocharging Success

How do you reframe your proposal to resonate with what ownership and/or the tenants actually care about?

Connecting efficiency/sustainability to 3 big dots...

1. Helping a property achieve market differentiation
2. Increasing tenant attraction and retention
3. Increasing property value and ROI

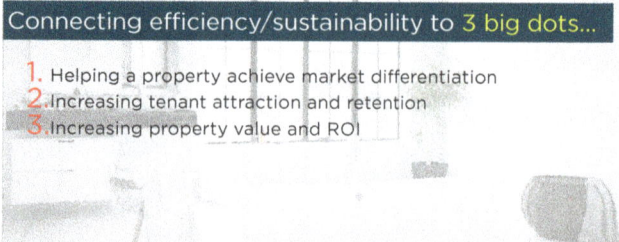

Important drivers to consider in your proposal...

1. Improved properties have to compete with new construction.
2. Millennials will have a big impact on the demand for "green" units.
3. ENERGY STAR® Labels for multifamily are still relatively new.
4. Leveraging rebates/incentives now help insulate against risks later.
5. Taking buildings from "brown" to "green" has proven to be profitable.

IDEAS & ACTIONS

_____

_____

_____

_____

Expanding the discussion to other stakeholders...

1. Include resident engagement in your upgrade strategies/tactics.
2. Provide tenants with a community-building feedback loop.
3. Contact corporate housing consumers re: green accolades.
4. Solicit media coverage on make-overs to support marketing.
5. Other...

Offering compelling comparisons...

1. Could you express the projected savings in terms of incremental units rented?
2. Could you express the projected savings in terms of an incremental increase in rental rates?

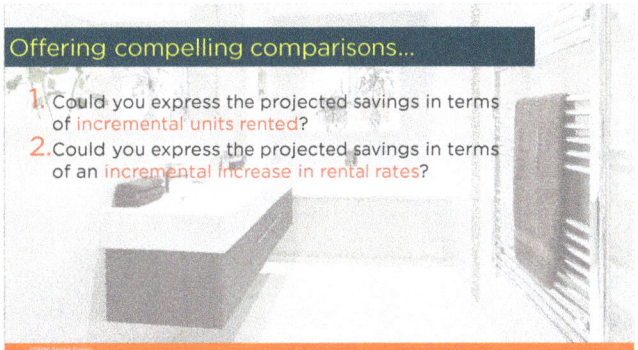

selling in 6™

Lesson 293
SUCCESSFUL SELLING IN RESIDENTIAL PROPERTIES
The 3-Sentence Solicitation™ for homeowners

Presented by
Mark Jewell
@SellingEnergy
info@sellingenergy.com

sellingenergy
Turbocharging Success

A **3-sentence solicitation** that gets the conversation started...

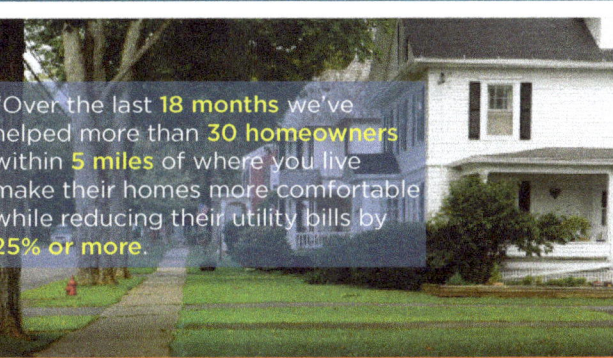

"Over the last **18 months** we've helped more than **30 homeowners** within **5 miles** of where you live make their homes more comfortable while reducing their utility bills by **25% or more**.

"Most of the homes in your neighborhood, including yours, were built by the **same developer** within the same 5-year period, and all of the homes we've worked on from that developer have needed the **same energy fixes**.

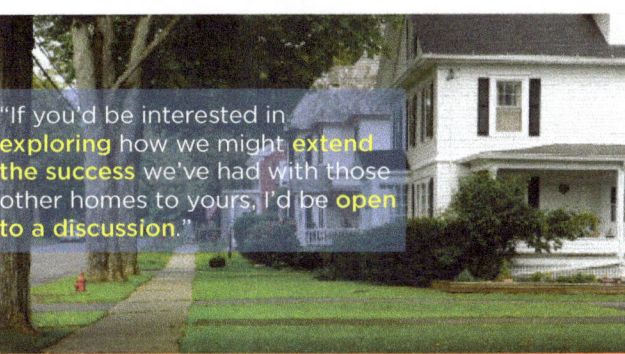

"If you'd be interested in **exploring** how we might **extend the success** we've had with those other homes to yours, I'd be **open to a discussion**."

EXERCISE
The 3-Sentence Solicitation

IDEAS & ACTIONS

Lesson 294
SUCCESSFUL SELLING IN RESIDENTIAL INCOME PROPERTIES
The 3-Sentence Solicitation™ for multifamily

Presented by
Mark Jewell
@SellingEnergy
info@sellingenergy.com

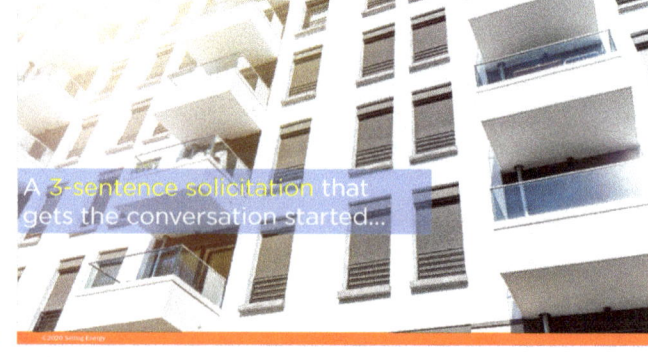

A 3-sentence solicitation that gets the conversation started...

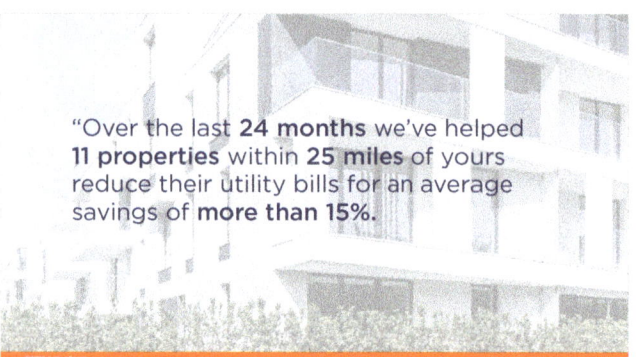

"Over the last **24 months** we've helped **11 properties** within **25 miles** of yours reduce their utility bills for an average savings of **more than 15%.**

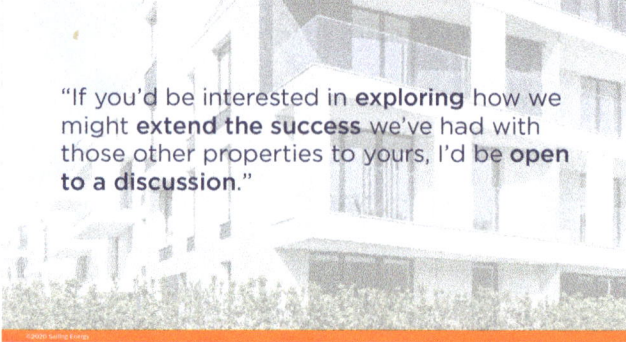

"If you'd be interested in **exploring** how we might **extend the success** we've had with those other properties to yours, I'd be **open to a discussion.**"

"It occurred to me as I was doing a nighttime drive-by that your exterior lighting is the **same system we removed from 9 of those other properties, at an average savings of 40% in lighting energy.**

EXERCISE
The 3-Sentence Solicitation

Lesson 295
SUCCESSFUL SELLING IN RESIDENTIAL & RESIDENTIAL INCOME PROPERTIES
Using fewer written words to drive more approvals

Presented by
Mark Jewell
@SellingEnergy
info@sellingenergy.com

Could using fewer written words lead to more approved initiatives?

IDEAS & ACTIONS _____

_____

_____

_____

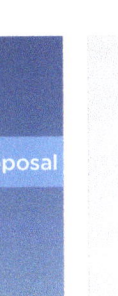

STEP 2. The One-Page Proposal

- "Succinctly expresses all the facts, reasoning, and conditions surrounding an undertaking or project.
- "Uses persuasive language to build a case for approval.
- "Proposes a specific course of action.
- "Fulfills all these qualifications within a single printed page."

What is it?

Adapted from The One-Page Proposal, Patrick G. Riley

"Identify a clear objective, focus on it, ferret out the pitfalls, sharpen your thinking, and pitch an idea perfectly."

Why only one page?

Adapted from The One-Page Proposal, Patrick G. Riley

"400 words will take an average reader 3 to 4 minutes to review – the attention span of many high-level decision-makers."

Why only one page?

Adapted from The One-Page Proposal, Patrick G. Riley

- **Title and Subtitle**
  - Label and define the entire proposal
- **Target (and Secondary Targets)**
  - Identify the goals of the proposal
- **Rationale**
  - Delineates why the proposed action is necessary

Adapted from The One-Page Proposal, Patrick G. Riley

- **Financials**
  - Quantifies the costs and benefits
- **Status**
  - States where things stand at the moment
- **Action**
  - Clarifies exactly what the recipient should do

Adapted from The One-Page Proposal, Patrick G. Riley

Lesson 296
SUCCESSFUL SELLING IN RESIDENTIAL & RESIDENTIAL INCOME PROPERTIES
The anatomy of a One-Page Proposal

Presented by
Mark Jewell
@SellingEnergy
info@sellingenergy.com

Q:
Who is the intended reader of your one-page proposal: a homeowner, members of a condo board, the COO of a portfolio of apartments, etc.?

IDEAS & ACTIONS

www.SellingEnergy.com

The format of your "one-pager" will depend on...

1. Your preferred level of formality
2. The amount of detail you intend to include
3. Your need to keep the proposal confidential

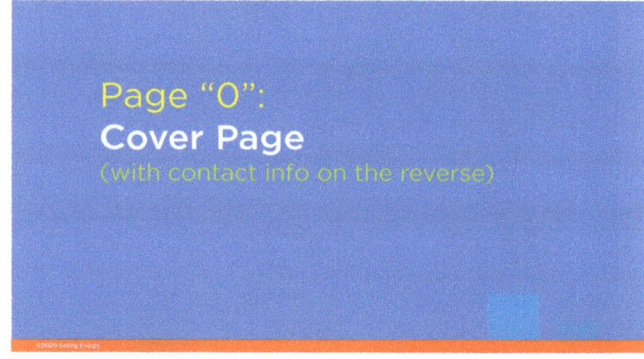

Page "0":
Cover Page
(with contact info on the reverse)

Page 1:
One-Page Proposal
(with reverse intentionally blank)

Page 2:
One-page financials
(with reverse intentionally blank)

Page 3:
Cost of delay
(with reverse intentionally blank)

Page 4:
Sheet of colored paper
("Technical Appendix")

Pages 5+:
Everything else...

EXERCISE
The One-Page Proposal

IDEAS & ACTIONS

Lesson 297
SUCCESSFUL SELLING IN <u>RESIDENTIAL & RESIDENTIAL INCOME PROPERTIES</u>
The weighted-average One-Page Proposal

Presented by
Mark Jewell
@SellingEnergy
info@sellingenergy.com

Q:

What successes have you had with customers who are similar to the targets you have decided to focus on?

Q:

Is there an opportunity to "clone" those successes by assembling every target that looks a lot like your past projects?

Q:

Could you produce a "weighted-average" one-page proposal describing the success you've had with other similarly configured customers?

EXAMPLE: A weighted-average condo board proposal

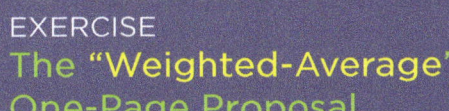

EXERCISE
The "Weighted-Average" One-Page Proposal

Lesson 298
SUCCESSFUL SELLING IN <u>RESIDENTIAL PROPERTIES</u>
Using one-page proposals for homeowners

Presented by
Mark Jewell
@SellingEnergy
info@sellingenergy.com

Q:

What kind of proposal are you currently using for homeowners?

IDEAS & ACTIONS

Q:

Considering that a true "proposal" has to "propose" something, and that the best way to propose something is to be persuasive, how persuasive is your current proposal template?

Q:

How might the format (and formality) of a one-page proposals differ when used with homeowners vs. owners/managers/board members of multifamily properties?

Benefits of one-page proposals for homeowners...

1. Quick to prepare using templates
2. Easy for the prospect to read and understand
3. Facilitates review with spouse or other influencers
4. Emphasizes compelling reasons to act now
5. Outlines the precise steps of the process
6. Other...

Does each proposal part apply to homeowners?

1. Title and subtitle
2. Targets
3. Rationale for change
4. Financials
5. Status
6. Action steps

Let's revisit the purpose of the one-page proposal...

1. Get the prospect interested in the process.
2. Ensure the prospect in motivated to take action.
3. Spell out pressing concerns to be addressed, credible fixes for known issues, compelling increases in comfort and convenience, etc.

Let's revisit the purpose of the one-page proposal...

4. Describe the financial costs and benefits.
5. Outline the upgrade process, including what steps have been completed so far.
6. Request the specific action(s) to be taken to make the upgrade a reality.

How simple should the financials be?

1. Costs and savings, including rebates/incentives
2. Chart showing cash flow over time (optional)
3. Savings-to-investment ratio vs. payback period
4. Comparisons that highlight the financial benefits
   a. Digits-to-Widgets™ analogy to hours worked
   b. Comparison to financial planner or "magical ATM"
   c. Projected early retirement of mortgage by repurposing savings
   d. Other

The one-page financial analysis itself can be an appendix.

Lesson 299
SUCCESSFUL SELLING IN RESIDENTIAL AND RESIDENTIAL INCOME PROPERTIES
Using fewer figures to drive more approvals

Presented by
Mark Jewell
@SellingEnergy
info@sellingenergy.com

IDEAS & ACTIONS _____

_____

_____

_____

_____

Q:

How might the format (and formality) of one-page financials differ when used with homeowners vs. owners/managers/board members of multifamily properties?

Tips for financial analysis for homeowners

1. People make emotional decisions and then justify them financially.

2. The rate of return earned by investments in energy solutions outpaces most other investment alternatives, particularly when viewed on an after-tax basis.

Tips for financial analysis for homeowners

3. While the returns can be compelling, complex financial analyses and metrics can be confusing to homeowners.

4. Doing the financial analysis and then excerpting the highlights – ideally with the help of easily grasped practical analogies – is typically the wisest approach.

Tips for financial analysis for homeowners

5. Keep the more detailed financial analysis handy to address any questions from the homeowner or their advisors.

Tips for financial analysis for condos/coops

1. Realize that decisions in these settings often involve multiple stakeholders with varying levels of sophistication.

2. As with homeowners, plan to keep the financial findings simple and compelling.

Tips for financial analysis for condos/coops

3. Keep the more detailed financial analysis handy to address any questions from the decision-makers or their advisors.

Tips for financial analysis in income property

1. Be sure to view the other lessons in this program related to landlord/tenant settings (including but not limited to the relationship between NOI and asset value).

2. Be sure to allocate each cash inflow and outflow, or portions thereof, to the landlord and the appropriate tenant(s) so that you can accurately represent who pays and who benefits.

Tips for financial analysis in income property

3. Realize that the level of financial sophistication varies among property owners (e.g., owners of single-family rentals vs. owners/managers of thousands of income-producing units).

IDEAS & ACTIONS

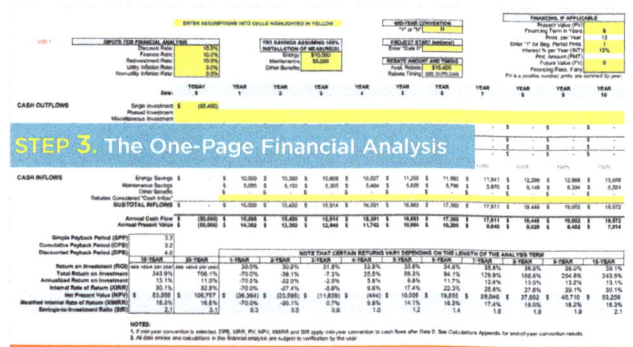

STEP 3. The One-Page Financial Analysis

Energy Savings	$	-	$	10,000	$	1
Maintenance Savings			$	5,000	$	
Other Benefits			$	-	$	
Rebates Considered "Cash Inflow"						
SUBTOTAL INFLOWS	$	-	$	15,000	$	1

Annual Cash Flow	$	(50,000)	$	15,000	$	1
Annual Present Value	$	(50,000)	$	14,302	$	1

Simple Payback Period (SPP)	3.3			
Cumulative Payback Period (CPB)	3.2			
Discounted Payback Period (DPB)	4.0			
	10-YEAR	**20-YEAR**	**1-YEAR**	**2-YEA**
Return on Investment (ROI)	see value per year	see value per year	30.0%	3
Total Return on Investment	243.9%	706.1%	-70.0%	-3
Annualized Return on Investment	13.1%	11.0%	-70.0%	-2
Internal Rate of Return (XIRR)	30.1%	32.8%	-70.0%	-2
Net Present Value (NPV) $	53,256 $	106,757 $	(36,364) $	(23
Modified Internal Rate of Return (XMIRR)	18.3%	16.5%	-70.0%	-2
Savings-to-Investment Ratio (SIR)	2.1	3.1	0.3	

Energy Savings	$	-	$	10,000	$	1
Maintenance Savings			$	5,000	$	
Other Benefits			$	-	$	
Rebates Considered "Cash Inflow"						
SUBTOTAL INFLOWS	$	-	$	15,000	$	1

Annual Cash Flow	$	(50,000)	$	15,000	$	1
Annual Present Value	$	(50,000)	$	14,302	$	1

Simple Payback Period (SPP)	3.3			
Cumulative Payback Period (CPB)	3.2			
Discounted Payback Period (DPB)	4.0			
	10-YEAR	**20-YEAR**	**1-YEAR**	**2-YEA**
Return on Investment (ROI)	see value per year	see value per year	30.0%	3
Total Return on Investment	243.9%	706.1%	-70.0%	-3
Annualized Return on Investment	13.1%	11.0%	-70.0%	-2
Internal Rate of Return (XIRR)	30.1%	32.8%	-70.0%	-2
Net Present Value (NPV) $	53,256 $	106,757 $	(36,364) $	(23
Modified Internal Rate of Return (XMIRR)	18.3%	16.5%	-70.0%	-2
Savings-to-Investment Ratio (SIR)	2.1	3.1	0.3	

BONUS LESSONS

SALES MANAGEMENT

selling in 6™

Lesson 300
SALES MANAGEMENT
Making Selling in 6™ a no-exceptions best practice

Presented by
Mark Jewell
@SellingEnergy
info@sellingenergy.com

sellingenergy
Turbocharging Success

Q:

Is Selling in 6™ ideal for new hires, veterans, or the entire team?

Q:

Is Selling in 6™ useful for traditional sales roles, non-traditional sales roles or both?

Q:

What is the ideal way to deploy Selling in 6™?

IDEAS & ACTIONS

_____

_____

_____

_____

Q:

How does a sales manager ensure employee engagement when deploying Selling in 6™?

Q:

What success tools should be incorporated into sales practices to yield a truly effective deployment of Selling in 6™?

Success tools to include in Selling in 6™ deployment

1. Segment-specific research
2. Elevator pitches
3. 3-sentence solicitations
4. One-page proposals
5. One-page financial analyses
6. Success Story Archives™
7. Objections Archives™
8. And more...

Lesson 301
SALES MANAGEMENT
Setting realistic sales goals

Presented by
Mark Jewell
@SellingEnergy
info@sellingenergy.com

Q:

What's the difference between market potential and sales forecasts?

Common methods used to assist with forecasting

1. Market Potential Method
2. Historic Method
3. Full-Time Equivalent (FTE) Method

Q:

What is the "Market Potential Method"?

Market Potential Method

$$\text{Total market} \times \left[1 + \text{Your \% guestimate of market growth} \right]$$

Realize that the "addressable market" is not the same as *your organization's share* of that market.

IDEAS & ACTIONS

Q:

What is the "Historic Method" for forecasting sales?

Historic Method

| Last year's sales | x | Your guestimate of your organization's market share |

Q:

What is the "Full-Time Equivalent Method" for forecasting sales?

Full-Time Equivalent (FTE) Method

| # of FTEs | x | Breakeven point plus a profit margin |

Q:

Have you taken the time to compare the results from two or more of these approaches?

Q:

Might there be an even more pragmatic way to set sales goals?

Identifying and cloning your best customers!

1. Identify your best customers.
2. Assemble into subsets by market segment and solution.
3. Design a three-sentence solicitation for each subset.
4. Assemble a Success Story Archive™ for each subset.

Identifying and cloning your best customers!

5. Prepare a weighted-average one-page proposal and one-page financial summary for each subset.
6. Assess the addressable market for each subset within an accessible territory.
7. Calculate each subset's revenue potential assuming "x" average deal size and "y" closing ratio.

IDEAS & ACTIONS _____

_____

_____

_____

Lesson 302
SALES MANAGEMENT
Setting SMART goals

Presented by
Mark Jewell
@SellingEnergy
info@sellingenergy.com

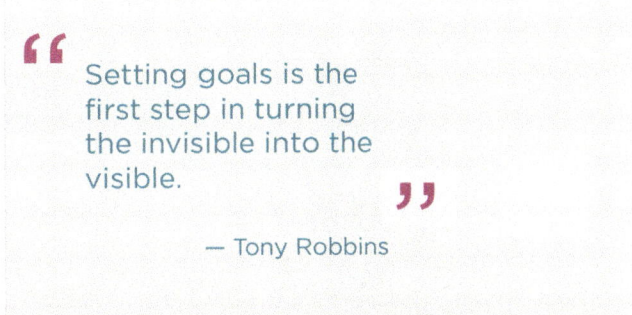

> Setting goals is the first step in turning the invisible into the visible.
>
> — Tony Robbins

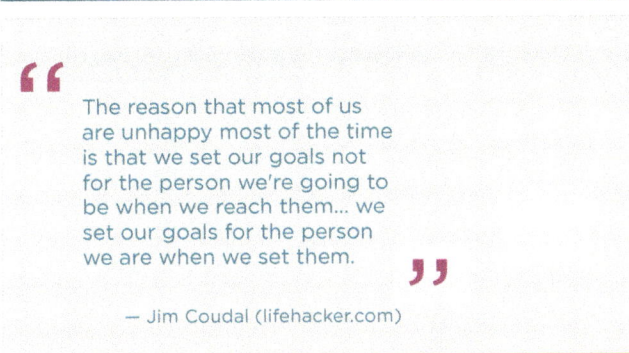

> The reason that most of us are unhappy most of the time is that we set our goals not for the person we're going to be when we reach them… we set our goals for the person we are when we set them.
>
> — Jim Coudal (lifehacker.com)

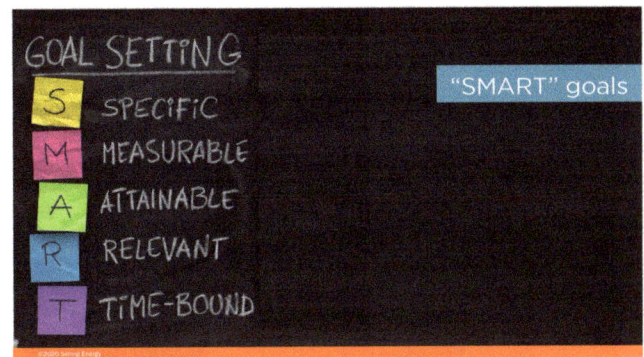

"SMART" goals

Specific

Measurable

Attainable

Realistic

IDEAS & ACTIONS

www.SellingEnergy.com

Time-bound

Q:

What are some of the pitfalls to avoid when setting sales goals?

Pitfalls to avoid when doing sales forecasts...

1. Managerial ambition may unrealistically inflate sales goals.
2. Forecasts sometimes get inflated as they rise through management levels as execs try to demonstrate organizational growth to their superiors.

Pitfalls to avoid when doing sales forecasts...

3. Certain product or market dynamics may be overlooked or ignored (e.g., production issues affecting capacity or changes in buying behavior among certain prospects or customers).

Q:

How do you secure buy-in for goal-setting and measurement?

Multiple levels of buy-in to ensure success...

1. The sales team's level of buy-in around their goal
2. Their level of confidence in attaining the goal
3. Potential roadblocks that could prevent goal attainment
4. The role they would prefer that their sales manager plays in supporting goal accomplishment

---

Multiple levels of buy-in to ensure success...

5. How the team would prefer to be managed around the goals
6. How the team prefers to be held accountable and how they would prefer to be approached if they fail
7. The structure(s) needed to manage the daily activity that will ensure consistent progress toward their goals

---

Q:

And how often should you and your team check on the progress you're making toward your sales goals?

IDEAS & ACTIONS

_____

_____

_____

_____

Q:

And how often should you and your team check on the progress you're making toward your sales goals?

HINT: The more frequently you measure, the easier it will be to make necessary adjustments.

Lesson 303
SALES MANAGEMENT
Addressing sales forecasting challenges

Presented by
Mark Jewell
@SellingEnergy
info@sellingenergy.com

Turbocharging Success

Q:

How often should you review progress toward achieving sales forecasts?

Bi-monthly pipeline review

1. Performed every two weeks
2. Reviews the top of the sales funnel
3. Evaluates whether the sales team has sufficient pipeline to achieve their sales goals

Weekly sales forecasting meeting

1. Performed weekly, ideally during the sales meeting
2. Reviews the middle to bottom of the sales funnel
3. Evaluates the health of pending deals and coaches reps to either win or purge stagnant ones from the pipeline

Q:

Which assumptions made in your sales forecast introduce the greatest potential for missing your numbers?

Beware of the following assumptions in your forecast

1. Deal timing
2. Deal size
3. Stalled engagements
4. Random deals

Q:

How can you incorporate more realistic assumptions regarding deal timing?

IDEAS & ACTIONS

Timing is everything...

1. Compare each deal's age vs. average win cycles.
2. Track all timing changes and beware if the projected deal closing date moves >3 times.

Q:

How can you incorporate more realistic assumptions regarding deal size?

Keep an eye on deal size...

1. Compare deal size vs. average deal size and beware if the projected deal size is >3x the average.
2. Also beware if the deal size has dropped >30% from the initial estimate.

Q:

How can you incorporate more realistic assumptions regarding stalled engagements?

Beware of stalled engagements...

1. If there has been little or no activity within the last two to four weeks, be careful.
2. Beware if there has been little activity in a later stage, which is when you'd expect activity to intensify.

Q:

How can you incorporate more realistic assumptions regarding random deals?

Random deals could lead to overzealous projections...

1. Carefully study randomly added deals that are >2x average deal size.
2. Be wary if deals are randomly added at the end of a fiscal period and then mysteriously removed at the beginning of the following period, which suggests someone may be gaming the pipeline for reporting purposes.

Lesson 304
SALES MANAGEMENT
Designing intelligent offerings

Presented by
Mark Jewell
@SellingEnergy
Info@sellingenergy.com

IDEAS & ACTIONS

Q:

What do we mean when we say "design intelligent offerings"?

The essentials of designing intelligent offerings...

1. Understand your buyer.
2. Be realistic regarding your competitive advantage.
3. Study your value equation and adjust as needed.

Q:

What does it mean to understand your buyer?

Taking the time to really understand your buyer

1. Each prospect must have the need, desire, authority and ability to buy from you.
2. Your value proposition has to resonate with all decision-makers and influencers.

Q:

What are your genuine competitive advantages?

What do you consider to be your "competitive advantage"?

3 categories of competitive advantage...

1. Low-price vendor
2. Value-differentiated
3. Focused on a niche market

Michael Porter (Harvard) as cited in "Hope is Not a Strategy" by Rick Page

You should build an arsenal of competitive advantage

Michael Porter (Harvard) as cited in "Hope is Not a Strategy" by Rick Page

IDEAS & ACTIONS

"Arsenal of Competitive Advantage"

Sales team	Trust, differentiation, strategy, linkage, expert product/industry knowledge, exec presence, strategic literacy
Industry focus	Industry expertise & network, market share, tailored solutions
Product/solution	Functionality, features, technology, quality, value, ease of use, availability, brand loyalty, advertising, price, speed
Service	Service, responsiveness, people, customer satisfaction, results, performance
Company	Brand loyalty, financial stability, reputation, quality, other products, experience

Adapted from "Hope is Not a Strategy" by Rick Page; ©2003 McGraw-Hill Education; based on Michael Porter's work at Harvard

How to determine your competitive advantage

Analyze your competition.
What are they doing and not doing?

What are they known for...
Good and bad?

You can be a hero by helping your prospects solve their puzzles...

Q:

Have you taken the time to fine-tune the value equation to stack the deck in your sales team's favor?

"The unassailable value equation"

"VALUE = BENEFITS MINUS COSTS"

Adapted from *Escaping the Price-Driven Sale* by Tom Snyder and Kevin Kearns

"The unassailable value equation"
"VALUE = BENEFITS - COSTS"

BENEFITS

"INSIGHT and DISCOVERY that the customer receives from the buying experience"

Adapted from *Escaping the Price-Driven Sale* by Tom Snyder and Kevin Kearns

IDEAS & ACTIONS

"The unassailable value equation"
"VALUE = BENEFITS - COSTS"

COSTS

"Not just price – from the standpoint of the buying experience itself, it is the **TIME and EFFORT** that the customer is devoting to being SOLD TO"

Adapted from *Escaping the Price-Driven Sale* by Tom Snyder and Kevin Kearns

---

"The *actual* unassailable value equation"

$$VALUE \; equals \; \boxed{\begin{array}{c} \text{BENEFITS} \\ \text{INSIGHT} \\ \text{DISCOVERY} \end{array}} \; minus \; \boxed{\begin{array}{c} \text{COSTS} \\ \text{TIME} \\ \text{EFFORT} \end{array}}$$

Adapted from *Escaping the Price-Driven Sale* by Tom Snyder and Kevin Kearns

---

Take price off the table by...

revealing an unrecognized problem...
finding an unanticipated solution...
creating/revealing an unseen opportunity...

Lesson **305**
SALES MANAGEMENT
Deputizing and motivating everyone to sell

Presented by
Mark Jewell
@SellingEnergy
info@sellingenergy.com

Turbocharging Success

Q:

Who in your organization other than your traditional salespeople interacts with your prospects and customers?

Q:

What if you deputized those non-traditional sales roles to act in ways that would support business development?

Q:

What are some of the ways that non-traditional sales roles could help drive business, which would support setting higher sales goals?

Empowering non-traditional sales roles to support goals

1. Provide above-and-beyond customer service.
2. Casually ask prospects/customers exploratory questions.
3. Look for opportunities to cross-sell and up-serve.
4. Contribute to goal-setting exercises.
5. Have a series of "elevator pitches" handy at all times.

IDEAS & ACTIONS

www.SellingEnergy.com

Lesson 306
SALES MANAGEMENT
Creating effective and efficient sales professionals

Presented by
Mark Jewell
@SellingEnergy
info@sellingenergy.com

What elements support sales professionals?

1. Informed hiring/onboarding
2. Emphasis on having personal and professional goals
3. Effective sales training
4. Ongoing sales coaching

What elements support sales professionals?

5. Credible approach to motivation
6. Contests and other awards that show you care
7. Success Story Archive™
8. Objections Archive™

What elements support sales professionals?

9. Constant focus on time management (more on that later)
10. Development/enforcement of pre-meeting protocols
11. Best practices re: prospect/client meetings
12. Proactive post-implementation follow-up

Lesson 307
SALES MANAGEMENT
Monitoring the cadence of sales follow-up activity

Presented by
Mark Jewell
@SellingEnergy
info@sellingenergy.com

Why post-implementation follow-up?

1. Ensure customer satisfaction
2. Discover non-utility-cost and non-financial benefits
3. Collect content for the Success Story Archive™

Why post-implementation follow-up?

4. Pursue cross-selling and up-serving opportunities
5. Support a structured approach to gain referrals
6. Demonstrate a differentiating level of professionalism

Q:
What is the best cadence for following up with a customer after the deal is sold?

IDEAS & ACTIONS

_____

_____

_____

_____

Lesson 308
SALES MANAGEMENT
Nurturing the sharing of success stories to clone

Presented by
Mark Jewell
@SellingEnergy
info@sellingenergy.com

Turbocharging Success

Q:
How many of the "wins" that your sales team has catalyzed (or even witnessed) have been catalogued so that everyone can benefit from the collective wisdom of the entire "sales tribe"?

Are you willing to create and maintain a **Story Archive**?

A **6-column worksheet** that allows anyone in your organization to leverage any of your best stories helping customers

1. Customer segment
2. Technology or approach
3. "The win" in 75 words or less
4. Location of the win
5. Where to get the whole story
6. Date added to the Archive

Making the Success Story Archive™ a living document

1. Require at least one story per week per salesperson.
2. Give recognition/rewards to most frequent contributors.
3. Quiz salespeople on most recently submitted content.
4. Leverage story trends to prospect more intelligently.
5. Ensure that your whole staff is actually using the stories!
6. Other...

Lesson 309
SALES MANAGEMENT
Optimizing meetings with prospects and customers

Presented by
Mark Jewell
@SellingEnergy
info@sellingenergy.com

Turbocharging Success

Making the most of prospect/customer meetings

1. Every meeting should have an agenda.
2. You have to be able to visualize a positive outcome.
3. Consider "power poses" and hand-clapping beforehand.
4. Start every meeting with a time check.

IDEAS & ACTIONS

www.SellingEnergy.com

Making the most of prospect/customer meetings

5. Which questions *must* be answered before adjourning?

"What is the 'Why?' that motivated this meeting?"
"How will the purchasing decision be made?"
"What projects have been proposed/approved in the past?"
"How easy was it to get those projects approved?"
"What next steps are needed to move the project forward?"

Making the most of prospect/customer meetings

6. Develop a culture of using C-level Talking Points™
7. Enforce diligent (and archived and shared!) note-taking.
8. Focus on and set next steps before adjourning.
9. Emphasize the importance of active listening.
10. And a lot more...

Q:

Have you made "24 Steps to an Effective Meeting" a no-exceptions best practice for all sales meetings?

Lesson 310
SALES MANAGEMENT
Maximizing the effectiveness of sales meetings

Presented by
Mark Jewell
@SellingEnergy
info@sellingenergy.com

Turbocharging Success

Making your sales meetings more effective

1. Set and share your sales meeting agenda beforehand.
2. Always start and end on-time, kick it off with an energizer, and limit the meeting to 60 minutes.
3. Share individual, team, and company progress, *ideally with the help of CRM entries and analyses to emphasize the importance of actually using the CRM in the ways it was designed to be used.*

Making your sales meetings more effective

4. Address any challenges encountered and praise recent wins.
5. Make sure *everyone* contributes to the meeting.*
6. Incorporate role-playing and practice telling success stories.

*Consider establishing a "no-devices" policy (except for attendees using their devices to take notes or retrieve info for the group).

Making your sales meetings more effective

7. Leverage Selling in 6™ and other personal and/or professional growth trainings and activities.
8. Only address topics that apply to everyone present.
9. Communicate supply-chain issues, volume updates, and other operating details elsewhere.

Making your sales meetings more effective

10. Table any off-agenda items to be addressed later.
11. Agree on action plans to address open issues (and revisit prior action plans to verify their progress).
12. Throughout the process, stay upbeat, motivate the team, and build the culture!

IDEAS & ACTIONS

_____

_____

_____

_____

Lesson 311
SALES MANAGEMENT
Ensuring the implementation of Selling in 6™ lessons

Presented by
Mark Jewell
@SellingEnergy
info@sellingenergy.com

Q:
How can you ensure that your team will engage with Selling in 6™ training and apply it in their daily activities to increase their sales?

Ensuring the implementation of Selling in 6™ lessons

1. Review your Selling in 6™ viewing reports each week.
2. Review the highlights of assigned Selling in 6™ lessons.
3. Ask attendees how they are applying what they learn.
4. Discuss the most recent Success Story Archive™ entries.
5. Incorporate role-playing and success story sharing.

Ensuring the implementation of Selling in 6™ lessons

6. Focus on challenges encountered and wins achieved.
7. Make sure *everyone* contributes to the discussion.
8. Encourage the use of audio-only lessons as reinforcement.
9. Encourage the use of Selling Energy's monthly coaching.
10. Invite Selling Energy to join meetings periodically.

Lesson 312
SALES MANAGEMENT
15 Deadly sins of ineffective account reps

Presented by
Mark Jewell
@SellingEnergy
info@sellingenergy.com

15 Deadly sins of ineffective account reps...

1. Lacking organization – the multiple legal pads and Post-It notes syndrome
2. Lacking leverageable focus – emphasizing the urgent over the important (and operating with a LIFO mentality)
3. Lacking documentation and systems that facilitate complete and timely follow-up

15 Deadly sins of ineffective account reps...

4. Relying too much on a relationship-builder approach
5. Talking too much when they should be listening
6. Focusing too much on sales targets with managing, forecasting and communicating future projects

15 Deadly sins of ineffective account reps...

7. Not taking the time to understand the segment and reframe the solution so its benefits could be measured with the prospect's yardsticks
8. Focusing too much on the What, How, How Much and When instead of the Why
9. Focusing on the rebates/incentives instead of the core value(s) of the proposed measure

IDEAS & ACTIONS

www.SellingEnergy.com

15 Deadly sins of ineffective account reps...

10. Offering free audits, rebates and technical details or focusing on lowest price rather than tapping an emotional reaction that motivates forward motion
11. Falling short on follow-through – customer satisfaction, unexpected (leverageable) benefits seen in the wake of the installation
12. Ignoring the sales potential at the account level

15 Deadly sins of ineffective account reps...

13. Spending too much time in customer support rather than pursuing new opportunities
14. Spending too much time on small opportunities
15. Not taking the time to identify all of the prospect's needs prior to recommending a solution

Lesson 313
SALES MANAGEMENT
Winning habits to instill in your salespeople

Presented by
Mark Jewell
@SellingEnergy
info@sellingenergy.com

Turbocharging Success

Helping salespeople maximize their productivity

1. Having a clear life purpose and goals that inspire action
2. Focusing on the important rather than the urgent
3. Staying organized, documenting and archiving everything*

*Emphasize consistent use of the CRM, which makes so many aspects of sales professionalism and productivity easier!

Helping salespeople maximize their productivity

4. Committing to complete and timely follow-up
5. Returning to ensure satisfaction, collect more info, etc.
6. Respecting metrics and the accountability they support

Helping salespeople with time management

1. Understanding the value of starting early and ending late
2. Reserving prime selling time for selling, not paperwork
3. Focusing on the long view, not short-term sales targets

Helping salespeople with time management

4. Prioritizing opportunities by magnitude and probability
5. Dedicating time to proactive hunting, not just farming
6. Balancing "customer service" with genuine selling

Helping salespeople with proper prep in advance

1. Investing effort in knowing your prospects' segments
2. Reframing your benefits to resonate with their yardsticks
3. Finding compelling needs with detailed pre-call planning

IDEAS & ACTIONS

Helping salespeople with proper prep in advance

4. Developing a list of questions that must be answered
5. Visualizing a positive outcome before every interaction
6. Developing active listening and note-taking skills

Helping salespeople maximize sales interactions

1. Identifying compelling emotional motivations to buy
2. Selling value, not free audits, rebates or price discounts
3. Focusing on selling the account, not just a transaction
4. Setting/recording commitments by seller/buyer with dates

Helping salespeople maximize sales interactions

5. Accurately reflecting sales probabilities in forecasts
6. Focusing on cross-selling, up-serving, referrals and cloning
7. Sharing written accounts of success stories, etc.
8. Sharing models of winning proposal templates, etc.

selling in 6™

Lesson 314
SALES MANAGEMENT
Designing effective compensation plans

Presented by
Mark Jewell
@SellingEnergy
Info@sellingenergy.com

sellingenergy
Turbocharging Success

Q:

What are the key principles of an effective compensation strategy?

Principles of effective compensation plans...

1. Understand the organization's growth strategy.
2. Reward behaviors that support that growth strategy.
3. Understand the links between corporate goals, sales strategies and tactics, and salesforce behaviors.

Q:

What behaviors support growth?

Behaviors that support growth...

1. New customer acquisition.
2. Current customer penetration (e.g., more departments, cross-selling, up-serving)
3. Current customer retention (e.g., steady project flow)

IDEAS & ACTIONS

Q:

What compensation strategies motivate these behaviors?

Compensation strategies that motivate desired behaviors...

1. Rewarding star performers
2. Promoting teaming with subject matter experts
3. Encouraging cross-selling and up-serving
4. Encouraging sales to new customers (including referrals)

Q:

What compensation structures are most common?

Examples of compensation strategies...

1. Profit-based
2. Revenue/quota
3. Balanced (based on volume, revenue, and quota attainment)
4. Team (everyone bonused when quarter-to-date goals are achieved)

Q:

How does a manager balance a sales rep's expectation for a living wage and still maintain a motivational component based on performance?

Lesson **315**
SALES MANAGEMENT
Advantages of sales territories

Presented by
Mark Jewell
@SellingEnergy
info@sellingenergy.com

selling energy
Turbocharging Success

Q:

What are the advantages of establishing sales territories?

Advantages of establishing sales territories...

1. Better allocate resources and assign quotas based on market opportunity.
2. Build markets vs. acquiring accounts.
3. Create local presences, which enable better support and establish key relationships.
4. Capitalize on local and competitive knowledge.

IDEAS & ACTIONS

www.SellingEnergy.com

Advantages of establishing sales territories...

5. Create the option to segment accounts within each territory to improve focus (e.g., enterprise, mid-market, SMB).
6. Decrease travel and increase selling time.
7. Increase effectiveness of sales operations with streamlined partnerships, lead assignments, and insights into local biz trends, needs and competition.
8. Reduce conflict between sales reps.

Lesson 316
SALES MANAGEMENT
Disadvantages of sales territories

Presented by
Mark Jewell
@SellingEnergy
info@sellingenergy.com

Turbocharging Success

Q:

What are the disadvantages of establishing sales territories?

Disadvantages of establishing sales territories...

1. Ambitious sellers are limited.
2. Specialization might be limited since a territory-assigned rep has to address all prospects in the region.
3. Personal referrals are limited in that the person who was designed to serve the referral cannot do so if referral is outside the original rep's territory.

Lesson 317
SALES MANAGEMENT
Best practices for staffing and territory configuration

Presented by
Mark Jewell
@SellingEnergy
info@sellingenergy.com
sellingenergy
Turbocharging Success

Q:

What are some best practices for establishing, staffing and managing sales territories?

Tips for territory creation, staffing and management...

1. Balance the territories based on anticipated workload, market potential and/or turnover.
2. Consider taking an approach based on location, product, or customer type/volume.
3. It is vital to match the proper customer with the right sales team at first contact.

Tips for territory creation, staffing and management...

4. Territory manager and sales rep(s) should collaborate on creating the sales plan.
5. Consider shrinking the territories to grow sales.

IDEAS & ACTIONS

Q:

What other staffing tips should you consider?

Estimated time required to cover various sized accounts:

1. Large tier: 750 hours per year
2. Medium tier: 250 hours per year
3. Small tier: 30 hours per year

How much sales time does a rep really have?

1. Available sales time = 75% × 2,000 hours/yr.
2. That 1,500 hours of selling time might enable the rep to cover 2 large accounts, 6 medium accounts, or 50 small accounts.

Lesson 318
SALES MANAGEMENT
Organizing territories by buyer decision-making practices

 Presented by
Mark Jewell
@SellingEnergy
info@sellingenergy.com

Q:

What other ways might your organization allocate sales reps?

Other "territory" approaches...

1. Segment-specific
2. Nano-vertical
3. National accounts
4. Other

Lesson 319
SALES MANAGEMENT
Keys to motivating salesforces

Presented by
Mark Jewell
@SellingEnergy
info@sellingenergy.com

Q:

Could the most effective coaching actually have "yin" and "yang" dimensions to it?

IDEAS & ACTIONS

Might the following coaching "yin" and "yang" work?

1. Monday to Thursday – "This is how you could be doing better..."
2. Friday – "You're great. Thanks for your contribution!"
3. Over the weekend, emails and voicemails thanking them for being part of the team.

Q:
Perhaps there are other creative ways to "shake it up" and capture your sales team's attention?

Consider the following ways to "shake it up"...

1. Give a prize for the person who hears the most "no's" in a week!
2. How about rewarding the person who recounts the most irrational objection heard – and how he/she overcame it?
3. Other ideas? Remember, think out of the box!

Q:
So what are the real keys to motivation among salespeople?

Research shows there are many keys to motivation.

1. Pleasant working environment
2. Connection to the larger "why"
3. Connection to *their own* "why"
4. Visibility on metrics
5. Competition and recognition

Research shows there are many keys to motivation.

6. Satisfaction of belonging to a winning team
7. Autonomy to find a path to the goal
8. Thrill of problem-solving
9. Training and professional development
10. Flexibility in working hours and/or locations

Q:
How about some unusual ways to motivate salespeople?

Some innovative ways to motivate salespeople...

1. Lower the sales quotas.
2. Sell it for them via a demonstrated path to cloning past successes and the tools and HQ support to do it.
3. Go bird watching!
4. Stop talking money; talk career growth, prestige, etc.

IDEAS & ACTIONS

Some innovative ways to motivate salespeople...

5. Ask them to focus on their personal goals (e.g., *Think and Grow Rich*)
6. Offer to shave your head if a certain goal is reached.
7. Make it more of a team sport.
8. Extrinsically motivated folks need at least 3 positive interactions for each negative one (some salespeople's ratios are as high as 11:1)!

Be careful with sales contests...

1. First of all, if cash did the trick, everyone would already be an "A" player and meeting their goals.
2. Any contest should be designed so that everyone has the opportunity to win somehow to prevent anyone from becoming disengaged and demotivated.

Q:

How can you help your salespeople get out of their own way?

Tactics for increasing sales productivity...

4. Clear your desk and maintain an organized workspace.
5. Handle each item once.
6. Create and use templates to shave time off repetitive tasks.

Q:

What about sales contests?

Lesson 320
SALES MANAGEMENT
Tactics for increasing sales productivity

Presented by
Mark Jewell
@SellingEnergy
info@sellingenergy.com

Tactics for increasing sales productivity...

1. Make a list of the 7 most important things to do tomorrow, and when tomorrow comes, do those things in order of priority!
2. Make a goal sheet – and a vision board!
3. Wake up earlier.

Tactics for increasing sales productivity...

7. Don't do anything that creates less value per hour than your annual income divided by 2000.
8. Stop working from multiple To Do lists and calendars.
9. Schedule meetings and avoid last-minute ones if possible.

IDEAS & ACTIONS

Tactics for increasing sales productivity...

10. Eliminate non-essential work.
11. Never squander prime selling time on non-prime-time tasks.
12. Use your drive time wisely (e.g., Selling in 6™)

Tactics for increasing sales productivity...

13. Do the tough stuff first.
14. Turn off your internet connection when you're working on a focused task.
15. Commit to taking/storing/sharing better notes.

Tactics for increasing sales productivity...

16. Always look at the call duration timer on your phone before hanging up to ensure your (and your prospect's!) time invested in that call was worth it.
17. Learn to write concise emails.
18. Use your CRM to the fullest: note-taking, to do items, reminders, performance tracking, etc.

Lesson 321
SALES MANAGEMENT
Sales manager coaching best practices

Presented by
Mark Jewell
@SellingEnergy
info@sellingenergy.com

Turbocharging Success

Q:

How much time management, productivity, motivation, software or other training is happening now in your organization?

Q:

Which of your people have embraced coaching and how it is performed now?

Q:

What are the three top skills currently being coached in the field today?

Q:

What are the three weakest skills currently exhibited by account reps?

IDEAS & ACTIONS

Q:

How is improvement tracked, analyzed and communicated, and how regularly?

What best practices would you like to institute?

1. Deliberate approach to coaching on time management, productivity, motivation, software and/or other training.
2. Vigilant tracking of sales skills before/after coaching.

Q:

How much time elapses between the office visit and/or field ride-along and the documented coaching report?

What best practices would you like to institute?

3. Regular measurement, analysis and communication of coaching-related outcomes to both the sales staff and management – with adjustments made as needed.

What best practices would you like to institute?

4. Timely filing of coaching reports following interactions with the sales staff.
5. And many others, no doubt...

Lesson **322**
SALES MANAGEMENT
Various dimensions of sales manager coaching

Presented by
Mark Jewell
@SellingEnergy
info@sellingenergy.com

Turbocharging Success

Q:

How many coaching paths exist?

There are plenty of coaching paths to consider...

1. Telephone strategies (duration, voicemail protocol, call logs, prime selling time calling)
2. Email effectiveness (grammar, five-sentence emails, proper signature lines, techniques to capture attention and get a response)
3. Business writing (grammar, tone, business acumen)
4. CRM use (planning, documenting, analyzing, sharing)

IDEAS & ACTIONS

_____

_____

_____

_____

_____

www.SellingEnergy.com

There are plenty of coaching paths to consider...

5. Note-taking (taking, archiving, reviewing, sharing)
6. Setting goals and To Dos (personal and professional)
7. Calendar management (protecting prime selling time)
8. Other professional development topics (Lynda.com, leadership, communication, business etiquette, business acumen, maximizing referrals/cross-selling/up-serving)

Lesson 323
SALES MANAGEMENT
Allocating coaching time across the sales team

Presented by
Mark Jewell
@SellingEnergy
info@sellingenergy.com

Q:
How can you create the most value coaching your top performers?

Creating value coaching top performers...

1. "You're a top performer and we certainly appreciate the contribution you're making here. From your perspective, what is it that you're doing to produce such outsized success that others on the team are not doing?"
2. "What do you think others around here could focus on to be more successful?"

Q:
How can you create the most value coaching your middle performers?

Creating value coaching middle performers...

1. "What are you doing that is most important to your sales success, and how do you keep track of how you're doing?"
2. "What is your perception of some of your peers here who are top-performers, and what do you think they're doing that is different?"
3. "What would you like to learn that you don't understand or don't yet feel comfortable with?"

Q:
How can you create the most value coaching your bottom performers?

Creating value coaching bottom performers...

1. "What do you think your peers here are doing that you should be doing to improve your sales performance?"
2. "Is there any aspect of your role that you feel uncomfortable with – any specific training needs, for example, that you'd like to share with me?"

IDEAS & ACTIONS

www.SellingEnergy.com

Creating value coaching bottom performers...

3. "Have you made an effort to mingle with the middle and top-performers here to ask them what they're doing differently so that you might start emulating some of those best practices?"

Q:

How often should you do sales meetings, and what part will coaching play in those meetings?

Consider including a rotation of topics in sales meetings.

1. Success Story Archive™
2. Objections Archive™
3. Assigned chapters in *Selling Energy*
4. Assigned lessons (and questions) in Selling in 6™

Consider including a rotation of topics in sales meetings.

5. Importance of migrating discussions from "popular" to "proper" financial metrics
6. Reviewing last week's sales challenges and victories
7. Brainstorming responses to competitive threats
8. Other

Lesson 324
SALES MANAGEMENT
Maximizing the value of a ride-along

Presented by
Mark Jewell
@SellingEnergy
info@sellingenergy.com

Turbocharging Success

Q:

What coaching roles could ride-alongs fulfill?

How much effort have you put into doing ride-alongs?

1. What is the goal of your ride-alongs now?
2. How often do you make a point of doing them?
3. How do you allocate your time for ride-alongs across various levels of salespeople?

Ride-alongs are useful in many ways.

1. Improving closing ratios among new and existing customers
2. Reinforcing the skills learned in Selling in 6™, etc.
3. Assessing how well those skills are being applied in the field

IDEAS & ACTIONS

_____

_____

_____

_____

Ride-alongs are useful in many ways.

4. Triangulating the sales rep's perception with new perspectives on the prospect's needs and reactions
5. Acquiring unvarnished feedback from prospects and customers
6. Communicating to prospects that sales management stands behind your offerings and is committed to a good outcome

Q:

What's the structure of an effective ride-along?

Planning for effective ride-alongs

1. Mark the date on your calendar and stick to it.
2. Leave at least 30 minutes between calls to debrief.
3. Consider doing an "unrehearsed" ride-along.
4. Occasionally surprise the rep by adding a second day!
5. Celebrate successes; share your own unsuccessful calls.
6. Limit the intended coaching outcomes to three.

Starting the day over breakfast...

1. Review who, when, goals, challenges (beware of vague answers).
2. Review previous calls/meetings (ideally using the CRM).
3. Review the objectives – what does a good job look like?
4. Consider potential objections and how to address each.

Starting the day over breakfast...

5. Review the elevator pitch, one-page proposal, one-page financial analysis, technical appendix, etc. as appropriate.
6. Review your evaluation form for coaching with the rep.
7. Agree on how your role will be explained to the prospect.

Who takes the lead? That depends...

1. Agree in advance and have a "high sign" for switching.
2. Take the lead throughout and demonstrate how it's done.
3. Share the lead, to save a call or demonstrate a skill.
4. Allow the sales rep to lead, even if he/she is failing.
5. If prospect asks a question, redirect attention back to the rep.
6. Make it clear the rep will remain the main point of contact.

What happens afterwards?

1. Discuss how the rep thinks it went. What went well?
2. What would the coach have done differently?
3. Where is this prospect headed and what are the next steps?

What if the rep missed a step (or two or three)?

1. Asking "Is there a reason you didn't do 'x'?" gives the rep the benefit of the doubt.
2. Prep a field coaching report immediately thereafter.
3. Follow-up with the rep via phone/email to discuss how the coaching outcomes are being applied.
4. Publicly praise the positive aspects of the ride-along in the next sales meeting, giving the rep (and others) a positive perspective on ride-alongs and coaching in general.

IDEAS & ACTIONS

Q:

What factors can impede effective ride-alongs?

Factors that impede effective ride-alongs...

1. Taking insufficient time to prep, perform, discuss, document
2. Thinking that "experienced" equals "trained"
3. Focusing on closing the sale rather than nurturing the rep
4. Limiting ride-alongs to best customers or "damage control"
5. Taking over the sales call, leaving the rep demoralized

Factors that impede effective ride-alongs...

6. Judging rather than coaching
7. Doing (and reporting on) ride-alongs without a system
8. Not coaching toward a process (or not having a process!)
9. Defaulting to the manager's favorite approach to selling

Q:

What are the most obvious sales rep shortcomings revealed during ride-alongs?

Sales rep shortcomings often revealed during ride-alongs...

1. Doing all the talking
2. Not asking enough questions
3. Focusing on the offerings rather than the prospect, segment or need

Lesson 325
SALES MANAGEMENT
Mistakes to avoid in the coaching process

Presented by
Mark Jewell
@SellingEnergy
info@sellingenergy.com

Q:

What mistakes should sales reps avoid when being coached by their manager one-on-one?

Mistakes sales reps should avoid when being coached...

1. Scheduling meetings only with easy prospects
2. Showing up unprepared
3. Shoving problems onto their manager
4. Speaking in generalities
5. Failing to make progress

IDEAS & ACTIONS

_____

_____

_____

_____

Q:

What mistakes should sales managers avoid when coaching their sales reps one-on-one?

Mistakes sales managers should avoid when coaching...

1. Showing up unprepared
2. Not building trust both initially and throughout
3. Running the ride-along as if it's an inspection

Mistakes sales managers should avoid when coaching...

4. Believing you know it all
5. Not using "how" questions to probe
6. Not using "what" questions to induce sales rep agreement

Mistakes sales managers should avoid when coaching...

7. Trying to coach on too many topics at a time
8. Always using the same room, agenda, time for coaching
9. Allowing phone calls, emails, etc. to distract you

Mistakes sales managers should avoid when coaching...

10. Not allowing the rep to direct key coaching needs
11. Not holding the rep accountable via an immediate follow-up email/call
12. Not starting each check-in by reviewing the last one

Lesson 326
SALES MANAGEMENT
Setting and enforcing expectations with metrics

Presented by
Mark Jewell
@SellingEnergy
info@sellingenergy.com

Turbocharging Success

Q:

What are the key steps to setting, tracking and enforcing sales metrics?

Key step to setting, tracking and enforcing sales metrics...

1. Determine which metrics to track based on goals.
2. Communicate expectations.
3. Monitor and manage specific behaviors.
4. Monitor results.
5. Provide transparency.
6. Give regular feedback, rewarding wins and coaching suboptimal behavior.

IDEAS & ACTIONS

www.SellingEnergy.com

Types of key metrics...

1. Activity metrics
2. Second-order metrics: effectiveness, pipeline, results

Basic activity-based metrics: Productivity

1. How many new leads did you generate this week?
2. How many of your interactions were with new leads?
3. How many follow-up calls did you make this week?
4. How many leads did you move through the sales cycle on average for the sales you made this week?

Basic activity-based metrics: Productivity

5. How many large accounts vs. single sales did you engage this week?
6. How many hours of prime selling time did you have this week?
7. Other

Basic activity-based metrics: Revenue Generation

1. How many conversions did you see this week?
2. What was your total dollar value of sales this week?
3. What was the value of sales in pipeline this week?
4. Other

Basic activity-based metrics: Personal Development

1. What new personal habits did you develop/reduce this week to increase productivity (and reach your goals)?
2. What coping methods did you employ this week to deal with the rejections you encountered?
3. How have you worked on developing a positive attitude?
4. Other

Basic activity-based metrics: Professional Development

1. Which webinars did you attend this month?
2. How many networking events did you attend this month?
3. Which drip-irrigation content reinforcement resources did you avail yourself of this week?
4. Other

Lesson 327
SALES MANAGEMENT
Results-based metrics

Presented by
Mark Jewell
@SellingEnergy
info@sellingenergy.com

Turbocharging Success

Q:

What are some key results-based metrics?

IDEAS & ACTIONS

_____

_____

_____

_____

Basic results-based metrics:

1. Open opportunities (total and per sales rep)
2. Closed opportunities (total and per sales rep)
3. Deal size
4. Win rate
5. Sales cycle
6. Other

Pipeline results-based metrics (historical):

1. Pipeline integrity (# changes to deal size, close date, etc.)
2. Sales funnel conversion (% deals passing to each stage)
3. Duration (length of sales cycle)
4. Win rate by opportunity
5. Slippage of expected value and/or close date
6. Other

Pipeline results-based metrics (forward-looking):

1. Pipeline by rep
2. Pipeline inflow/outflow
3. Metrics-driven sales forecast
4. Other

Sales results-based metrics:

1. Closed sales vs. goal (how many deals need to close?)
2. Won/lost by opportunity close date (closing fast enough?)
3. Won/lost by reason (preemptive remedies needed?)
4. Sales cycle by rep (share best practices?)
5. Other

Lesson 328
SALES MANAGEMENT
Alternative approaches to metrics

Presented by
Mark Jewell
@SellingEnergy
info@sellingenergy.com

Turbocharging Success

Q:

Are metrics different for inside sales?

Popular metrics to track for inside sales...

1. Revenue per rep
2. Average sale price
3. Lead response time
4. Rate of contact when cold-calling
5. Number of times reps follow-up
6. Average call duration
7. Number of emails sent
8. Usage rate of marketing collateral
9. Other

Q:

What metrics give you the confidence that you know how your sales team is performing, both in terms of activities and results?

IDEAS & ACTIONS

_____

_____

_____

_____

www.SellingEnergy.com

Lesson 329
SALES MANAGEMENT
5 Metrics other than sales to measure team progress

Presented by
Mark Jewell
@SellingEnergy
info@sellingenergy.com

Turbocharging Success

Q:
What are some metrics other than sales to measure your team's performance?

Metrics other than sales to measure performance...

1. Customer retention
2. Ave. # of calls to close a deal (more efficient or more persistent?)
3. Customer satisfaction ratings
4. Length of sales cycle

And a variety of non-sales metrics related to activities...

1. Make "a" customer contacts per day, month, quarter
2. Build "b" dollars of sales pipeline
3. Cross-sell product "c" to customers already using "d"
4. Increase face-to-face customer visits by "e%" over last year

---

Q:
What are other factors to keep an eye on when measuring your team's sales performance?

What is the quality of the deals in your current pipeline?

1. Has the rep verified need, desire, authority and ability?
2. Is the prospect likely to buy something from anyone?
3. Do we have a reasonable chance of winning?
4. Do they fit our profile of a good customer?

IDEAS & ACTIONS

Printed in the USA
CPSIA information can be obtained
at www.ICGtesting.com
JSHW070747110823
46265JS00002B/6